The Global Offensive

OXFORD STUDIES IN INTERNATIONAL HISTORY

JAMES J. SHEEHAN, SERIES ADVISOR

THE WILSONIAN MOMENT
*Self-Determination and the International Origins
of Anticolonial Nationalism*
Erez Manela

IN WAR'S WAKE
Europe's Displaced Persons in the Postwar Order
Gerard Daniel Cohen

GROUNDS OF JUDGMENT
*Extraterritoriality and Imperial Power in Nineteenth-Century
China and Japan*
Pär Kristoffer Cassel

THE ACADIAN DIASPORA
An Eighteenth-Century History
Christopher Hodson

GORDIAN KNOT
Apartheid and the Unmaking of the Liberal World Order
Ryan Irwin

THE GLOBAL OFFENSIVE
*The United States, the Palestine Liberation Organization,
and the Making of the Post–Cold War Order*
Paul Thomas Chamberlin

The Global Offensive

THE UNITED STATES, THE PALESTINE LIBERATION
ORGANIZATION, AND THE MAKING OF
THE POST–COLD WAR ORDER

Paul Thomas Chamberlin

OXFORD
UNIVERSITY PRESS

OXFORD

UNIVERSITY PRESS

Oxford University Press is a department of the University of Oxford.
It furthers the University's objective of excellence in research, scholarship,
and education by publishing worldwide.

Oxford   New York
Auckland   Cape Town   Dar es Salaam   Hong Kong   Karachi
Kuala Lumpur   Madrid   Melbourne   Mexico City   Nairobi
New Delhi   Shanghai   Taipei   Toronto

With offices in
Argentina   Austria   Brazil   Chile   Czech Republic   France   Greece
Guatemala   Hungary   Italy   Japan   Poland   Portugal   Singapore
South Korea   Switzerland   Thailand   Turkey   Ukraine   Vietnam

Oxford is a registered trade mark of Oxford University Press
in the UK and certain other countries.

Published in the United States of America by
Oxford University Press
198 Madison Avenue, New York, NY 10016

Chamberlin, Paul Thomas.
The global offensive : the United States, the Palestine Liberation Organization,
and the making of the post-cold war order / Paul Thomas Chamberlin.
p.   cm.
Includes bibliographical references (p.) and index.
ISBN 978-0-19-981139-7 (hardcover : alk. paper); 978-0-19-021782-2 (paperback : alk. paper)
1. Palestinian National Authority.   2. Munazzamat al-Tahrir al-Filastiniyah.
3. Terrorism.   4. Palestinian Arabs—Politics and government—20th century.
5. Arab-Israeli conflict—Influence.   6. Middle East—Foreign relations—United States.
7. United States—Foreign relations—Middle East.   I. Title.
DS119.7.C4625 2012   327.7305609'04—dc23   2012016066

Some material in this book is drawn from Paul Chamberlin, "A World Restored: Counterrevolution,
Religious Fundamentalism, and the Search for Order in the Middle East,"
Diplomatic History 32, 3 (June 2008): 441–69, used here by permission of Blackwell Publishing,
and
Paul Chamberlin, "The Struggle Against Oppression Everywhere: The Global Politics of Palestinian
Liberation," *Middle Eastern Studies* 47, 1 (January 2011): 25–41,
used here by permission of Taylor & Francis Publishing.

To my parents and my brother

{ CONTENTS }

Acknowledgments ix

Introduction: Palestinian Liberation and the Dawn of
the Post–Cold War Era 1

1. The Struggle Against Oppression Everywhere 14

2. The Storm 43

3. Nixon, Kissinger, and the Terror of a Postimperial World 76

4. The Jordanian Civil War 108

5. A Worldwide Interlocking Terrorist Network 142

6. "The Torch Has Been Passed from Vietnam to Us" 175

7. The Diplomatic Struggle 218

Conclusion 257
Notes 269
Bibliography 311
Index 319

{ ACKNOWLEDGMENTS }

A project such as this book would have been inconceivable without the support of a number of individuals and institutions. I was fortunate enough to receive several Foreign Language Area Studies Fellowships through the Middle East Studies Center at the Ohio State University, which allowed me to study Arabic at the American University in Cairo and the University of Damascus. Generous grants from the Mershon Center and the Department of History and the Society for Historians of American Foreign Relations played crucial roles in supporting my research for this project. I benefited immensely from a fellowship in the International Security Studies program at Yale University and conversations with John Gaddis and Paul Kennedy. A fellowship at Williams College also helped me transform my dissertation into a book manuscript and gave me the chance to interact with a wonderful group of scholars in the History Department and the Stanley Kaplan Program in American Foreign Policy. Among them, James McAlister, Jessica Chapman, Magnus Bernhardsson, and Chris Waters deserve special thanks. This project also benefited from the National History Center's Decolonization Seminar and the advice of William Roger Louis, Jason Parker, John Darwin, Pillarisetti Sudhir, Philippa Levine, and my fellow participants. The staff at the Library of the Institute for Palestine Studies in Beirut deserves special mention for their assistance during the summer of 2007, as do Dan Walsh and the Palestinian Poster Project, who helped track down a number of the images used in this book and for its cover.

My undergraduate advisor, Nick Cullather, introduced me to the study of diplomatic history and shepherded me through my first attempts to produce a serious research paper. I could not have asked for a better dissertation committee than the one I had at Ohio State. Kevin Boyle encouraged me to be a better writer and a more critical thinker. Stephen Dale spent many hours explaining Islamic history to me in between stories of his travels around the Muslim world. Robert McMahon held my work to his exacting standards, pushing me to be a better scholar and inspiring me with his commitment to the field of diplomatic history. Peter Hahn acted as my advisor and mentor from the beginning of my time at Ohio State, encouraging me to study Arabic, travel overseas, and do my best to live up to his example as an international historian. It is to him that I owe my greatest professional debt. I also owe a substantial debt to other scholars in my field who read and commented on various versions of this manuscript. Salim Yaqub, Erez Manela, Doug Little,

James Goode, Brad Simpson, Vijay Prashad, Nathan Citino, Guy Laron, Matt Jacobs, Zach Levy, and Yezid Sayigh have earned my gratitude, as have the anonymous referees who read this manuscript. Their suggestions saved me from a number of embarrassing mistakes and helped make this a much stronger book. Susan Ferber, my editor at Oxford, spent many long hours helping me to transform my manuscript into a more polished book. It is a far better work because of her efforts. In 2010, I had the privilege to join a wonderful group of colleagues in the History Department at the University of Kentucky and the opportunity to get to know George Herring. It is both an honor and a pleasure to teach and work with them in Lexington.

I was fortunate to spend my time at Ohio State with an exceptional cohort of graduate students. Alex Poster, Chapin Rydingsward, Ryan Irwin, and Kate Epstein contributed to this project in countless ways during the last six years. I am privileged to call them both friends and colleagues. My wife, Lien-Hang Nguyen, who was there to watch me transform my dissertation into this book, has been a source of inspiration, encouragement, and love. For all this, no amount of thanks could be sufficient. The arrival of our daughter, Leila, in the final stages of this project has been a special joy and a most welcome distraction. Finally, my parents, Tom and Connie, and my brother, Dan, were a constant base of support. I hope that I have made them proud.

The Global Offensive

Introduction: Palestinian Liberation and the Dawn of the Post–Cold War Era

On 28 March 1970, a Chinese military aircraft left the Beijing airport for Hanoi with a delegation of Palestinian liberation fighters that included Yasir Arafat, the chair of the Executive Committee of the Palestine Liberation Organization (PLO), and his deputy, Salah Khalaf. Although the two men had tried to attract as little attention as possible when they arrived—Arafat dressed in a conservative business suit rather than his trademark black and white kuffiyah—they were seen off by a crowd of thousands. The delegation arrived at Hanoi's heavily fortified Gia Lam Airport on the eve of a series of North Vietnamese attacks on U.S. and South Vietnamese positions that shattered the relative lull in fighting that had prevailed in the region over the previous eight months. After disembarking, Arafat and Khalaf were met by members of the Politburo and escorted into a reception room for several hours of discussion. During their two-week stay in North Vietnam, the Palestinians would tour factories, military bases, training camps, schools, and missile batteries and would enjoy an audience with General Vo Nguyen Giap, Hanoi's preeminent military strategist. "The Vietnamese and Palestinian people have much in common," Giap told the delegation, "just like two people suffering from the same illness."[1]

Giap was not the only leader thinking in these global terms. A few months later, President Richard Nixon sat down in a Los Angeles television studio—nearly eight thousand miles from Hanoi—for an interview with journalists from the three national networks. Nixon warned the millions of Americans who watched the broadcast that night that the critics who had begun to denounce as obsolete the domino theory—which argued that a communist takeover of one state was likely to lead to the overthrow of other governments in the region—had not "talked to the dominoes." The president explained that American success in South Vietnam could mean the difference between freedom and a communist takeover for millions of people throughout East Asia.

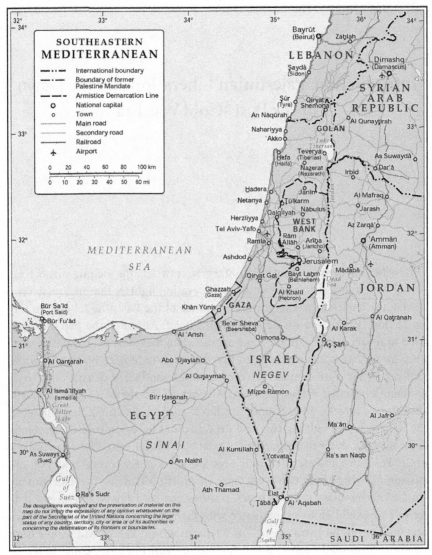

FIGURE O.1 *Southeastern Mediterranean, map no. 4013, July 1997. Courtesy of the United Nations.*

Further, a communist victory in South Vietnam would surely encourage Moscow and Beijing to pursue their revolutionary ambitions in other parts of the world. The conversation then turned to the Middle East: "You cannot separate what happens to America in Vietnam from the Mideast or from Europe or any place else," he explained. The Soviets were moving into the area, which was already torn by conflicts between Israel and its neighbors and between moderates and radicals in the Arab world. Making matters worse, there now appeared to be an even more revolutionary force in Arab politics, the Palestinian guerillas. Important as the struggle for Southeast Asia had been, Nixon warned at the end of the broadcast, the stakes and the dangers in the Middle East were even greater.[2]

Nixon, Arafat, and Giap each recognized that they were operating on a global field. While the Cold War superpowers worked to maintain and extend their influence in every region of the world, small states and guerilla groups sought to exploit a proliferating array of transnational connections that criss-crossed the globe. For insurgents such as Arafat and Giap, these global networks presented new spaces to be infiltrated and contested; for leaders such as Nixon, they represented lines that must be defended. Though they were not the first to target this interstate terrain, Palestinian fighters—driven by necessity as much as design—would orchestrate a campaign to seize this transnational space using a revolutionary set of tactics and strategies never before seen in history.[3] In doing so, the PLO emerged as the world's first globalized insurgency and became a seminal influence on other rebellions in the following decades.[4] At the same time, the United States, in its efforts to defend its front lines against insurgents such as the PLO, worked to strengthen its existing network of strategic relationships around the world. Ultimately, as the two sides fought over the physical and conceptual space that was Palestine, they helped to remake the art of revolution and the structure of global power in the late Cold War world and beyond.

This book traces the changing face of national liberation at the end of the twentieth century. It is a history of the PLO's formative years and the organization's impact on U.S. policy toward the Arab-Israeli conflict. It is also a history of the PLO's international strategies and their impact on the emerging international order of the 1970s. Palestinian guerillas launched an offensive on many fronts: they fought across the arid floodplains of the Jordan Valley and in the climate-controlled corridors of United Nations headquarters in Manhattan, amidst the modernist high-rises of West Beirut and inside the pressurized cabins of commercial jetliners. Palestinian cadres presented their credentials to communist leaders in both Moscow and Hanoi and were greeted by throngs of cheering supporters in the public squares of Beijing and East Berlin; the violence they unleashed touched upscale apartments in Paris as well as the blisteringly hot side streets of Khartoum. As Palestinian fighters made these crossings, as both guerillas and diplomats, they helped to transform the regional order in the Middle East and the shape of revolutionary politics in the wider world.

Accordingly, this book locates the Palestinian armed struggle within the broad complex of liberationist forces scattered throughout the international system of the Cold War world. Viewed from this perspective, the era's myriad insurrections, revolts, and rebellions appear not as discrete episodes but as a linked, and at times even coordinated, series of assaults on the structures of global power. They were part of a unique moment in history when it appeared

FIGURE 0.2 *Fatah poster, "I Did Not Die," c. 1967. Courtesy of the Palestinian Poster Project Archives.*

as if progressive guerilla movements might seize control of the postcolonial world, in which more than 70 percent of the earth's population resided. More than just isolated reactions to local circumstances and superpower politics, these uprisings had in common a vision of revolutionary politics drawn from a shared culture of Third World national liberation.[5] This is not to say that these movements were monolithic—indeed, a staggering diversity existed within their ranks over both time and space—but rather to draw attention to the many transnational connections, exchanges, and crossings that character-ized national liberation. Guerilla fighters from Palestine, Algeria, Vietnam, Cuba, and a dozen other locales can be understood as a sprawling constella-tion of revolutionary networks. Viewed from a distance, they appear as an international force in their own right, a global offensive against the bastions of state power in the Cold War system.

While Palestinian fighters recognized these global networks as a new field on which to wage their war of national liberation, U.S. policy makers came to understand this transnational terrain as a new front that had to be fortified. Victory in the Cold War, according to many in Washington, could not be achieved if the United States was in retreat throughout the global South. For the United States and its allies, holding the line on the Third World battlefields of the 1960s and 1970s would mean finding some way to halt the guerillas' advances. Thus, just as Cuban and Vietnamese fighters can be seen as comprising the western and eastern wings of a worldwide guerilla offensive, U.S. moves to contest the advance of national liberation movements from Latin America to Southeast Asia can be understood as part of a long campaign to win the Cold War in the Third World. These global dynamics came into play in every theater of the Cold War as the European empires of the pre-1945 world collapsed. In this way, policy makers in Washington came to understand the Cold War as a struggle for influence across physical, political, and conceptual battlefields in every region of the world.

Thus, the PLO's global offensive, which began in earnest in the Middle East in late 1967 and reached the world stage by the end of 1974, was only one front in this larger story. As Palestinian military and diplomatic operations unfolded on a series of four main stages concentrated on the cities of Nablus, Amman, Beirut, and Geneva, the guerillas emerged alongside Vietnamese and South African liberation fighters at the vanguard of the struggle of national liberation in the 1970s. These victories on the world stage would also help to make the PLO a key player in the Arab-Israeli dispute. During this same period, the U.S. government developed its official position on the PLO, which sought to bal-ance the resurgence of Palestinian nationalism with evolving priorities in the region and the wider Cold War. In this way, the Johnson, Nixon, and Ford administrations would move toward a policy of diplomatic containment of the PLO coupled with military suppression of the fedayeen—literally, "those who sacrifice themselves," used to refer to the Palestinian guerilla fighters—at the hands of regional police powers. Thus, as Palestinian fighters gained ground in the international arena, the United States and its allies in the region reinforced their defenses.

Moving beyond the confines of the Israel-Palestine dispute, the PLO's global offensive carried a threefold significance in twentieth-century international history. The Palestinian experience of the 1960s and 1970s represented a watershed in the worldwide struggle for national liberation. As they tapped into the transnational culture of Third World liberation, Palestinian fighters became adept at traversing the revolutionary networks of the Cold War international system and became a cause célèbre for progressive movements around the world. By late 1973, Arafat could claim to have taken up "the banner of the global struggle" from the Vietnamese revolution, marking the passage to a new phase in the twentieth-century wars of decolonization.[6] As the "global struggle" moved from the jungles of Southeast Asia to the mountains, plains, and cities of the Middle East, however, its character changed. If the victory of Vietnamese communist forces in 1968–75 was one of the last great triumphs in a broader wave of postcolonial wars of national liberation, the Palestinian armed struggle during those same years can be seen as one of the first great stalemates. The PLO's experience thus marked the end of an era characterized by triumphant wars of national liberation around the global South and the beginning of a new chapter in the history of the Third World. The global offensive straddled this divide—rather than produced it—and its fate would presage the balkanization of the Third World revolution in the coming decades.

This battle for Palestine marked a turning point in the global Cold War whereby guerilla campaigns throughout the developing world would confront a new configuration of U.S. power. As their position in Vietnam deteriorated in the face of a concerted guerilla assault, officials in Washington scrambled to find the means to reinforce U.S. commitments throughout the Cold War periphery; they struggled to produce a post-Vietnam containment strategy for the developing world of the 1970s and beyond. The Nixon Doctrine, as this new configuration came to be known, was designed to hold the line against the string of guerilla offensives around the developing world through the creation of a network of local police powers. At the same time, Washington established a defensive position in the chambers of the United Nations, where it sought to counter the tide of Third Worldism—an amorphous, left-leaning political movement among the developing nations that emphasized the North-South divide in international affairs and sought to create greater solidarity among the nations of the postcolonial world—that was sweeping through the organization. Nowhere would these diplomatic and strategic transformations be more focused than in the Middle East, where the Nixon administration fortified its special relationship with Israel through enormous infusions of military aid and mobilized its veto power to shield its ally in the UN Security Council. Meanwhile, Henry Kissinger's diplomatic approaches to the Arab-Israeli conflict worked to accomplish a power shift in the Arab world away from alignment with Moscow and toward a new relationship with Washington.

Finally, the contest between the PLO and the United States was one of a series of events that marked the beginning of what some commentators have called the age of globalization. At the same time that they navigated the world-wide revolutionary networks of the 1960s and 1970s and gained diplomatic support in international forums such as the United Nations, Palestinian fighters employed a new set of transnational guerilla tactics, which indicated the increasing power of nonstate actors in the international system and introduced the concept of "international terrorism" into the modern lexicon. In doing so, the PLO's struggle signaled the beginning of a new age of security interdependence in which international cooperation, military partnerships, and stronger international organizations would be necessary to deal with increasingly global and transnational threats. This multilateralism was accompanied by a militant new unilateralism designed to combat the PLO's global offensive. To this end, Israeli security forces developed an array of counterterrorism techniques that would provide a blueprint for the special forces operations of the twenty-first century. Ultimately, the PLO's war would have more in common with the types of conflicts that would break out at the turn of the twenty-first century than with the battles of the Cold War era.

Although this book is first and foremost a study of the United States and the Palestinian liberation struggle in the late 1960s and 1970s, its arguments engage in broader debates about international history, the Cold War, decolonization, and U.S. foreign relations. Until recently, international history was all but synonymous with the history of the great powers. Local peoples and states were minor participants in a story dominated by the architects of empire, little more than aspects of the terrain over which the policies of Western statesmen moved. In this version, the great powers served as the "driving force of history," while "indigenous actions [were reduced] to mere strategies of subversion and survival."[7] Upon closer inspection, however, the picture becomes more complicated: these actors exercised a considerable amount of power and harbored their own ambitions; they crafted their own grand strategies and advanced their own foreign policies.[8]

Thus in recent years, historians of foreign relations have moved beyond their traditional focus on the making of state policy in Western capitals, working to incorporate local actors as fully rendered agents in the making of the contemporary world order. Far from being merely supporting players on a stage dominated by presidents and prime ministers, indigenous non-Western peoples were active participants in the complex set of negotiations that created the modern world. This new scholarship endeavors to treat their agency not as the background to the real drama unfolding in places such as Washington and Moscow but rather as an essential component of a genuinely international story. It recognizes that the history of the Cold War in the Middle East, Latin America, Asia, and Africa is inseparable from the history of the states and peoples that constitute those regions.

As ever more multilingual, multiarchival studies appear, a more complete picture of international history is emerging that highlights the complex interplay of forces and agents across a truly global spectrum. Some of the most impressive scholarship in recent years has used European archives to deepen understandings of the Cold War in its transatlantic context, underscoring the role of the United States as merely one participant in a field crowded with rival powers, small states, and transnational actors all working toward their own ends. For studies of the postcolonial world and the global South, much more remains to be done, especially on those peoples and parts of the world that once fell under—or managed somehow to evade—the power of Western imperialism. Work utilizing non-Western sources has begun to move beyond the transatlantic focus on the great powers to incorporate Third World actors as dynamic agents in the creation of contemporary history. [9]

This effort is still in its early stages, however. A sizable majority of international histories written in English on the Arab-Israeli conflict, for instance, make virtually no use of Arabic materials. For decades, this was rationalized by citing the lack of official archives in Arab countries. This and similar explanations effectively silenced and ignored the voices of the majority of the human population whose affairs are not meticulously documented by the well-funded bureaucracies of the modern, usually Western state. In truth, the carefully preserved national archives maintained in places such as London, Paris, and Washington, DC, represent the exception, rather than the rule, in human history. And in recent years historians have produced whole schools of historiography on groups, such as Native Americans, that lacked the ability to produce and sustain official archives.[10] In fact, the contemporary Middle East offers troves of materials that have gone virtually untouched by international historians, although the sources may appear somewhat barren in comparison to those available in the United States and much of Western Europe.[11] Until historians begin to make use of such sources, the Middle Eastern side of events will remain sorely underrepresented in Western scholarship.

Middle Eastern actors play a central role as dynamic agents in the chapters that follow. The roles of the great powers are not ignored, but this book underscores the interactions between guerillas, international organizations, nonstate groups, and small powers that long remained hidden on the Cold War "periphery." Rather than being a comprehensive account of all involved participants, this book fits within the new international history in integrating the perspectives and roles of central—though previously neglected—players in world affairs.[12] In this spirit, it does not aim to present international history as an all-encompassing picture of every belligerent in the Arab-Israeli conflict. Key participants such as Israel, Egypt, and the Soviet Union appear frequently, but they are not the principal subjects. Rather, the book's main objective is to analyze the international strategies of the groups that would form the PLO, situating them in the broader context of U.S. foreign policy, the Cold War, and the global movement for national liberation. In doing so, it treats Palestinian fighters not as bit players but as central agents in the construction of the regional and international order that emerged in the 1970s and beyond.

By approaching the PLO in this manner, this work departs from the existing literature on the topic. One strand, represented by Middle East specialists, includes a number of excellent studies of Palestinian politics and society to which this work is deeply indebted. These works represent a Palestine-centric approach to the subject, which this study is not.[13] The second group, consisting of historians of foreign relations and scholars of the Arab-Israeli conflict, tends to approach their subjects from U.S. and/or Israeli perspectives. Rather than focusing on Palestinian international history per se, these scholars concentrate on U.S.–Middle East relations or on the history of the Arab-Israeli conflict itself.[14] A third body of work that deals extensively with the PLO focuses on the issue of "international terrorism." Its focus on tactics does little to illuminate the larger dimensions of the Palestinian liberation movement that were central to its history. In contrast to these three types of works, this study moves beyond the regional framework of the Arab-Israeli conflict to focus on the international dimensions of the Palestinian armed struggle and place the PLO in the global context of revolutionary change during the Cold War era. In doing so, it seeks to return the story of the Palestinian liberation struggle to its appropriate place in the history of the twentieth-century world.

Given the highly politicized nature of the discussion that follows, some definitions are in order. The first concerns "terrorism," which appears in the following pages as a historical concept rather than an analytical or objective one. The value of the term is vastly outweighed by the baggage it carries. "Terrorism" is problematic for a number of reasons. There is no definition of the term that is acceptable to most, let alone all, of the parties interested in its use. The concept has most often been employed as an accusation by groups seeking to undermine the legitimacy of their political opponents. If it can be said to have a usable definition as a military tactic or mode of violence, "terrorism" has a tendency to essentialize its subjects. Complex organizations with broad political platforms, aspirations, and goals and a wide range of constituents are reduced to "terrorists." These three properties—ambiguity, delegitimation, and essentialization—have historically made the term a powerful rhetorical weapon. Thus, the charge of "terrorism" has been leveled by and against all of the major actors mentioned in the following chapters in connection with actions that do not fit most common definitions of the term. Instead, as journalist Robert Fisk has argued, "terrorism" is no longer an analytical concept but "a political contrivance. 'Terrorists' are those who use violence against the side that is using the word."[15] Still, there are those who argue that the concept can be rescued with the application of an objective, technical definition. Even if such a definition could be found and accepted, "terrorism" would still be subject to rampant misuse in mainstream parlance and would still be weighed down by decades of historical baggage. Even when used in the most careful and dispassionate manner possible, the term invites misinterpretation. For these reasons, this book historicizes the term, treating "terrorism" as a historical artifact rather than as a legitimate concept to be applied objectively.

While I approach the topic of this book as a scholar and not as an activist, I fear that the politics of the Israel-Palestine dispute are likely to distract from my scholarship. For that reason, I feel that it would be helpful to establish my position at the outset. I agree with the prevailing precepts of international law that Israel has a right to exist and that the Palestinian people have a right to a sovereign state in the West Bank and Gaza Strip. Moreover, like political scientist Mark Tessler, I believe that the conflict "is not a struggle between good and evil but rather a confrontation between two peoples who deserve recognition and respect, neither of whom has a monopoly on behavior that is either praiseworthy or condemnable."[16] During the period covered in this book, Israel was a state fighting for what it considered to be its very survival. At the same time, Palestinian fighters were struggling for their own national survival. Both groups faced what they believed were threats to their existence as nations; both groups behaved ruthlessly in defense of their claims and were responsible for acts of terrible violence against civilians. An honest treatment of the conflict must accept that neither side's actions were the product of irrational hatreds or sectarian bloodlust. Rather, violence in the Israel-Palestine conflict was the result of considered—though at times misguided—strategies that the various parties followed in the hopes of maximizing their chances for national survival in a dangerous environment. These points should not be read as justifications for the bloodshed, nor do they imply some sort of judgment about the moral balance between the two sides. Instead, they serve as explanations that are essential for understanding the history of the conflict. The ideologically committed on both sides of the spectrum will disagree with this position, but nothing short of polemic is likely to satisfy such readers in any case.

The territory that has come to constitute Israel-Palestine also demands definition. The borders of Israel-Palestine were constructed in several stages over the course of modern history. The land of Palestine historically represented the area between the Jordan River and the Mediterranean Sea and formed three districts (*sanjaqs*) within the province (*vilayet*) of Syria under the Ottoman Empire. In 1920, Great Britain and France divided Ottoman Syria into separate mandates, with the French establishing the entities of Syria and Lebanon to the north and the British establishing Palestine and Transjordan in the south. These mandate boundaries would form the basis of the system of independent states that appeared after the departure of European imperial powers. Under British rule, two distinct communities had risen in Palestine, one Jewish and one Arab. While the Jewish population of Palestine constituted some 10 percent of the total at the turn of the century, by the late 1940s, as the British prepared to leave, it had risen to around 30 percent as the result of significant immigration from Europe, spurred in no small part by the horrors of the Holocaust. In 1947, under strong pressure from the United States, the new United Nations put forward a plan for the partition of Palestine into two states. The proposed Jewish state would receive approximately 56 percent of Palestine, while the Arabs, who constituted some two-thirds of the population, would be left with only about 44 percent. The Arab population—who favored a one-state solution in which they would enjoy a controlling majority rather than a partition that would leave them with less than half of their homeland—rejected this plan for partition, citing the principle of self-determination, and the seeds for the First Arab-Israeli War were sown. That conflict, which lasted in various forms from 1947 to 1949, resulted in a victory for the newly formed state of Israel and the expansion of its borders to comprise some 78 percent of the former mandate of Palestine. The 1949 armistice lines became the de facto borders of Israel, the West Bank, and the Gaza Strip. The total area of historic Palestine represented some 10,418 square miles, of which Israel constituted approximately 8,019 square miles, the West Bank just over 2,260 square miles, and the Gaza Strip approximately 139 square miles. These lines would come to be known as the 1967 borders and stood more or less intact on the eve of the Third Arab-Israeli War, which marks the beginning of this book.[17]

Finally, a short definition of the PLO and its constituent groups. The PLO is an umbrella organization first created in 1964 that brought together a number of different bodies. Prior to 1968, the PLO was largely under the control of the Egyptian government. Meanwhile, Fatah, created in 1959, brought together Palestinian nationalists such as Arafat who hoped to carve out an independent political role for their people. The third major force on the scene prior to 1967 was the Arab Nationalist Movement (ANM), which sought to marry the cause of Palestinian liberation to the wider pan-Arab struggle. While Fatah would continue to grow through the 1960s, the ANM declined, giving birth to the Popular Front groups, most notably George Habash's Popular Front for the Liberation of Palestine (PFLP) and Nayaf Hawatmeh's Democratic Front for the Liberation of Palestine (DFLP). During the period in question, there were also myriad smaller guerilla groups, most of which existed for only a short time or were essentially proxies of Arab governments in the region. The most notable of this latter group were Al-Saiqa and the Arab Liberation Front (ALF), controlled by the Syrian and Iraqi Ba'ath parties, respectively. While these other groups appear, this book is primarily a study of the PLO, Fatah, and the PFLP. Finally, it should be noted that all of these groups were overwhelmingly secular; Islamic guerilla groups such as Hamas did not appear until later decades.

The following chapters are organized in a roughly chronological manner beginning in the wake of the 1967 Arab-Israeli War and concluding at the start of the Lebanese civil war in 1975. The first two chapters look at the emergence of the Palestinian fedayeen into mainstream Arab politics in the wake of the

1967 war and Washington's initial response. By combining a vision of national liberation adopted from the Algerian, Vietnamese, Chinese, and Cuban examples with a series of guerilla operations, Palestinian fighters were able to gain regional and international prominence as well as the attention of U.S. officials, who were becoming increasingly concerned about the potential for the guerillas to destabilize the region. The fedayeen's political victory at the Battle of al-Karama would serve as a sort of Palestinian Tet Offensive, energizing the movement and guaranteeing the survival of the armed struggle. Chapter 3 analyzes the Nixon administration's response to the increasingly global threat of the Palestinian liberation struggle and the problem of revolutionary upheavals around the world. The president and his national security advisor, Henry Kissinger, set about laying the foundations for a post-Vietnam containment strategy that would hold the line against what appeared to be a series of revolutions in the developing world and erase the PLO from the global map of national liberation fighters. Chapter 4 examines the climactic 1970 showdown between the PLO and the U.S.-backed Hashemite monarchy in Jordan. Although Jordanian security forces maintained control of the kingdom, the conflict demonstrated the urgency of Palestinian nationalism as a force in the Arab world and thrust Arafat and the PLO onto the international stage.

Chapters 5 and 6 chart the shift in the PLO's strategies in the wake of the Jordanian war, the emergence of the Black September Organization—responsible for the 1972 Munich Olympics massacre—and the U.S. response to the problem of international guerilla warfare. This new stage of the conflict would be marked by the full internationalization of the PLO's armed struggle and the rise of the "terrorism versus freedom fighter" controversy in forums such as the United Nations. Meanwhile, the United States and Israel would work to introduce unilateral tactics—diplomatic and military—to deal with the challenge of the PLO's global insurgency. The final chapter examines the period from the end of the 1973 Arab-Israeli War to the beginning of the Lebanese civil war. As the PLO secured the political high ground in the international sphere, winning world recognition as the sole legitimate representative of the Palestinian people, it grappled with the challenge of moving its armed struggle into the diplomatic sphere and worked to establish an official dialogue with Washington. Meanwhile, the United States and its allies established political and military authority in the region and moved to lock the PLO out of the official peace process spearheaded by Henry Kissinger. The resulting stalemate between the opposing sides would continue for decades. As the Israeli-Palestinian conflict hardened, Lebanon descended into civil war, and hopes for a post-1967 settlement faded away.

The PLO's paradoxical fate would be a bellwether for the national liberation struggles of the post-Vietnam era. The new generation of Third World revolutionaries would run up against superpower-proxy forces trained and equipped to wage low-intensity conflicts, sparking a string of bloody but indecisive guerilla wars around the global South. In Angola, warring factions supported by the United States, the Soviet Union, China, Cuba, and South Africa would fight one of the longest civil wars of the Cold War era. Right-wing regimes would use military aid from Washington to wage a series of brutal counterinsurgencies against left-wing guerillas in Guatemala, El Salvador, and Colombia. The Reagan White House pushed these low-intensity conflict strategies one step further in the 1980s, when it began channeling funds and weapons to guerilla forces in Nicaragua and Afghanistan fighting against left-wing governments in Managua and Kabul. Meanwhile, as the PLO was pulled into the carnage of the Lebanese civil war, the goal of Palestinian statehood grew more distant and the impetus for liberation shifted to new segments of Palestinian society that would challenge the PLO in the decades to come. While it appeared as if Washington and its allies around the developing world had found the means to stop the revolutionary dominoes from falling, the post–Cold War era promised to be every bit as fraught with conflict as the half century that had preceded it.

What follows, then, is a history of the PLO's global offensive, the U.S. response, and the making of the contemporary international order during the pivotal years between 1967 and 1975. It examines the way that a group of Palestinian refugees managed to launch a national liberation movement that seized the world's attention and helped to rewrite the rule book for revolutionaries around the globe. It also explains how the world's greatest superpower recalibrated its international security strategies to meet the challenges of this global offensive and shore up its position throughout the global South. In the end, it is neither a story of triumph nor a tale of defeat but rather a chronicle of stalemate and the origins of a guerilla war that would last into the twenty-first century.

The Struggle Against Oppression Everywhere

The 1967 Arab-Israeli War was over in less than a week. A devastating air attack against the Egyptian air force on June 5 had all but guaranteed the Israel Defense Forces (IDF) control of the air for the rest of the conflict. It would take Israel only five more days to cut a swath through the Egyptian, Syrian, and Jordanian armies, occupy the West Bank, the Gaza Strip, the Golan Heights, and the Sinai Peninsula, and lay waste to Egyptian president Gamal Abdel Nasser's pan-Arabist dreams. Nasser's tragedy would open the door for a new revolutionary force in the region, however. While he could hardly have been happy with the situation, Yasir Arafat recognized the opportunity that unfolded as the guns fell silent. Arafat had spent a good deal of the previous summer locked up with several of his comrades in Syria's al-Mezzah prison after running afoul of Defense Minister Hafiz al-Assad. The yoke of Egyptian and Syrian patronage weighed heavily on the guerilla leader's shoulders: while the Arab states lauded Palestinian commandos in public and supplied them with much-needed cash and weapons, leaders such as Nasser and Assad expected obedience and defer-ence from the fedayeen. As the shattered Arab armies gathered their wounded and marched back to their respective capitals, Arafat and his comrades moved to throw off the crumbling remains of Nasserism and push their own version of revolutionary Palestinian nationalism to the fore. As Arafat would console a fellow guerilla commander, "This is not the end. It's the beginning."[1]

Although his small stature did not fit the image of the fearsome guerilla com-mander that he hoped to project, Arafat was a sort of Palestinian everyman. Born in Cairo in 1929 to a Gazan merchant and a woman from Jerusalem, the young Arafat witnessed the final decades of British colonial rule in the Middle East. While he spent several years in Jerusalem, Arafat came of age in Cairo, the puls-ing heart of the Arab world and one of the centers of the global movements against European colonialism. He became involved in politics early, joining pop-ular demonstrations against British rule on the streets of Cairo at the age of ten.

In 1948, he joined units of the Ikhwan Muslimun (Muslim Brotherhood) fighting in Gaza against Zionist forces in the First Arab-Israeli War. After returning to Egypt and his engineering studies at Cairo University, Arafat became involved in the Palestinian Students Union (PSU) and was elected its president in 1952. His work with the PSU—for which he gained a reputation as a skilled organizer—brought him into contact with a number of other young activists as well as the Egyptian secret police, who were suspicious of possible challenges to the new revolutionary regime. In 1957, after earning his degree, Arafat left Cairo for the less stifling political atmosphere of Kuwait. Like many members of the Palestinian diaspora, he found success abroad but still longed for a homeland. Arafat ran a successful construction company, developed a fondness for fast cars, and continued his political activities, founding the Palestinian National Liberation Movement, known by its reverse acronym, Fatah. Espousing a nebulous ideology of Palestinian nationalism mixed with revolutionary Third World liberation and left-wing social thought, Fatah called for a guerilla war designed to liberate Palestine and for the creation of a Palestinian state. The group's clandestine activities were originally limited in scope, but by publishing a number of periodicals and having its members travel widely, it was able to win an increasing number of Palestinian recruits as well as international supporters.[2]

Fatah was not the only competitor for political leadership of the Palestinian diaspora, however. The biggest challenge came from the Arab states themselves and the Palestine Liberation Organization, created in 1964 as a means for the Arab regimes—Cairo in particular—to retain a measure of control over the Palestinians and the issue of Palestinian liberation. By creating the PLO as an essentially toothless organization, Nasser had hoped to bolster the perception that his regime was working toward Palestinian liberation when it was in fact retreating from the more radical dimensions of Arab nationalism. The organization functioned largely as a foil led by the volatile Ahmed Shuqairy, famous for his pledge to "drive the Jews into the sea." Indeed, it was in response to the creation of the PLO—and the fear that the cause of Palestinian liberation would continue to be overshadowed by the larger cause of Arab nationalism—that Arafat was able to convince his colleagues in Fatah to begin a series of guerilla attacks against Israel in January 1965. Such fears were not unreasonable. Prior to the mid-1960s, the Palestinian liberation movement had been largely subsumed under the umbrella of Arab nationalism. While tensions between Jews and Arabs had dominated Palestinian politics during the 1940s and 1950s, the major Arab states including Syria, Egypt, and Iraq had experienced social revolutions that had brought new elites to power, replacing the traditional classes of urban notables who had dominated Arab political life under the Ottoman sultans and the European mandate system. Thus, while Nasser's star rose in Cairo and Ba'athist officials consolidated power in Damascus and Baghdad, post–World War II Palestinian society lacked clear political leadership.[3]

This was the sociopolitical atmosphere in which Arafat came of age. Although his troubles with Cairo and Damascus made his task more difficult—he needed to look no further than his recent incarceration in a Syrian prison—Arafat had the advantage of being connected to a number of international networks of political, material, and ideological exchange. From his youth, Arafat had witnessed a surging anticolonial movement that linked groups around the non-Western world. The shared experience of colonialism and common struggle against European imperialism had laid the foundations for what would become known as the Third World during the post-1945 era. Likewise, his experience fighting in Gaza alongside members of the Ikhwan Muslimun had exposed the young Arafat to cultural currents that flowed across national boundaries and united groups around the Middle East. His work with the PSU during his time at Cairo University brought him into contact with socialist and communist groups that were at the forefront of nationalist movements around the region and the developing world. Finally, his time working as a businessman in Kuwait left Arafat with an awareness of the power of international finance and the growing role of oil money in the Arab world. The net effect of these experiences created a man who was well acquainted with the dominant transnational political forces of the Palestinian, Arab, and developing worlds. Arafat was not the only player looking to lead the way to Palestinian liberation, however.

Born into a family of Greek Orthodox merchants in the Palestinian city of Lydda in 1926, George Habash showed a great deal of promise, leaving his homeland to study pediatric medicine at the American University of Beirut. On a visit home in 1948, Habash was caught in the Jewish attack on Lydda and, along with his family, forced to leave the city in the mass expulsion that came to be known as the Lydda Death March. He returned to Beirut as a refugee to finish his studies, graduating first in his class in 1951. The following year, he became a founding member of the Arab Nationalist Movement, a left-wing anti-imperialist organization that sought to create a revolutionary vanguard in the Arab world. That same year, the man who was to become known as the "doctor of the Palestinian revolution" moved to Amman, where he opened a clinic for refugees. Like many of his contemporaries, Habash was attracted to Nasser and his message of Arab unity. By the early 1960s, the ANM had become a principal competitor to Arafat's group. In contrast to the more narrowly Palestinian Fatah, the ANM embraced a pan-Arab vision aimed not just at establishing an Arab state in Palestine but also at bringing about a political revolution throughout the Arab world. The Arab defeat in 1967 dealt a devastating blow to Habash and the ANM, however, leading to the fragmentation of the movement and a turn away from Arab states such as Egypt. In December 1967, Habash and several of his colleagues created the Popular Front for the Liberation of Palestine.[4]

Beyond opening the door for new leaders such as Habash and Arafat, Nasser's humiliation raised fears that the Arab powers might abandon the

Palestinian cause by granting recognition to Israel in exchange for the return of territories occupied by the IDF during the war. If Israel could be persuaded to return to its prewar frontiers, Cairo, Damascus, and Amman might cut their losses and accept a political settlement with Israel. Such a settlement appeared a very real possibility in late 1967, as both the United States and the Soviet Union agreed to set aside their differences and back UN efforts to bring about a negotiated peace. Security Council Resolution 242, passed in November 1967, established a framework for peace based on the principle of the exchange of land for political recognition. Under the efforts of Swedish diplomat Gunnar Jarring, the United Nations encouraged Israel to evacuate Arab territories occupied during the June War in return for peace with the Arab states. The resolution called for a settlement of the refugee problem, but not the recognition of Palestinian political aspirations. While seemingly minor, this semantic distinction was fundamental to the issue of Palestinian nationalism: Arab refugees could be resettled in any one of the many Arab states, while Palestinians were a nation entitled to sovereignty and self-determination. Indeed, the reference to the Palestinians as Arab refugees could lead to the denial of their very existence as a people. To this end, the struggle to secure recognition as a nation functioned as the first and most basic goal of the Palestinian resistance movement. Had the Jarring Mission succeeded, Palestinian hopes for self-determination might have been left out in the cold.[5]

The Jarring Mission would run into a number of obstacles, however. The most basic dilemma arose from Israel's lopsided victory in 1967, which left the Jewish state with too much leverage in any potential negotiations. Israeli leaders, with some justification, fell into the habit of thinking that their state was militarily invincible. Thus, while they were amenable in theory to the land-for-peace settlement, the particulars of any prospective settlement presented significant hurdles to progress. Growing pressure within the Jewish state to consolidate control over occupied Arab territories compounded matters. Control of the Sinai, the Golan Heights, and the West Bank increased Israel's strategic depth dramatically: future wars, should they break out, would be fought on these battlefields rather than within Israel itself. The presence of Judaism's holiest shrines in Jerusalem and cultural attachments to the West Bank—manifest in a growing political constituency that demanded annexation of these lands—made the wholesale return of that territory even more difficult to accomplish. These forces became stronger as Israeli settlers began seizing Arab territory, usually without state support, with the intention of creating Eretz Yisrael (a greater Israel) upon the conquests of the June War. On balance, at the end of 1967, Israeli leaders faced as much or more pressure to retain control over Arab lands as they did to return them.

Conversely, this situation provided little incentive for Arab regimes in Egypt and Syria to seek a political settlement in which they would be negotiating for the return of their territory from a position of extreme weakness. Better to wait until the situation became more favorable to their interests, leaders in Damascus and Cairo concluded. Hence, at the September 1967 Khartoum Conference, the Arab League issued the famous "three noes": no peace with Israel, no recognition of Israel, and no negotiation with Israel. At its most basic, the dilemma between Israel and the Arab states focused on the fact that Israel had too much leverage in the negotiations with its Arab neighbors; neither side felt inclined to press for negotiations. For their part, officials in Washington were preoccupied with the war in Southeast Asia. The Johnson administration thus did not throw its full weight behind Jarring's efforts, seeking to manage rather than resolve the regional situation. The fedayeen would emerge as the strongest Arab critics of the Jarring Mission.

From Arab Refugees to Third World Liberation Fighters

As the dust settled from the June War, Arafat and several of his lieutenants slipped across the Jordan River and into the Israeli-occupied West Bank. Convinced that the defeat of the Arab armies confirmed the necessity of waging a protracted guerilla war of attrition against Israel, Arafat made his way to the old quarter of the city of Nablus to set up a base of operations. Fatah's operations in the summer of 1967 marked a watershed around the region, one that would be followed by revolutionary transformations in Libya, Egypt, Lebanon, Syria, and Iraq, but few groups were more deeply affected than the nearly 1 million Palestinians in the West Bank and Gaza who suddenly found themselves living under Israeli military occupation. For these Palestinians, the experience of the 1967 war represented a new tragedy. Scattered since the 1948 war, the Palestinians had been geographically separated, with an estimated 600,000 living in the West Bank, 300,000 in Gaza, and 300,000 in Israel, and another 880,000 living in refugee camps in Jordan, Syria, and Lebanon. Some 280,000 Palestinians were spread around the Arab world—mainly in the oil-rich gulf states of Kuwait and Saudi Arabia—with approximately 150,000 others living outside the Arab world.[6] The largest concentration of Palestinians, on the West Bank, had lived under Jordanian rule for nearly two decades; Gazans lived under Egyptian authority. The greater part of the diaspora—like most of their fellow Arabs—had been gripped by Nasser's pan-Arab message since the mid-1950s. This enthusiasm for Cairo combined with the absence of any formal state structures to create a lack of clear leadership over Palestinian society. Traditional social elites—the urban notables—still held a considerable amount of power on the West Bank. Their influence was eroding under the new IDF occupation, however, as it became clear that they could do little to contest Israeli control. The pressure of occupation would become a catalyst for change in the diaspora. While the old elite families of the West Bank had been losing power, the dynamic political force of radicals in the refugee camps had been growing. It was out of this milieu that groups such as Fatah, the ANM, and the PFLP would emerge. In the years following the 1967 war, Palestinian society would become a battleground between the forces of traditional authority and their revolutionary challengers.[7]

If they were to build an enduring political movement, upstarts such as Arafat and Habash needed to establish their political legitimacy in such a way as to offer a viable alternative to the largely discredited Arab nationalism emanating from Cairo and Damascus. Thus both Arafat and Habash would look further afield for examples of successful revolutionary movements to serve as models for the rising Palestinian armed struggle. This was an auspicious time for aspiring guerillas. Radical movements, social protest, and political turmoil were on the rise around the world in the late 1960s as the postwar generation came of age in the First, Second, and Third Worlds. While the First and Second Worlds split into two opposing blocs in the Cold War rivalry, the Third World emerged as the product of decolonization. Composed of dozens of postcolonial states, the Third World functioned more as a political project than as a geographic space. In its most general sense, that project represented the demands of the formerly colonized nations for political equality, but its character was in a nearly continuous state of flux.[8]

The first wave of postcolonial nationalism—the Bandung Generation—had lost much of its energy by the mid-1960s. Meanwhile, rising on the Third World political scene was a younger set of postcolonial leaders who were less enamored with the visions of state-based development and nonaligned foreign policy than their predecessors. The Cuban and Algerian revolutions had added a new revolutionary flavor to the cause of Third World liberation, while the spectacle of the Vietnamese people challenging American military might in Southeast Asia had become a rallying cry for revolutionaries around the world. To some observers, the nature of social revolution seemed to be changing as its pace quickened: the Cuban and Algerian experiences suggested the possibility of a new model of revolution built around the concept of urban guerilla warfare rather than a mass proletarian uprising. Under this new model, the guerillas operating in the cities would create the conditions for the revolution rather than waiting for them to materialize on their own.[9] These wars of national liberation in the Third World spawned a radical literature that quickly circulated through the international system and became a sort of canon for revolutionaries. Palestinian fighters sought to apply the principles of writers such as Frantz Fanon, Mao Zedong, Vo Nguyen Giap, and Che Guevara to their own liberation struggle.

Leaders such as Arafat would gravitate toward these models of national liberation through guerilla war. In their one meeting with Che Guevara in 1964 at the Hotel Atteli in Algiers, Fatah officials apparently charmed the Argentine guerilla commander, who expressed his surprise that the Palestinians had not started their own armed struggle and promised Cuban solidarity if they did.[10]

This association with Third World revolutionaries would shape the ideological orientation of groups such as Fatah and serve to differentiate them from Arab states such as Egypt and Syria. In August 1967, Fatah published fourteen pamphlets under the series title *Revolutionary Studies and Experiences*, outlining the basic policy positions of the resistance movement. In addition to titles such as *How to Launch the People's Armed Revolution* and *The Revolution and the Road to Victory*, the series contained three pamphlets devoted to the Chinese, Vietnamese, and Cuban revolutions, plus a shorter study on the Algerian revolution. The booklets portrayed the group as a fundamentally cosmopolitan organization with spiritual ties to revolutionaries around the Third World; the Palestinian resistance identified its struggle as one front in a global war against the forces of imperialism and neoimperialism taking place around the Third World. The booklets were part of a concerted effort by the guerillas to bolster the transnational dimensions of their movement. That a struggling resistance movement should devote such substantial resources to the study of the wider world reveals the importance of international events in shaping regional politics in what was becoming an increasingly global order. Arafat was intent upon the goal of liberating the Palestinian movement from the "stranglehold of Arab tutelage" under which it had operated for the previous two decades. Another pamphlet from late 1967, entitled *The Relationship of the Palestinian Revolution with the Arab Revolution and the World Revolution*, also tried to distance Palestinian nationalism from its wider Arab counterpart and explain the links between Palestinian and Third World revolutionary movements.[11]

More than simply propaganda, these manuals constituted a clear articulation of Fatah's strategy of revolution—if not military tactics. This shift away from Cairo and Damascus as model struggles underscored the fundamental differences between the Palestinian guerillas and the older Arab nationalists, reinforcing arguments for an independent Palestinian nationalism. Likewise, Fatah began its study of revolutionary warfare with the Chinese example rather than the Bolsheviks. Using Mao's example of a people's liberation war as a starting point, Palestinian cadres then turned to the Cuban model of *foco* warfare, Algerian theories of urban guerilla war, and finally the Vietnamese innovations of people's war that called for the creation of a general offensive and uprising. These examples of revolutionary war in the Third World inspired Palestinian fighters. In time, the fedayeen would join the ranks of these theorists of revolutionary warfare with their own version of guerilla war.[12]

Both the PFLP and Fatah's writings reflected this revolutionary cosmopolitan worldview. As they published newspapers, magazines, and books, the guerillas narrated their own national experience and, in doing so, reimagined the Palestinian community as a stateless nation of liberation fighters rather than a group of Arab refugees and a propaganda tool of the regimes in Cairo and Damascus. As the guerilla press constructed a vision of the outside world, it self-consciously represented the Palestinian struggle as a Third World resistance movement, circulating throughout the Palestinian diaspora notions of radical liberation through armed struggle. The idea that Palestinian activists would embrace Chinese, Vietnamese, and Cuban leaders as the ideological inspiration for their revolution represented a rebellion against the imagined geography of the Cold War order. Geographic distinctions had been set in place as Western empires extended political control over the larger world and divided it into regions. These geographical units were demarcated as much by Western interests and conceptions of the world as they were by actual boundaries. Just as this process of mapping accompanied the extension of European empires, the retreat of those empires witnessed a process of de-mapping as postcolonial actors imposed their own geographies. The fedayeen's appropriation of transnational revolutionary ideologies was in many ways symptomatic of the rise of a new vision of global order and of a wider transnational political consciousness.

An awareness of this consciousness is evident in the publications of the guerilla press, which targeted a diverse range of audiences. The first of these consisted of the fedayeen themselves. The various guerilla organizations produced publications intended for military and political training, indoctrination, and news. The guerillas also published for the wider Palestinian diaspora in the refugee camps, the occupied territories, and the Arab world. The other Arab states and their populations represented a third audience for the fedayeen's public information apparatus. These publications were not published solely in Arabic; a substantial portion of the guerillas' public materials appeared in English and French and was aimed at the broader world community and designed to engender support for the fedayeen's struggle. Likewise, the guerillas' public diplomacy efforts in international forums such as the United Nations, the Non-Aligned Movement, and the Organization of African Unity were directed toward a global audience. Although guerilla leaders were initially skeptical about the ability of these global information campaigns and the international community to redress their grievances, these efforts would develop into a key dimension of the Palestinian struggle in later years.

While the superpower rivalry dominated Western visions of international affairs, actors in the developing world focused on the divide between rich and poor nations and the split between the postcolonial world and the former imperial powers. Arafat embraced this new global political geography. The Palestinians together with the Cubans, Chinese, Algerians, and Vietnamese were associated with the forces of liberation, while Israel—with its ties to the United States, Rhodesia, and South Africa—was allied with the forces of imperialism.[13] "As we know," Salah Khalaf (aka Abu Iyad), Fatah's second in command, explained, "the world is in practice divided into three parts: The Eastern Camp, the Western Camp and the Third World."[14] Here was a worldview that moved beyond the binary Cold War divide to focus on the importance of the global South.

Paradoxically, this emerging cosmopolitan consciousness would play a key role in cementing Palestinian claims to nationhood as the fedayeen sought to frame their own struggle within the broader context of global decolonization. Arafat addressed Arabs, Muslims, and Third World revolutionaries "in Africa, Asia and Latin America who consider our struggle as part of the struggle against oppression everywhere." "Our struggle is part and parcel of every struggle against imperialism, injustice and oppression in the world," Arafat went on to say. "It is part of the world revolution which aims at establishing social justice and liberating mankind." As Arafat envisioned it, the alliance of neoimperialist powers facing the Palestinians stretched from Israel to the United States to the reactionary regimes of southern Africa. Israeli visits to South Vietnam to study the counterinsurgency in that country reinforced Arafat's conviction that Israel was "playing the new role of the East India Company in the Middle East."[15]

Indeed, to many radicals in the Middle East, the United States appeared to be the new imperial power in world affairs. The PFLP argued that, following World War II, the colonial-imperialist forces of the world had gathered behind the leadership of the United States. This new formulation of global power under Washington's leadership had developed the techniques of neoimperialism through which it hoped to limit the expansion of the socialist camp and to destroy movements of national liberation around the world. Events in Vietnam, Cuba, and other places had shown that when native peoples resisted, Washington would not hesitate to send in military forces to crush the insurrection. In order to resist these attempts to isolate and neutralize the Palestinian revolution, Arafat asserted, the fedayeen must launch a popular liberation war and "enter into a full alliance with all revolutionary forces on the world level." Arafat continued:

> The major conflict experienced by the world of today is the conflict between exploiting world imperialism on the one hand and [the peoples of Africa, Asia and Latin America] and the socialist camp on the other. The alliance of the Palestinian and Arab national liberation movement with the liberation movement in Vietnam, the revolutionary situation in Cuba and the Democratic People's Republic of Korea and the national liberation movements in Asia, Africa and Latin American is the only way to create the camp that is capable of facing and triumphing over the imperialist camp.

Ultimately, the liberation forces of the world must be brought into alignment with the wider forces of the global revolution.[16]

The Palestinian fedayeen seized on the promise of liberation through revolution in the Algerian, Cuban, and Vietnamese models. National liberation struggle would be the means by which the Palestinians would secure their national rights, restoring Fanon's sense of dignity to the oppressed in an

FIGURE 1.1 Cover of Fatah newspaper *Hisad al-'Asifa*, "1948 Refugees—1965
Revolutionaries." Courtesy of the Library of the Institute for Palestine Studies, Beirut.

attempt to redirect their energies toward armed struggle.[17] This image of the
Palestinian guerilla as a national liberation fighter would soon become an icon
of the movement. A 1969 issue of Fatah's newspaper, *Hisad al-'Asifa*, bore the
caption "The Palestinians: refugees [*al-'aja'un*] 1948, revolutionaries [*thuwar*]
1965." The words were scrawled over an illustration of an elderly Palestinian
woman clinging to the breast of a young guerilla fighter with an AK-47 slung
over his shoulder. The two stood in front of a refugee camp with children playing in the background.[18] The guerillas insisted that they had been pushed into
the armed struggle as the only means of securing their national rights:

> For twenty years most of the Palestinians have lived in a diaspora of
> shabby tents, misery and the humiliation of a meager dole. In this schizo-
> phrenic world of ours the rights of Africans, Asians and Polynesians
> were recognized and espoused, while Palestinian rights were disregarded
> and forgotten. Not even the tragedy of the heroic Angolans, South Africans
> and Zimbabweans equaled theirs. For alone among these people, the
> Palestinians were totally uprooted from their land and completely denied

the right to live on it and enjoy its fruits.... We refuse to accept misery and diaspora as our fate, and we refuse charity and compromise as solutions to our problem. We shall overcome: through a long-term liberation revolution to destroy the bases of colonialist aggression that frustrate the exercise of our inalienable rights, and bring an end to the racist militarist regime that oppresses our people.[19]

Fatah officials were convinced that the world respected only the strong. For the past twenty years, the image of the Palestinians had been that of refugees, but by launching an armed struggle, the guerillas had "completely transformed the picture of these crowds into that of combatants who bear arms in quest of freedom."[20]

Further, guerilla struggle seemed the only means available to Palestinian activists to resist their present situation. Fatah leaders explained that their political and military efforts represented two parts of a single struggle, and their separation would lead to failure of the revolution. Because they could not muster the military power necessary to confront conventional Israeli forces, the guerillas must widen their political base. At the same time, a political movement divorced from military operations would remain impotent and vulnerable to military attack. By linking the armed struggle to a wider political movement, however, the guerillas hoped to survive the confrontation with Israel. These connections must move beyond the local population and win the backing of revolutionary groups around the world. Fatah's political struggle must therefore continue to push forward on both the regional and international fronts.[21]

The fedayeen recognized the importance of winning the support of the world community, and to this end, fedayeen leaders kept a vigilant eye on the world press, publishing regular articles in guerilla newspapers on international reactions to resistance activities.[22] A 1969 Fatah pamphlet dedicated to the international media explained that world opinion was slowly gathering behind the guerillas as the Palestinians were becoming associated with the European resistance movements of World War II. Reproducing articles from the *Guardian*, the *Times* of London, the *Observer*, *Life* magazine, the *Daily Star*, and the *International Herald Tribune*, Fatah reiterated British and American statements that drew parallels between Palestinian fighters, European partisans, and the South Vietnamese National Liberation Front. Such efforts to recast the Palestinian resistance as a cosmopolitan political movement rather than simply a refurbished Arab nationalism were central to the fedayeen's strategies of establishing links with the wider world while maintaining independence from the Arab states.[23]

The fedayeen paid special attention to the issue of human rights as well. In an open letter to the UN General Assembly in October 1968, Fatah claimed the status of a legitimate national resistance movement fighting for self-determination—as set out in the UN Charter and the Universal Declaration of Human Rights—against a colonialist apparatus that had been in place since 1918. Having launched a resistance in the same spirit as the anti-Nazi resistance groups of World War II France, Italy, Czechoslovakia, and the Soviet Union, Fatah leaders called for international recognition of their legitimate rights as a people living under hostile military occupation.[24] Addressing the United Nations Conference on Human Rights, Fatah asserted that if

> human rights, fundamental freedom, justice and morality have one and the same value for human beings the world over, then the all-important question that arises is whether men and women of good will should not accept the challenge and give new impetus to their ideals and ethical precepts; indeed whether they should not translate into practice the self-evident truths which they see before their own eyes!

Fatah explained that it was a movement struggling to achieve the same ideals that formed the basis of the Universal Declaration on Human Rights. "The truth of the matter is," the Fatah representative stated,

> that all of the full-scale Israeli attacks, the so-called reprisals, search and destroy operations, the destruction of villages, and the massacre of civilians, "border tensions" and the prevailing strife and misery in the Arab world, particularly against Palestine Arabs, are the logical corollary and by-product of a larger and by far more serious phenomenon; a part of a long-range Zionist imperialist policy.

The Palestinian problem was at its core a problem of human rights, and its solution must be rooted in the restoration of those rights, as set out in the UN Charter. "What we are asking for," explained the representative, "[is an] application of the rules and principles of international law and a respect for the worth and dignity of the human person."[25]

Fatah appealed to concepts of international law and justice, explaining that the government of Israel had violated the basic human rights of Palestinians living under occupation and as refugees. Because international organizations such as the United Nations had not enforced their own rulings, the Palestinians had no choice but to launch their own struggle. The goal of the Palestinian resistance was thus in keeping with those of its counterparts "throughout the world, wherever Fascist and imperialist aggression is being perpetrated—in Vietnam, South Africa, Angola, Bolivia or elsewhere."[26] The image of the fedayeen cadre as Arab Che Guevaras challenged Orientalist constructions of the Arab militant as a backward, anti-Semitic religious fanatic.

This conception of a world in the grip of revolutionary ferment framed the fedayeen's vision of its own struggle. The war in Vietnam had shown the world the ability of a people's army to stand up to superior force and to struggle for liberation. Similar insurgencies in Laos, Burma, Thailand, Guinea, and Eritrea were all part of a single global struggle against imperialism through the act of people's war.[27] Multiple revolutions had appeared on the global horizon in which oppressed peoples rose up against injustice to claim control over their own lands and wealth.[28] As one of these national liberation movements, Fatah called upon the rest of the world to come out in support of the fedayeen and "provide the Palestinian people with such material and moral aid as they give to liberating revolutions in Vietnam, Rhodesia, Angola, and other armed popular revolutions."[29]

Fedayeen newspapers devoted considerable coverage to revolutionary struggles in the wider world. *Filastine al-Thawra* ran a regular section entitled "Reports of the Revolution in the Last Half Month," which covered armed struggles in Southeast Asia, Africa, and Latin America. "Decolonization is always a violent phenomenon," insisted Fatah officials, borrowing a phrase from Fanon. Arafat insisted that the Palestinian liberation struggle was a progressive movement that embraced the right to self-determination for all nations, had ties to revolutionary and leftist movements around the world, and was part of a worldwide movement for social justice.[30]

Although leaders such as Nasser loomed large in Western consciousness as symbols of nonaligned resistance, by the late 1960s the archetype of anticolonial struggle in the Arab world was the Algerian Front de Libération Nationale (FLN). The strategic implications of the Algerian war of liberation—especially the notion of urban guerilla war and the importance of winning international support—would play a key role in the ideological construction of the Palestinian struggle.[31] Salah Khalaf explained that the younger generation of Palestinians had been inspired by the success of the Algerian revolution, which served as a model for the fedayeen.[32]

Salient as the Algerian experience had been, no liberation struggle generated more enthusiasm than the one taking place in Southeast Asia as a population of peasants fought the world's greatest power to a standoff. The PFLP argued that the Vietnamese revolution had demonstrated that by mobilizing the masses, studying the art of revolutionary warfare, and building international alliances, a movement could achieve victory over imperialism.[33] In the face of IDF military superiority, the Palestinians had no choice but to adopt the Vietnamese and Cuban models of guerilla warfare, thus turning the Middle East into "a second Vietnam."[34] The fedayeen might even manage to turn one of the surrounding Arab capitals—Amman and Beirut being the most likely candidates—into what the PFLP described as an "Arab Hanoi," a base for revolutionary action self-consciously modeled on the South Vietnamese experience.[35]

Fatah seized on the massive antiwar demonstrations that took place throughout the United States on 15 October 1969 as part of the Moratorium to End the War in Vietnam as an opportunity to air its own grievances. "Vietnam today is the personification of the suffering and pain that the 'Free World' is inflicting on peoples in a mad parody of the absurd," *Fateh* wrote, arguing that the antiwar protests should be understood as an "expression of Revolution" in the United States. The newspaper insisted that "death in Vietnam and occupied Palestine is real and ugly. But the dollars and advisors, the B-52's and Phantoms, and the new interpretations of dual citizenship which are being pumped by the US Establishment to the puppet regime in South Vietnam or the Zionist settler-state in Israel are uglier."[36]

This technique of framing the Palestinian struggle within the context of the Vietnamese experience went deeper than antiwar sentiment, however. When reports of the My Lai massacre broke in late 1969, Fatah announced the news in its newspaper in a story entitled "Vietnam Has Its Deir Yassin." The story drew clear parallels between the 1968 massacre of Vietnamese peasants by U.S. soldiers and the slaughter of more than a hundred Palestinian peasants by members of the Irgun and Lehi paramilitary groups in the village of Deir Yassin twenty years before.[37] The 1948 massacre was one of the central myths of the Palestinian nation prior to 1968, a story of mass suffering and exile that gave meaning to the Palestinian plight as refugees and served as a rallying cry for the resistance. By transposing the images of My Lai into the narrative of Deir Yassin, Fatah linked the two powerful symbols and reinforced the notion of a common struggle against global forces of oppression.

The Vietnam allegory also served as a response to criticisms that the fedayeen were jeopardizing the Middle East peace process and threatening to spark a superpower conflict. "We are a liberation movement," insisted Khalaf. "Why is such talk about world peace not tendered to the liberation movement in Vietnam for instance? Vietnam likewise could threaten to cause a world war."[38] At the same time, the idea that the events of Vietnam would spill over into other parts of the world, the Middle East in particular, ran strong in many of the guerillas' messages. Slogans such as "Revolution today in Vietnam and tomorrow in Palestine" suggested that American fears of the domino theory were perhaps not entirely off base.[39]

This effort to associate themselves with the Vietnamese resistance not only served as an inspiration to fedayeen cadres but also functioned as a way of accessing international networks of Third World radicals. Although they might be hopelessly outgunned by the IDF and desperately squeezed by the political machinations of the Arab states, Palestinian fighters could win support in the international community by casting themselves as a heroic resistance movement striking against the forces of global imperialism.[40] Communist regimes in Cuba and North Korea also appeared as common points of interest in fedayeen propaganda, as did the series of conflicts unfolding in sub-Saharan Africa.[41] As events in the latter region become increasingly violent, increasing numbers of guerillas and outside observers would begin to note similarities between Palestine and places such as Rhodesia and South Africa.[42] The guerillas had, in their own words, "been able to penetrate the iron curtain imposed by the Zionist movement on world public opinion," exposing the "falsity of fabrication and lies" that had been leveled at the fedayeen.[43] It would also put them at odds with the United States and two of its key allies in the region.

A Worldwide Phenomenon

It was only the second day of the June War, but U.S. ambassador Dwight Porter had his hands full. Between the angry Lebanese mob outside the embassy's doors and the eight Marine guards itching to "lock and load" their weapons, it was all Porter, an Oklahoma native and graduate of Grinnell College, could do to keep the situation from boiling over into a major international incident. The regional center for U.S. cultural and commercial relations with the Arab world, the U.S. embassy in Beirut was about to become even more important for Washington's operations in the region. In the following days, six Arab capitals, including Cairo and Damascus, would sever relations with Washington, leaving Beirut as the hub for American diplomatic and intelligence activities in the region. For the time being, however, the embassy was under siege. As the crowd burst through the enormous glass door to the building, the commander of the small police unit reinforcing the Marine guard seized one of the rioters, threw him against the wall, and killed him. The shocked crowd recoiled and then retreated. The U.S. mission to Lebanon was not yet safe, however. The surge of anti-Americanism that followed the 1967 war put tremendous pressure on Beirut to join its fellow Arab states and break relations with Washington. Porter suggested a different approach to Lebanese officials: rather than close down their embassies, Beirut and Washington would take the more moderate action of recalling their ambassadors. While Porter would go home, a skeleton staff of Americans would remain. The ambassador would spend the summer pushing his superiors to throw their weight behind the effort to achieve a general peace in the Arab-Israeli conflict, and then in the fall he would join the trickle of Americans returning to Beirut.[44]

The scene outside the embassy in Beirut was not so different from similar events taking place around the world. While authorities confronted mounting upheaval in cities around the United States, Foreign Service officers sensed a rising tide of anti-Americanism abroad. In the broadest sense, the changing geopolitical landscape of the 1960s presented policy makers in Washington with a new set of global challenges. Analysts working for the Central Intelligence Agency (CIA) explained that as new actors emerged in an increasingly complex international order and political and economic troubles continued to plague the developing world, both superpowers were likely to lose authority and influence. Adding to this erosion of superpower authority, analysts warned, was the fact that "the old ideologies are losing much of their impact, and new forms of radicalism are emerging." It was thus becoming increasingly difficult to predict future events. "Some of the poorer nations could collapse into anarchy or be overcome by their economic weakness," the CIA report noted. In the coming decade, the smaller nations of the world would be more likely to buck great-power authority and strike out on their own.[45] These fears of anarchy and revolution bred of structural collapse would prove to be an enduring theme as U.S. policy makers speculated about the 1970s.

American intelligence analysts warned that the developing world was likely to experience a wave of revolutions that would be, for the most part, noncommunist in origin yet still anti-American. This alone was a source for worry that the binary distinctions of the Cold War would have less relevance in a globalizing world system. While the Third World was being swept by a wave of revolutions, advanced countries would experience persistent social upheaval brought on by the collapse of old ideologies and the rise of student unrest and social protest. These tensions were likely to "open deep fissures in modern society and threaten existing political and social institutions."[46] The Third World was in a state of revolutionary upheaval, the agency explained, as "Nehru's idealism, Sukarno's new Emerging Forces, Nkrumah's Pan-Africanism, and Nasser's Pan-Arabism have all faded away." The CIA predicted that "new nationalist ideologies, perhaps of a radical character, will probably arise as time goes by." Both Washington and Moscow were losing power and influence as groups and nations around the world increasingly began to pursue their own nationalistic interests.[47]

The Soviets' fears that they were witnessing the beginning of a global counterrevolutionary offensive in the developing world mirrored Washington's anxieties. The collapse of Sukarno's regime in Indonesia, Nkrumah's fall, the mounting U.S. counterinsurgency in Vietnam, the June 1967 war, and a succession of intrigues in Damascus stoked Moscow's worries and led Soviet leaders to adopt a hard-line approach to the Middle East.[48] While American-backed counterrevolutionaries threatened the Soviet position from the right, Maoist radicals—backed by Beijing's rhetoric as well as its weapons—threatened from the left. The People's Republic of China was becoming an increasingly important player in world affairs and a potential wild card in East-West relations. In a 1963 report, the CIA noted China's growing influence over the international communist movement. While Moscow maintained its overwhelming authority over international communism, Beijing's influence was growing, a fact that surely unsettled the Kremlin.[49] The Sino-Soviet split had pushed both countries into a position where each power sought to outbid the other for legitimacy as the patron of world revolution. At the same time that the Soviets continued to back the regimes in Cairo and Damascus, leaders in Beijing hoped to use the fedayeen to gain a foothold in the Middle East and thereby frustrate the plans of both U.S. "imperialists" and Soviet "revisionists," who no longer stood for the true ideals of the communist revolution. While the Cultural Revolution would lead to a general withdrawal of Chinese forces around the world, Beijing's support for the PLO would remain largely intact. This tension created opportunities for the Palestinians and other nonaligned actors to play the communist powers off one another in hopes of gaining support from one or more of the great powers.[50]

While the Soviets, Chinese, and Americans jockeyed for position, the social upheavals—particularly among the younger generation—presented a threat to the status quo both locally and globally. The CIA reported in 1968 that student dissidence was "a worldwide phenomenon. It is shaped in every instance by local conditions, but nonetheless there are striking similarities." The report explained that although students had represented an important force for political change throughout the modern period, Americans tended to dismiss student demonstrations in different parts of the world as unconnected events that had little impact on U.S. interests. This social unrest should be taken more seriously, however. Opposition to U.S. foreign policy in Vietnam and around the world added fuel to the fires of student unrest in Western Europe, Latin America, and the Middle East. The violence that had broken out in the Middle East, Japan, Latin America, and Europe was now creeping into student movements in the United States. While they might reap some short-term gains from student protest against U.S. policies, the CIA suggested, communist states faced analogous problems from their own youth. Young people around the world had come to embrace thinkers such as Frantz Fanon and revolutionary

FIGURE 1.2 *Italian students, photo from Fatah's newspaper* Fateh. *Courtesy of the Library of the Institute for Palestine Studies, Beirut.*

heroes including Mao Zedong, Fidel Castro, and Che Guevara, in addition to writers such as C. Wright Mills and Herbert Marcuse. Although they were largely separate and local in origin, radical student movements maintained contacts with one another that might one day be formalized.[51]

Just as a new generation came forward in the First and Second Worlds to demand a greater share of sociopolitical power, new nations in the developing world voiced louder demands for power and influence in the international community. As the CIA explained:

> The pace of change in the world is accelerating, and there has been a marked increase in the interaction of political events in different parts of the world. Conflicts or rebellions in one area encourage dissidents in others, and major changes in a nation's political life can occur quite suddenly. Important departures from present world trends are almost certain over the next ten years.[52]

The entrenched hegemony of the superpowers over both domestic and international society that had been a feature of the early Cold War era was slipping, and now the global superpowers resorted to more coercive measures to shore up their faltering control. Thus, as the 1960s came to an end, Third World crises increasingly became sites of contestation where new notions of social reality developed. Adding to the global stakes tied up in these Third World flash points, the increasing quantity and depth of transnational connections in the international order ensured that conflicts in one part of the world carried important implications for societies in another. At the same time that societies around the world become more connected, new players complicated the international system.

This growing integration of global events was of paramount concern to American intelligence officers. "Wars, revolutions, and political crises in one place will impinge more and more upon the national fortunes of those not directly involved," noted the report's authors. Although still susceptible to great-power influence, Third World leaders would increasingly follow their own interests, which would likely result in more upheaval. While it was not the most probable outcome, the CIA warned, substantial portions of the developing world could "fall into complete chaos." Washington and Moscow would have to find new ways to project their power over a global environment in which terrorism, guerilla warfare, and counterinsurgency would be more common than conventional warfare. There would be a greater need for clandestine operations and military advisors and less call for traditional military units and expeditionary forces.[53]

Washington and Moscow shared many of the same interests in managing threats to the status quo and containing radical challenges to the global system. The logic of superpower détente became more compelling as Third World radicals demonstrated that the gap between the developed and developing worlds was often as salient as the divide between Washington and Moscow, if not more so. Great-power rivalries proved difficult to set aside, however, especially in light of emerging risks and opportunities in the Third World. Thus, even as détente became a strategic priority, the United States and the Soviet Union continued and at times accelerated their competition on the periphery. Moscow and Washington sought both order and influence in the Third World even when these goals conflicted.

The Middle East was a key battleground in this struggle for the Third World as well as a region of substantial strategic interest for the United States, given the presence of oil, its proximity to the Soviet Union, and its strategic position in the Mediterranean and at the crossroads of Europe, Africa, and Asia. The onset of the Cold War and the decline of British and French imperial power in the region had made the Middle East an important theater of the early Cold War. By the end of the 1960s, however, American policy makers' biggest fears revolved around the area's potential to trigger a superpower confrontation—a concern shared by Moscow—and the prospect of creeping Soviet influence in the region. For example, a CIA estimate from 1965 explained that the collapse of the European empires and the emergence of local social protest movements had opened the nations in North Africa, the Middle East, and South Asia to Soviet influence. Another report, circulated on the eve of the June War, warned of Moscow's growing influence in the Mediterranean basin and Soviet leaders' desire to forge an alliance "between the 'socialist camp' and a broad front of revolutionary forces to constrict and weaken the world position of the Western powers." The Cold War was in the process of transforming from a contest over Europe into a long-term struggle on many fronts around the developing world.[54]

The 1960s witnessed the consolidation of a close relationship between Israel and the United States. Both John F. Kennedy and Lyndon Johnson nevertheless sought—at least publicly—to remain even-handed in the Arab-Israeli dispute. Kennedy laid the foundations for what would become the U.S.-Israeli "special relationship" in 1961. Kennedy brought an admiration of Zionism to the White House but nevertheless hoped to achieve a resolution of the Arab-Israeli conflict. At the same time, Kennedy was preoccupied with the issue of nuclear proliferation and the very real fear that the Israel might decide to use its reactor at Dimona to produce nuclear weapons. To this end, the president resolved to provide U.S. weaponry—specifically Hawk surface-to-air missiles—to the Jewish state in hopes of dissuading Israel from going nuclear. While Kennedy would be remembered for providing weapons to Israel, his efforts to make progress on the Arab-Israeli conflict would achieve little.[55]

Lyndon Johnson continued down the road of improved relations with Israel. Johnson was closer to American pro-Israel groups than Kennedy had been, and he was considerably less tolerant of Arab radicals such as Nasser. Moreover, Johnson seems to have had a set of prejudices that cast Arabs as backward and untrustworthy. Historian Douglas Little argues, for example, that Johnson tended to view the Arab-Israeli dispute along the lines of Israeli cowboys and Arab Indians. Nevertheless, Johnson, like Kennedy, remained reluctant to open American military stores to the Jewish state. At the same time, he did little to restrain Israel's leaders as the 1967 crisis began to mount. While historians argue about whether Johnson gave Israel a "green or yellow light" to launch its preemptive strike against its Arab neighbors, it is clear that he did not flash a red one.[56]

As Ambassador Porter and his counterparts around the region could see, however, the June 1967 war changed the political landscape of the Middle East. Both Moscow and Washington recognized that the Arab defeat had the potential to radicalize the Arab world by chipping away at Cairo's influence, exposing the failures of Arab nationalism, and opening space for new groups to enter the political mainstream. Historians of the Arab world have argued that the fallout from the 1967 war played a key role in discrediting secular Arab nationalism and encouraging more-radical forms of political and religious thought.[57] At the same time, the post-1967 situation raised the possibility of a genuine peace in the region under the auspices of a land-for-peace agreement.

The Dowry Pleases You but the Bride Does Not

The years between 1967 and 1973 would witness the formation of an Israeli approach to the PLO and the Palestinians. Inside the newly occupied territories of the West Bank and Gaza, the Israeli government found itself facing a novel challenge: how to control nearly 1 million Palestinians. This task fell to Israel's minister of defense, Moshe Dayan. Born in Ottoman Palestine in Kibbutz Deganya Alef in 1915, Dayan had been introduced to a martial life early. He joined the Haganah—the Jewish militia in Palestine and precursor to the IDF—at the age of fourteen and was arrested in 1939 by British authorities. After his release in 1941, he participated in joint British-Haganah operations in Lebanon, where he lost his left eye. During the 1948 war, he rose to prominence and became a national hero for his role in commanding IDF forces in the 1956 Sinai campaign. He retired from the IDF to enter politics, joining the Mapai Party in 1959. Seven years later, Dayan would famously tour South Vietnam, where he would inspect the U.S. counterinsurgency and publish his observations. As tensions mounted in 1967, Prime Minister Levi Eshkol brought Dayan back into the Israeli government as minister of defense. Israel's spectacular victory helped to renew his military fame.[58]

Dayan would be the dominant figure in shaping Israel's approach to the PLO during these early years, and he would do so primarily in the interests of maintaining security in the occupied territories. Foreign Minister Abba Eban would call the 1967–73 period the "era of Moshe Dayan."[59] In his memoirs, Dayan argued that the biggest sources of friction in the occupation came not from the Arab residents of the occupied territories—who quickly adjusted to the IDF's presence—but rather from the guerillas living outside of the military's control, particularly those in the Jordanian "sector." These attacks were seen mainly as a nuisance, the acts of loosely organized "terrorist cells" and "sabotage squads" who harassed Israeli farmers and kibbutzim. "Though the big war was officially over," Dayan recalled after a visit to a settlement in early November 1967, "we clearly had to prepare ourselves in this sector for a new phase and style of hostilities." Dayan responded by moving IDF units closer to the border to provide a measure of defense. He blamed the incursions on King Hussein's failure to stop the guerillas and suggested the remedy of attacking the Jordanian army in an effort to induce Amman to tighten its control over the fedayeen. This would be the basis of Israel's post-1967 approach to the Palestinian fedayeen. Dayan put forward four basic principles of Israel's counterguerilla operations. First, the control of Fatah "terrorists" was to be considered a Jordanian obligation under the most recent cease-fire agreements. Second, Israel would not stop at the Jordanian border; if the fedayeen crossed into Israeli-controlled territory, the IDF would not refrain from crossing into Jordanian territory. Third, counterguerilla operations were to be understood as "military moves in a [prolonged] campaign." Finally, villages along the frontier must be militarized and integrated as part of a broader security network.[60]

At the most basic level, however, Dayan and the Israeli government misunderstood the threat that the PLO represented as being primarily military, rather than political in nature. Like the majority of the international community circa 1967, Israel viewed the Palestinians primarily as Arab refugees. Palestinian nationalism was treated as a fabrication, part of a broader Arab plot to destroy the Jewish state. Indeed, the Arab regimes frequently used the Palestinian issue as a cause to rally domestic support and distract from their internal failures. Deeper tendencies to homogenize the peoples and states of the Arab world only made this dismissal of an autonomous Palestinian political consciousness easier in Israel and elsewhere. The Israelis also incorrectly judged Palestinian guerilla fighters—usually referred to as "terrorists"—as a nuisance, but hardly a significant national security threat compared to the armies of Syria, Egypt, Jordan, and Iraq. Indeed, Israel was at pains to refute inflated guerilla claims of military success. Israeli leaders also tended to view the guerillas as appendages of the Arab states from which they operated. Whether they were proxies of or challengers to neighboring Arab regimes—and they could be either—fedayeen groups were the responsibility of their host governments. These three principles led to a succession of Israeli governments that treated the rising power of the PLO primarily as a military threat. Moreover, to focus on the rising political and diplomatic influence of the PLO seemed, to many Israeli officials, tantamount to acknowledging the validity of Palestinian claims.

Thus, the Eshkol, Golda Meir, and Yitzhak Rabin governments each fell into the trap of dismissing the growing political power of the PLO in favor of working to crush its military wing. The PLO's military operations actually functioned in support of its diplomatic and political offices rather than the reverse. In hindsight, one officer of the Shin Bet, Israel's internal security service, would lament that perhaps the greatest failure of the war against the PLO had been to focus on counterterrorism rather than political activity among the Palestinian population.[61] Whether Israel could have done anything to counteract the PLO's rising influence in the region and the wider world remains open for debate, but on the question of the primacy of politics and diplomacy in the PLO's struggle—as well as the ultimate independence of groups such as Fatah and PFLP from the Arab states—there is little doubt now.

None of this was clear, however, in the initial weeks following the 1967 war. The IDF's stunning victory in the war left Israel in possession of substantial tracts of Arab land, which might be used as bargaining chips in obtaining official recognition and peace treaties from its Arab neighbors. The Israeli cabinet was torn over what course to take in the wake of this spectacular victory. Returning the territories would effectively sacrifice the strategic depth that they added to Israel, along with a more defensible eastern border and the holy sites in Jerusalem. Gaza could not be returned to Egyptian control, since the IDF occupied the Sinai Peninsula. The matter of the West Bank was even more complicated. Significant segments of Israeli society—specifically the adherents of Revisionist Zionism—called for the wholesale annexation of the West Bank, arguing that "Judea and Samaria" belonged to Israel. The problem, however, was that these combined territories contained more than 1 million Palestinians. If Israel annexed the West Bank, it would be forced to contend with this population. Giving West Bank Palestinians citizenship would erode the Jewish demographic majority in Israel; denying them citizenship would force Israel to establish a military occupation for the foreseeable future. The option of returning the territory to Jordan so soon after the 1967 war was also unappealing. As far as Israeli policy makers were concerned, there was no ideal solution. As Prime Minister Eshkol explained to Golda Meir, "The dowry pleases you but the bride does not."[62]

Initial discussions thus focused on the best means of returning the West Bank to Arab control. Two options—the Palestinian and the Jordanian—emerged in cabinet discussions through the end of 1967. The Palestinian option envisioned the creation of a semiautonomous Palestinian ministate; the Jordanian option called for the return of the territory to Jordanian sovereignty. Eshkol initially leaned toward the Palestinian option. Progress toward this end quickly ground to a halt, however, as the prime minister found that the traditional West Bank leaders favored full independence, not limited autonomy.

Moreover, the younger generation of Palestinians had become increasingly enamored with the exploits of the fedayeen. The Jordan option ran into difficulty with King Hussein, who was reluctant to break ranks with the rest of the Arab world so soon after the June defeat, especially if doing so entailed the loss of large chunks of the West Bank. As Minister of Labor Yigal Allon would later explain, the king "would rather leave Israel under international criticism in possession of all the West Bank than take on himself the responsibility of ceding 33 percent of it to us."[63] Thus, the government of Israel shifted to a platform of opposition to the creation of a Palestinian state, which it would maintain until the 1990s.

In light of the ad hoc nature of this new situation and the reality that the fedayeen were a nonstate group, the Israeli government did not formulate a clear foreign policy regarding the Palestinian resistance. Indeed, because the guerilla organizations were not states—and the Foreign Ministry focused on states—the government of Israel elected not to treat its interactions with the fedayeen as a diplomatic matter. Responsibility for dealing with the guerilla organizations thus fell to three groups: the IDF, the Shin Bet, and the Mossad, Israel's foreign intelligence service. Under Dayan's Ministry of Defense, the IDF would continue its policy of counterinsurgency and reprisals against suspected guerilla sanctuaries, in part as an attempt to compel Israel's neighbors to police the fedayeen groups. The Shin Bet was charged with surveillance and control in the occupied territories, while the Mossad was tasked with infiltrating Palestinian organizations abroad. Colonel Shlomo Gazit was put in charge of coordinating intelligence operations against Palestinian fighters in the occupied territories. The primary aim of these activities was to "isolate the terrorist from the general population and deny him shelter and assistance even though the natural sympathy of that population is with the terrorists and not the Israeli administration." Aided by initial Palestinian incompetence and the capture of a large cache of Jordanian intelligence files on the Palestinian resistance organizations, Shin Bet's activities on the West Bank would prove devastatingly effective.[64]

Thus, with the prospect of the creation of a Palestinian state closed, the Israeli government returned to its standing policy on the Palestinians. As had been the case prior to 1967, the Eshkol government would mediate the issue of the Palestinians through neighboring Arab governments whenever possible, rather than engaging in direct diplomacy with Palestinian leaders. Amman emerged as the centerpiece of this approach, owing to the concentration of guerilla groups inside Jordan and a history of working relations between the Israeli government and King Hussein. Although Israel would engage with the Palestinian population in the occupied territories directly, the international implications of Palestinian nationalism would be negotiated through Jordan. Successive Israeli governments hoped that IDF strikes against the fedayeen along with coordination with Amman might help to bring the guerillas—who were a security concern for both regimes—under control. At the same time, military reprisals against the Syrian and Lebanese governments would keep the pressure on Damascus and Beirut to tighten their control over Palestinian fighters on their soil.

The Next Generation of Arab Leaders

Meanwhile, both Washington and Moscow hoped to achieve a settlement that would stabilize the region in the wake of the June War while leaving their interests intact. This marked the beginning of the post-1967 Arab-Israeli peace process. The Johnson administration's initial thinking complemented dovish positions in Israel. This strategy embraced the notion that by rendering itself virtually impervious to attack, the state of Israel could compel its hostile neighbors to abandon irredentist aspirations and sue for peace. The IDF's performance in the June War—not to mention its occupation of vast tracts of strategically vital territory, such as the Sinai and the Golan Heights—transformed this strategy into a reality. Johnson and doves in Israel hoped that, having secured a position of such indomitable strength, the Israeli government might move quickly to trade land for peace.[65]

This was a high-stakes game, however, and the White House was not in a position to give it full attention. President Johnson was preoccupied with events in Vietnam, the upheavals within the Democratic Party, and the approaching presidential election. The State Department, which bore the brunt of the responsibility for formulating U.S. policy toward the region, worried that in the absence of concerted executive effort, the 1967 defeat had the potential to force the leadership of the Arab world away from Cairo and into the hands of more radical forces such as the regime in Algiers. It warned that this shift from Egypt to Algeria could represent a major change in the political order and magnitude of the Arab revolution.[66]

The State Department's fears about the future of the Arab world and the danger of growing radicalism were validated by phenomena occurring in the global system. Arabists warned of a generational shift in the Arab world that mirrored similar demographic changes in the West. In late January 1968, Majid Khadduri, a professor at the American University of Beirut, told Undersecretary of State Eugene Rostow that the leadership of the Arab world was "passing to the hands of a new generation." The first generation of Arab leaders had won their independence from Turkish, British, and French imperialism; the second had been influenced by the West as well as by Marxist and Soviet ideas in its search for progress. The current generation was clashing with the previous two and turning against the West. Washington's close relationship with Israel was overshadowing U.S. attempts to reach out to the Arab world and risked creating a permanent break. "The West must not lose the third generation in the

Arab Near East," Khadduri insisted. If the United States could not find a way to strengthen moderate elements in the region, "extremists would expand their position and seek to purge Arab society of Western values and concepts." For the time being, the United States simply was not doing enough to support these moderates.[67]

Rumblings of the change in regional affairs continued to reach Washington, which remained surprisingly ignorant of the power of Palestinians' aspirations for independence. The June War transformed the Palestinian situation by placing their remaining homelands under control of the IDF. National Security Council staff member Harold Saunders seemed genuinely surprised after a meeting in March 1968 with a Lebanese politician who urged recognition of the Palestinian movement. While most Westerners saw the Palestinian question as a refugee problem that needed to be resolved by the existing states in the region, the Arabs—according to the politician—believed that the matter could not be settled without Palestinian participation. "I have not heard expressed before as strongly the notion that the Palestinians must have a responsible voice in the peace settlement," Saunders noted afterward.[68] Viewed in hindsight, officials in the Johnson administration were witnessing a watershed moment in regional affairs.

The rising power of the Palestinian resistance movement signaled the onset of a crisis. Some observers in Washington and London warned that although direct challenges had been contained by Israeli security forces, Palestinian fighters had the potential to foment a massive resistance movement among Palestinians living inside Israel and to push the Arab governments toward greater militancy.[69] While the Arab states needed peace to regain territory and credibility lost in 1967, local leaders were not strong enough to stand up to criticism from neighboring governments and their own publics in order to endorse a settlement with Israel. Even as Washington continued its calls for support of UN peace efforts, some observers in the region predicted that only the leader of a unified fedayeen movement could muster the credibility to achieve a genuine settlement.[70] Policy makers in Washington were understandably wary of fedayeen appeals. Palestinian claims threatened the regional status quo in no small part because of the diffuse nature of the Palestinian diaspora; indeed, America's three closest allies in the region—Israel, Jordan, and Lebanon—controlled territory with substantial populations of potentially subversive Palestinians.

Furthermore, deep fears about the possibility of a global domino effect from guerilla victories in places such as Algeria and Vietnam haunted policy makers trying to devise strategies to deal with the problems of an increasingly interconnected world. The war in Vietnam—and the knowledge that such revolutionary pangs were not unique to Southeast Asia—drove home the transnational repercussions of local insurgencies. This had indeed been the case in Southeast Asia: like the Algerians before them, Vietnamese communists were working to marshal world opposition against U.S. action in Indochina. As a 1966 CIA report explained, liberation struggles and civil unrest in other parts of the world bolstered Vietnamese morale and demonstrated that the Vietnamese communists were "not alone in their opposition to Western 'imperialism and colonialism.'" The report warned that other national liberation movements, world opinion, and opposition in the United States could play a significant role in encouraging the insurgency in South Vietnam.[71] If Palestinian fighters could do the same, they might very well represent the next incarnation of a guerilla insurgency against U.S. interests in the Third World.

While the guerillas' public appeals gained support with audiences in the nonaligned world, State Department officials interpreted the fedayeen's growing popularity, Moscow's recent support for resistance movements, and Third World support for national liberation struggles as a new danger to U.S. interests in the region. In their eyes, Israel's occupation of the West Bank had sparked a growing Palestinian resistance similar to anti-Nazi resistance movements during World War II and contemporary ones in the Congo, Vietnam, and Algeria. They warned that "should the Arabs, either by themselves or with Soviet support and advice, succeed in shifting the ideological underpinnings of the Middle East conflict away from the old-fashioned concept of 'terrorism' and toward the newer notion of a legitimate resistance movement against foreign occupation, Israel and her friends will face an accelerating erosion of support for their current diplomatic positions." The American experience in Vietnam had shown the danger that international sympathy could create for powers seeking to resist the tide of revolutionary upheaval in the developing world.[72] In this regard, U.S. fears mirrored fedayeen hopes that a global audience might provide the basis for continuing resistance activities.

Ironically, many of the first members of this audience were nonstate groups and individuals in the Western world. As the June 1967 war drew to a close, intellectual Jean-Paul Sartre's journal, *Les Temps Modernes*, published a special issue on the Arab-Israeli conflict that aimed to establish a dialogue between pro-Arab and pro-Israeli scholars. One essay in particular, by French Orientalist Maxime Rodinson, stood out. A public intellectual, Marxist, and director of the Sorbonne's École Pratique des Haute Études, Rodinson was recognized as one of Europe's leading scholars of Middle East history. His article "Israel, Fait Colonial?" argued that the state of Israel represented a colonialist-settler state. Locating the history of Zionism within the broader context of European-American expansionism and its "civilizing mission," the essay insisted that Israel was the product of "colonial conquest, justified by an ethnocentric and racially exclusive ideology." In this respect, Israel should not be differentiated from other products of European colonialism such as the white regime in South Africa and French-ruled Algeria. Rodinson argued that an awareness of the "colonial character of the State of Israel" was necessary for understanding the Arab-Israeli conflict. The Arab reaction to this situation had been the same as the reaction of those "peoples of the Third World who are in the same situation."[73]

The French weekly *Jeune Afrique* also devoted continuing coverage to the emerging fedayeen movement in the wake of the 1967 war. The publication described the post-1967 PLO as the Palestinian FLN.[74] By May 1968, Fatah had made the cover of the journal, which boasted the first interview with Yasir Arafat, "the Palestinian 'Che'" and leader of the "secret Palestinian army." Arafat insisted that the Palestinian battle was part of the Third World struggle and the entire world's fight "against imperialism, racism and colonialism." Fatah had borrowed elements of the politico-military struggle from other revolutionary movements with which it was in contact, as well as sending representatives to the cultural congress of Havana, voicing a strong identification with the experiences of African Americans, and embracing the concept of black power.[75]

The Palestinian cause aroused interest on the other side of the English Channel as well. British philosopher Bertrand Russell's last public statement, read to the International Conference of Parliamentarians meeting in Cairo in February 1970, addressed the issues of Israeli "aggression" and peace in the Middle East. Comparing the conflict between Israel and its neighbors with the war in Vietnam and German bombing raids over Great Britain during World War II, Russell attacked the idea that IDF reprisals would lead to an Arab surrender. The state of Israel was an aggressive expansionist force in the region, behaving in "the traditional role of the imperial power, because it wishes to consolidate with the least difficulty what it has taken already by violence. Every new conquest becomes the new basis of the proposed negotiation from strength which ignores the injustice of the previous aggression." Meanwhile, the Palestinian refugees had entered their third decade of exile. "No people anywhere in the world would accept being expelled en masse from their own country; how can anyone require the people of Palestine to accept a punishment which nobody else would tolerate?" Russell called for a "world campaign...to help bring justice to the long-suffering people of the Middle East."[76]

The PLO also won the attention of members of the American left. American Jewish intellectual Noam Chomsky, known for his pioneering work in linguistics at the Massachusetts Institute of Technology and a prominent critic of the Vietnam War in 1967, began to speak on the issue of Palestine. While he had identified with Zionist-socialist ideas in earlier decades, by the end of the 1960s Chomsky included Washington's relationship with Israel in his larger critique of U.S. foreign policy. By the time he published *Peace in the Middle East? Reflections on Justice and Nationhood* in 1974, Chomsky had identified American support for Israel as "a sort of magic slate rewrite of American failure in Vietnam." American liberals and the left, once critical of Washington's support for the South Vietnamese government, ought to denounce the analogous set of policies that formed the basis of the United States' relationship with

Israel.[77] By 1976, the editors of the University of California, Berkeley, newspaper *The Jewish Radical* were arguing that the time had come for Israel to open negotiations with the PLO. If "Israel continues on its present course," they warned, "it will become progressively more isolated on the international scene, and it will also make it appear that the Palestinian nationalist movement has nothing to gain from moderation."[78]

Although the question of Palestine did not become a central issue for the American civil rights movement, it did receive some attention after the 1967 war. The July 1967 issue of the Student Nonviolent Coordinating Committee's (SNCC) newsletter contained commentary and several images suggesting an association between Zionism and imperialism. One image showed a hand carrying a Star of David and holding nooses around the necks of President Nasser and Muhammad Ali. In the background, a black arm labeled "Third World" and holding a sword labeled "Liberation Movement" was raised in a position to sever the ropes.[79] The two-page spread prompted a harsh reaction from a number of groups within and outside SNCC, which in turn led an SNCC spokesman to respond that "Israel is and always has been the tool and foothold for American and British exploitation in the Middle East and Africa." In a speech at the 1968 convention of the Organization of Arab Students, former SNCC chairman Stokely Carmichael condemned Israel as an "unjust and...immoral state" that had exploited the memory of the Holocaust to justify the expropriation of Arab land and used charges of anti-Semitism to shield itself from criticism. "If white people who call themselves revolutionary or radical want our support," Carmichael insisted, "they have to condemn Zionism."[80]

The recent war and the rising influence of African American groups—many of whom identified Arabs as one of a number of Third World peoples suffering under imperialist oppression—in the American left combined to inject new criticism into domestic discussions of the Arab-Israeli issue. The African American caucus at the New Politics Convention held in Chicago in September 1967, for example, insisted that the June War be condemned as an "Imperialistic Zionist War."[81] Indeed, some African American groups were even more explicit in their criticism of Israel. The Nation of Islam had been openly critical of the Jewish state since the 1956 Suez Crisis, arguing that Israel was an agent of Western imperialism in the Middle East and an analogue of the white regime in South Africa.[82] The Black Panther Party condemned Israel as a racist, imperialist state and voiced support for Arab guerillas:

The Israel government is an imperialist expansionist power in Palestine. The government is at fault, not all Jews. There are many non-Jews who support what Israel is doing. Pig Johnson is one of them. The term, Israel, is like saying racist United States, and it has the same policy as the US government has in the Middle East.

Moreover, there was, according to some of the Panthers, a direct line between racial oppression in Palestine and the United States: both came as the result of U.S. imperialism. Israeli state policy operated at "the height of chauvinism and ethnocentrism."[83]

While the guerillas may have found an enthusiastic group of supporters in the United States and Western Europe, it was becoming clear by late 1968 that the fedayeen and the U.S. government were on a collision course. As they began to establish political and cultural hegemony within the diaspora, the fedayeen implanted their vision of worldwide revolution in the social terrain of Palestine. In this regard, the guerillas represented a global revolution from the inside out: the revolution was international not because it was unfolding all around the world but rather because Palestinian fighters self-consciously positioned themselves at the junction of the global forces of revolutionary change in the 1960s in an effort to lay claim to notions of national sovereignty, human rights, and social justice that were no longer under the purview of either superpower. These connections with the wider would, in turn, provide the foundation for the fedayeen's success in internationalizing its struggle during the following decade.

State Department views on the fedayeen had also begun to solidify. Fear that the guerillas would be instrumental in radicalizing the Middle East and destabilizing the region combined with frustration over Israel's unyielding position and rising levels of violence to lend a sense of urgency to the seemingly stalled peace process. A State Department paper prepared at the end of 1968 for a National Intelligence Estimate explained that the question of Palestine lay at the heart of the Arab-Israeli conflict. Disillusioned with the inability of the Arab states to address their grievances and inspired by other revolutionary groups' successes, the fedayeen had taken matters into their own hands. "As long as the examples of China, the Viet Cong, and similar movements continue to be influential," the paper added, "it is unlikely that the Palestinians will accept the idea of Israel's permanent existence."[84] This global dimension represented one of the most worrisome aspects of the Palestinian struggle for U.S. decision makers. Fueled by the winds of global change, the fires in Palestine were starting to rage out of control.

{ 2 }

The Storm

Salah Khalaf was roused at dawn by one of his men with the news that Fatah's sentries had spotted Israeli tank columns moving across the Jordan River toward the refugee camp at al-Karama. Located in a hilly area some four miles from the river, the camp had become an operational headquarters for the Palestinian fighters who had launched a string of guerilla attacks against Israelis on the occupied West Bank. Determined to crush the commandos, the IDF sent a large force of tanks and several thousand men across into Jordan. Three days earlier, on 18 March 1968, Khalaf and Yasir Arafat had met with a Jordanian general who warned them that the IDF was mobilizing for a large-scale raid against the guerilla base. Arafat and his deputy took the news back to the guerilla commanders, who resolved to take positions in the caves and hillsides surrounding the camp. Although some groups elected to fall back—using conventional guerilla tactics of attack and retreat—the leaders of Fatah made the unprecedented decision to stay in their bases. "Our duty was to set an example," Khalaf explained, "to prove that the Arabs are capable of courage and dignity." Arafat was even more dramatic, vowing to turn Karama into a "second Leningrad." As the armored columns drew closer, Israeli artillery began shelling the camp and IDF helicopters dropped parachute troops behind fedayeen positions. As some 15,000 Israeli troops converged on Karama, Palestinian forces began firing back, mounting a stiff resistance that would include hand-to-hand fighting and reports of suicide attacks against Israeli tanks. In perhaps the most memorable incident, seventeen guerillas entrenched themselves in the path of the Israeli forces and began a suicidal defense with rocket-propelled grenades at close range. Arafat would name his elite security unit Force 17 in their honor. The battle would carry a symbolic importance far beyond its tactical dimension by cementing the fedayeen's image as heroic resistance fighters, helping to propel Khalaf and Fatah to a leading position in the PLO, and putting the fedayeen on the global map of Third World revolutionaries.[1]

Khalaf, whose nom de guerre was Abu Iyad, was born into a middle-class family in the port city of Jaffa in Palestine in 1933. When Jewish forces seized the city in 1948, Khalaf and his family fled to Gaza. He enrolled in teacher's college in Cairo, where he met Arafat. The two men grew close, with Khalaf serving as Arafat's deputy and then successor in the Palestinian Student Union. He earned a degree in philosophy in 1957 and then returned to Gaza. Two years later, he joined Arafat in Kuwait as a founding member of Fatah. Khalaf would serve as a sort of liaison between the more moderate Fatah and left-wing groups such as the PFLP. As one of Arafat's principal deputies, Khalaf moved from Kuwait to Syria and then relocated to the occupied West Bank following the 1967 war.[2]

The Battle of al-Karama represented something of a reversal for Fatah's fortunes, which had been dismal in the preceding months. Khalaf and Arafat's initial attempts to launch an insurgency in the West Bank in 1967 buckled under the full weight of Israeli security. By the end of the year, Palestinian fighters had been driven across the river into territory that remained under King Hussein's jurisdiction. The rapid defeat of Fatah's insurgency in the occupied territories was the result of extremely proficient IDF counterinsurgency operations in conjunction with the reality that the guerillas—most of whom came from refugee camps—were moving among a population that had only recently been placed under military occupation. While the West Bankers were largely sympathetic to the fedayeen, they hardly shared the guerillas' sense of desperation and consequent willingness to sacrifice everything in the pursuit of liberation. Likewise, guerilla recruits had difficulty blending into the wealthier population of the West Bank, which had not spent the last generation in the camps. By the end of the year, Arafat himself—disguised as a woman carrying a baby—was forced to flee across the frontier.[3] In many respects, the fiasco of the 1967 insurgency in the West Bank would become the most glaring failure of the resistance, forcing the fedayeen to rely on what would become a largely symbolic struggle.

The Battle of al-Karama

Faced with this defeat in the occupied territories, the fedayeen turned their focus to cross-border raids on Israeli forces from bases on the East Bank in Jordan, thus initiating the Amman phase of the PLO's war. This new strategy introduced another layer of complexity into the conflict: although Palestinian fighters on the East Bank enjoyed some protection against the IDF, they were subject to periodic crackdowns by Jordanian security forces, who sought to control the guerillas' actions. The Jordanian government recognized the fedayeen as a potential threat to its domestic sovereignty and a major irritant in its already tense relationship with Israel. Faced with this increasingly difficult situation, leaders in Amman tried to keep a lid on the guerilla war that was simmering along their western border. Thus, in early March 1968, Jordanian agents—using information reportedly passed to them by the CIA—warned fedayeen leaders that a major Israeli strike on their bases along the Jordan River was imminent.[4]

The pretext for the anticipated Israeli attack came on 18 March 1968, when a land mine planted by a group of fedayeen near Eilat exploded beneath an Israeli school bus, killing two and wounding eight. As they prepared to mount their largest military operation since 1967 across the Jordan River, Israeli officials told Washington that Fatah was planning a spring offensive in hopes of making a "big echo, something like [the Tet attacks in] Saigon." They warned that the Vietnamese example had become an increasingly powerful source of inspiration in the Arab world and explained their determination to intervene before the situation got out of hand. Following the failure of its initial attempts to reach out to moderate Palestinian leaders on the West Bank, the Israeli government reverted to traditional means of dealing with the issue of Palestinian nationalism: it would treat the Palestinians as an Arab problem. Israel would deal with the Arab states, and the Arab states would deal with the Palestinians. While the IDF engaged the fedayeen, the Foreign Ministry would attempt to persuade Amman, Damascus, and Beirut to adopt stricter control over guerilla units inside their respective borders.[5]

To this end, the IDF had developed a number of measures to deal with the threat of the Palestinian guerillas. Within the occupied territories, Israeli units engaged in nighttime sweeps, searched caves and orchards for fedayeen and weapons caches, and instituted a system of massive retribution against suspected sympathizers that included house demolitions. To deal with the threat of infiltration, the IDF fortified the Jordanian frontier with forward bases at river crossings, barbed-wire fences, minefields, electronic surveillance measures, and a smudge trail that would reveal the tracks of guerillas crossing the border.[6] These countermeasures supplemented an aggressive defense strategy based on aerial raids, artillery attacks, and massive reprisals against fedayeen bases on foreign soil. While effective in an immediate sense, this approach overlooked the long-term dangers represented by the resurgence of the fedayeen. As Ian Black and Benny Morris argue, Israel's principal goal in these operations was to provide a short-term solution to what it expected to be an ephemeral threat.[7]

The Karama operation—the largest of its kind since before 1967—was designed as a knockout punch to the guerillas that might force the Jordanian government to crack down on the fedayeen. As IDF chief of staff Chaim Bar-Lev commented, the attack was designed to "help Hussein screw Fatah." It would not go as smoothly as the IDF hoped.[8] The invasion force met heavier resistance than initially expected, both from guerillas in defensive positions and from Jordanian military forces on the hills above the town. Nevertheless, the IDF managed to gain control of the camp by early afternoon and began pulling its troops out as evening approached. As the strike force moved out of Jordan, Prime Minister Levi Eshkol announced triumphantly to the Israeli parliament, the Knesset, that their forces had "cleaned up the nests of the gangs and destroyed their bases." Israeli forces accomplished their military objectives, but they had stumbled into a political trap: the guerillas seized on the battle as a victory, transforming a military defeat into their first major salvo in a renewed resistance against Israel. Years later, Aharon Yariv, a general with the IDF, would voice a different assessment: "After Karameh, we understood that we had on our hands a serious movement."[9]

Although Jordanian units probably inflicted most of the Israeli casualties, it was Fatah that managed to capitalize on the propaganda victory. In a matter of days, the organization began running images in its newspaper of destroyed IDF vehicles and captured weapons; here, less than a year after the humiliation of the 1967 war, was the face-saving victory for which the Arabs had been waiting. Fatah's telling of the Karama skirmish transformed the battle into a narrative counterpoint to the massacre at Deir Yassin: while the latter signaled the onset of the period of Palestinian suffering and dispossession, the former announced the beginning of a new chapter in the history of Palestine in which resistance and liberation would be the dominant themes. The battle at al-Karama and ongoing guerilla operations served to complicate the picture of the Palestinians as refugees with the image of the Palestinians as liberation fighters.[10]

In the minds of the fedayeen and many international observers, Karama became the Palestinian Tet Offensive. The guerillas demonstrated their ability to inflict damage on Israeli forces even if they could not prevail on the battle-field. Palestinian recruits might not be marching on Tel Aviv anytime soon, but they were strong enough to give the IDF a bloody nose and live to tell about it. This seemed to fulfill the basic proposition of the modern insurgency: the gue-rillas could win as long as they did not lose. Indeed, if the Algerian and Viet-namese experiences were any guide, the crucial issue was that the fedayeen would continue to fight even if victory seemed unattainable. To this end, Fatah established a Palestinian branch of the Red Crescent, a humanitarian assis-tance group; an economic wing designed to provide vocational training for refugees; and the Ashbal, or Cubs, program, designed to train children—the next generation of fedayeen—in guerilla tactics.[11]

Moreover, defeat on the battlefield could be less important than political victory on the world stage. The Algerians reinforced these comparisons and encouraged the Palestinians to follow the FLN's example by making the fight for international opinion a focus of their resistance struggle. The *New York Times* wrote:

The Algerians remember that an important part of their struggle for independence was fought at the United Nations, in the offices of American newspapers, in African capitals, and at innumerable African-Asian

FIGURE 2.1 *Fatah poster by Shafiq Radwan, "Revolution Until Victory," c. 1968. Courtesy of the Palestinian Poster Project Archives.*

conferences, where Algerian envoys won moral—and in many cases practical—support for their provisional government in Tunis.

Al-Karama marked a turning point in the fedayeen's struggle for regional and international recognition and would remain one of the central rallying points in the armed struggle. As thousands of volunteers overwhelmed Fatah's recruiting capacity in the spring and summer of 1968, international observers took note of the fedayeen's growing prominence.[12]

Fatah's international profile received another boost when the battle sparked a heated debate at the United Nations. The Israeli retaliation had been launched against the guerillas from the occupied West Bank—territory that was internationally recognized as falling under Jordanian sovereignty—and sparked a confrontation with a third party that happened to be a sovereign state. For many, this sort of action seemed to confirm Arab accusations of aggressive Israeli expansionism. Making matters worse, Amman had notified the Security Council that an attack was likely and thereby portrayed Israeli actions as being especially calculated.[13]

The Security Council debate showcased the stark divisions over the Palestine question and the Arab-Israeli dispute. U.S. ambassador Arthur Goldberg sought to limit the political damage to the United States and Israel in the fallout from the raid. Keeping to a theme that would dominate Washington's approach to UN debates on Israel and the Palestinians, Goldberg argued for a resolution that would balance the Israeli reprisal with the fedayeen attacks that had sparked it: the problem was not aggressive action by the IDF but rather Arab "terrorism," which threatened the fragile cease-fire in the region. By framing the issue in this way, U.S. policy makers sought to contain the fedayeen threat and steer attention back to the political process. Although Israel must be restrained, King Hussein would also need to establish firmer control over his frontier in order to limit cross-border attacks.[14] U.S. policy garnered loud criticism, however, from Palestinian supporters.

Algerian ambassador Tewfik Bouattoura was among Goldberg's critics, articulating an argument that would become familiar at the United Nations. Bouattoura criticized the United States for its unwavering support of Israel and argued that events in Palestine must be framed not within the context of terrorist attacks and state reprisals but as a question of colonial aggression. The Palestinian resistance was no different from anticolonial movements around the world. "The Palestinian liberation movement," he emphasized, "notwithstanding the traditionally colonialist epithets with which it has been labeled this morning, is leading its people towards their destiny, as in Vietnam and Rhodesia." The representative from Pakistan went further, comparing Israeli actions to those of the South African government, while the representative from Hungary suggested that the IDF was applying counterrevolutionary techniques that it had learned from the U.S. experience in Vietnam. While militarily effective, Israel's reprisal strategy allowed the Palestinians to gain international sympathy by casting the IDF as the aggressor. The Jordanians also insisted that the situation be understood in terms of colonial aggression rather than terrorist attacks, complaining to State Department officials that Israel's "explanation that its intervention was [a] police action rather than [a] retaliation evoked outmoded colonial concepts which should be embarrassing to all." Comparisons to the French resistance fighters during World War II reinforced the argument that the fedayeen were not the terrorists that they had been made out to be.[15] The fedayeen's case that they must be understood as a national liberation movement had entered the debate at the United Nations.

The Wave of the Future

While debates at the United Nations raged, officials at the U.S. embassy in Tel Aviv noted disturbing parallels between the guerilla war along the Jordan River and the ongoing insurgency in Vietnam. As the war in Southeast Asia became a rallying point for the fedayeen and their supporters, Ambassador Walworth Barbour worried that Palestinian fighters might create a similar situation in the Middle East. As guerilla operations increased, embassy officials in Tel Aviv warned that the fedayeen were starting to resemble the South Vietnamese National Liberation Front. Because reprisals such as the Karama raid seemed ineffective, Israeli officials were faced with the prospect of changing their tactics, either to an occupation of Jordanian territory or to Vietnam-style search-and-destroy missions.[16] Foreign Service officers from around the region echoed these reservations about the potential power of the Palestinian guerillas to provoke destabilizing Israeli reprisals. Although Vietnamese guerilla tactics were not suited for the physical and human terrain in the Middle East, such sentiments were widespread at the time.

Likewise, U.S. officials in the Jerusalem consulate warned of growing support for the guerillas in the West Bank. Rejecting the ludicrous suggestion that Palestinians preferred Israeli to Jordanian occupation, consulate officers explained that, given the Israeli policies of "land requisitions, house demolitions, indefinite detention incommunicado without charge or trial, massive military retaliation against the East Bank, and the exclusion of refugees, Arab discontent becomes deeper, admiration of terrorists becomes greater, and [the] mutterings of [the] population become more ominous." As a result, Fatah had begun to attract better-educated, more motivated, and more dangerous recruits than had been the case in previous years. At the same time, the fedayeen had turned to more dangerous and less controllable attacks. From the State Department's offices in Foggy Bottom, Assistant Secretary of State Lucius Battle warned that the cycle of terrorism and reprisal now represented the most dangerous threat to regional peace. Making matters worse, fedayeen tactics had evolved in recent months, creating new threats and dangers. In addition to expressing concerns over the changing nature of the conflict and the increase in the number of commando organizations, Battle warned of the growing popularity of these "so-called resistance groups" among educated Arabs. Actors on all sides must resist this cycle of mounting violence and work through diplomatic channels to achieve a negotiated settlement, he said.[17]

The appearance of the Palestinian guerillas as an independent force created headaches for Soviet leaders as well. While Third World revolutionaries were no friends of the United States, they could threaten Soviet assets in a given region or might be more sympathetic to Beijing than Moscow. The fedayeen's volatile relationship with Cairo and Damascus and willingness to accept Chinese aid made the Kremlin wary of extending support to the guerillas. The PLO also appeared poised to create more trouble in the Middle East. The organization called for the destruction of Israel, placed its faith in a military solution to the conflict instead of a political one, espoused a nationalist political orientation instead of a socialist one, and aligned itself with Beijing.[18] Still, Soviet leaders were quite willing to play upon the issue of the Israeli victory to attack U.S. interests in the region. In early January 1968, the Soviet vice premier delivered a speech in Egypt portraying the Arab world as the focus of the struggle between the "forces of imperialist reaction and the national liberation movement." The Israeli government and its allies were bent on destroying the progressive forces in the Arab world, he said, and the Soviets pledged their "solid support for the just cause of [Egypt] and the other Arab countries in their struggle against imperialism and colonialism, to get rid of the consequences of the Israeli aggression."[19] While seemingly supportive of the fedayeen, such statements suggest that Moscow hoped the PLO would remain under the yoke of friendly Arab powers such as Egypt and Syria.

The Kremlin expressed a growing sympathy for the Arab struggle against the Israeli occupation and charged Washington with complicity in Israeli expansionist designs. *Pravda* argued that Israel and its American backers were creating a situation in the Middle East that mirrored the struggle in Southeast Asia between imperialist forces and national liberation fighters. Despite Moscow's rhetoric, State Department intelligence analysts believed that the Soviets still viewed the guerillas as irresponsible and were particularly wary of the PLO's relationship with Beijing. Nevertheless, if the Palestinians developed an effective resistance, Moscow's sympathies—tempered by the Soviet experience under German occupation in World War II—could evolve into more substantial support.[20]

Moscow's rhetoric concerning the PLO changed as the Soviet press began describing fedayeen as "partisans." The burgeoning relationship between the guerillas and the Kremlin was a tactical necessity given the post-1967 regional status quo. By the end of the year, the fedayeen represented a political and military reality in the Middle East. Even so, Soviet leaders voiced skepticism regarding the prospects for liberation of the occupied territories through guerilla operations and remained critical of the PLO's refusal to entertain possibility of a compromise solution.[21] In July 1968 Nasser brought Arafat to Moscow, where the guerilla leader was introduced to Foreign Minister Alexei Kosygin, Chairman Leonid Brezhnev, and President Nikolai Podgorny. Despite their reservations, Soviet leaders agreed to send the guerillas some $500,000 in weapons through Egyptian intermediaries over the next several years. Beijing remained the PLO's principal source of military aid, however.[22]

In late 1969, *Pravda* ran an article referring to the PLO as a "national liberation anti-imperialist struggle" and promised support for the "fifth front of the Arab struggle against Israel aggression." This was followed up with an official visit by a PLO delegation to Moscow in February 1970. Roland Dannreuther attributes these improved relations to the Kremlin's concerns about Egyptian losses in the War of Attrition with Israel and the hope that public support for the fedayeen could help demonstrate the Soviet commitment to the Arab world and, potentially, provide some slight leverage in the superpower contest in the Middle East.[23]

Such rhetoric stoked American anxieties that the Soviets were in the process of stepping up their operations in the Middle East in an attempt to recoup their losses from the June War and erode Washington's position in the region. Of particular concern were Moscow's efforts to increase its influence in Jordan through offers to resupply the Jordanian military after its losses of June 1967. For their part, the Jordanians looked to play on American fears of Soviet gains in the region in order to secure more aid from Washington. General Amer Khammash, commander of Jordanian military forces, told Harold Saunders that the Soviets were looking to move into Jordan "in a big way." If Moscow was able to increase its influence in Amman, Khammash warned, the regime could very well fall under the influence of leftists who would then chart a course toward the Eastern bloc. Furthermore, the continuing Israeli occupation of the West Bank was feeding the growth of Arab "terrorists" whose "guerilla-type activities" were making them more and more popular.[24] The growing influence of radical forces could coalesce to present a major threat to Western-oriented regimes and to Washington's position in the region.

If the fedayeen were to mount a serious threat to Israel, however, groups such as Fatah and the PFLP would have to secure foreign patronage while remaining functionally independent. Although support for the Palestinian cause was overwhelming on the Arab street, many Arab leaders were less than thrilled by the prospect of an independent Palestinian guerilla movement. This ambivalence stemmed from the defeat of the Arab states in the 1948 and 1967 wars. The 1948 defeat had swept away the existing regimes in Cairo and Damascus and brought to power a new generation, which vowed to right the wrongs of its predecessors by liberating Palestine. That the Palestinian refugees would be forced to do this for themselves after an even more humiliating defeat highlighted the failure of the Arab leaders to deliver on these pledges. Added to this disgrace, Palestinian cadres represented a threat to the status quo on both the internal and regional levels: while the diasporic nature of the community meant that substantial Palestinian populations in Lebanon, Syria, Jordan, and the Gulf States might develop loyalties to the fedayeen leadership as opposed to their host governments, the dynamism and charisma of men such as Yasir Arafat and George Habash threatened to upstage leaders in Cairo and Damascus. A vibrant guerilla movement controlled by the Palestinians themselves would add instability to an already tumultuous regional system.

While Syrian, Egyptian, and Jordanian interests were often at odds with the resistance, North Africa and the Gulf States were more ready to embrace the fedayeen. Libya, the Gulf States, and Saudi Arabia were the beneficiaries of rising oil prices and contributed large amounts of financial aid as well as public support for the Palestinian struggle. Although the conservative Saudi regime traditionally had been inclined to side with Washington on regional issues, the loss of the Islamic holy places in Palestine and Washington's seemingly one-sided support for Israel had led many conservative Arabs to reconsider their position toward the United States. Washington's relationship with Israel, beyond underwriting the occupation, now seemed to represent a key source of disruption that was contributing to the spread of communism and radicalism in the region. As officials in Riyadh began to refer to the fedayeen as an "Algerian-type" resistance movement, U.S. observers warned that the "guerillas have captured [the] imagination of [the] Saudis."[25]

Algeria provided the most immediate source of inspiration for the Palestinian armed struggle. The fedayeen saw Algeria as a model for their revolution, a source of political and material support, and—in Arafat's words—the "window through which we appear to the West." Fatah looked to the Algerian FLN as the archetype for its own public diplomacy campaign, adopting Algerian principles and relying on Algerian tutelage in its efforts to gain worldwide support. Articles in the New York Times, L'Express, and Time had convinced Algerian officials that their efforts to represent the Palestinians to the West were making headway.[26]

Indeed, North Africa was fast becoming a power base for the Palestinian fighters. While the fedayeen looked to the Algerian revolution as a model, quoting liberally from Frantz Fanon and making frequent state visits to Algiers, Algerian leaders saw the Palestinian movement as a protégé of the Algerian struggle for independence and began to provide Fatah with weapons, training, and support in winning global opinion. Meanwhile, Libya had become a key financial backer of the guerillas, and even the moderate regimes in Morocco and Tunisia had been compelled to make gestures of solidarity toward the guerillas. As their own movement matured, fedayeen leaders continued to look outward for examples of successful revolutions. On a state visit to Libya, Arafat made allusions to the importance of a rising revolutionary bloc, forged in the image of Algeria and Vietnam and reliant on the strength of the Arab people.[27]

Algerian support for the guerillas was all the more valuable in light of that country's impressive anti-imperialist credentials. "Since the Palestine problem is the result of a colonialist-imperialist plot," the Algerian FLN explained, "it must be seen in its proper context, that of the struggle for national liberation in which the Palestinian people is engaged." The state of Israel was for all intents and purposes a military outpost of neocolonialism in the heart of the Arab world, according to Algerian president Houari Boumedienne. Algiers endorsed the Palestinian armed struggle—which could only be accomplished by the Palestinians themselves—as "an inseparable part of the world-wide movement for the liberation of all peoples."[28] This diplomatic backing gave the fedayeen immediate credibility with many of those who had supported the FLN in its earlier struggle against the French.

Like their neighbors, the Tunisians applauded the emergence of the resistance. President Habib Bourguiba remarked that the Palestinians, with the emergence of the fedayeen, had become self-reliant. It was therefore imperative that Palestinian concerns be taken into account in any attempts to solve the problems in the Middle East. Ultimately, he stressed, colonialism in the region must be eliminated, as had been the case in Tunisia, Algeria, Morocco, and Kenya.[29] At a banquet with President Lyndon Johnson, Bourguiba stressed the need for the United States to push for a political solution in the Middle East and drew comparisons between the Balfour Declaration of 1917 and the "Congress of Berlin and other conferences through which the European powers have cut up in pieces and divided among themselves the countries of Africa and Asia." By sanctioning the partition of Palestine, the UN and the great powers had turned their backs on Woodrow Wilson's Fourteen Points and the principle of self-determination. While the Arab regimes had unwisely sought to reverse the partition, the emergence of the Palestinians presented an opportunity to right past wrongs and achieve a lasting peace in the region. Bourguiba thus implored the leaders of the world powers to recognize this new situation in the Middle East.[30]

Even Nasser had begun to follow the fedayeen's lead, at least in public. Indeed, both Cairo and Damascus provided weapons and training to the guerillas in hopes of establishing a measure of influence over the organizations. Nasser met with Fatah leaders in November 1967 in a now famous episode in which Arafat was allowed to keep his pistol and gunbelt. "My intelligence people are telling me that you insist on bringing your gun because you intend to kill me," the president told the guerilla leader. "Mr. President," Arafat replied, lifting his pistol out before him, "your intelligence people are wrong. I offer you my freedom fighter's gun as proof of that fact." Nasser smiled and said, "No. You keep it. You need it, and more." After the meeting, Nasser allowed

Arafat's group to set up a radio station in Cairo, began sending modest amounts of aid to the group, and gave Fatah officers training in Egypt as "rocket gunners, frogmen, commando instructors, and intelligence officers." As Muhammad Heikal, Nasser's public information chief, explained, the fedayeen would be independent of state control, functioning as the Arab governments' "irresponsible arm." The PLO would function as the "Stern Gang or Irgun" to the Arab states' equivalent of the Jewish Agency.[31]

Although Egypt had used the Palestinian issue opportunistically prior to 1967, the guerillas had since overshadowed Nasserism as the leading edge of Arab nationalism. Though American observers in Cairo did not yet feel that Palestinianism had "become the wave of the future," the continued growth and success of the movement would likely represent a major obstacle to a political settlement of the Arab-Israeli dispute. Realizing that he could not control the guerillas, Nasser had voiced public support for the movement and encouraged it to seek support from the wider world. However, he was also cutting them loose and, in doing so, giving himself the opportunity to pursue diplomatic initiatives aimed at recouping Egypt's losses in the 1967 war. By acknowledging the existence of multiple paths to Arab victory, U.S. officials argued, Cairo effectively disowned the fedayeen in order to chart a separate course toward a political solution. While such a strategy bought Nasser some room to maneuver, the Palestinian resistance could grow into an Algerian-style movement and Cairo's influence would be fully eclipsed should the standoff continue indefinitely. State Department officials asserted that only a political solution— which was complicated both by the existence of the fedayeen and by Israeli reprisals—could create the circumstances necessary for Nasser to regain his lost prestige.[32]

"Surrounded by Assassins"

Harrison Symmes was an unlikely choice for Washington's ambassador to Jordan. Although the North Carolina native was a career Foreign Service officer and Arabist who had served in posts in Egypt, Syria, Kuwait, and Libya, he had been responsible for a minor scandal in the U.S. intelligence community. Symmes had written a memo suggesting that Washington might consider dropping its support for King Hussein because the monarch did not enjoy a popular mandate in Jordan. He argued that continued support for the Hashemite monarchy in Jordan might prove detrimental to long-term U.S. interests in the region. When his memo was leaked, he assumed that his relationship with the kingdom was irrevocably damaged. All this changed in the wake of the 1967 Arab-Israeli War, however. Hussein's disastrous decision to join the belligerent Arab states in the early stages of the war had angered policy makers in Washington and led some to consider efforts to assert more control over the monarch. The State Department dispatched Symmes to take charge of the U.S. mission to Amman.[33]

Not surprisingly, the ambassador got off to a rocky start with the Jordanians. Symmes' first official meeting with King Hussein concerned Jordanian threats to seek military aid from the Kremlin. Although Symmes was able to talk the king down, tensions would remain high throughout his time in Amman. The problem of the fedayeen in Jordan was possibly the most intractable. As Symmes recalled:

> When we got there the Fedayeen had decided that they were really going to try it on. They were collecting money from people. They'd stop you on the street and ask for money, they'd stop your car and ask for money. They were walking around with Tommy-guns and ... AK-47s and camouflage suits and so on. And making a general nuisance of themselves, firing feu-de-joie up in the air. We'd find spent bullets in the embassy residence garden lying on the pavement. You could just pick them up.

The king was in a tremendously difficult position: while Arab observers outside the guerillas' immediate sphere of operations could stand aside and watch the fedayeen's exploits, Jordan was caught in the eye of the storm. A sense of gloom hung heavy over leadership in Amman as the prospects of international efforts to broker an Arab-Israeli peace appeared increasingly bleak and the regime became embroiled in the fighting. According to one State Department official, King Hussein was "literally surrounded by assassins." Impotent in the face of Israeli reprisals and the continuing occupation of Jordanian territory, Hussein's government was becoming estranged from the Jordanian people. The rising popularity of the Palestinian fighters had made it impossible for the government to bring them to heel and was threatening to make them the "dominant force" in the kingdom.[34]

Despite the grave threat they posed to his regime, King Hussein could ill afford a confrontation with the guerillas. As time passed, the fedayeen were coming to be seen by many in the region as the only force that was still fighting against Israeli domination. Although Hussein still controlled the army, popular support for the resistance had crept into the junior officer corps, and Amman's inability to repulse Israeli attacks had created a sense of frustration in the military. Resentment in the occupied West Bank was feeding the popularity of the resistance. As hopes for a quick settlement faded away, traditional Palestinian notables on the West Bank were slowly losing their influence. More and more residents of the occupied territories were coming to the conclusion that resistance offered the only option that might result in an Israeli withdrawal. One influential West Banker warned that the window of time in which an acceptable settlement might be reached was fast closing: in three or four months, the relative calm could give way to a full-blown revolt. The king could not hope to move against the guerillas without sacrificing his remaining support in the West Bank. The king's own advisors predicted that if pressure from the fedayeen continued to mount, he was destined to fall, as were leaders in Baghdad and Damascus. Even Nasser was now "only a shadow." The Arab world's sole hope seemed to rest in making common cause with the fedayeen, turning the resistance into the "vehicle of all [the] Arabs." Hussein would have to walk a fine line if he hoped to prevent an uprising.[35]

While the fedayeen posed the most serious threat to the regime, the presence of Iraqi troops inside Jordan made matters even worse. The Jordanian army could likely handle a showdown with the guerillas, but a confrontation with the Palestinian fighters *and* Iraqi units would overwhelm the king's forces. Ideally, Fatah could be incorporated into Hussein's own military forces as a means of harnessing the fedayeen and preserving the king's authority. However, the prospects for this dwindled as the guerillas grew stronger. If the situation continued, Amman might even be forced to accept Soviet weapons as a means of preserving internal security.[36]

Added to these concerns was the ever-present threat of Israeli reprisals for guerilla attacks. The IDF's policy of retaliation was designed to induce Amman to bridle the fedayeen by punishing the Jordanian government—and often the Jordanian people—and rested on the proposition that, by failing to police the cease-fire lines, Amman was in violation of international law and therefore subject to Israeli retribution. The situation was more complicated than it initially seemed, however, due to Israel's continued—and illegal–occupation of the West Bank. While Israel insisted on Amman's legal responsibilities to prevent guerilla attacks from its soil, Jordanian authorities argued that policing the armistice lines was tantamount to a Jordanian defense of the Israeli occupation. Any subtlety in Amman's attempts to control the guerillas, moreover, was undermined by periodic Israeli reprisals that brought the issue of the Palestinian fighters to the forefront of Jordanian public opinion. When artillery duels between Jordanian and Israeli forces broke out in February 1968, State Department officials warned that the clashes would damage King Hussein's ability to control the fedayeen. Moreover, the Jordanian public was increasingly coming to view the guerillas as "patriotic resistance fighters" and the IDF reprisals as evidence of Israeli disregard for Arab life. As the clashes continued without decisive action by the monarch, internal unrest and erosion of public authority became a threat to the regime.[37]

All of this made life more difficult for policy makers in Washington and Foreign Service officers in friendly Arab capitals. Although Israel was its closest ally in the eastern Mediterranean, Washington maintained strong interests in and close relations with Jordan and Lebanon, both of which were being pulled into a state of low-level war with Israel by continuing fedayeen operations. The situation on the ground was far from a straightforward conflict between Arabs and Israelis, as State Department officials such as Symmes and Dwight Porter struggled to explain to their superiors in Washington. As the cycle of violence accelerated, U.S. policy makers tried to encourage their three allies to cooperate against their common enemy, the fedayeen. These efforts met limited success, however, as they failed to account for the exceedingly difficult position of the Jordanian and Lebanese governments vis-à-vis the Palestinian guerillas. Washington's efforts to discourage Israeli reprisals were equally ineffective, as Israel repeatedly demonstrated its determination to maintain complete control over its own defense policies rather than bow to U.S. pressure to accommodate Beirut and Amman.

The stakes were exponentially higher for the moderate Hashemite kingdom in Jordan, however. According to some in Washington, Jordan formed a linchpin in U.S. Middle East strategy: geographically, the kingdom split a potential bloc of pro-Soviet Arab states such as Egypt, Syria, and Iraq that might threaten moderate governments in the region, including those in Saudi Arabia and Iran. By diverting pressure away from King Faisal in Saudi Arabia and the shah of Iran, Hussein's kingdom helped to insulate U.S. interests in Middle East oil and strategic facilities in the region. Moreover, Washington hoped that Jordan—the "most realistic and least intransigent" of the Arab states—might play a key role in a potential settlement with Israel. Further, the collapse of the regime likely would lead to an inter-Arab war that would surely be accompanied by an escalation in the Arab-Israeli dispute, which might ultimately spark a superpower conflagration. Beyond strategic calculations, Amman played a crucial role as a symbol of moderation, an example of how the Arabs could benefit from alignment with the West. King Hussein's overthrow would be a major blow to American and British interests in the region.[38]

Walworth Barbour, U.S. ambassador to Israel, warned that the Jordanian population was heralding the fedayeen as national heroes. He told Israeli foreign minister Abba Eban that King Hussein was doing all he could to rein in the guerillas, but Israeli attacks were not helping those efforts. Beyond being counterproductive, State Department officials insisted, Israeli reprisals were morally questionable, as they amounted to a policy of killing innocents and individuals who had nothing to do with guerilla operations. Israeli officials answered by explaining their intention to hold Amman responsible for the actions of militants operating from Jordanian territory. The "problem was between governments, not individuals. If Jordan would not let Israel live in peace," Israeli ambassador Yitzhak Rabin told State Department officials, "then Israel would not let Jordan live peacefully."[39] For the time being, rising tensions between Israel and Jordan would occupy much of the attention of U.S., Israeli, and Jordanian diplomats. Although King Hussein professed common cause with the PLO, Ambassador Symmes explained, he was "walking the fence," publicly acquiescing to the resistance movements while privately building up his security apparatus. In the meantime, the Jordanian government appeared to be heading toward confrontation with the fedayeen. As an uneasy quiet settled over the streets of Amman, young Jordanian men kept a low profile in order to avoid King Hussein's recent conscription efforts. Increased government surveillance at police checkpoints sought to root out the vehicles carrying armed guerillas throughout the city. Fatah and the PFLP continued their public rejection of a political solution and called on the population to rally to the guerilla cause and rebuff Amman's attempt to control fedayeen actions.[40]

As the king struggled to regain control of Jordan, he found himself in the unenviable position of Washington's second-favorite ally in the region. He was thus forced to sit back and watch as the IDF—outfitted with some of the latest U.S. weapons—carried out one punishing raid after another on his territory. Moreover, these reprisals boosted the guerillas' image and hampered his regime's ability to reestablish a military presence on the Jordanian frontier. Even when they mustered the strength to launch operations against the fedayeen, Jordanian units deployed against the guerillas ran the risk of being hit by IDF aircraft using napalm against suspected Palestinian forces near the border.[41]

Amman's approaches to Washington on the subject of Israeli hostility had little immediate effect. Jordanian complaints that Israeli inflexibility and military reprisals were scuttling the peace process were met by explanations that Israel was exercising restraint. The State Department went on to suggest that Amman should judge U.S. policy toward the Middle East "in terms of what we have not done [i.e., increased arms sales to Israel] rather than what we have done." The Jordanian ambassador shot back cynically, "You mean it could be much worse." Furthermore, State Department officials warned Amman not to expect any change with the transition to a new U.S. administration in 1969. Jordanian pleas for Washington to pressure Israel to grant concessions in hopes of achieving some future settlement were met with similar rebuffs.[42]

Not far away, the government of Lebanon faced deeper, if less immediate, problems than Amman. As the next target in line after Amman, the moderate government in Beirut recognized that unrest in Lebanon was likely to increase as King Hussein clamped down on the guerillas in Jordan. Although the United States would have preferred closer cooperation between the two moderate regimes, Beirut chose to approach fedayeen leaders in Amman and Cairo, pleading with them to refrain from using southern Lebanon as a base for commando operations. A strong guerilla presence would threaten the nation's precarious confessional balance, invite Israeli intervention, and expand Syrian influence in Lebanon. Lebanese leaders judged that their best chance of survival lay in avoiding a direct confrontation.[43] This attempt at accommodation led to the creation of the Cairo Agreement on 2 November 1969, which would form the foundations of what some have called the PLO's state-within-a-state in Lebanon. In exchange for a promise to respect Lebanese sovereignty, the fedayeen were given authority within the refugee camps and secure routes to the Israeli frontier and to Syrian supply sources. In the coming years, a Palestinian state-within-a-state would emerge in the suburbs of Beirut and south Lebanon, transforming Israel's northern neighbor into the center of PLO activity.[44]

State Department officials were well aware of Lebanon's precarious situation. Ambassador Porter noted that the "Lebanese are watching developments in Amman with understandable fascination—they could be next." While the fedayeen butted heads with King Hussein, political factions in Lebanon began to choose sides. One Lebanese leader told the State Department that the fedayeen were the "wave of the future" and the new heart of the pan-Arab movement. While the PLO had been discredited by its close associations with Cairo and Damascus, Fatah was seeking to chart a separate path, independent of both Washington and Moscow. Although he still hoped for the rejuvenation of the Ba'ath Party, this official remarked, he was now devoting 99 percent of his time to the commandos.[45]

Support for the fedayeen was also running high on the streets of Beirut. Student demonstrations in the capital on 6 November in support of the guerillas spread to Tripoli in the north and Sidon and Tyre in the south. Demonstrators calling for the government to open Lebanon to fedayeen operations broke out into brawls, with elements from the right-wing Christian Phalange Party raising concerns over the possibility of larger confessional clashes. By 9 November students in most of Lebanon's large cities were protesting and the threat of a general strike loomed large. The Lebanese government, wary of fanning the flames of protest, chose to tolerate the demonstrations but sent large numbers of gendarmes into the streets to keep them under control. After the immediate threat passed, a brewing unrest remained. Ambassador Porter warned that "the radical, anti-US elements have captured the 'street element' of the commando supporters" and that if Amman fell to the guerillas, Beirut would be forced to shift its support to the resistance.[46]

Lebanese military leaders worried that growing pressure from the public, and youth in particular, to sanction the guerillas was putting their forces in an increasingly difficult situation. While government forces were probably strong enough to ensure internal security or to prevent cross-border commando raids, fulfilling both missions was out of the question. Beirut insisted that the Syrian-backed guerillas were a greater threat to Lebanon's security than to Israel's, as Damascus hoped to create popular unrest in Lebanon. Lebanon was caught in a vicious circle: fedayeen-bred internal disorder would force the army to pull its units off the Israeli border, leaving the frontier open to guerilla attacks; these attacks would then invite Israeli reprisals, which would, in turn, fuel the internal disorder. Beirut had no choice but to pay "lip service to the fedayeen cause" while at the same time trying to dislodge the sources of guerilla power in Lebanon and hoping that Israeli and Syrian meddling would not spark a civil war along confessional lines.[47]

Porter noted that it was unreasonable to expect the relatively weak Lebanese army to seal its border with Israel to all guerilla attacks. Moreover, the Lebanese were struggling to contain fedayeen influence in their nation, which seemed to rise after each IDF reprisal. He insisted that the Israeli government must realize that its reprisal strategy was risky and probably counterproductive. Continued military strikes on Lebanese soil would merely "inflame public opinion, reinforce Arab suspicions of Israeli designs on South Lebanon, and throw [an] embarrassing glare of publicity on [the] Lebanese military's sensitive campaign to suppress infiltration." As moderates in the region lost power, U.S. influence in the Arab world was bottoming out. Porter urged his superiors to push Israeli leaders toward acceptance of UN Security Council Resolution 242 (the land-for-peace blueprint established in the wake of the 1967 war). But Israel made no move toward accepting the resolution, and the situation soon worsened.[48]

Washington's greatest concern remained its overall position in the Middle East. To this end, U.S. officials worried that the Israeli attacks would fan the flames of the resistance: referring to the U.S. experience in Vietnam, Rostow pleaded with Israeli officials to focus on political as well as military considerations. Other observers noted that continued reprisals seemed to strengthen the hand of the "terrorists," made it more difficult for Amman to control the fedayeen, and might eventually encourage the guerillas to move against the Western-oriented governments in Amman and Beirut.[49] As violence escalated, the Arabs and Israelis were becoming more intransigent, and hopes of a quick post-June settlement—which seemed to be in everyone's interest, with the exception of the PLO—seemed to be receding. Increasing guerilla activity was leading many Israelis to see all "able-bodied West Bank Arabs as potential terrorists." One intelligence report explained:

> The sensitivities, frustrations, and infatuations of the Arabs are well enough known. The drives that show most intensely in the *fedayeen* are to be found to some degree even in most of the moderates, whose room for maneuver is thus circumscribed by limits of temperament as well as by political feasibilities. The correspondingly extreme Israeli attitudes are less familiar, perhaps because the Western origin of so many Israelis raises expectations that they do not attach to recogniz[ab]ly un-Western Arabs.

Officials remarked on the general sense of superiority to Arabs felt by most Israelis and noted the disconcerting similarity between Israeli attitudes toward the Arabs and "the 19th Century European view of colonial peoples." Furthermore, State Department intelligence warned that Israeli leaders might be seeking to dethrone King Hussein. Having demonstrated his inability to control the fedayeen, the king seemed like a growing liability to Israel. Some in Israel might wish to topple the regime in Amman to clear the path for a new government that would not be on such friendly terms with Washington, thus gaining the Israelis a free hand to deal ruthlessly with the new regime. For their part, the guerillas appeared to be an independent force in the region, outside the control of local governments. Riding a wave of popular opinion, the fedayeen might one day overthrow leaders such as Hussein and Nasser. "Then," the intelligence officers warned, "anarchy and violence will truly rule in the Middle East."[50]

British officials echoed these reservations about Israeli reprisals, especially Karama. The raid had been a "grave mistake," they told Secretary of State Dean Rusk; "it was costly and it had put Hussein in pawn." Rusk explained his view that terrorism could not be controlled without peace, and if it could not be "controlled, the risks are unimaginable." From Beirut, Ambassador Porter warned that Fatah had benefited enormously from Karama and was now threatening to take control of the Palestinian legislative body, the Palestinian National Council (PNC). He argued that Israel ought to focus on the likelihood that it was witnessing the emergence of a genuine Palestinian political entity that would function independently of the Arab states. Meanwhile, Symmes warned that because the fedayeen were in essence a grassroots political movement, they could no longer be dealt with simply as a security problem.[51]

Third World Liberation Fighters

While they propelled the fedayeen into a position of regional power, Fatah's diplomatic and military operations also helped to generate international publicity for the Palestinian cause and win support from the global community throughout 1968. Many observers in the nonaligned world came to see the guerillas as a viable political force in international politics. Fedayeen efforts to identify their struggle with the larger movement against imperialism in places such as Beijing, Hanoi, and Havana were intended to secure foreign patronage and represented a key component of fedayeen international diplomacy. Evidence from IDF-fedayeen clashes confirmed that much of the support for the guerillas went beyond the rhetorical. In a post-Karama briefing with the U.S. defense attaché, the IDF displayed captured Palestinian weapons of Soviet, Chinese, Czech, Yugoslavian, French, British, and even American origin. An IDF spokesman also warned of the possibility of a fedayeen–Viet Cong connection and noted that the IDF was interrogating a guerilla leader who had received training in China.[52] Public statements by some fedayeen commanders suggested that North Vietnamese might be serving as military advisors to the guerillas as well.[53]

Palestinian fighters had managed to tap into a number of Third World international networks that functioned outside the scope of the U.S.-Soviet rivalry. By late summer of 1968, Fatah had sent more than four hundred volunteers to Algeria for guerilla training and dispatched some thirty officers in a five-month leadership course in the People's Republic of China (PRC). After completing their studies, the contingent returned to Jordan—along with several hundred Chinese-manufactured rifles. Beijing became Fatah's main source of arms, directing shipments of AK-47s, mortars, and rocket-propelled grenades through Syria and Iraq to guerilla units in Jordan. This flow of arms increased exponentially in the late 1960s, allowing Fatah to equip 2,000 men in 1968, 7,000 in 1969, and 14,000 in 1970. By the end of 1969, China had shipped an estimated $5 million in weapons to the fedayeen, much of it through Basra and then overland into Jordan. Algiers and Cairo would also become important sources of arms for the guerillas; a steady stream of weapons scavenged from the battlefields of the June War by local Bedouin found their way into fedayeen hands as well.[54]

The Fatah-PRC link had been established early. After Arafat and Khalil al-Wazir (the latter a co-founder of Fatah and its chief military strategist) made a 1964 visit to Beijing as part of an Algerian delegation, the Chinese leaders began encouraging Fatah to launch an armed struggle modeled on the South Vietnamese National Liberation Front.[55] While Chinese motives involved hardheaded power politics and an effort to gain leverage in the triangular competition with the United States and the Soviet Union, Beijing's words reflected the ideals of Third World internationalism and the language of anti-imperialism. Pitting the fedayeen against the forces of U.S. imperialism and Israeli militarism, the government weekly *Peking Review* insisted that the Palestinians stood alongside Asian, African, and Latin American peoples in their struggle against colonialism. Palestinian fighters could take heart in the knowledge that "U.S. imperialism has had its head broken on the Vietnam battlefield and it is beset with worsening political and economic crises." As an important source of weapons, training, and financial aid, Beijing received frequent praise from the PLO as its first supporter among the great powers. On the other end of the PRC-PLO relationship, officials in Beijing praised the Palestinian fighters as the key force in the Arab revolution and as proof that Mao's vision of armed struggle remained the correct path toward national liberation. Likewise, Beijing blasted "U.S. imperialism, Soviet revisionist social-imperialism and the running dogs of both" in the Middle East. A May 1968 story in the *Peking Review* told the tale of one Palestinian fighter who had been mortally wounded in a raid in Gaza but managed to pull himself to a house in a nearby village and "with the last drops of his blood" wrote out the slogan "Down with U.S. imperialism!" While drenched in hyperbole and Maoist rhetoric, Beijing's propaganda was representative of widespread Third World sentiment.[56]

Meanwhile, Vietnamese leaders expressed camaraderie with the Palestinian fighters in their public statements, condemned Israeli attacks as outgrowths of U.S. imperialism, and called for the recognition of Palestinian national rights. "The Vietnamese people fully support the Palestinian people's liberation movement and the struggle of the Arab peoples for the liberation of territories occupied by Israeli forces," announced Ho Chi Minh. In private, they offered advice on waging a people's liberation war. "Stop talking about annihilating Israel,"

FIGURE 2.2 *Cover of PFLP's newspaper* Al-Hadaf, *"Anniversary of the Victory of the Chinese Revolution." Courtesy of the Library of the Institute for Palestine Studies, Beirut.*

General Vo Nguyen Giap told Arafat, "and instead turn your terror war into a struggle for human rights. Then you will have the American people eating out of your hand."[57]

The Cubans joined this revolutionary group, providing material assistance as well as moral support for the fedayeen. Like Hanoi, Havana publicly embraced the Palestinian cause and the guerillas who sought to further it. Warming relations between Algiers and Havana were leading to increasing cooperation between the two states in efforts to support revolutionary movements in the Third World. Cuban officials denounced what they saw as U.S.-backed Israeli aggression as well as the "Arab forces of reaction" that were endorsing peace efforts designed to extinguish the spark of revolution in the Arab world. Rather, the example of the Palestinian resistance presented the only legitimate response to imperialist moves in the region. Havana saw global implications arising from the struggle in the Middle East: as an imperialist coalition comprising the United States, Great Britain, West Germany, Israel, and reactionary Arab forces massed in the region, the Palestinian fighters had launched their struggle, which represented "a major and most significant front in the struggle of African, Asian and Latin American peoples against imperialism, colonialism and neo-colonialism." Reports of Palestinian fighters training in Cuba surfaced throughout 1969.[58]

At the same time that revolutionary states in the Third World sought to assist the fedayeen with military aid and training, the guerillas gained important diplomatic victories with the Non-Aligned Movement. After the PLO's visit to a meeting in Belgrade, the heads of state of the nonaligned countries chose to endorse restoration of Palestinian rights in the occupied territories and announced their full support for the fedayeen in their "struggle for liberation from colonialism and racism and for the recovery of their inalienable rights."[59] In the last week of April, Zakir Husain, president of India, made a speech at a dinner in honor of Ethiopian emperor Haile Selassie calling for Israeli withdrawal from the occupied territories. A joint communiqué released the same day by Yugoslav president Josip Broz Tito and the government of Iran echoed this call for an Israeli withdrawal from occupied Arab territory.[60]

The French chimed in early in April, declaring their belief that the Israeli occupation of the West Bank and Gaza was responsible for Fatah's rise and citing parallels between Palestinian actions and French resistance to German occupation.[61] In subsequent years, Paris would come to play an important role in bridging the gap between Western powers and the Arab world. France— once Israel's principal arms supplier—emerged after the war as one of the most vocal Western critics of Israeli policies. In August 1967, President Charles de Gaulle publicly denounced the "scandalous fate of the refugees in Jordan" and warned, "The Israeli occupation of the territories it captured cannot continue without oppression, repression, expulsions, nor without the emergence over time of a resistance it will then label as terrorism."[62] He added that Israel would become "more imperialistic" as long as no settlement was achieved; the Israelis would "go to the Nile, to Beirut and to Damascus."[63] France's motives in its relations with the Arab world reflected both past experience and contemporary interests. No stranger to counterinsurgencies in the Third World, France had become a critic of Third World interventions in the wake of the Algerian war. The French also maintained an attachment to the peoples of its former mandates in Syria and Lebanon. The latter country especially was seen by many French as an example of the success of *la mission civilisatrice*. At the same time, Paris had cynical reasons for supporting the Palestinian cause. By embracing the Palestine issue, France gained credibility and sympathy throughout the Arab world. In addition to raising French stock in global politics, this sympathy carried the prospect of an economic payoff in the form of favorable oil prices and arms contracts with the oil-producing Arab states. The motives for French Middle East policy would remain a subject of debate for observers in Washington and London into the 1970s.[64]

By the end of 1968, the fedayeen had managed to state their case to the world community and to establish themselves as a growing force in regional affairs, confounding many of the existing categories and established frameworks in Middle East politics. Palestinian fighters enjoyed a wide base of support from states with a diverse set of motivations. While many foreign governments identified with the revolutionary rhetoric emanating from groups such as Fatah and the PFLP, others were simply more sympathetic to the humanitarian plight of the Palestinian refugees. Meanwhile, some governments understood their endorsement of the PLO to be a strike against Israel and/or the United States. While statements of support from France, Pakistan, Algeria, Yugoslavia, India, Ethiopia, and China would not give the Palestinians a homeland, they did point to the growing support for the Palestinian cause in the international community and the importance of transnational radical politics in the Palestinian search for a state.

The Tide of World Opinion

Mounting support for the cause of Palestinian liberation complicated Washington's plans for the Middle East. At the United Nations, U.S. policy makers found themselves in a difficult position for a number of reasons. The growing power of the nonaligned bloc presented an obstacle to U.S. policies in the Middle East, especially on the issue of national liberation. Nations in the postcolonial world that had strong memories of their own struggles for self-determination were often sympathetic to the types of arguments that the PLO made. At the same time, the evolution of international norms regarding issues such as human rights, state violence, and resistance struggles around the world provided a vocabulary within which Palestinian activists could couch their claims. Israel's stunning victory in the June War, its ongoing occupation of Arab territory, and the increased flow of high-tech weapons from the United States led many in the world community to question assumptions about a weak Jewish state surrounded by hostile neighbors.

While these issues remained important in their own right, frequent outbreaks of violence along the Jordanian and Lebanese frontiers pushed the Palestinian question onto the floor of the Security Council. On 4 August 1968 Israeli forces carried out air strikes against two locations near the ancient town of as-Salt in Jordan. Citing evidence obtained through prisoner interrogation, the IDF claimed that the two sites were being used as "terrorist" headquarters and explained that Israeli actions were aimed at the bases, not the town. After the first wave of jets had finished their attack, however, Israeli artillery launched a second strike. During the short pause between the attacks Jordanian villagers had begun efforts to recover the dead and wounded. Thus, the second attack struck many civilians and several ambulances. In response, Amman called for an urgent meeting of the Security Council in order to discuss the violation of the cease-fire.[65]

At the Security Council, the Jordanians presented pictures of civilian casualties, claimed that the as-Salt raid represented a premeditated attack against civilian population centers, and asserted that it had been designed to intimidate Jordan. The Israeli representative responded that the actions had been necessary acts of self-defense against "terrorist bases." The Algerian representative insisted that the "basic problem of the Middle East was the conflict between an aggressive power, which was supported by imperialist interests, and the Palestinian nation, which was determined to regain its rights." The only possible solution, he suggested, was for the United Nations not to place the complaints of the victim and the aggressor "on equal footing." Moscow agreed that Israel's justifications were groundless in light of its continued occupation of Arab territories. "The people of those territories," commented the Soviet representative, "had every right to resist that occupation and wage a just struggle for their freedom and independence." To make matters worse, this latest attack had come—as had the Karama raid—at a crucial moment in Gunnar Jarring's UN peace efforts. The council therefore had an obligation to take punitive action against the aggressor.[66]

U.S. efforts to draft a resolution that placed equal blame on both sides met fierce resistance from a number of states that pointed to the fundamental disparities between the two sides. The Jordanians rejected Israeli attempts to deflect attention away from the reprisals by issuing countercharges against the guerillas and the Jordanian government. Amman maintained that so long as the occupation continued, acts of resistance would persist:

Resistance against occupation had precedents in every country [that had been] occupied....The situation in Angola, Southern Rhodesia and

South Africa was no different from the struggle of the Arabs of Palestine. Europeans had resisted Nazi occupation in similar manner and millions of them had lost their lives in the struggle to regain their homelands. Jordan would not stop acts of a people's national resistance against Israeli occupation.

Much like its counterparts from Jordan and Algeria, the Pakistani delegation attacked attempts to balance the actions of the two sides. The representative explained that to "equate the small, sporadic and spontaneous acts of resistance of the people of the occupied territories with the carefully planned and large-scale military operations of Israeli forces was to ignore a startling disparity of magnitude and quality and to confer equal rights on the aggressor and its victim."[67]

The highly aggressive nature of the Israeli attacks troubled international observers, as did the fear that such actions might set a precedent for other states. Linking the attack on as-Salt to the Karama raid, the French voiced their deep concern over the pattern of violence in the region. Such attacks were acts of reprisal rather than self-defense and could only lead to more violence and jeopardize international attempts to reach a political settlement. The Canadians, too, called on all parties to refrain from further acts of belligerence. The representative from Senegal warned that the Security Council's decisions might set a dangerous precedent for other nations. "Leaders in Portugal, Southern Rhodesia, and South Africa were watching the Security Council's reaction to the Israeli interpretation of the concept of self-defense." The Indian delegate also insisted that the Salt raid, like Karama before it, must be condemned, as ultimately there could be no peace in the region until Israeli forces withdrew from Arab territories.[68]

Meanwhile, the State Department encouraged the U.S. ambassador to the United Nations, George Ball, to stick as closely as possible to the position his predecessor had taken following the Karama raid in March. Ball should stress the connection between terrorist attacks and Israeli retaliation, seek a balanced resolution that would place fedayeen provocations alongside Israeli retaliations, and articulate Washington's objections to all violations of the cease-fire. At the same time, the United States must take care not to isolate itself from the rest of the Security Council in an attempt to shield Israel.[69]

In private meetings with State Department officials, Amman expressed its belief that Washington could prevent Israeli attacks if it chose to do so. Indeed, in the as-Salt raid the IDF had used American-built aircraft that had been delivered to Israel after it occupied Arab territory. Although the United States had previously assured Amman of its intentions to push for UN Resolution 242, Washington was now seeking to equate the actions of a few Palestinian guerilla groups with a coordinated attack by the Israeli armed forces. Many in the Arab world were coming to see Washington's actions as unabashedly pro-Israel given the disproportionate nature of the attacks. Furthermore, King Hussein faced a serious credibility problem, as Jordanians and others around the Arab world began to question Amman's ties to Washington. "Such ties are becoming very dangerous for him in the concrete sense," explained the Jordanian ambassador, who pleaded with State Department officials to put more pressure on Israel to reach a political settlement. Israeli leaders announced defiantly that they had little regard for world opinion so long as they maintained the support of the U.S. government. It was therefore imperative that the U.S. government make some gesture of support for its friends in the Arab world if Washington hoped to maintain close relationships with its Arab allies in the region.[70]

Symmes made it clear to his superiors that Jordanian civilians had suffered the most in Israel's most recent raid. High civilian casualties combined with the psychological shock of watching the IDF enjoy unrestricted use of Jordanian airspace for three and a half hours had taken their toll. Rumors were circulating of more than a hundred casualties, with some estimates as high as four times that number. Hospitals in Amman were filled with wounded and were resorting to triage systems. Moreover, locals reported that many of the fedayeen had in fact survived by taking shelter in caves and a nearby forest.[71]

Watching the debates from Amman, Symmes cabled Rusk to note his concern that Washington was becoming isolated at the United Nations as the sole supporter of a balanced resolution. Recent Israeli reprisals and unilateral attacks had swung world opinion in favor of the fedayeen and against the Israeli government. Compounding matters, Israeli reprisals punished the Jordanians, who were in fact trying to control the fedayeen. Reprisals strengthened the guerillas and undermined King Hussein's efforts to reassert his control. Symmes argued for a resolution that "would put Israel on notice that the tide of opinion is flowing against her," in hopes of convincing the Israeli leadership that future raids would only exacerbate the problem of world opinion and render it more difficult for Washington to continue its support and protection.[72]

Ambassador Porter warned that the current fedayeen-Israeli violence was putting Washington's position in the eastern Arab world in jeopardy. If the U.S. government continued on its present course, Amman would become estranged from Washington. Internal pressures could force King Hussein to turn against the United States, leaving Beirut as the only Arab capital still on friendly terms with Washington. Should it become the sole U.S. ally, Lebanon would face tremendous pressure to align itself with its fellow Arabs in opposition to the United States. American interests would best be served by Washington's support of a Security Council resolution condemning the most recent reprisal. The push for a balanced resolution ought to be abandoned in favor of a condemnation of the as-Salt raid and pressure on Israel to make some conciliatory gesture in order to keep the peace process rolling forward. This latter approach would facilitate King Hussein's efforts to control the fedayeen and stem the rising tide of anti-Americanism in the Arab world.[73]

In the end, officials in Washington chose to ignore the advice of State Department officers in the field, electing instead to go easy on Israel. After exhaustive efforts at the UN, Ball managed to achieve a more balanced resolution regarding as-Salt, featuring terms similar to those voiced after the Karama raid. Following the debates, Ball reiterated his belief that while the resolution had focused on the Israeli attacks, all parties in the region were responsible for maintaining the cease-fire. In response, the Algerian representative expressed his regret that such balanced resolutions were rendering the Security Council largely ineffective.[74]

Israeli prime minister Levi Eshkol remained adamant, however, that Israel would not tolerate guerilla attacks. Eshkol's secretary suggested that there were "many in the cabinet who believed that retaliation was the only language that the Arabs would understand." While U.S. officials had become accustomed to this sort of saber rattling, even more disturbing signals were coming out of the Israeli government. In mid-August, an Israeli embassy official informed the State Department that his government viewed King Hussein's friendly relations with Washington as an obstacle. If the king were to fall and be succeeded by a radical regime, the IDF would be free to launch an invasion across the Jordan River designed to crush Fatah and the Jordanian Army.[75]

Meanwhile, the rising power of the fedayeen continued bleeding into internal politics in Lebanon. In mid-August the U.S. embassy in Beirut reported signs of growing resentment toward Israel and increasing confessional tensions in Lebanon, with the growing stature of the commandos leading sympathizers to call on the Lebanese government to join the fedayeen in their struggle against Israel. The Lebanese government was increasingly in peril, as the stalemate in the region exposed the weakness of the Arab regimes. As the Arab governments came to appear more and more impotent, Porter wrote, "commando activities are taking on an increasing luster." Even some Lebanese Christians—among the most Western-oriented Arabs—were applauding the PFLP's recent hijacking of an Israeli airliner. Lebanese officials feared that the fedayeen movement would soon race beyond their control and that radicalization of the Arab world would ensue. Israeli reprisals had failed to intimidate the Arabs; rather, they increased the power of radical factions in the region. Porter reported that the "Arab humiliation of 1967 has ushered us into a third and more ominous phase [of the Arab-Israeli conflict]—that of guerilla warfare." Israeli reprisals had strengthened the PLO's image. Porter feared that trends were leading toward a fourth phase of the conflict, when the commandos might establish control over some of the Arab governments. He warned that the "major seismic effects of the June War may still be ahead of us. Today we are enjoying a period of relative calm which may represent the last chance for constructive intervention."[76]

Failure to Create a United Front

Although their stock was rising in the international arena, the guerillas still faced division and dissension from within the diaspora. In part to address these divisions, Fatah convened a meeting of the various guerilla organizations in January 1968 that laid the groundwork for fedayeen participation in the upcoming meeting of the PNC. In a sign of things to come, the PFLP boycotted the meeting. The following month, Habash and Wazir met in Beirut, where they agreed to coordinate their activities. This cooperation was short-lived, however. In the wake of the Battle of Karama, Fatah began criticizing the PFLP for its withdrawal in advance of Israeli forces. Arafat was working to undermine Habash and thereby marginalize a rival for leadership of the fedayeen.[77]

With their prestige and influence on the rise following Karama, the fedayeen set their sights on taking control of the PNC. At the fourth meeting of the legislative body in July, Fatah managed to parlay its recent successes into a dominant political position. On 17 July 1968, the congress released its new Palestinian National Charter, which reflected the expanded role of the guerillas in the PLO. Although the old bourgeois notables of the West Bank continued to draw respect from the Palestinian population, the fedayeen were the principal source of energy and dynamism within Palestinian politics. Guerilla control of the organization was established once and for all with Arafat's ascension to chairmanship of the PLO in February 1969.[78]

The new charter placed armed struggle at the center of the Palestinian liberation movement and insisted on Palestinian rights of sovereignty and self-determination. Liberation would come not from the actions of the Arab states but through the efforts of the Palestinian fedayeen. Likewise, the end goal of the Palestinian resistance would be the creation of an independent Palestinian state rather than the annexation of Palestinian land by its Arab neighbors.[79] These political transformations indicate the importance of guerilla operations and arms to the budding movement. Guerilla operations reshaped the structure of Palestinian national identity and provided the "currency" for political competition between rival factions.[80]

While the guerillas came to dominate the PLO by late 1968, no single group could claim to control the fedayeen. Although Arafat's Fatah gained the lion's share of international attention and a preeminent position in the PLO, other guerilla groups remained vocal in the movement. George Habash and the PFLP had been eclipsed in the months following al-Karama by the larger and more powerful Fatah. Thus, while Arafat and Fatah were preoccupied with training guerilla fighters to engage in cross-border raids against the Israeli occupation and establishing the concept of a Palestinian resistance separate from the Arab struggle, the PFLP sought to carry out more spectacular operations designed to spark a people's war of liberation. Guerilla raids were not enough, the group insisted, to oppose Zionism and its American imperialist backers.[81]

Even as Fatah consolidated its position in the PNC, the PFLP laid plans to seize the world's attention and establish itself as a leading voice in the Palestinian resistance.

Fatah failed to recognize the danger of the uncontrolled growth of rival guerilla organizations. Rather, Arafat welcomed fellow guerilla groups and competing political ideologies into the PLO.[82] Middle East specialist Alain Gresh attributes this array of guerilla groups to the realities of Palestinian existence up to 1968: diaspora and the varied backgrounds of the leaders and groups associated with the movement, a strong sense of individualism in Palestinian cultural values, the relatively high levels of education among Palestinians (which contributed to their susceptibility to a variety of ideological currents), and the interference—direct and indirect—of the Arab states.[83]

In short, Fatah failed to capitalize on its opportunity in 1968 to create a united front. In the months following Karama, Arafat's group enjoyed preeminence among the fedayeen and the political backing of many of the Arab states. Indeed, during 1968 and 1969, Egypt, Saudi Arabia, Kuwait, and Qatar all encouraged Fatah to take full control of the PLO. Arafat declined, however; his goal was rule by consensus, rather than majority. This decision was partly the result of caution. Prior to 1968, the PLO had been a tool of the Arab regimes, and so Arafat sought to foster allies among fellow guerilla groups in the event that Arab states sought to reassert their control over the organization. Likewise, Fatah's leaders feared that any move to consolidate their control over the PLO would lead to bloody internecine conflicts and destruction of the organization. Rather than risk civil war between the fedayeen, Fatah chose to incorporate the guerilla groups into the PLO in their full diversity. Arafat also cited his desire to maintain the democratic character of the movement: "If we had used the guns to solve such problems," he later explained, "we would have made a nonsense of our democracy and our masses would have lost confidence in us." This decision would carry a heavy price. By the end of the decade Fatah had lost its opportunity, as the power of the Arab states grew and rival groups strengthened their positions.[84] The fragmented structure of the PLO had a profound impact on the nature of the armed struggle and the rise of guerilla operations against civilians. The immediate effect on the ground was the creation of redundancies and competition between and within the various guerilla groups, weak security, poor organization, and no clear strategy to military operations. "It was action for action's sake," reported one senior Fatah officer.[85] This fragmentation would also play a role in directing guerilla violence against civilians, as soon became evident.

On 23 July, an Israeli passenger jet departed Rome on its way to Tel Aviv. Twenty-five minutes after takeoff, two PFLP commandos broke into the plane's cockpit and ordered the pilot to change course for Algiers, while a third, armed with an unpinned grenade and a revolver, kept watch over the passengers. The PFLP insisted that the hijacking of the El Al plane constituted a legal act of resistance, explaining that Israel used the airline and its pilots to transport soldiers and military equipment during times of war, thereby making the aircraft a military target. During a conversation with American embassy officers in Beirut, a PLO official applauded the hijacking, explaining that it would put Algeria in the position of having to prove whether it was willing to back up its statements of support for the fedayeen with action. He said there would be no peace until "the racialist state of Israel was eliminated" and warned Washington not to depend upon its "client-state" to protect its interests in the region. Such policies had been "discredited in the eyes of the rest of the world [and] in Viet-Nam, and the United States should not make the same mistake in the Middle East."[86]

The hijacking signaled a new direction in the armed struggle, with alarming implications for an increasingly interconnected international system. By attacking civil aviation, Third World liberation fighters had transferred their guerilla war "from the forests to the skies." This new strategy exploited recent communications technology and the growing interconnectedness of the late Cold War world, targeting global networks of transportation. In so doing, the PFLP moved its regional struggle into the international sphere not just in the ideological dimension, as Fatah had already done by associating itself with the ideals and examples of postcolonial liberation, but in a physical sense. Palestinian gunmen began to move across a terrain that was inherently transnational; civil aviation existed quite literally in the space between nations, and it was here that the commandos would strike, effectively circumventing the IDF's counterinsurgency tactics and contributing to the internationalization of the Palestinian question. The PFLP thus blazed a trail that other groups would follow. Many guerilla groups tended to be more wary of hijacking and similar types of "external operations," however. Aside from the public relations problem that such attacks created, larger organizations including Fatah recognized that many of these operations were designed to increase the relative influence of extremist groups such as the PFLP at the expense of more moderate fedayeen.[87]

One of the earliest justifications for fedayeen attacks against civilians centered on the idea of reciprocity: the Israeli occupation of the West Bank and Gaza had unleashed a wave of military violence against the Arab population, and the guerillas, by attacking Israeli civilians, were merely responding in kind. Beyond this philosophical justification, however, lay a practical calculation: civilian targets were far easier to hit than military ones. As Palestinian fighters discovered the high cost of operations against Israeli armed forces, the guerillas began to shift their attention to civilian or "soft" targets. While the PFLP was outclassed by Fatah in nearly every metric of guerilla power—men under arms, access to weapons, foreign aid, international allies—its spectacular external operations dramatically increased the organization's prestige. Because they involved a relatively small number of guerillas and garnered a large amount of publicity, these attacks were an important component of the organization's arsenal. Thus, external operations became an important means of demonstrating the power and continuing relevancy of various guerilla organizations.[88]

The July hijacking was followed, on 26 December, by an attack on the Athens airport in which two guerillas from the PFLP opened fire on an El Al jetliner as it sat on the tarmac, killing one passenger and wounding a flight attendant. Beirut newspapers praised the attack, calling it a justifiable reprisal carried out by freedom fighters in response to the brutality of Israeli occupation in the Palestinian territories. The Lebanese government found itself in a difficult position amidst the public cheers, as the PFLP was based in Beirut. Although it condemned the attack against a civilian aircraft, the government of Lebanon could not openly criticize the fedayeen for fear of stirring volatile domestic tensions. Worried that the Athens attack would invite an IDF reprisal, the Lebanese government approached U.S. officials, insisting that it bore no responsibility for the attack. Although Ambassador Porter tried to reassure the Lebanese that Israel was unlikely to retaliate against Lebanese aircraft, he warned that Israeli actions were ultimately impossible to predict.[89]

The Israeli government reacted harshly. Prime Minister Eshkol fumed that "the mark of Cain shall be on the brow of those who carried out this criminal act and those who sent them to do it." Explaining that these terrorist attacks were a threat not just to Israel but to the entire civilized world, he added that those who supported the attackers were well known to his government. By sending agents to attack Israeli interests, Eshkol warned, the Arab states had exposed themselves to future retribution. The Israeli minister of transportation added that his government would hold the government of Lebanon responsible for the attacks, since they were organized on its soil.[90] In a meeting of his top security staff, Eshkol decided to stage a retaliatory assault on Lebanese aircraft. Although the operation was originally designed to attack no more than four planes, Defense Minister Moshe Dayan expanded its scope.[91]

At eleven-thirty the following evening, four Israeli helicopters descended on Beirut's al-Khaldah International Airport, opened fire on the runway, and landed near the hangar of Middle East Airlines, Lebanon's national carrier. Not wishing to create unnecessary bloodshed, Israeli soldiers ordered bystanders to take cover in the hangars and then placed and detonated explosives on thirteen Lebanese aircraft. In the raid's aftermath, Prime Minister Eshkol announced that the operation had been carried out in retaliation for the Athens attack and the July hijacking of the El Al jet. "States that make it possible for the terrorist organizations to organize and perpetrate acts of terror bear the responsibility for the aggression," as stipulated by international law, Eshkol said.[92] Few international observers would share the Israeli interpretation of the raid, however.

The al-Khaldah reprisal released a firestorm of international criticism. Algerian newspapers argued that the raid was the "cynical reward" for Beirut's policy of moderation toward Israel and that the attack demonstrated the unfeasibility of a political solution. The British press condemned the raid, arguing that the attack had dragged the moderate Lebanese government into the Arab-Israeli conflict, squandered any diplomatic advantage in the aftermath of the Athens attacks, and demonstrated that Israeli hawks were "clearly in control." The *Financial Times* suggested that the Israeli government had lost a sense of the "regional realities" in attacking Beirut and noted the possible effects on British insurance firms—Lloyd's of London was the principal insurer of the aircraft—of what could become the largest aviation claim in history. Even American officials were harshly critical, at least in private, of the latest reprisals. Beyond the immediate outrage, however, it became clear that the transnational nature of civil aviation meant that the attacks carried out by both the Israelis and the Palestinians carried international repercussions and ultimately demanded a global response. In key respects, the United Nations was the only organization capable of dealing with the sorts of issues that the dispute over Palestine was beginning to raise.[93]

The storm over the latest violence quickly made its way to the UN Security Council, where the Lebanese demanded that Israeli actions be condemned and that the government receive compensation for the destruction of its aircraft. Israeli officials argued that Beirut, by providing safe haven and encouragement to the fedayeen, had opened itself up to attack. Citing the recent Athens incident, the Israeli representative claimed that his nation was merely responding in kind and that the Beirut airport attack had to be seen as a part of the wider guerilla war against the fedayeen and their Arab supporters.[94]

While U.S. and British representatives criticized the Athens attack, they refused to accept the idea that the reprisal was justified and noted that the Beirut raid was in any case disproportionate to the Athens incident. Criticism of the reprisals—especially considering Beirut's record of moderation—from Brazil, India, Canada, China, Denmark, France, Paraguay, and Senegal soon gave way to more virulent attacks from the Soviets, Algerians, and Hungarians. The Pakistanis insisted that the latest raid was merely the most recent instance of an aggressive Israeli defense strategy that relied on indiscriminate use of force against its neighbors. As a resolution condemning Israel took shape, U.S., British, and Danish representatives expressed concern about the need to place Israeli actions within the wider context of violence and the specific aftermath of the Athens attack. Canadian delegates responded that the Athens attack must also be judged within the context of violence in the region.[95]

Controversies such as those over the al-Khaldah, al-Karama, and as-Salt raids helped to crystallize international perceptions—growing since the end of the 1967 war—that Israel's defense strategies were overly aggressive and dangerous to its neighbors. Meanwhile, the Security Council debates shed light on the growing divide between the part of the world community that sympathized with the Palestinian struggle and those governments—particularly British and American—that sought to shield Israel from international criticism. While they condemned Israel's actions in private, Washington and London insisted that Israeli reprisals be viewed within the context of guerilla violence. At the same time, they played down the violent context of military occupation that had initially fueled the rise of the fedayeen movement. The framing of the Palestinian struggle—already a crucial component of fedayeen diplomacy—had emerged as the most hotly contested issue in the global debate over the increasingly international question of Palestine; it would also prove to be one of the most intractable. While the Battle of al-Karama had effectively placed the fedayeen on the global map of national liberation movements, other powers were conspiring to wipe them off.

Nixon, Kissinger, and the Terror of a Postimperial World

Henry Kissinger was an ambitious but frustrated young man. The son of Jewish parents from Bavaria, Kissinger had come to the United States in 1938, fleeing Nazi oppression. He distinguished himself in World War II as an interpreter working in counterintelligence and, after his return to the United States, gained admission to Harvard. He graduated summa cum laude in 1950 and then earned a doctorate in 1954. His plans to stay on in Cambridge as a tenure-track professor and member of the esteemed Society of Fellows were derailed when the dean of the faculty, McGeorge Bundy, denied his request. Kissinger was instead offered temporary employment as an instructor, a position that he grudgingly accepted while he began searching for employment elsewhere in academia. In the midst of this angst, on a stroll across Harvard Yard, he ran into the historian Arthur Schlesinger Jr., who gave Kissinger a paper he had been writing about U.S. nuclear weapons policy. The young instructor read the paper and wrote up a response over the weekend. Schlesinger was so impressed with Kissinger's feedback that he forwarded it to the international relations journal *Foreign Affairs*, which agreed to print a revised and expanded version.[1]

Kissinger's first published essay on national security, "Military Policy and Defense of the 'Grey Areas,'" focused on the need for the United States to develop the capacity to wage low-intensity conflicts in a world characterized by nuclear parity. As Moscow's nuclear strength grew, Washington would find that its standing policy of massive nuclear retaliation was inadequate for the defense of peripheral interests in the Third World. Although these gray areas were not important enough to risk sacrificing a major city such as Chicago or New York in a Soviet counterstrike, the young Harvard instructor argued that the defense of the periphery must remain a major priority for Cold War decision makers. Thus, rather than an all-or-nothing approach to national security, Kissinger made the case that Washington must develop the capacity to defend areas that did not warrant a nuclear showdown. In the coming years, as Kissinger established his credentials as a defense intellectual and the United States became mired in the war in Vietnam, the ideas outlined in his 1955 article would come to seem prescient.[2]

"The Dominoes Appeared to Be Falling"

By the late 1960s, the conflict in Vietnam had come to dominate public discourse in the United States. As Washington's counterinsurgency efforts gave way to a war of attrition in Southeast Asia, a growing number of Americans searched for a way out of the quagmire; Richard Nixon was one of them. The former senator turned vice president turned failed presidential candidate from Whittier, California, was staring at a very real chance of winning the White House. Whoever emerged victorious from the campaign would confront an array of challenges, however. At home, student protesters had turned university campuses into sounding boards for their revolutionary appeals, while racial tensions threatened to transform some of the nation's largest cities into war zones. Abroad, the new president would have to deal with one of the most intractable wars in the republic's history and cope with a rapidly changing international system. Nixon was convinced that one of the Johnson administration's biggest mistakes was allowing the conflict in Vietnam to dominate the administration's foreign and domestic policies. If given the chance, the Republican front-runner was determined to take a broader approach. Rather than being bogged down by concerns in any single region, he hoped to craft an integrated global strategy designed to strengthen Washington's position in the international system. On 5 November 1968, after one of the most contentious elections in the nation's history, a slim plurality of the American people decided to give Nixon his chance.[3]

Kissinger admitted his general ambivalence about the presidential candidates, Nixon and Hubert Humphrey. Kissinger had been working with Nixon's Republican rival, Nelson Rockefeller, when he was first approached by the campaign with an offer to serve as a foreign policy advisor. Kissinger declined, explaining that he could be of more help if he "worked behind the scenes." The nature of this assistance would spawn a controversy over Kissinger's alleged collusion with the Nixon campaign to spoil the 1968 peace negotiations in Vietnam by encouraging the South Vietnamese delegation to hold out in anticipation of getting a better deal under Nixon. Controversies aside, Kissinger was still hesitant about the president-elect when, on November 22, he received a phone call from Nixon's staff. In an awkward conversation in person three days later, Nixon expressed his determination to wrest control of foreign policy from the State Department, placing it firmly in the hands of the White House. After discussing the offer of a position within the administration with his colleagues at Harvard and at the urging of Rockefeller, Kissinger accepted.[4]

The president-elect and the young professor had much in common in their approach to diplomacy, which Nixon recognized in 1968 after reading Kissinger's *Nuclear Weapons and Foreign Policy*. Both believed in a realpolitik approach to foreign policy that backed diplomacy with force.[5] Further, both men pushed for a foreign policy that integrated regional issues into a single global strategy. This conviction came to form the basis for the "linkage" tactic that sought to globalize relations with Moscow, connecting issues such as arms limitation and bilateral trade with negotiations over Cold War flash points such as Vietnam, the Middle East, and Germany. Ultimately, both Nixon and Kissinger saw the need for the creation of an overarching global strategy that would bolster Washington's position in the Cold War, address the disastrous situation in Vietnam, and hold the line in hot spots around the Third World while at the same time refraining from committing American ground forces in peripheral areas.[6]

Although his interests now turned on current policy, Kissinger had devoted much of his early career to the study of European diplomatic history in search of the universal maxims that governed state-to-state relations. He would later translate this understanding of history and political science into an official U.S. foreign policy. Kissinger revered post–Congress of Vienna Europe as the only example of a functioning balance-of-power system and the historical archetype for a stable world order. In this same spirit, he considered Klemens von Metternich and, to a lesser extent, Otto von Bismarck ideal statesmen. While he respected Bismarck's willingness to exercise power in defense of state interests—his realpolitik—Kissinger viewed Metternich as the mastermind behind the most successful diplomacy the world had ever seen. The Austrian count had managed to construct a peaceful international order based on a set of shared values between the European powers. He had ensured that legitimacy would remain safely in the hands of the established European monarchs and sought to suppress the forces of liberalism, nationalism, and revolution in nineteenth-century Europe.[7]

At the same time, Kissinger's model statesman was one of history's greatest counterrevolutionaries. Metternich considered democracies dangerous and unpredictable. The furor of revolutionary France had demonstrated that the masses could not be trusted to create reasonable, pacific foreign policies. Revolutionary change and liberal ideals led inevitably to disorder and conflict. Traditional legitimacy—in the form of monarchical dynasties rather than liberal values—was the element that had held the international order together and prevented major warfare. In contrast, leaders such as Woodrow Wilson, who sought to construct a peaceful international order based on shared liberal values and ethnic nationalism, ultimately undermined the cause of peace.[8]

Kissinger's vision of a stable international system required that the great powers balance security with concepts of justice: to accept the status quo, states must not feel threatened by it and must believe in its ultimate fairness. This understanding of balance of power in international relations would shape Kissinger's conception of détente. Ultimately there must be a broad consensus between the great powers, which would then cooperate to maintain world order.[9] Second- and third-tier powers would naturally take a secondary role.

In the same manner, nonstate groups that rose to challenge the status quo had no place within this international system. Rather, these groups fell into the category of internal subversion and threatened to undermine the world order by eating away at domestic sources of legitimacy. The incoming administration needed to look no further than the streets of Washington, New York, Chicago, and Berkeley to find such threats of subversion. Further complicating matters, antiestablishment radicalism was a transnational concern in an increasingly interconnected global system. As Kissinger wrote, by "the late 1960s, the violent protest of the students had grown into a global phenomenon." As a result of the breakdown in domestic order and consensus, the Nixon administration had come into office under "near–civil war conditions."[10]

The president and his national security advisor shared this conservative-globalist vision. Indeed, the incoming administration faced the novel challenge of dealing with an international system that was more interconnected than ever before and undergoing radical transformations. As Nixon had said to an audience in 1967, "We live in a new world. Never in human history have more changes taken place in the world in one generation." He predicted that with advances in communications and transportation technology, the world would be one "great city" by the end of the century.[11] Kissinger expanded on this idea when he wrote:

> For the first time, foreign policy has become global. In the past, the various continents conducted their foreign policy essentially in isolation. Throughout much of history, the foreign policy of Europe was scarcely affected by events in Asia.... Today, statesmen face the unprecedented problem of formulating policy for well over a hundred countries. Every nation, no matter how insignificant, participates in international affairs. Ideas are transmitted almost instantaneously. What used to be considered domestic events can now have world-wide consequences.

The appearance of so many new players on the world stage, the pace of technological change, and the expanding interest in international affairs had, in Kissinger's eyes, revolutionized the global system.[12] The war in Vietnam energized this global turmoil. Kissinger would later write that the conflict had threatened to spark a revolutionary change in the global order. Radicals around the world were inspired by the communist victory in Vietnam. The U.S.

collapse in Southeast Asia caused a surge in Soviet advances around the Third World.

> Cuban military forces had spread from Angola to Ethiopia in tandem with thousands of Soviet combat advisers. In Cambodia, Vietnamese troops backed and supplied by the Soviet Union were subjugating that tormented country. Afghanistan was occupied by over 100,000 Soviet troops. The government of the pro-Western Shah of Iran collapsed and was replaced by a radically anti-American fundamentalist regime.... Whatever the causes, the dominoes indeed appeared to be falling.

While this moment in fact marked the beginning of communism's unraveling, Kissinger noted that it appeared to contemporaries as the "nadir of America's international position."[13]

In order to reconstitute the bases of Washington's power in this increasingly globalized world order, Nixon and Kissinger needed to accomplish a number of objectives. The first remained simply to recognize the limits of U.S. power. Revolutions tended to succeed, Kissinger wrote, when the "established order is unable to grasp its own vulnerability." The Vietnamese experience had signaled the need for a reassessment of Washington's role in the wider world and the necessity of finding a sustainable means of maintaining U.S. influence in the developing world. The Nixon administration was determined, in Kissinger's words, "to get beyond Vietnam without suffering geopolitical losses" and to move the struggle against communism to more important arenas. American resolve must not be squandered in a losing war in the jungles of Southeast Asia but ought to be redirected toward more efficient activities in more important regions. Overextension in the Third World and the Cold War stalemate were draining American resources and resolve. In light of the complex set of challenges that confronted it and the finite nature of American resources, the new administration worked to craft a global strategy designed to manage the international system rather than dominate it.[14] Nixon said that as he watched communism spread to the Third World in the form of socialism and through wars of national liberation, he feared that the Soviets were gaining the upper hand. What was needed was a revitalized containment strategy designed to preserve Washington's power and authority both at home and abroad.[15]

At the same time that they developed this revised containment strategy, Nixon and Kissinger introduced a new structure to the White House's foreign policy bureaucracy. This organizational framework represented a dramatic expansion of the powers of the national security advisor at the expense of the Secretary of State and resulted in a considerable amount of confusion during Nixon's first term.[16] Using his exceptional bureaucratic skills and growing charismatic appeal—to say nothing of his sycophantic relationship with the president—Kissinger quickly emerged as the key foreign policy advisor in the administration.

The Nixon Administration and the Middle East

There was one region, however, in which Kissinger would, in theory, take a backseat to Secretary of State William Rogers: the Middle East. Nixon deemed it a secondary interest for the incoming administration and judged that its complexities could be left to the State Department for the time being. Moreover, Nixon's anti-Semitic tendencies—which his national security advisor would be forced to endure—initially made him suspicious of Kissinger's ability to remain impartial when dealing with Israel. Kissinger, however, was determined to establish control over the whole of the foreign policy apparatus and had no intention of being locked out of any region. The seeds were sown for an intra-administration clash.

This budding internal rivalry was manifest in early disagreements over the shape of Nixon's foreign policy toward the Middle East and the Arab-Israeli conflict. While State and Defense proposed more conventional approaches that sought to account for the unique dynamics of the region, Kissinger pushed for a strategy based on his own foreign policy maxims and integrated into U.S. geopolitical efforts in the larger world. The region presented a particularly troubling set of challenges to the new administration: Israel remained a difficult and fiercely independent ally with the support of strong interest groups within the United States, King Hussein's regime in Jordan was being squeezed by the guerilla war between the PLO and Israel, and Lebanon was suffering from some of the same tensions that plagued Jordan and widening sectarian divisions. At the same time, the growing power of the PLO and the threat of Moscow's creeping influence raised U.S. concerns about the potential for further radicalization in the Arab world.[17]

Divisions within the administration appeared in late January 1969 when the National Security Council (NSC) established a basic outline of the new administration's Middle East policy. The NSC outlined eight key points that encapsulated U.S. goals in the region. Washington must avoid a situation that would spark a military clash with the Soviet Union. As part of this goal, policy makers should be careful to keep U.S. military forces out of the Arab-Israeli conflict, remain aloof from local wars, and prevent the introduction of nuclear weapons into the region. At the same time, the United States should ensure that the state of Israel maintained its armed forces, safeguard continued access to communications and military facilities in the region, protect American oil interests, and keep up good relations with moderate Arab states, Iran, Greece, and Turkey.[18]

More ambiguous goals included the establishment of an effective posture toward the radical Arab states and the containment of the threat of increased Soviet influence in the region. While many policy imperatives were fairly straightforward, the U.S. posture toward the Arab-Israeli dispute, Arab radicalism, and Soviet influence in the region was less clear. The operative U.S.

stance toward Gunnar Jarring's efforts to implement UN Resolution 242 lay at the heart of the matter. The State Department posed the basic question of whether Washington should accept the improbability of a negotiated settlement in the region or move into a more aggressive stance by supporting a negotiated settlement. The former choice would result in little or no change in present U.S. policy and could very well lead to increased Soviet influence in the region, the development of Israeli nuclear capacity, and the collapse of moderate Arab regimes. Moreover, such an approach could be misconstrued as a signal of U.S. disinterest in the region.[19]

Nearby in Foggy Bottom, the State Department argued for increased U.S. efforts to bring about a negotiated settlement by putting greater pressure on Israel to make concessions to the Arab states and establishing a cooperative relationship with Moscow on regional policy. While Washington was the only player that could hope to influence Israeli policy, the Kremlin was the only actor that could force concessions from the radical Arab states. The superpowers would have to work together in order to move their allies toward peace. Moreover, cooperation with Moscow in working toward a peaceful settlement would fulfill a number of key U.S. goals. In addition to decreasing superpower tension over the Middle East—a primary objective in itself—this approach would signal continuing U.S. interest in working with the Arab states, shoring up moderate elements and stabilizing relations with radical regimes in an effort to incorporate them into the status quo. Ultimately, the State Department argued that a multilateral approach offered the best option for accomplishing the necessary conditions—Arab recognition of Israel's right to exist and Israeli evacuation from the occupied territories—for a lasting political settlement.[20]

Although the Israeli leadership was not taking orders from the White House, Washington did, according to many accounts, enjoy significant leverage over the Jewish state. The State Department intelligence section observed that U.S. support was a crucial component of Israeli security. While they were willing to strike out on their own, Israeli leaders understood that a substantial break with Washington could be catastrophic. State Department diplomats were not the only observers in Washington who supported the idea of putting greater pressure on Israel to move toward some sort of political settlement with its Arab neighbors.[21]

The Pentagon supported the idea that the region's problems demanded engaged diplomatic efforts. A Department of Defense study of U.S. interests in the Arab-Israeli conflict laid out some of the basic difficulties facing Washington in its approach to the region. The study identified the effects of the 1967 war and the status of the Palestinians as central obstacles to a stable peace in the Middle East. Having established semiautonomous status through guerilla activities, the Palestinian fighters threatened other parties in the region. Moreover, the report held that as a great power priding itself on a regard for human rights, the United States should be more concerned about the plight of the Palestinian refugees.[22]

Israeli security strategy was, in many respects, at odds with these assessments: the Israeli government tended to see offensive operations and retaliatory strikes as an integral component of its national defense strategy. Secretary of Defense Melvin Laird explained that the "IDF has been very successful with the blitzkrieg-type war," which was ultimately beyond Washington's power to control. The present policy of selling Arab governments inferior weapons while outfitting the IDF with state-of-the-art equipment did not appear to be working. While the U.S. government urged both sides to accept a peaceful settlement, its most tangible role in the region was as Israel's primary arms supplier. Moreover, Laird went on, it was difficult to argue that the flow of U.S. weapons into the region supported the peace efforts. He insisted that the United States back up its diplomatic initiatives with proof that it was not functioning as an arsenal for Israeli expansionism. Otherwise, U.S. efforts to seek a negotiated settlement to the Arab-Israeli conflict would go nowhere.[23]

At the same time, the U.S. government should seek to maintain and expand its relations with the Arab world. Because its underlying interests lay in preventing the Soviet-backed radicalization of the Middle East, Washington should find some means of establishing contact with the Palestinians. "Reaching the Palestinian Arab population should be of paramount concern for the United States," Laird wrote. Washington must not underestimate the power of its cultural, economic, and military influence in regions such as the Middle East.

> Where one area might be closed, another area of endeavor, such as economic cooperation, might be opened. In any event, loss of the Middle East to some form of revolutionary power which is antithetical to America's cultural traditions would be disastrous for the United States. The development of some new form of Leninism or Maoism in the Arab world is a possibility which could very well develop after years of humiliation and defeat. Present Arab leadership does not represent this extreme form of politics, but Soviet and Chinese plans for the area clearly envisage something along these lines. Before this disaster occurs, it is worth considering alternatives in American policy toward the Middle East which can guide political change and prevent these extreme developments.

Officials in the Pentagon thus advocated stricter controls over the U.S. supply of arms to Israel and the expansion of American contacts with Palestinian groups with an eye toward expanding Washington's diplomatic influence.[24]

While analysts in the Department of Defense were pleading for reconsideration of Washington's posture in the Middle East, the report's recipient, Henry Kissinger, had other plans. In its contribution to the incoming administration's review of Middle East policy in January 1969, Kissinger's NSC staff included a paper arguing that the region was not vital to U.S. interests in the same sense that other regions such as Western Europe were. Rather, the United States should be more selective in its approach to the Middle East. Washington should accept the reality that tensions in the Arab-Israeli dispute would remain high and that the region would remain volatile for the foreseeable future. The only reasonable progress that could be made lay in the area of Israeli-Jordanian relations:

> Although late indeed to make the attempt, it is still worth the effort and risk to push Jordan and Israel together, while recognizing that, even if Israel offers Hussein a sufficiently generous deal for him to accept, the terrorists may assassinate him. It is a gamble that we advocate because a continuance of present trends means that he probably will be eliminated in any case, and our arming of both [Israel and Jordan] becomes harder to explain and defend.

Support and military aid for Israel must continue, but Washington should refrain from defending every Israeli action, while still limiting formal criticism of Israeli retaliations. In particular, the United States should seek to dispel the impression that it was working closely with the Israeli government, especially in international forums such as the United Nations.[25]

In tandem with these efforts, the paper argued, Washington should seek to use the current break with the radical Arab states to its diplomatic advantage. The United States was now "in the position of uncommitted listener to their importunities, diatribes, and endless requests for assistance." Washington could neither solve the Arabs' domestic problems nor achieve Arab diplomatic goals vis-à-vis Israel. Kissinger was clear that it was not in Washington's interest to rush to reestablish diplomatic ties to the Arab world. If and when they were reestablished, Washington should do so on its own terms. In the meantime, the United States should take advantage of an "unexcelled opportunity" to distance itself from the problems of the radical Arab world.[26]

President Nixon seemed to lean toward this approach. He later spoke of his desire "to construct a completely new set of power relationships in the Middle East—not only between Israel and the Arabs, but also between the United States, Western Europe, and the Soviet Union." While supporters of Israel might be concerned about this overhaul of U.S. Middle East policy, Nixon was of the opinion that what Israel (and Washington) needed most was a far-sighted strategy designed to give the United States the means to maintain a long-term commitment in the region. Critics of the administration, he argued,

> must recognize that our interests are basically pro-freedom and not just pro-Israel because of the Jewish vote. We are *for* Israel because Israel in our view is the only state in the Mideast which is *pro*-freedom and an

effective opponent to Soviet expansion. We will oppose a cut-and-run policy either in Vietnam or Cuba or the Mideast or NATO or anyplace else in the world. This is the kind of friend that Israel needs and will continue to need, particularly when the going gets very tough in the next five years.

The president was particularly troubled by the fact that many of Israel's staunchest supporters were critical of the war in Vietnam. "We are going to stand up in Vietnam and in NATO and in the Mideast," he wrote, "but it is a question of all or none."[27] Ultimately, as he pointed out to Israeli ambassador Yitzhak Rabin, Israel ought to be invested in what Washington was doing in Vietnam, for if it failed in Southeast Asia, the U.S. public might become more isolationist and demand a reduction in American engagement with other nations, such as Israel.[28]

Writing years later, Kissinger argued that the administration's Middle East policy aimed at the larger geostrategic design of reducing Soviet influence in the Arab world by creating a diplomatic stalemate. The White House hoped to show that while Moscow could create tension and precipitate crises in the region, it lacked the ability to create positive progress toward a political settlement in the Arab-Israeli dispute. Kissinger pointed out that since the 1967 war, Israel had held all the diplomatic cards in the Arab-Israeli dispute.[29] In what amounted to a strategy of active disengagement, the Nixon White House would put a diplomatic freeze on the Arab-Israeli dispute at what may have been one of the most auspicious moments for a political solution in the history of the conflict. The PLO, however, represented a wrinkle in Kissinger's strategy: so long as the fedayeen remained heroes in the Arab world, they postponed the sense of despair that might drive the Arabs away from Moscow and toward Washington. This would come to represent a central flaw in Kissinger's Middle East strategy and a major source of instability in the Arab world. Ultimately, the PLO's symbolic victories presented an impediment to Kissinger's vision of a regional order tied to U.S. interests.

The stage was thus set for the contest between Rogers and Kissinger over the Nixon administration's policy toward the Arab-Israeli conflict. In December 1969, Rogers proposed an outline for a political solution centered on UN 242's land-for-peace scheme. Relegated to the Middle East as the one region where he and the State Department were supposed to enjoy preeminence over Henry Kissinger, Rogers had devoted substantial efforts to creating a plan that would seek to accomplish the implementation of UN 242. If successful, the Rogers Plan might achieve the elusive goal of resolving the state of war between the Arab powers and Israel based upon the exchange of land for peace. In essence, Washington would lean on Israel and the Arab regimes to commit to the Jarring Mission and press for a "just settlement" to the Palestinian refugee problem.

The plan faced major opposition, however, from actors inside and outside the U.S. government. While Rogers advocated a comprehensive peace plan to end the Arab-Israeli dispute, Kissinger projected a vision of realpolitik onto the region, seeking the maximum gain for the United States. Kissinger scoffed at the basic principles of UN 242. He recalled that upon first hearing them in February 1969, fourteen months after they were articulated, he thought someone was "pulling [his] leg." He preferred instead to plan for a strategic overhaul of U.S. policy in the Middle East through the perpetuation of a stalemate in the Arab-Israeli conflict, a notion shared by the president. He proposed the equivalent of standstill diplomacy toward the Arab-Israeli conflict, a set of tactics engineered to stonewall Jarring's progress, isolate pro-Soviet Arab regimes, reinforce Israel's defenses, and make the United States the only superpower with the ability to generate momentum in the Arab-Israeli peace process. With this in mind, Nixon and Kissinger effectively torpedoed the Rogers Plan at its inception in December 1969 by privately informing Israeli officials that the administration was not inclined to support the initiative.[30]

This was neither the first time nor the last that Kissinger would insert himself into the Nixon administration's Middle East policy process. Declassified documents suggest that the national security advisor was slowly extending his influence into what was intended to be Rogers' domain. Kissinger was convinced of the necessity to clean up the State Department's mess in the region, stepping in at the last minute to override Rogers' rejection of Israeli arms requests—for fear of the domestic ramifications of such a decision—and, by mid-1970, to press Nixon for a general reorientation of U.S. policy toward the region. Under Foggy Bottom's guidance, he insisted, the United States had been losing ground in the Middle East. Moscow's influence was rising while the Arab states increasingly found themselves under pressure from the radical fedayeen. The fundamental flaw in the State Department's policy rested on the mistaken assumption that a solution to the Arab-Israeli conflict would dissipate the power of Arab radicalism and the Soviet Union in the Middle East. Kissinger argued that, to the contrary, the land-for-peace formula upon which the Rogers Plan was founded would address only one in a long list of grievances that animated Arab radicalism. If Rogers succeeded in negotiating a return of Arab lands, radical forces in the region would merely turn their energies against other U.S. and Israeli interests in the Middle East.[31]

In essence, Kissinger was seeking to derail multilateral negotiations with the Arab states. Rather, he believed that the United States should dramatically increase arms shipments to Israel—including state-of-the-art Phantom and Skyhawk warplanes—thereby undercutting the ability of the Arab states to place military pressure on the Jewish state. Once said pressure was removed, Washington—as the sole source of leverage with the Israeli government—would become the only actor capable of creating a settlement in the Arab-Israeli conflict. Although he warned that such an approach was liable to enrage much of the Arab world, Kissinger was adamant that it represented a geopolitical opportunity that the White House should not pass up.[32] The State Department's efforts must be foiled.

Standstill diplomacy in the Middle East was only part of what would become the administration's approach to the challenges of the Third World in the 1970s. The need to develop the capacity to wage limited war in the developing world was a key concern for Nixon and Kissinger. As the latter had articulated in the 1955 essay for *Foreign Affairs* that had helped launch his policy career:

> The strategic problem of the United States has two aspects: to create a level of thermo-nuclear strength to deter the Soviet bloc from a major war, or from aggressions in areas which cannot be defended by an indigenous effort; but to integrate this with a policy which does not paralyze the will to resist in areas where local resources for defense do exist.[33]

Kissinger's *The Necessity for Choice* (1960) returned to the same territory as this article, namely, the idea of limited war as a crucial component of U.S. foreign policy. Washington must not seek to avoid confrontation out of fear over escalation to a superpower conflict, he wrote. Rather, the United States must be prepared to fight smaller wars in defense of its global credibility. In the same vein, Kissinger argued that U.S. influence was dependent on international perceptions of its willingness to back policy with force. U.S. weakness in the face of challenges would only "'embolden' its adversaries, 'dishearten' its allies, and diminish its 'credibility.'" Washington must defend its interests and image aggressively and punish any power that would test U.S. resolve.[34]

For Kissinger, this logic held true even in situations where the United States did not expect to emerge victorious. As he admitted in an article for *Foreign Affairs*, Washington had lost public support for the war in Vietnam. However, even in the midst of a hopeless situation, Washington could not accept defeat and pull its forces out of Southeast Asia. Rather, the United States must maintain its credibility. As Kissinger biographer Walter Isaacson suggests, "This argument would be at the heart of [Kissinger's] thinking on Vietnam and on every other global struggle for the rest of his career."[35]

Confronted with a collapsing Saigon, the Nixon administration required a new blueprint for fighting brushfire wars in the developing world, a "post-Vietnam counterinsurgency doctrine." Washington needed a way to maintain its global commitments even as its relative power declined and domestic enthusiasm for military interventions bottomed out. The most visible application of this new strategy emerged in Southeast Asia and became known as the Nixon Doctrine. First articulated in late July 1969, it called for a reliance on local forces—supported by infusions of U.S. military and economic aid—on Third World battlefields rather than direct intervention by U.S. troops. The doctrine "aimed at utilizing foreign countries as proxies and regional police," which could either "overthrow 'undesirable' Third World governments or underpin the stability of 'friendly'" regimes. Such a strategy would not only lower the risk of a direct superpower confrontation but also insulate national security policy from domestic opponents of intervention.[36] Although Nixon did not introduce the notion of using regional partners in the Cold War in the Third World, the doctrine's emphasis on these allies represented a key dimension of the administration's efforts to revamp its strategies for the 1970s.

Active Defense

Following Levi Eshkol's death in 1969, Kissinger found a partner in this hard-line approach at the helm of the Israeli government. Golda Meir, Israel's "Iron Lady," was born in Kiev in the spring of 1898, the daughter of a carpenter. In search of employment, her father left for the United States in 1903. The rest of the family joined him in Milwaukee in 1906. There she attended school, worked in her mother's grocery store, and developed a strong will and an independent mind. By 1915 she had embraced Labor Zionism and become active in the local movement in Milwaukee. In 1921, along with her husband and sister, Meir moved to Kibbutz Merhavyah in the Jezreel Valley in Palestine. There she became active in politics, serving as the kibbutz's representative to the Jewish labor union, the Histadrut, and eventually she moved to Jerusalem. By 1936 she had become head of the organization's political department, a position that placed her at the forefront of Zionist politics as Mandate Palestine headed toward dissolution and the wider world moved toward the horrors of the Holocaust and World War II. When its secretary was arrested in the summer of 1946, Meir became acting head of the Jewish Agency's Political Department. This post put her in a position to negotiate both with the British government as it sought to liquidate its mandate in Palestine and with Transjordan's King Abdullah. From Israel's independence until 1965, Meir served as minister of labor in the Mapai Party, putting her in a crucial position among the founders of Jewish state. As general secretary of Mapai, Meir played a seminal role in the formation of the Labor Party, becoming its first leader. After the death of Levi Eshkol, Meir became the fourth prime minister of the Jewish state. She brought to the office a fierce determination and an unwavering resolve to defend Israel against any and all of its challengers.[37]

At her swearing-in ceremony in March 1969, Prime Minster Meir announced her intention to prosecute a new strategy of "active defense" against the PLO. Rather than responding to guerilla attacks on a tit-for-tat basis, this new policy amounted to a de facto military campaign against the fedayeen. The IDF would undertake ongoing offensive military action against suspected centers of guerilla activity. Active defense would thus supplement Israel's standing policy of reprisals against its neighbors in an attempt to compel Amman, Damascus, and Beirut to tighten their control over the guerillas.[38] Thus, by early 1969 the

Israeli government had implemented a strategy that combined preventative, preemptive, and retaliatory operations, which it would stage as a response to the general threat from the PLO rather than in response to specific guerilla attacks. In addition to cross-border raids against Jordan and Israel, the IDF set up "ambushes, artillery barrages and air raids" based on intelligence reports. These operations proved to be "generally ineffective" as a deterrent against further guerilla attacks but did have the positive effect of bolstering "Israeli morale" and creating "the impression of a concerted effort against terrorism."[39]

Meanwhile, Meir "remained unremittingly hostile toward Palestinian nationalism," which she viewed as the "irreconcilable enemy of Israel." She was adamantly opposed to the creation of a Palestinian state on the grounds that such an entity would not be viable. The creation of "an additional state between Israel and Jordan, would not succeed, because [it] would not have an adequate geographic or demographic base," former aide Simcha Dinitz explained. Rather, the only conceivable solution would be the Jordan option, which would place control over the Palestinian people in Amman's hands. "Consequently," Dinitz added, "in order to arrive at a solution to the Palestinian problem, a link with Jordan had to be forged. Hence all the meetings and discussions with Hussein." This Meir-Hussein dialogue would form the basis of Meir's approach to the Palestinian question and yield a number of benefits. Indeed, both Israel and Jordan wished to curb the PLO's rising political and military power, which led to cooperation against the fedayeen on multiple fronts. Permanent borders on the West Bank would remain a point of contention between the two states, however.[40]

Meir made it clear, however, that she had no intention of returning Israel to its pre-1967 borders and that Israel would return occupied land only after the direct negotiation of peace treaties with its neighbors. In the absence of such progress, she would continue to strengthen Israel's hold over Arab territory. This amounted, according to historian Avi Shlaim, to a policy of "immobilism." The general election held in Israel at the end of October 1969 reaffirmed the Israeli government's intentions to maintain control over the territories occupied since 1967 as "secure borders" and its continuing rejection of UN 242 as a blueprint for peace. "Sharm el-Sheikh without peace is better than peace without Sharm el-Sheikh," Moshe Dayan insisted.[41]

Meir's policies thus dovetailed with Kissinger's designs. In regard to Israeli national security, Meir became "a hawk who listened only to other hawks." Under her leadership, Moshe Dayan and the IDF general staff gained influence in the Israeli government at the expense of the doves in the Foreign Ministry. Abba Eban, a longtime foreign minister, recalled that Meir tended to "blindly accept" recommendations from the IDF in cabinet meetings. As senior officers gained primacy within the Israeli government under Meir, diplomacy took a backseat to military strategy. Shlaim describes the result as a policy of "military activism and diplomatic immobility." Mordechai Gur, who became chief of staff in 1974, lamented the "reliance on force as the almost exclusive factor in the formulation of policy." Meir's views on the Palestinians were even more bellicose. Unlike Eshkol, Meir rejected any notion of negotiations with the Palestinians, whose existence as a people she famously denied. Under her leadership, the PLO would be treated as a security problem to be contained and crushed, not a diplomatic issue.[42]

Thus, the Meir government did not develop a diplomatic policy toward the PLO, because it elected to treat the fedayeen as a military and intelligence problem, rather than a foreign policy issue. This ultimately fit into the existing approach that Israel had taken to the Palestinian question over the previous two decades. Rather than dealing with Palestinian Arabs directly, the Israeli government treated them as the responsibility of the various Arab states. Indeed, this had been the only means of engaging with those Palestinians outside Israel's borders in the years between 1948 and 1967, when the West Bank and Gaza were under Jordanian and Egyptian jurisdiction, respectively. After 1967, however, this situation changed. Palestinians living in the West Bank and Gaza came under the control of the Israeli occupation—and thus were monitored by the Shin Bet—while those living outside of the occupied territories were still treated as the responsibility of the Arab states in which they operated. Insofar as the government of Israel engaged with the PLO, it did so by placing pressure—through diplomatic and military means—on states such as Jordan, Lebanon, and Syria to crack down on guerilla activities. As far as Israeli leaders were concerned, the fact that armed guerilla groups were launching attacks on its assets and population hardly seemed like a good reason to craft a diplomatic approach to the PLO. Indeed, it would be the political mobilization of the Palestinian diaspora through the means of armed struggle—which the Israeli government called "terrorism"—that would prompt the first discussions in forums including the United Nations on whether the Palestinians should receive recognition as a nation rather than merely being treated as a group of refugees.

Hence, discussions in the Israeli government focused not on whether to recognize Palestinian national aspirations—as expressed by the PLO—but on how best to implement countermeasures against the guerillas. To this end, the Israeli government adopted two basic tracks, one defensive and one offensive. Defensively, the IDF sought to limit the number of attacks, establishing infantry patrols, electronic surveillance, and helicopter sweeps to detect fedayeen infiltrations. The Israeli government burned the vegetation along the Jordan River, erected electronic security fences, and set up closed-circuit cameras to monitor the frontier.[43]

In offensive terms, Israel reverted to the strategy of limited reprisals against Arab states that had been part of its arsenal stretching back to the days of the British Mandate. The Israeli government and IDF were faced with the need to respond to guerilla attacks—and domestic pressures for retaliation—in some manner that fell short of full-scale war. In late 1953, following a disastrous raid into the West Bank that killed some sixty Palestinian civilians, the IDF altered its reprisal strategies. The new policy targeted the regimes that harbored guerillas, rather than the guerillas themselves. "We shall hit the enemy where and how we choose," read an IDF directive on the new policy, "even if the objective does not exactly match the enemy's crime." This change was designed in part as an effort to limit civilian deaths among the Arab population by engaging clearly marked military and police assets rather than focusing on guerillas seeking to avoid detection. Perhaps the most dramatic example of this type of operation came in 1966 with the massive IDF attack on the West Bank village of Samu, which drew Jordanian forces into a skirmish with Israeli units. IDF reprisals against Jordan following the 1967 war, however, reverted to the earlier focus on attacking the guerillas. According to scholar Zeev Maoz, the decision was made not to place too much pressure on King Hussein. Secret exchanges about the possibility of a Jordanian-Israeli peace agreement, pressure from Washington, and increasing military exchanges with Egypt on the Suez front in mid-1968 may also have factored into the decision not to retaliate too forcefully against Amman.[44]

This same restraint did not apply to Syria and Lebanon. In regard to its northern neighbors, the Israeli government maintained its pre-1967 policy of holding its neighbors responsible for guerilla attacks launched from their territories. In addition to having a basis in international law, this approach worked to turn Beirut and Damascus into reluctant partners in the maintenance of Israeli border security. While the strategy of bringing the guerillas under control or suffering the consequences had been generally effective prior to 1967, the emergence of an increasingly autonomous PLO guerilla movement in the wake of the war introduced new complications. Continued Israeli reprisals against Syria and Lebanon for Palestinian attacks would begin to draw ever greater criticism in the international community as well as producing diminishing returns in terms of the Arab states' ability to police the guerillas operating on their soil.

Although Israel was never Washington's proxy and was not addressed as one of the principal beneficiaries of the Nixon Doctrine, its position in the Middle East squared with this logic of relying on local forces to underpin U.S. power in the global South. Indeed, the IDF's impressive military record exemplified the type of effective force that the Nixon administration hoped to maintain in support of U.S. interests in the developing world: a partner in defense and a strategic asset in a troubled region. Moreover, the new government's policy of "active defense" seemed to present an answer to Washington's counterinsurgency problems: here was a pro-Western state waging a successful campaign against Third World guerillas. Using a combination of air strikes and deep-penetration commando raids, the Israel Defense Forces had adopted a strategy designed to make fedayeen actions so costly that the guerillas would choose to scale back their attacks. Israel sought to maintain an element of surprise and unpredictability against their Arab neighbors, a tactic that the Nixon White House employed in its diplomatic strategies as well. Although retaliatory raids and preemptive strikes had long been an integral part of the IDF's repertoire, the new strategy of active defense took an increasingly preventive approach to counterinsurgency.[45]

Although Israel claimed that its active defense strategy was playing a decisive role in hindering fedayeen activities, State Department officials were skeptical in the absence of any clear evidence that this was the case. While periods of calm had sometimes followed major IDF reprisals, each reprisal seemed to spur popular support for the guerillas and add legitimacy to their image as liberation fighters. Moreover, Israeli counterstrikes convinced PLO leaders that their actions were having an effect on Israel. Thus, while Israeli raids might have resulted in some short-term tactical gains, they had the long-term effect of fueling the growth of the fedayeen movement and giving it an element of political cohesion.[46]

Paradoxically, international efforts to restrain Israel merely convinced the state of its isolation and the subsequent need to take matters into its own hands. State Department intelligence observed that international criticism of Israel's attack on the Beirut airport and a perceived dearth of sympathy for the Athens attack had "reinforced the Israelis' view that they can count on no one else." As opposition to its actions mounted in forums such as the Security Council, Israel was coming to rely more and more on these active defense strategies. Within Israel itself came calls for the creation of counterterrorist squads that would employ "terrorist" tactics in fighting the fedayeen. Pressure to occupy more Arab territory in an attempt to restrain guerilla actions was also a concern for State Department observers.[47] The United States was coming to be implicated in this policy as the strikes continued and Washington remained Israel's only major defender at the United Nations and its principal arms supplier.

Africa, Asia, and Beyond

A grisly revelation in early 1969 cast doubt as to whether anyone could contain the fedayeen threat through police measures. On the morning of 24 February, Israeli warplanes entered Syrian airspace en route to two locations outside of Damascus. The attack came in retaliation for a bombing that had taken place three days earlier in a Jerusalem supermarket that killed two Israelis and wounded another twelve. After engaging with a group of Syrian MiG-17s, the Israeli jets struck two Palestinian bases at Hama and Massilun. While State Department officials were never happy to see more violence in the troubled region, the reports that followed the attack contained what might have been the most disturbing information. Sources reported that the Israeli air strikes had done more than just kill Palestinian guerrillas. Bodies recovered from the wreckage in the camps appeared to belong to Eritrean Liberation Force commandos who had been training with Chinese military advisors alongside Palestinian fedayeen. If Eritrean separatists fighting against the Ethiopian government were working in conjunction with PLO fighters in Syria, the political repercussions of the Palestinian armed struggle might spread beyond the Arab world.[48]

While the fedayeen and their radical supporters could create problems for U.S. interests in the Middle East, officials worried that their influence might not stop there. Fears about the wider repercussions of the conflict in the Middle East made the situation all the more urgent.[49] Like other radicals in the Third World, the Palestinian guerillas threatened to move across state boundaries and spread revolutionary unrest. Decision makers in Washington were only too familiar with the picture of revolutionary movements coming to power and seeking to spread their revolution to their neighbors. Soviet influence in Eastern Europe, Chinese and North Korean influence in Asia, Hanoi's influence in Southeast Asia, Cuba's role in Latin America, and Algeria's influence in the Middle East raised concerns in the United States about the appearance of more radical regimes in the developing world. Palestinian radicals were even more threatening because they did not represent any single state. Rather, as a diaspora spread through North Africa, the Levant, and many of the Gulf States, the Palestinians had come to embody the threat of transnational radicalism everywhere.[50]

Indeed, Africa was fast becoming an area of particular interest not only for the Cold War superpowers but also for the regional players in the Middle East. Algerian moves toward the government of Mali raised U.S. concerns about growing Arab interest in sub-Saharan Africa as a potential theater for revolutionary action. The Algerians and Palestinians had not been the first actors in the Middle East to turn their attention to Africa, however. Nasser had granted African exiles permission to establish offices in Cairo during the 1950s, when many sub-Saharan states were consumed with their own national liberation movements against European colonialism. The Egyptian leader pressured African liberation movements to embrace the Palestinian cause as well. Nasser conceived of a political geography surrounding Cairo composed of three circles: Arab, Islamic, and African. After most of Africa had achieved independence in the 1960s, Nasser stepped up his attempts to gain support in the Arab-Israeli conflict, arguing that Israel represented a "Trojan horse" of Western imperialism in the Third World. But prior to 1967, African support for the Palestinian cause had been tepid at best.[51]

In the wake of the June War, however, African support for Arab issues began to increase. The conflict had transformed Israel's image—in Africa and elsewhere—from a small state surrounded by hostile neighbors to a regional superpower waging a military occupation beyond its frontiers. The Arab-Israeli issue appeared frequently at the summits of the Organization of African Unity (OAU) from 1967 onward. Likewise, voices in global forums such as the Conference of Non-Aligned States and the United Nations gradually took a more critical stance toward Israel. As the Palestinian question came to be seen as the focus of the Middle East conflict and Israeli expansion into Palestinian territory came to be seen as analogous to European expansionism in southern Africa, African sympathy grew stronger.

The Israeli government had its own foreign policy goals in Africa. The Jewish state's first prime minister, David Ben-Gurion, had called for the construction of an outer ring of states—such as Iran, Turkey, Sudan, and Ethiopia—allied with Israel with the intention of "establishing a strong dam against the Nasserist Soviet torrent."[52] State Department officials detected signs of Israeli concern over the "growing rapprochement" between African states such as Chad—which might serve as "a potential point from which to harass the rear of Israel's Arab enemies"—and the Arab world, along with Israeli attempts to drive a wedge between the Arabs and the Africans.[53] Israeli officials floated the idea of creating a "security entente between the United States, Ethiopia, Israel, and Iran in hopes of countering Soviet moves in the region," but American officials were skeptical. The only unifying factor in this entente, explained one State Department officer, was hostility toward the Arabs.[54]

Africa was also becoming an important site for PLO diplomacy. In an open letter to its African brethren, Fatah pledged its support for solidarity with African liberation movements and identified Israel as a common enemy in the struggle against imperialism.[55] Fatah warned that Israel was channeling its political, military, economic, and cultural influence toward Africa in an effort to limit Arab power.[56] States such as the former French colony of Upper Volta in West Africa found themselves pulled in two directions by Arab representatives—often from Algeria—who urged them to take a harder line vis-à-vis Israeli diplomats who could offer aid programs to developing nations.[57] Palestinian fighters also found allies in the revolutionary Free Officers government of Sudan that had come to power in May 1969. On an official visit to Khartoum in June, Yasir Arafat heralded the Sudanese revolution as another victory in the Arab struggle against "Zionism, imperialism and neo-colonialism" and a victory for the "forces of progress and freedom" in the Arab world. The Free Officers released a statement announcing that they shared the attitude of the fedayeen toward the liberation of Palestine and the creation of a democratic state under the leadership of the PLO, and that the PLO had agreed to establish relations with the revolutionary government of Sudan.[58] The PFLP also paid close attention to African affairs, reporting regularly on fighting in Biafra and warning of imperialist moves in Nigeria.[59]

Although they were hardly a strategic priority in the eyes of American policy makers, the African states constituted an ever more important diplomatic bloc in the world community, one that was flirting with the idea of diplomatic alignment with the Arab world. The 1969 vote by the African Labour Ministers Conference to brand "Israel—along with South Africa, Rhodesia, Portugal and [South] Vietnam—as a 'racist and fascist regime' which constitutes a 'grave danger for the rest of the African continent' "—was a sign of things to come as more African states began to take an engaged role in international affairs. Tensions remained, however, as states such as Ghana were torn between lucrative relationships with Israel and a desire to maintain solidarity with the African bloc.[60] Ethiopia found itself in a particularly difficult position as it struggled with its own guerilla war against Eritrean separatists. Ethiopian officials thus sought publicly to maintain an even-handed approach to the Arab-Israeli dispute even as U.S. observers suspected that they were privately pro-Israel.[61] Although Israeli technical aid programs had been a substantial help to the Ethiopian government, U.S. officials observed that Ethiopia must live alongside its Muslim neighbors. The government was being careful not to embark "on [a] course which could lead to burning its bridges with Arab states and possibly to ... serious retaliation."[62]

This exchange was not merely one-sided, however. In a state visit to Damascus in late 1968, Mauritanian president Moktar Ould Daddah criticized the "Zionist-imperialist conspiracy against the Arab homeland" and affirmed Mauritanian support for the recovery of Palestinian rights in their homeland and the reversal of the 1967 Israeli victory. Moreover, both governments endorsed the view of Israel as a "racialist colonialist base established by imperialism in the heart of the Arab homeland to ensure military, political and economic domination and control" of the region and confirmed the need to gain world support for the struggle to liberate Palestine.[63]

In early 1969, State Department officials in Eritrea warned that local rebels had created an elite cadre of resistance fighters trained in the same manner as Fatah guerillas. If Eritrean fighters were able to build an urban guerilla force on Fatah's model, they might become a serious threat to U.S. interests and installations in the region. At the same time, Chinese advisors had moved from Sudan into Eritrea.[64] Reports of Eritrean rebels training in Fatah camps in Syria in March 1969 raised more concerns that commando activities in the Middle East were creating instability in Africa.[65]

While Palestinian radicalism might spread geographically to neighboring areas, it could also follow cultural lines to move throughout the Islamic world. Muslims around the world expressed sympathy for their coreligionists in the Middle East and worried about the effects of Israeli military control of Muslim shrines. In late 1968, the First Meeting of the International Islamic Organizations in Mecca released a statement arguing that the "cause of Palestine is not only an Arab cause, but the cause of the whole Islamic world." The conference called upon all Muslims to join a jihad to recover Muslim holy sites in Jerusalem and all other Palestinian and Arab territories occupied by Israel. Such a jihad was, according to the delegates, a religious obligation for all Muslims. The conference also called upon all Islamic nations to sever relations with the state of Israel and suggested that an approach be made to the United Nations regarding the status of Jerusalem.[66] The arson at Al-Aqsa Mosque in Jerusalem the following year by an Australian evangelical exacerbated concerns that Muslim holy sites were jeopardized by the occupation. Israeli officials warned Washington that Arab governments were using the arson attack "in order to transform their political dispute with Israel into a religious war and to drag [the] entire Muslim world into the dispute." This new dimension of "unbridled religious fanaticism" threatened to make the conflict even more dangerous. Israeli foreign minister Eban voiced concern over this recent development, which threatened to bring the Muslim masses into conflict with Israel.[67]

Official visits by PLO leaders to Pakistan in early 1969 raised fears that the fedayeen might channel their influence along religious lines into central and south Asia. The visits received celebratory press coverage in Pakistan as well as the endorsement of Islamic fundamentalist groups in Pakistan.[68] The prospect of Fatah opening offices in Karachi and Lahore came as an unwelcome but more or less inevitable development for U.S. officials.[69] Noting the appearance of pro-fedayeen posters on the walls near the U.S. consulate in Peshawar, State Department officers worried that Pakistani students on break for a religious holiday might have too much time on their hands.[70]

As support for the Palestinians mounted in the world's second-largest Muslim nation, pro-guerilla sentiment was also on the rise in the most populous Islamic country. Indonesian newspapers announced Fatah's plans to open offices in Jakarta in early January. State Department officials noted that although the government of Indonesia had no desire to become involved in the Middle East conflict, "domestic political considerations have compelled it to articulate a relatively militant stance regarding the Arab-Israeli dispute."[71] Fatah representatives in Malaysia created similar headaches for U.S. officials wary of nascent radical movements in the Third World.[72] In an international system characterized by proliferating interconnections between different regions, the spread of revolutionary contagions appeared all the more threatening. U.S. officials would have to find some means of preventing the dominoes from falling around the world in the aftermath of the fiasco in Vietnam.

A Secular Democratic State in Palestine?

The PLO's internal politics were rapidly evolving as the organization gained influence. Paradoxically, as Palestinian guerilla operations expanded, the rhetoric emanating from groups such as Fatah and the PFLP began to soften. This change was indicative of fundamental transformations within the organization.

As it developed into an authentically Palestinian political movement, the PLO's need for explosive, often anti-Semitic rhetoric declined. This turn away from inflammatory discourse was a reflection of central debates taking place within the ranks of the fedayeen over the question of the Jewish inhabitants of Palestine/Israel. In contrast to Ahmed Shuqairy's bluster—the infamous call to push the Jews into the sea—the fedayeen-led PLO announced that it would seek to reach some sort of accommodation with the Jewish population. Fatah had hinted in its first press release in January 1968 at its vision of a Palestine where Jews and Arabs lived side by side. In October of that same year, Salah Khalaf announced Fatah's plan to transform a liberated Palestine into a nonsectarian, democratic society where Muslims, Christians, and Jews would enjoy equal rights. Fatah reiterated this plan in January 1969 in a press statement calling for the "restoration of an independent and democratic Palestinian state in which all citizens, of whatever religion, will enjoy equal rights." The fifth Palestinian National Council, held the following month, codified this objective as official PLO policy.[73]

Certainly, the effort to come to terms with the Jewish population of Israel would be no simple matter. It was on this point that the guerillas emphasized the distinction between Palestinian Jews and Jewish settlers. Whereas the former group had lived in Palestine prior to creation of the Zionist movement, the latter group had arrived during the nineteenth and twentieth centuries and were thus seen by many in the Palestinian liberation movement as colonial settlers. The PLO's original position circa 1964 had stated that the permanent Jewish residents of Palestine would remain while the settlers would be expelled. Fatah maintained this position—modified with a measure of ambiguity—through 1968 but began to change it in early 1969. In January of that year, a Fatah leader explained to the *Tribune Socialiste* that the organization recognized "the right" of a large and growing Jewish population in Palestine to remain after liberation.

> We reject the formula that the Jews must be driven into the sea. If we are fighting a Jewish state of a racial kind, which had driven the Arabs out of their lands, it is not so as to replace it with an Arab state which would in turn drive out the Jews.... We are ready to look at anything with all our negotiating partners once our right to live in our homeland is recognized.

While this position remained somewhat ambiguous—and was not likely to win a ringing endorsement from Israeli leaders—it attested to a growing degree of moderation among Fatah's leadership on the question of the Israeli population. It also sparked a wave of condemnation through the ranks of Fatah's rivals. However, as area specialist Alain Gresh explains, the "right of the Jews to remain in Palestine was gradually asserting itself in Palestinian political thought."[74]

The most radical position emerged from the Popular Democratic Front for the Liberation of Palestine (PDFLP), a splinter group of the PFLP, in a draft resolution to the sixth PNC in 1969. The group rejected "chauvinistic solutions" of both Jewish and Arab origins, calling instead for the creation of a multicultural state in Palestine in which Jews and Arabs would enjoy equal rights. The PDFLP's proposal would lead Fatah to clarify its position on the Jewish question in the coming months.[75] The following year, Fatah published a treatise on the Jewish question entitled *La révolution palestinienne et les juifs* in which it sought to outline its political program for a liberated Palestine:

1. It concerns the whole of Palestine: there can be no question of a "rump state" in the West Bank and Gaza

2. It is not an Israel Mark Two; it will be a non-racist and non-sectarian state.

3. It can only result from the destruction of the Zionist state and armed struggle.

4. The new state will accept all the Jewish settlers who so desire.

5. It will not be a state like Lebanon or Cyprus.

6. We cannot go into details of the solution since we are only at the beginning of our struggle.

Thus, while a great deal of ambiguity remained, Fatah was working to establish a clear political program. The reclamation of the whole of Mandate-era Palestine through armed struggle remained at the center of this vision, but the ultimate elimination of Israel would not, in theory, entail the elimination of the Jews in the area. Likewise, Fatah envisioned a liberated Palestine as including an Arab majority, as the Palestinian birthrate would eclipse that of the Jewish population. Zionism as a political ideology would be eliminated, but Fatah was clear that it intended to allow the Jewish population of Palestine—native and settler—to remain. Indeed, in what was surely an exaggeration but still a telling statement of his position, Arafat told *Le Monde* in February 1969, "We have been very hurt by the extremist declarations of the Arab world...since we are very attached to our Jewish friends."[76]

Although it envisioned a place for a Jewish population in this new state, the PLO was still calling for a maximalist solution and rejecting all political solutions—including the Rogers Plan and the Jarring Mission—along with the prospect of a ministate in the West Bank and Gaza. The fedayeen were opposed to the creation of such an entity for a number of reasons. First among these was the fear that such a state would owe its creation and continued existence to Israel. As such, it would be at the mercy of its dominant and potentially hostile neighbor. Likewise, such a state would be under strong pressure from its Arab neighbors, which had already shown a tendency to meddle in Palestinian affairs. Should such a ministate be created, it might thus be used as a vehicle for the destruction of the nascent Palestinian national movement. Finally, acceptance of a rump Palestinian state would represent a major concession that the budding guerilla movement was not willing to make.[77]

FIGURE 3.1 *General Union of Palestinian Students, "Towards a Secular Democratic State in Palestine," c. 1975. Courtesy of the Palestinian Poster Project Archives.*

As the PLO began its slow shift toward a more pragmatic position, it emerged as an ever-larger wrinkle in Washington's geostrategic vision for the Middle East. However, transnational Palestinian violence would take center stage as the most immediate manifestation of the revolution sweeping through the diaspora. Indeed, no issue was more controversial than that of the PLO's external operations. Fedayeen attacks against international civil aviation were of particular concern to the United States. Described by many—especially in the United States and Israel—as "terrorism," these operations exploited new transnational transportation networks, moving the heretofore local violence of the Israel-Palestine conflict into the global system. Not only did such attacks represent a threat to American lives and interests abroad, but they were also especially difficult to control. Nation-states first appeared in a world in which few citizens ever ventured far from the place of their birth. Borders, though usually porous, were generally fixed and policed. National laws were developed to create legal control over this world system rather than the one that emerged in the second half of the twentieth century. International aviation moved people and goods faster than ever across borders and deposited them not in the hinterland or the frontier but in the heart of major cities. The guerillas' status as nonstate actors and their ability to move at will from nation to nation confounded conventional attempts to police them, just as it rendered military retaliations against Arab host countries largely ineffectual.

When PFLP fighters attacked an El Al jetliner in Zurich in February 1969, the question of fedayeen violence returned to the world's attention. Washington told Israeli leaders that it was doing all it could to keep attention on the hijacking and pushing for a multilateral response in the Security Council and the International Civil Aviation Organization (ICAO). Israeli officials warned Washington that local morale was low. Still reeling from recent criticism in the Security Council following the attack on Beirut's airport and increasingly concerned in the wake of the Zurich attack, the Israeli government feared that outside powers would seek to force a political settlement on the Arab-Israeli dispute that might compromise Israel's security interests.[78]

The Israeli government's tendency to conflate the PFLP with other guerilla groups as well as the Lebanese government annoyed State Department officials. They pointed out that the guerillas who carried out the Zurich attack had trained in Jordan, flown to Europe from either Amman or Damascus, and issued the communiqué accepting responsibility for the attack from Amman. With these facts in mind, U.S. ambassador Dwight Porter expressed dismay over Israel's continuing insistence on blaming the government of Lebanon for the actions of the PFLP. It seemed that the Israeli government was merely using the assumption that Beirut, the PFLP, and Fatah were part of a single entity as a convenient justification to attack Lebanon at will. Ultimately, the guerillas posed a far greater threat to Jordan and Lebanon than they did to Israel, and both Amman and Beirut were "fighting a running battle to keep [the] fedayeen under control."

Indeed, the PFLP was dedicated to the destruction of both Amman and Beirut and thus received negligible support from local governments.[79] The larger issue was, of course, rooted in the problem of attribution for transnational violence. Guerillas fighters who trained in Jordan, owed allegiance to an organization based in Beirut, and attacked Israeli assets in Switzerland did not fit neatly into the structure of the nation-state system.

"The Palestinians Must Learn the Secrets of the Vietnamese"

On the afternoon of 29 August 1969, Eleanor Glenn, a State Department personnel officer assigned to South Vietnam, left Rome for Saigon aboard TWA flight 840. Some forty minutes into the flight, Glenn noticed that the flight attendants seemed alarmed. Soon after, she heard a woman's voice over the aircraft's intercom, announcing that the plane had been "kidnapped" by the PFLP. The voice said that the plane had been hijacked because "imperialistic America" had sided with Israel against the Arab world (specifically, with a recent sale of F-4 fighter aircraft to the IDF), adding that the guerillas had received word that an Israeli assassin was on board. The woman on the intercom ordered all first-class passengers to move to the back of the plane and remain seated with their hands behind their heads. The hijackers instructed the pilot to change course, flying over Greece and then Israel, where the plane was met by Israeli fighter jets. The pilot forced the Israeli jets to disperse by threatening to crash-land the plane, then proceeded to Damascus. The woman on the intercom warned the passengers that the jetliner was rigged with explosives set to explode after landing, prompting Glenn and the others to make an emergency evacuation as soon as the plane had touched down and come to a stop. After all passengers and crew had disembarked, the guerillas detonated an explosive that destroyed most of the cockpit, and they began firing machine guns at the fuselage in hopes of igniting the plane's fuel reserves. Shortly thereafter, Syrian authorities established control over the situation, herding the passengers, crew, and hijackers onto two airport buses. Seated on the bus with the two hijackers, Glenn was taken with the woman, whom she described to her superiors as being "extremely attractive."[80]

That woman was Leila Khaled, soon to become one of the world's most famous "terrorists" as the media seized upon her striking appearance and her distinction as the first woman to hijack an airplane. Khaled was born in 1944 in the city of Haifa on the northern coast of Palestine. Like many of her fellow guerillas, she had fled from her home in 1948, settling in the north in Lebanon. At fifteen, she joined Habash's Arab Nationalist Movement and later became a member of its offshoot, the PFLP. Inspired by the Algerian and Vietnamese examples, Khaled watched as a "small nation in black pyjamas" fought and defeated the strongest empire in human history. "The Palestinians must learn the secrets of the Vietnamese," she would write. "We had to do it, unless we wished to remain contemptible 'refugees.'" Khaled was determined to carry on the revolutionary struggle against what she described as a U.S.-led counter-revolutionary offensive taking place in every corner of the developing world. "The 1960s was indeed America's decade," she explained. "The 1970s shall be the decade of its dismantlement and complete undoing." She watched as the Arab forces were humiliated in the 1967 war with Israel; several months later, she fell into despair upon hearing the news that Che Guevara had been killed by CIA-trained commandos in the jungles of Bolivia. The latter event convinced her to join the Palestinian revolution. After her political training in Kuwait, Khaled joined the Che Guevara Commando Unit of the PFLP, named to signify that the Palestinians were "part of the Third World and the world revolution."[81]

The Syrian government promptly released all passengers and crew except for six Israelis, whom it planned to exchange for Syrian pilots being held in Israel. While TWA tried to work with the Syrians to secure the release of the six passengers, the Israeli government brought considerable pressure on the company to reject any offers short of the release of all of them.[82] Washington defended the company's actions, explaining that it was unreasonable for TWA to force any of the six who were released to remain in Damascus, and warned Israel not to squander its "favorable position vis à vis world opinion" by taking overly aggressive actions in response to the hijacking.[83]

However, the State Department officials who continued to work for the release of the Israeli passengers seemed to be the only individuals in the U.S.-Israeli camp interested in taking into account the wide range of interests that the situation might affect. Even Congress was beginning to make noise regarding some sort of action designed to secure the release of the remaining Israeli hostages.[84] State Department officials concluded that, regrettably, it appeared that there were no remaining alternatives to the prisoner swap that Damascus was demanding. Such actions were now a part of life.[85] Moreover, the regime in Damascus was embroiled in internecine power struggles and might not be able to afford the unilateral release of the hostages. Pressure from the United States or Israel would only exacerbate the domestic repercussions of releasing the hostages in the absence of reciprocal gestures from Israel.[86]

While the State Department struggled to navigate the minefield of inter-Arab politics, Nixon and Kissinger had other plans. Despite admissions that he knew little about Middle East politics, Kissinger insisted, after meetings with the Israeli ambassador, that Washington must increase its efforts to secure the release of the hostages without an equal exchange. Kissinger and the ambassador recommended that Washington take steps to prevent Syria's election to the Security Council and warn other world governments that the United States was considering diplomatic sanctions against Damascus. Rejecting contrary advice from the State Department, Nixon agreed to his national security advisor's recommendation.[87]

The TWA hijacking introduced a new level of complexity to the problem of transnational guerilla warfare. Stateless guerillas attacking American-flagged jets in Europe and holding hostages in Syria presented a confusing chain of culpability that was not immediately reconcilable with traditional state-to-state relations. Moreover, private attempts—such as those of TWA—to solve the crisis infringed on what traditionally had been considered state interests. This increasingly international problem seemed to demand some new type of response from the global community. At the institutional level, the United Nations seemed the clear choice to establish a measure of control over matters of widespread global concern. However, global responses to issues such as transnational guerilla warfare were some of the most difficult to arrange. Nixon's distaste for the United Nations did little to help matters.[88] Notably, the split between the Cold War powers and the Third World created opposing stances on the issue of the fedayeen. While Washington and, to a lesser extent, Moscow tended to see the guerillas as disruptive if not criminal, many governments within the developing world understood the fedayeen within the framework of their own experience, as resistance fighters struggling against foreign domination.

In the aftermath of the February 1969 Zurich attack, a number of Western governments approached the Security Council to express their concern over the threat of attacks on civil aviation. The Israeli government also appealed to the Security Council, arguing that the failure of previous resolutions to condemn similar incidents had established an atmosphere in which extremists could act with impunity. It was now time, the representative from Israel argued, for the UN secretary-general to act in order to prevent future attacks. Although UN authorities supported the improvement of international police measures to prevent and punish transnational violence, the Israeli delegate insisted that such actions were not enough. He asserted that previous attacks had been carried out not by individuals but by extremist organizations with the support of Arab states.[89] Intelligence reports from Israel's own allies, however, remained dubious in regard to the involvement of the Arab states in the guerilla attacks.

Israel's demands were met with skepticism in the Security Council. Given that Israeli forces continued to occupy Arab territory in violation of international law and in the face of demands from many in the world community for withdrawal, the government of Israel had difficulty claiming to be an innocent bystander. Israeli reprisals against Jordan continued to be a tense topic in New York, with Jordanian representatives arguing that retaliatory strikes targeted mainly civilians.[90] The record of debates at the United Nations shows that more and more states had come to see fedayeen actions as those of resistance fighters. While support for Palestinian fighters remained predictably strong in the Arab world, growing numbers of African and Asian states, from Zambia to Nepal, were coming out in support of the Palestinian right to struggle and self-determination.

Paris and Madrid added their concern over Israeli reprisal policies that seemed to exact an unduly harsh toll on civilian populations.[91]

Meanwhile, the Saudi government voiced private concern over the anti-Arab tilt of U.S. Middle East policy. Riyadh's foreign minister explained that even as the world community was coming to recognize the patriotic motives that fueled the fedayeen movement and even as international sympathy for Arab peoples was on the rise, U.S. policy seemed to favor Israel. Indeed, he argued that only in the United States did public opinion still seem to favor Israel, and he wondered if this was a reflection of a "basic American 'hate for Arabs or Muslims'" or a result of "Jewish control over US public media." Even though it had been Israel that had attacked, the U.S. media still portrayed the Arabs as the aggressors and Israel as the victim.[92] Conspiracy theories aside, Saudi officials were correct in pointing out that the United States found itself in a shrinking pool of supporters of Israel.

Indeed, U.S. officials were in a difficult position at the United Nations, especially in light of the approaching round of Middle East peace talks. As previously noted, Israel had initiated a preemptive defense policy that sought to strike suspected fedayeen bases at will rather than responding to guerilla attacks on a case-by-case basis. Such tactics were sure to lead to significant civilian casualties. American Foreign Service officers warned that although Washington would defend Israeli actions in the Security Council, its efforts to balance this new policy against the persistent guerilla attacks not only were unlikely to succeed but also would damage the image of the United States as an impartial broker just as the four-power talks approached in April. The U.S. government was now forced to act as the "main champion of Israeli interests and yet we must now appear in [the Security Council] on complaint where Israel's actions will put her in [a] most unfavorable public light."[93]

These problems with Arab-Israeli issues at the United Nations were indicative of deeper changes at the UN that fed a growing American disillusionment with the organization.[94] Washington was simultaneously in the process of scaling back its commitments to the UN. In particular, the U.S. delegation was considering opting out of its involvement with the Committee of 24, a group charged with the task of dealing with the problems of decolonization. Although the United States had enjoyed a reputation as a champion of decolonization in the early Cold War, in recent years—especially after its counterinsurgency in Southeast Asia became a major international issue—Washington had been cast as a neocolonialist power in the Third World. The committee had thus, in the eyes of the U.S. mission to the United Nations, become a forum for "trumped up anti-Western charges" and a stage for a "grand exercise in vituperation against Western countries by radical [Asian and African countries] and [the] Soviets." While it might not withdraw from the committee completely, the U.S. government could use selective disengagement as a means of expressing its discontent with the current tilt of the group.[95]

Beyond its criticism of the United States, the Committee of 24 was in the process of recognizing national liberation movements in Africa at a series of meetings held in Kinshasa, Lusaka, and Dar es Salaam in May, which urged support for liberation fighters and called for the termination of international assistance to the government of South Africa.[96] This movement in the committee was part of a larger process in the United Nations whereby the organization would recognize the liberation struggles of peoples in the developing world and grant increased recognition to leaders of guerilla movements. General Assembly Resolution 2908, adopted in November, voiced concern that twelve years after the UN's Declaration on the Granting of Independence to Colonial Countries and Peoples, "millions of persons still lived under conditions of ruthless colonialist and racialist repression." The resolution reaffirmed the rights of colonized peoples, especially in Africa, and called upon UN member states to aid those peoples while at the same time withholding support for the governments of Portugal, South Africa, and Southern Rhodesia. The United States, not surprisingly, voted against the resolution.[97]

Although it was aimed at Africa, UN 2908's implications for the Middle East conflict were apparent to both the PLO and its opponents. While the conversation about African liberation groups had been brewing at the United Nations, Arafat had told reporters that Fatah was seeking foreign aid from any entity that wished to see a liberated Palestine, whether it was a group that had religious reasons or "those revolutionaries in Africa, Asia and Latin America who consider our struggle as part of the struggle against oppression everywhere." Lauding Palestinian ties with liberation movements in Cuba, China, Algeria, and Vietnam, Arafat restated the importance of international support. "Our struggle is part and parcel of every struggle against imperialism, injustice and oppression in the world," he remarked. "It is part of the world revolution which aims at establishing social justice and liberating mankind." The alliance of neo-imperialist powers facing the Palestinians stretched from Israel to the United States and to the reactionary regimes of southern Africa: "We have only to look at the support [Israel] receives from the United States, at its close links with the racist Republics of South Africa and Rhodesia." Israeli visits to South Vietnam to study U.S. counterinsurgency reinforced Arafat's conviction that Israel was a bridgehead of imperialism in the Middle East.[98]

World support for the Palestinian resistance continued to mount as the push to recognize national liberation movements gained strength. "Imperialist and reactionary forces are obstinately trying...by interfering in the internal affairs of foreign countries and even by inciting local wars," warned Yugoslav president Tito, "to arrest or delay the inevitable march of events towards the political and economic progress of peoples." Peace and stability were possible only in a world where all nations respected basic human rights and national sovereignties, he said, adding that nowhere was this more apparent than in the Middle East in the wake of the 1967 war. Peace could only be achieved through the return of all occupied Arab territory and the recognition of the legitimate rights of the people of Palestine.[99] While Belgrade called for all parties to commit to UN 242 with added provisions for the Palestinians, the PRC praised the fedayeen and condemned imperialism and neocolonialism as the "common enemy of the Afro-Asian peoples." Beijing warned that U.S. imperialist aggression was taking place on a global scale.[100] It was thus becoming increasingly clear that if it hoped to police the PLO, the White House would have to find some party besides the United Nations to act as its partner.

Even more than its predecessor, the Nixon administration appeared resolved to contest the PLO and its agenda in the Arab world. As a nonstate group, the fedayeen were not entitled to a voice in international politics, nor should nations such as the United States and Israel cave in to the demands of criminals and thugs who happened to cross state lines. Moreover, the appearance of the PLO threatened—in the guerillas' own words—to create a second Vietnam in the Middle East. Nixon and Kissinger were determined to prepare the United States for a long-term global struggle against the forces of revolution and thus hardly could have looked favorably upon the fedayeen and their supporters in international institutions, including the United Nations. Although Vietnam-style counterinsurgencies were essentially off the table, Nixon and Kissinger had no intention of backing down from revolutionary movements in the developing world, regardless of how much support the latter gained at the United Nations. Instead, local policemen would serve as agents of American influence in the Third World, while the White House provided military and diplomatic support and managed great-power relations through the process of détente.

The administration combined these new containment strategies with an overhaul of the foreign policy bureaucracy that channeled influence away from the State Department. Regional specialists and diplomats would not be allowed to interfere with the geostrategic frameworks being assembled in the White House. While this restructuring contributed to the drama of the geopolitical spectacle, it showed a certain disregard for the difficult task of appreciating specific regional situations, particularly in the Third World. Nixon and Kissinger were reluctant to engage with local problems that might interfere with the broad outlines of geostrategy and maxims of great-power diplomacy they had established on entering the White House. While no president could claim expertise in the sociopolitical backgrounds of every nation in the world, the Nixon administration chose to marginalize the area specialists who could. Put simply, Nixon and Kissinger did not understand the dynamics of the situation in the Middle East and had little use for anyone who did.

These factors would help to push the Nixon administration away from the more balanced policies of earlier administrations vis-à-vis the Arab-Israeli conflict and toward a strategic partnership with Israel and Jordan. In hindsight, no other nation could have provided a better prototype for the Nixon Doctrine's local policeman-style strategy than the State of Israel. Israel's penchant for active defense rather than diplomatic efforts appealed to realists in the White House who were determined to reshape the political landscape of the Middle East by showing the Arab states that alliance with Moscow was ultimately futile. Moreover, Nixon, Kissinger, and Meir were all invested in making sure that the PLO did not come to occupy a prominent position in that landscape. Thus, the White House declined to push for a negotiated settlement to the Arab-Israeli dispute, concentrating instead on other major issues such as détente and Vietnam. Rather than capitalizing on one of the most promising opportunities for political progress in the Arab-Israeli conflict during his first term, the president—with Kissinger's encouragement—chose to let tensions fester. Indeed, the administration would not devote its full attention to the Middle East until the Black September crisis of 1970, which would complete Israel's transformation into America's principal strategic asset in the Middle East.

The Jordanian Civil War

Shortly before 6:00 p.m. on 1 September 1970, a group of armed men opened fire on a motorcade carrying King Hussein and his daughter to the airport in Amman. Escaping unscathed, the king ordered the shelling of fedayeen positions around Amman. The guerillas denied involvement with the attack on the king and argued that the entire event had been "fabricated" as a means to justify the regime's assault on the resistance. King Hussein called on the fedayeen to abandon their activities and look to the Jordanian security forces to carry on the struggle against Israel. To accomplish this goal, the king explained, he was granting special authority to the government to restore order by disarming the fedayeen.[1] The Jordanian civil war of 1970 had begun. The clash between the guerillas and the government of Jordan would engage the full attention of both Nixon and Kissinger for the first time and serve as a turning point for U.S. policy in the region. It would also mark a watershed in the history of the Palestinian resistance, bringing the Amman chapter of the fedayeen offensive to an end and ushering in the next phase of the struggle in Beirut and the wider world. The war in Jordan would also help to cement the PLO's position as a leading force among Third World revolutionaries around the globe.[2]

Superpower Diplomacy, Third World Support, and the Road to War

The clash between the PLO and King Hussein was precipitated by superpower diplomacy in the summer of 1970. It began with what came to be known as the War of Attrition: armed clashes between Egyptian and Israeli forces along the Suez Canal, consisting of artillery barrages and dogfights between Israeli and Egyptian jets—with some of the Egyptian aircraft apparently flown by Soviet pilots. This, combined with rising tensions in Jordan, led Secretary of State William Rogers to propose a cease-fire initiative in late June. Rogers called for an immediate end to hostilities and for the resumption of talks under the Jarring Mission. Israeli leaders initially rejected the proposal, but Ambassador Rabin declined to deliver the official rejection and instead pressed the Meir government to sign. On July 22, Nasser accepted Rogers' proposal; just over a week later, after receiving promises from Nixon of increased arms shipments and assurances that Washington would not press Israel to accept the "Arab definition" of UN 242, Meir accepted.[3]

Nasser's decision to accept Rogers' initiative in July sent shock waves through the PLO and elicited immediate condemnations from the major guerilla organizations. In addition to its other problems—for example, the failure to address Israeli concerns over the emplacement of Egyptian antiaircraft missiles along the Suez—Rogers' efforts aggravated tensions between the guerillas and the Arab governments because they did not include the Palestinians as an independent political force in regional affairs. The PLO issued a statement denouncing UN 242 and the Rogers activities, insisting that they were designed to strengthen Israel by destroying the Palestinian resistance and undermining the cause of Arab unity. The PLO called upon "the Arab masses that had struggled against colonialism and secured many great victories" to reject the proposals and "play their effective role in facing the battle of destiny and imposing their will in steadfastness and liberation."[4] On 25 July, Arafat dismissed the prospect of a peaceful solution to the occupation. Equating settlement to surrender, he announced, "Victory or death lie ahead of us, we welcome either."[5] PFLP leader George Habash added his voice the same day, insisting that the resistance movement would not allow itself to be butchered. The principal enemy of the Palestinian people was U.S.-backed imperialism. Washington was eager to impose a political settlement, he said, "because it knows very well that the resistance movement will make the whole of this part of the world—not only Jordan or Lebanon, but the whole of the Arab world—a second Vietnam."[6]

PLO commanders were not the only opponents of the plan. The announcement of the acceptance of Rogers' initiative was met with large protests in Jordan on 31 July and in Lebanon on 2 August. The protest in Amman was the largest ever held in the city, with tens of thousands of Palestinians and guerillas filling more than three miles of city streets. Energized by this public outpouring, Arafat pledged to fight the proposal and insisted that the PLO would speak for itself.[7] Fatah leaders charged the Arab states that had accepted the initiative with implicit acceptance of Israel's existence. The organization reasserted its position that the goal of Palestinian liberation required a political, economic, social, and cultural revolution in the Arab world. The existing regimes had joined with Israel and the forces of imperialism to enforce peace in the region, which amounted to the suffocation of the Palestinian revolution and national liberation. The goal of the fedayeen must be to overturn this state of affairs, thus opening the door to a wider armed resistance. Still, Arafat was reluctant to move to topple the regime. Unlike many of his officers, he remained convinced that liberation could not be achieved by attacking King Hussein or any other regime.[8] In a statement released on 9 August, the PLO's Central Committee warned that its enemies had mobilized against the resistance. King Hussein's forces were preparing for a siege against Palestinian forces in Amman in an effort to crush the fedayeen between the Jordanian military and the IDF. The stage was set for a "fourth campaign of encirclement and annihilation and the organization of a terrible and bloody massacre."[9]

While this rejection of the negotiation process placed the fedayeen at odds—in principle—with the two superpowers, the guerillas were supported by more-radical voices in the nonaligned world.[10] Palestinian supporters in the Third World denounced Rogers' efforts and any cease-fire that stopped short of achieving the PLO's goals. Beijing attacked the Rogers initiative as a new Munich in which Moscow and Washington hoped to divide the Middle East into two spheres of superpower influence and force the resistance to abandon its cause of national liberation. Chinese leaders also took aim at the Kremlin for instructing its "propaganda machines to grind out counter-revolutionary trash lauding" the plan, and accused leaders in Moscow of working with American forces to betray the Arab people and destroy the Palestinian armed struggle.[11]

The PLO's rejection of the Rogers efforts challenged its still precarious relationship with the Soviet Union. Moscow had a considerable amount of capital invested in the peace process, which the PLO's defiance threatened to undermine. The Kremlin criticized the PLO's move as inexplicable, insisting that the Arab-Israeli conflict could only be solved by political—not military—means. This disagreement marked perhaps the most crucial and enduring difference between Moscow and PLO.[12] Arafat met with Soviet intelligence in Damascus on the eve of the war in Jordan, where he explained his conviction that, if a showdown with the king took place, the fedayeen would surely prevail. He expected the Iraqi units inside Jordan to intervene on the PLO's behalf, and he assumed that large numbers of the Jordanian military would defect to the guerillas. Moreover, if Israel were to intervene, Arafat said, "the entire Arab world would become a second Vietnam."[13]

The mounting crisis in Jordan presented a problem for Moscow as one set of allies, Syria, Iraq, and the PLO, agitated against joint Soviet-Egyptian efforts to achieve progress toward a political solution. Further, although the Kremlin could not count Amman among its allies in the region, Soviet leaders had no desire to see King Hussein deposed and replaced by radicals within the PLO who were aligned with Beijing. Such a development would not only introduce a new element of instability into the already volatile region but also deprive Nasser of a potential ally in his efforts to seek a negotiated settlement. Thus Moscow criticized the "extremist" factions among the fedayeen who sought to escalate the crisis, while praising those "moderates" who were working to defuse tensions. Indeed, Soviet leaders recognized a key distinction between moderate and radical elements within the PLO, which many leaders in Washington would overlook. Contrary to Washington's fears of Soviet-backed Arab radicalism—Nixon and Kissinger believed, mistakenly, that Moscow was behind the crisis in Jordan—the Soviet Union was working to resolve the crisis.[14]

In contrast to this rocky relationship with Moscow, fedayeen public statements highlighted the continued close relationship between Beijing and the PLO. The PRC's vice chairman, Tung Pi-Wu, informed guests at a banquet in honor of a visiting Yemeni delegation that Washington's counterrevolutionary tactics against the Palestinians and the other revolutionary people of the world were a symptom of U.S. desperation.[15] In a speech given on 13 August, Salah Khalaf expressed his gratitude to Moscow for supporting the forces of national liberation but criticized Soviet pressure on Palestinians and applauded Chinese aid. "We have received arms from China," he added, "more than we have received from all the Arab countries." Khalaf added that the fedayeen were willing to die to defend their inalienable rights of national sovereignty.[16]

While China was the principal source of material aid, left-wing states in East Asia provided significant symbolic support for the Palestinian struggle. Radio Hanoi denounced the Rogers initiative as a treacherous attempt to strengthen Israeli claims to Arab territory. "Standing on the forefront of the struggle against U.S. imperialism," Hanoi announced, "the Vietnamese people have followed with deep concern the fight of the Arab people, their intimate comrades-in-arms and brothers."[17] PLO delegation visits to China, North Vietnam, North Korea, and Malaysia were designed to encourage the Asian regimes to maintain their support of the fedayeen and probably helped to distract international attention from the worsening situation in Jordan.[18]

Nonstate groups also announced their support for the fedayeen and guerilla movements throughout the world. The Sixteenth World Conference Against Atomic and Hydrogen Bombs, held in Tokyo on 3 August, pledged to "support the heroic struggle" of the Palestinians among other groups and called for the solidarity of the world's peoples in opposing the use of nuclear weapons and for opposing oppression and neocolonialism around the world.[19] In the midst of these rising tensions, the Second World Conference on Palestine met in Tunis to extend its support to the resistance against Portuguese imperialism in Africa and to call for "unity among the different liberation movements in colonial territories to make the struggle against colonialism more effective."[20]

This nonstate people's diplomacy provided broad—although not always deep—support for the Palestinian cause. In early September, delegates from around the world met in Amman for the Second World Conference on Palestine, sponsored by the General Union of Palestinian Students. Representatives from resistance movements in Vietnam, Angola, South Africa, Mozambique, and Eritrea met with delegates from student movements in Yugoslavia, France, the United States, Czechoslovakia, Italy, and the United Kingdom and with communists from China. In addition to listening to speeches from Arafat and Khalaf, representatives visited refugee camps, fedayeen bases, and PLO schools and clinics. The participants condemned the forces of Zionism and imperialism and pledged support for the Palestinians as well as national liberation struggles throughout Africa, Asia, and Latin America, and promised solidarity with the "Black Movement in the United States."[21]

While criticism from Third World governments bolstered the PLO's arguments, the State Department hoped that Rogers' efforts would appeal to a more moderate "silent majority" in the Palestinian population. This silent majority consisted of West Bank Palestinians among whom American officials detected signs of strong support for the initiative. While they maintained sympathy for the fedayeen and understood that the refugees constituted the core of the Middle East problem, Palestinians on the West Bank placed priority on simply ending the occupation rather than liberating the whole of Palestine. Ultimately, however, the only truly viable settlement would require the total withdrawal of Israeli forces behind the 1967 lines. Furthermore, the American consulate in Jerusalem reported that the Palestinians must have a voice in any potential political settlement and, at the very least, see the creation of an autonomous—if not independent—Palestinian entity.[22]

U.S. officials hoped that these differences between the fedayeen and West Bank Palestinians might form the basis of a political approach to the Palestinian question. In a conversation with a Lebanese journalist, State Department official Talcott Seelye explained Washington's belief that the "silent majority" of Palestinians would support a settlement based on UN 242—which would presumably lead to the realization of Palestinian aspirations through association with Jordan. He went on to suggest that the United States would consider opening formal contacts with the fedayeen if the latter accepted the resolution and showed a willingness to participate in a negotiated settlement. Seelye added, however, that the increasing frequency of U.S. public references to the Palestinians ought to be interpreted not as an indication of U.S. support for the PLO but merely as an attempt to deflect criticism that Washington was not giving sufficient attention to the Palestinian issue. Nevertheless, the possibility of some sort of recognition seemed to be in sight.[23] Other voices argued against the idea of a Palestinian entity. Senator William Fulbright called upon Israel's neighbors to absorb the Palestinian population. While Israel should take back some of the refugees, it would be impossible to accommodate most of the displaced Palestinians. Rather, the Arab states—with financial assistance from Israel—should be expected to settle the refugees.[24]

Israel's official position on the Palestinians remained firm throughout 1970, although the Palestinians were hardly its primary foreign policy concern. Minister Eban told the *Jewish Chronicle* that there was ultimately no need for the creation of another state in the region because Jordan was, for all intents and purposes, Palestine. Moreover, Israel had no conceivable motivation for taking "the lead in disrupting the recognized international structure of the Middle East," especially if the result would be to place in power groups that would regard Palestine as a "substitute for Israel, not a neighbor to it."[25] Reacting to a fedayeen attack in May that killed a number of schoolchildren, Deputy Premier Yigal Allon fumed that the PLO was a group of "murderers, not freedom fighters," and insisted that Beirut ultimately bore responsibility for the attack, which was launched from its territory.[26] Meanwhile, Ambassador Rabin warned that Israel should not be surprised if one day the United States decided to open a channel to the PLO. "The United States is sitting at a negotiating table," he said, "with a 'Fatah' which is killing Americans—with the Viet Cong.... [W]e should not be surprised if they are prepared to accept a 'Fatah' which is killing not Americans but Israelis."[27]

Likewise, Prime Minister Golda Meir insisted that the Palestinians—if they could be said to exist as a distinct people at all—were the Arab states' problem. "We carry no responsibility for the creation of the refugee problem," she asserted, adding that the Palestinian question "could have been settled very, very easily, with no question of people going into foreign lands, among foreigners, a different language, a different religion, a different way of life." While Meir had no objection to the idea of an eventual state named "Palestine-Jordan" or "Jordan-Palestine," she declared that her government would negotiate only with other governments. "We negotiate only with states, and heads of states," she insisted. "No organization, certainly just because there are terrorist organizations and their ideal is to kill Jewish men, women and children and attack buses with children, does not make them eligible for negotiations."[28]

Although Meir remained firm, there were signs that Israeli opinion might be evolving. In January 1970, the secretary-general of the Israeli Labor Party stated that he believed Israel should recognize the Palestinians as an "infant nation. It is there," he explained. "We have to recognize them. The sooner we do it, the better it will be for us, for them, for eventual peace."[29] A State Department intelligence report released at the end of August noted changing attitudes toward the Palestinians in Israel. The "pre-1967 fedayeen had appeared to the Israelis as a band of thugs in the employ of the intelligence services of the established Arab governments," while the "refugee problem had always been billed as a humanitarian problem rather than an emerging nationalism." Many in Israel still held this view, but the occupation of the West Bank had led some to consider the possibility of creating some sort of Palestinian entity. While events on the Suez front (between Egypt and Israel) had moved into the limelight over the summer and interest in the Palestinian issue had waned, as of August 1970 the State Department concluded that the greater part of Israeli opinion favored the notion that "Palestine is Jordan."[30]

Meanwhile, there were indications that the Palestinian issue was becoming more dangerous for the moderate regimes in Lebanon and Jordan. Embassy officials in Beirut warned that mounting tensions unleashed by the June War were posing a serious threat to the survival of the Lebanese government. A total of eight Arab states had been taken over by radical regimes since 1945. "These circumstances suggest a trend which may eventually encompass the entire Arab world." Western ideas such as democracy and socialism, facilitated by new communications technology, emigration, and education, had reshaped the social field in the Arab world and culminated in the rise of new ideas and the collapse of traditional regimes in Algeria, Egypt, and Syria. Officials noted the appearance of a new breed of Arab radicalism in Lebanon that drew its inspiration from Moscow and Beijing and added to the precarious balance between sectarian interests, the military, and pressures exerted by the fedayeen.[31]

As demands for change mounted in Israel and the Arab world, officials in Washington continued to hedge on the issue of Palestinian sovereignty, despite indications of the gravity of Palestinian desire for self-determination and signs that time would only increase the power of Palestinian nationalism. U.S. policy makers still hoped that the Palestinian question might be solved within the existing regional state framework. The most optimistic projections put forward the idea that the Palestinians might somehow come to accept a Palestine-as-Jordan option, thereby eliminating the need to revise the framework of the Jarring Mission. While U.S. officials debated over the nature of a theoretical Palestinian state, however, the crisis in Jordan broke open.

"We Are Calling the Shots in Jordan"

Although he was reluctant to provoke a full-scale civil conflict in his own country, King Hussein was hardly a victim of circumstances beyond his control. Rather, a significant amount of his authority rested on his ability to speak in some part for the Palestinians, owing to the fact that the majority of his subjects could claim to be Palestinian nationals. As the U.S. government discussed the possibility of granting recognition to some sort of autonomous Palestinian entity, King Hussein would have felt the pressure to reassert his authority over both population and territory. This drive, combined with pressure from the United States and Israel to crack down on the guerillas, would have provided a strong incentive to force a confrontation.

Observers in the British Foreign Ministry suspected that Washington had a hand in fomenting the crisis. "I have little doubt that the Americans have been discr[eet]ly egging [King Hussein] on to such a confrontation," cabled one British officer, "presumably in the hope that if the fedayeen could be smashed, it would be easier to 'deliver' the Israelis."[32] Moreover, although U.S. leaders were resolved in their support for the king, they were loath to bring the guerillas into their designs for a long-term Middle East settlement. Thus, while it may not have amounted to the conspiracy envisioned by the fedayeen and Beijing, the

September crisis did seem to represent the sort of confrontation between the regime and the PLO that Israeli and U.S. officials had been calling for.

Indeed, Israeli reprisal policies were engineered to force Amman to crack down on the guerillas as much as they were intended to inflict real damage on the fedayeen themselves. State Department intelligence noted that since 1968, voices in Israel had been calling for the destruction of King Hussein's regime as a way of simplifying the fedayeen problem. With the king out of the way, the IDF would no longer need to worry about harming a U.S. ally in its retaliations against the guerillas. Some opinions also suggested that the responsibility of running a government might have a moderating effect on the guerilla leadership. Successive crises in Amman had "strengthened the hand of those who believed that King Hussein's survival was not particularly useful to Israel."[33] According to this line of reasoning, King Hussein must either bring the fedayeen under his control or move out of the way so that the IDF could.

The king also faced strong pressure from within the ranks of his own military, which resented the PLO's presence in Jordan as well as the damaging Israeli reprisals that this presence invited. By late summer 1970, Jordanian security forces were itching for a fight with the fedayeen. Defying standing orders, army units had begun launching minor provocations in hopes of sparking the anticipated conflict with the guerillas. Meanwhile, individual commanders grumbled about the possibility of a mounting a coup against King Hussein if the king refused to move against the PLO. Chafing under mounting pressure from the government and sporadic attacks from Jordanian military units, the guerillas ratcheted up their rhetoric, declaring both sides of the Jordan to be a "single arena of struggle" and announcing their intention to transform the Hashemite Kingdom into a "stronghold" of the revolution.[34]

In response to the worsening situation in Jordan, the PFLP concluded that the time was right for drastic action. PFLP leaders announced that actions were being taken in response to efforts by Jordanian security forces to destroy the resistance. The group intended to resist the imposition of the Rogers initiative, a political settlement that, as they saw it, was designed to destroy Palestinian aspirations and ensure the survival of the state of Israel. On 6 September, PFLP guerillas hijacked a Swissair DC-8, a TWA Boeing 707, and a Pan Am Boeing 747, with a total of nearly 500 passengers. The guerillas flew the Pan Am flight to Cairo, released the passengers, and then destroyed the plane. The Swissair and TWA aircraft were flown to Dawson Field (which guerillas dubbed "Revolution Airfield") in Jordan and wired with explosives. A fourth hijacking was foiled by El Al security officials, and a fifth plane, a British VC-10, was captured by PFLP gunmen on 9 September. From Dawson Airfield, the PFLP announced:

> The government can do nothing to stop us. If they move the army closer to the planes, they will be responsible for the consequences. We are

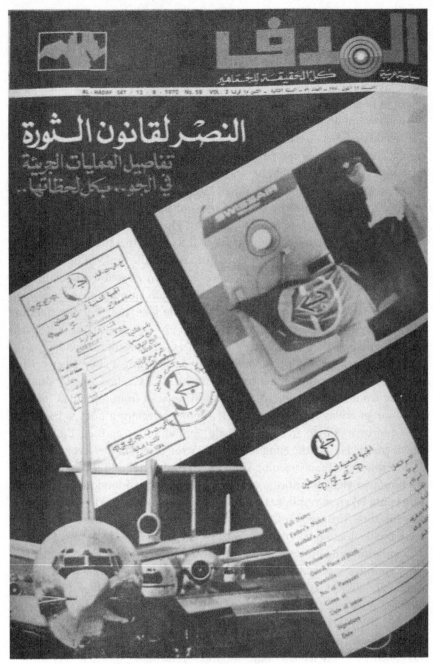

FIGURE 4.1 *Cover of PFLP's newspaper* Al-Hadaf, *"The Victory of Revolutionary Law."*
Courtesy of the Library of the Institute for Palestine Studies, Beirut.

calling the shots in Jordan, not the government. As for world opinion, where was world opinion when a million of our people were hijacked out of Palestine by the Israelis? The world didn't care about us, so why should we care about anybody? Now let world opinion—and King Hussein—understand the drastic measures we are prepared to take to dramatize our cause and win back our land.

The guerillas demanded the release of all Palestinian prisoners being held in the United Kingdom, Switzerland, and Israel in exchange for the hostages at Dawson Field.[35] They also declared their indifference to voices in the international community that decried the hijackings. "World opinion has not helped us in our case during the last twenty-five years.... The important thing about the operations is that they ask the world a question: Why?"[36]

While spectacular, the hijackings overplayed the guerillas' hand and alienated many of the moderates in the PLO. On 12 September, sensing that the tide was turning against the fedayeen at Dawson Field, an irate Arafat suspended the PFLP's membership in the Central Committee and announced a desire to remain uninvolved in the current affair. "I begged Habash and the other leftists not to make such a demonstration," Arafat later explained. "I was completely against it." The committee insisted that the PFLP's actions had endangered the revolution and distracted the resistance from the real enemy. The committee must "protect the humane image of the revolution [as well as] the lives and security of the civilian passengers who had nothing to do with the policy of their colonialist governments."[37] As the ranks of the fedayeen began to split, Washington and Amman might have had the opportunity to reinforce a moderate position among the guerillas. However, the PLO's expulsion of the PFLP from the Central Committee came too late to avert the impending crackdown.

The 1970 crisis was the most dramatic repercussion to date of Fatah's failure to create a united front. Whereas Arafat's group embraced the principle of nonintervention in the affairs of the Arab states, other fedayeen groups did not. The PFLP's pan-Arab aspirations marked conservative monarchies like the one in Amman as enemies. Meanwhile, the PDFLP called for the creation of revolutionary councils or soviets in the region and worked to undermine internal Jordanian stability.[38] All along, Arafat had argued that the creation of a united front would not be necessary. As he told a Lebanese newspaper in January 1970, Fatah would not follow the path of the Algerians in attacking rival Palestinian guerilla organizations. Rather, Arafat's organization took as an example the Vietnamese National Liberation Front, which included twenty-one organizations clustered around the "backbone" of the Viet Cong; Fatah would be the PLO's backbone. An attack on competing organizations not only would be antithetical to Fatah's beliefs, according to Arafat, but also would amount to a rejection of the Arab world's diversity, of which the PLO was a reflection. Moreover, such a move would risk confrontation with the various

Arab states that supported Fatah's rivals in the PLO. Ultimately, Arafat believed, a purge might not even be necessary, since twenty-three of the thirty-three organizations constituting the Palestinian revolution had already dissolved themselves peacefully.[39] Further, the Algerian approach would be extremely difficult considering the geographical dispersion of the guerilla groups and their patron states throughout the Arab world. How, for instance, could Fatah destroy the Arab Liberation Front if the latter remained sheltered in Iraq?[40]

As temperatures climbed in Amman, the Third Conference of Non-Aligned Countries convened in Lusaka, Zambia. The participants were notably sympathetic to the fedayeen, identifying the Jordanian government as the aggressor and calling for recognition of Palestinian sovereignty. Yugoslav president Tito drew parallels between foreign interventions in Indochina and the Middle East, criticizing Israel and its refusal to abide by Security Council resolutions— although he did not discuss the PLO's rejection of UN 242. He argued that events had shown that Israel was acting out of a desire for territorial gains rather than out of fears about its national security. Tito argued that Israel's acceptance of Rogers' initiative was a diplomatic ploy designed to disguise its refusal to make concessions. He called on the international community to bring about the withdrawal of Israeli troops from occupied land and provide for the recognition of Palestinian rights in order to prevent further violence.[41]

The conference's participants also identified the conflict in the Middle East as a manifestation of imperialism and neocolonialism, judging that the Palestinians had much in common with other postcolonial actors around the world who had struggled to achieve independence. President Marien Ngouabi of the Congo warned that words were not enough in the face of imperialist aggression. When all was said and done, he asserted, the basic problem in the Middle East remained the existence of the Palestinian people, and any feasible peace plan must recognize this.

> We have talked about the problem of apartheid, the problem of the minority regime in South Africa, the racist regime in Rhodesia, the problem of the colonial regime of Portugal in Africa; we have spoken of Zionism, we have spoken of American imperialism in Asia, we have referred to economic problems. But in actual fact, what are we really doing here?[42]

The representative from Guinea warned the assembled nonaligned countries of the threat posed by imperialism. Israel was an imperialist bridgehead, he noted, and had shown its true colors in the occupation of Arab territory and its refusal to abide by UN and OAU resolutions. This threat to the nonaligned world was global and manifest in multiple regions. Likewise, he called for the withdrawal of U.S. forces from Southeast Asia.[43]

The conference proceedings revealed a growing recognition of the Palestinians as a national group entitled to independence and self-government. The

Nigerian delegation voiced concern over the global menace to liberty and pledged support for any "region of the world where people are fighting to regain their rights of sovereignty, freedom, national unity and [patrimony]," be it "in Africa or in the Middle East, Indochina or [elsewhere]." Nigerian foreign minister Okoi Arikpo was particularly concerned about Israel's refusal to participate in the peace process despite the OAU's recent endorsement of UN peace efforts.[44] Indian prime minister Indira Gandhi also voiced support for UN mediation efforts and the recognition of Palestinian national rights.[45] Representatives from communist states came out in support of the Palestinians as well. The Cubans reaffirmed their full support for the Palestinian struggle against Israeli imperialism and called for the immediate withdrawal of Israeli forces from the occupied territories and the "unconditional recognition of the Palestinian people whose intrepid devotion and tenacity constitute a source of pride and encouragement for the peoples of Africa, Asia, and Latin America."[46]

An appeal to the universality of human experience and recognition of a common set of human rights undergirded wider visions of international order embraced by many states in the Third World. Said the Peruvian foreign minister:

> There is no nation in the world that at one time in the course of its history has not had to fight for its independence or for the respect of its national personality. No one can consciously deny the legitimate right to freedom of those countries which are as yet subjects of a foreign State. On the other hand, all men on earth, whatever their racial characteristic may be, belong to the same human gender and as such they have equal rights, obligations and aspirations. Therefore, it is repugnant to the very conscience of mankind to see any form of aggression, discrimination, or racial segregation that ignores or affects the dignity of human beings.[47]

The final resolution on the Middle East adopted at the conference affirmed support for the UN's efforts to resolve the conflict and denounced Israel's continuing occupation of Arab territory and its use of force against its neighbors, as such actions were incompatible with the spirit of peace negotiations. Furthermore, the nonaligned heads of state cited the recognition of Palestinian rights as a necessary component of any peace in the region and confirmed the support of the nonaligned world for the Palestinians' "struggle for national liberation against colonialism and racism."[48] Although the conference showcased the ideals that lay beneath a nonaligned vision for peace in the Middle East, professions of solidarity and support for universal human rights did little to resolve the immediate crisis in Jordan.

While the various delegations debated in Lusaka, the PFLP's dramatic simultaneous hijackings generated both criticism and defense in the court of world opinion. The Algerian press followed the hijackings closely, stressing the need to focus on the circumstances that framed the guerillas' actions. The official daily, *Moudjahid*, argued that the hijackings were justifiable because they represented the only means at the disposal of the Palestinians to achieve the release of their comrades being held in Western prisons. Moreover, the Algerian media openly criticized Egyptian papers that denounced the hijackings and remained silent over Amman's crackdown against the PLO.[49] Beijing cheered on the guerillas and reaffirmed its scorn for Rogers' efforts. "The Palestinian guerillas, which have become a strong force in the Arab national-liberation movement," remarked the Chinese vice premier, "enjoy a high reputation among the people of the world." In the Chinese view, the Rogers initiative was a superpower plot designed to reopen the region to outside control.[50]

The guerillas found Western sympathizers as well. Historian Arnold Toynbee wrote an editorial that appeared in Fatah's newsletter on the subject of the hijackings. While he did not excuse the PFLP's actions, Toynbee argued that "the blood of any innocent victims of Palestinian Arab commando operations is not on the commando-fighters' heads alone; it is also on the heads of the world itself, since without its constituents' acquiescence the Establishment could not sit enthroned." Since the pronouncement of the Balfour Declaration in 1917, he wrote, the Palestinians had been forced from their land and made to live under military occupation. "To all this...the world has turned a deaf ear." Deprived of power and influence, the Palestinians had been "made to pay the bill for wrongs inflicted on Jews, not by Arabs, but by Westerners." While they appeared as terrorists in the West, the fedayeen were seen as heroes in the eyes of other Arabs and fellow anticolonialists. Toynbee went on to compare the commandos to Jews who had fought against the Roman Empire, French guerillas in the Franco-Prussian War, and European resistance movements during World War II.

> The Palestinian Arabs have an understandable vendetta against the Israelis, but they also have a grievance against all the rest of us. Half a century of massive indifference to their wrongs has had the same exasperating effect on them as a century of similar treatment has had on the black citizens of the United States. The Palestinians are now in the mood for sacrificing their lives if by wrecking the pillar, they can bring the roof down on their Israeli enemies' heads; and if the crashing masonry were incidentally to stave in the skulls of the rest of the human race, why should the Palestinian Arabs care? What have the rest of us done to deserve consideration from them?

Toynbee warned that the fedayeen's present tactics were designed to prompt Israeli reprisals, which might in turn bring about a renewed war in the Middle East. Such a war could very well spark a clash between the superpowers and result in a nuclear conflagration. While he by no means condoned fedayeen violence, he regretted that the current state of affairs had led them to such acts.[51]

The outpouring of support for the Palestinian fighters hinted at the degree of worldwide identification with the PLO's struggle, but other observers were less moved by the plight of the Palestinians and the historical antecedents to the guerillas' actions. As the White House set about trying to secure the release of American and Israeli hostages on the jets, Nixon told Kissinger that he hoped to use the hijackings "as a pretext to crush the fedayeen." However, Kissinger warned of a greater threat: if the fedayeen were able to "destroy the authority of the King—one of the few rulers in the region distinguished by moderation and pro-Western sympathies—the entire Middle East would be revolutionized."[52]

On 11 September, President Nixon announced his plans to combat the growing menace of hijacking by implementing a new regime of surveillance over air transportation. In addition to stationing armed government officers on commercial U.S. flights, Nixon directed the Department of Transportation to increase its use of electronic surveillance in airports and conduct searches of passengers. These new measures would take place not only in U.S. airports but in foreign countries as well, so long as they chose to comply. Nixon also called on the world community to cut off air travel to countries that refused to comply with the convention.[53]

"There Must Be Peace or War"

Nixon's contempt would be the least of the PLO's worries, however. By mid-September, with tensions mounting on all sides, King Hussein made the fateful decision to move against the fedayeen. In response, the PLO denounced the king's actions and called for an end to additional security procedures inside Amman. Although it insisted on the right to defend itself, the organization maintained that it had no desire to provoke a confrontation with the government. The king formed a military government and called for the guerillas to lay down their weapons. "The situation can't go on," King Hussein was quoted as saying. "There must be peace or war." The PLO reacted by naming Arafat commander in chief of the fedayeen and calling for a general strike to overthrow the new government. At dawn the next morning, 17 September, Jordanian security forces—with support from CIA officials—launched an offensive against PLO positions in Amman. The war had begun.[54]

As the Jordanian army attacked fedayeen-controlled neighborhoods and refugee camps, plumes of smoke rose above Amman's skyline. Eyewitnesses reported heavy street fighting and widespread devastation in the nation's capital as guerillas, carrying small arms, engaged with the king's armored forces. "Hundreds of Palestinians and Jordanians were butchered," Fatah announced, as the "revolutionaries moved to repel a fierce military onslaught by King

Hussein and his newly appointed military cabinet." The guerillas warned that the king sought to crush the resistance once and for all.[55]

In Washington, the Jordanian crisis appeared as part of the larger global struggle between the forces of order and revolution.[56] In a lecture at Kansas State University on 16 September, President Nixon condemned the hijackers, asserting that they were part of a wider wave of global radicalism that was plaguing societies around the world. As "they held their hundreds of passengers hostage under threat of murder," he declared, "they sent shock waves of alarm around the world to the spreading disease of violence and terror and its use as a political tactic. The same cancerous disease has been spreading all over the world and here in the United States," he commented, pointing to a recent bombing at the University of Wisconsin as evidence of a "moral and spiritual crisis in the universities." The United States "cannot stand successfully for the rule of law abroad unless we respect the rule of law at home in the United States."[57]

In the president's mind, revolutionary violence and instability were an increasingly dangerous threat to the world order. Thus, the forces of order must stand up against this deluge of anarchic violence both at home and abroad: "A nation that condones blackmail and terror at home," he intoned, "can hardly stand as the example in putting an end to international piracies or tensions that could explode into war abroad." The struggle for order against radical forces in the world was, according to the president, a truly global undertaking: "Those who bomb universities, [who] ambush policemen, who hijack airplanes, who hold their passengers hostage, all share in common not only a contempt for human life, but also the contempt for those elemental decencies on which a free society rests—and they deserve the contempt of every American who values those decencies."[58]

Arab states including Algeria and Egypt pleaded for an end to the Jordanian conflict. Algerian president Boumedienne condemned the conspiracy against the Palestinian resistance as an example of Arab forces turning against one another. "We stand with all our resources behind the Palestinian revolution which is holding out against colonialism and imperialism and the hostile force," he said, adding that "Algeria will remain loyal to its principles and will maintain its attitude to the struggling Palestinian people and its victorious revolution."[59] Others in the Arab world preferred to chart a more moderate course that acknowledged the king's position in Jordan. On 19 September, Nasser cabled King Hussein and Arafat, calling on both men to agree to a cease-fire between Jordanian and Palestinian forces.[60]

The explosive situation in Jordan was not a welcome development for either superpower. Moscow maintained its focus on Cairo as its primary ally in the Arab world and denounced the hijackings, which might upset the regional status quo. *Pravda* argued that the "regrettable hijackings by extremist groups of the Palestinian guerillas" had played into Israeli hands by diverting "attention from the gist of the matter and inflat[ing] the anti-Arab campaign." Rather, the real concern remained the efforts by Israel to frustrate the progress of the Jarring Mission.[61] On 18 September, the Soviets expressed to the State Department their hopes for a peaceful solution to the present crisis and a political settlement to the situation in the Middle East along the lines set out in UN 242. Rodger Davies, deputy assistant secretary of state for Near Eastern affairs, confirmed Soviet intentions to urge restraint from Damascus and Baghdad and make all possible approaches to the Palestinian leadership.[62]

The White House was concerned with the implications of the crisis for the wider Arab world. The Washington Special Actions Group (WSAG), convened by Kissinger on 18 September, considered a list of possible outcomes of the Jordanian crisis, concluding that the most likely positive scenario involved King Hussein reestablishing control over urban centers in Jordan and "reassuring a large proportion of Jordanians who have been concerned about the breakdown of law and order in the cities." Moreover, reestablishing control over the cities would send a message to the silent majority of Jordanians and Palestinians who, according to WSAG, still looked to King Hussein to speak for the Palestinians. If the king could demonstrate this authority, it might serve to demoralize the fedayeen. Even Nasser, the group suggested, would welcome a blow to the movement. Finally, WSAG suggested that a victory for King Hussein would almost certainly contribute to Beirut's efforts to rein in the fedayeen in Lebanon.[63]

Nevertheless, this would not be the "wholesale rollback" of the fedayeen that some had hoped for; indeed, it would probably result in increased conflict along the cease-fire lines with Israel. Moreover, repression in Jordan was likely to radicalize moderate elements in the fedayeen such as Fatah and the mainstream PLO. King Hussein's efforts to regain Jordanian cities were likely to spark a confrontation with all of the guerilla organizations within the PLO. Should the monarch be forced to compromise with the fedayeen, he would be left in an especially dangerous position. The fedayeen might spin an eventual compromise as a political victory, an act that probably would gain them even more adherents. Moreover, if the king struck a conciliatory pose, he might face dissension from his own military and find his power further circumscribed.[64] The situation grew more explosive on 18 September when Syrian tanks crossed the Jordanian border and began moving south toward Amman. Under pressure from the United States, Israel mobilized its air force and prepared to intervene in order to halt the Syrian advance. Israeli leaders also requested the White House's blessing for a ground assault should air strikes prove insufficient. Facing resistance from Jordanian forces and the prospect of Israeli intervention, Damascus blinked, pulling its forces back on 22 September.[65]

The White House remained focused on the wider implications of the crisis, suggesting that Moscow may have been behind Syrian actions.[66] Ever the globalist, Kissinger stressed the importance of not focusing on the September crisis in a "purely Jordanian context." Indeed, the repercussions of King Hussein's showdown with the fedayeen reached beyond Jordanian frontiers. "If Syrian forces remained in Jordan," Kissinger said, "the King would be faced with the tragic dilemma of having to protect both the cities against guerillas and the country against main forces to the north. The same dilemma faced by the South Vietnamese."[67] Pulling back even further, the White House interpreted the events in Jordan in the global context of what it understood to be Soviet advances with the election of Salvador Allende in Chile and, more alarming, the construction of a Soviet submarine base in the Cuban port of Cienfuegos. From the perspective of the White House, the conflict in Jordan was just one episode in a series of crises—fueled by the Cold War—taking place around the world.

This preoccupation with the broader consequences of the situation in Jordan attested to the White House's perception of a precarious balance between radicals and moderates in the Arab world. The administration grossly miscalculated the effects of the crisis in Lebanon—assuming that the king's actions would contribute to stability in the republic—but its predictions that the crisis would radicalize Fatah were more accurate. At the same time, by backing King Hussein's crackdown on the Palestinians, Washington effectively underwrote what came to be seen as one of the most brutal expressions of state reaction in the Arab world and deepened the divisions between radicals and moderates in the region. Rising tensions in the region could also provide an opening for outsiders. State Department analysts noted that the present division of forces in the region provided the PRC with an opportunity to boost its image on the cheap. While the PRC's influence with the fedayeen was limited and its support of the guerillas was incomplete, Beijing hoped that by backing the Palestinians, it could sustain tensions in the region that might provide an opening for Chinese influence.[68]

While they kept a suspicious eye on each other, U.S. and Soviet officials shared this concern over Beijing's role in the region, particularly the possibility that China might be trying to use Arab extremists to provoke a crisis between Washington and Moscow.[69] To this end, U.S. contacts in Hong Kong reported the arrival of Syrian and Iraqi military delegations in Beijing in late September. Moreover, the Iraqis had been seen in the company of the Palestinian representative to Beijing, raising worries about the nature of the Chinese presence in the Middle East.[70] For its part, Beijing accused the United States of goading Amman into assaulting the fedayeen in an effort to destroy the Palestinian revolutionaries. The Chinese government condemned Washington's efforts and cheered the Palestinians in their struggle.[71] The Cold War and the Sino-Soviet split were still major forces in the Middle East.

A Political Fact

The events of September cast an international spotlight on Arafat and the PLO and convinced many observers that the split between Amman and the Palestinians was complete. Far from serving as the Palestinians' representative on the international stage, King Hussein now appeared as their biggest enemy. As Arafat wrote in a 22 September cable to the Arab leaders meeting in Cairo: "Amman is burning for the sixth day," and "The bodies of thousands of our people are rotting beneath the rubble." Despite efforts to achieve a settlement with the Jordanian military, "artillery and tanks are still shelling and destroying. . . . It is a massacre unparalleled in history." The Fatah commander insisted that Amman had betrayed the Palestinians and reneged on its promises to the Arab states. Nevertheless, he vowed to continue the struggle. In private, Arafat had another message for the PFLP: "You refused my ideas. Here are the results. You are responsible for what has happened."[72]

King Hussein's crackdown drew condemnation from voices throughout Europe, many of whom seemed to recognize the Palestinians as a national group. State Department officers noted that London newspapers were largely sympathetic to the Palestinian case. The *Sunday Times* argued that the Palestinian question remained at the heart of the Middle East conflict and insisted that the Palestinians must be given a voice in the international peace process.[73] The French spoke out in support of the Palestinian position as well. In a letter dated 21 September, President Georges Pompidou condemned the Syrian intervention but expressed his great concern over the prospect of a U.S. intervention. He also pressed his conviction that the great powers had been wrong to ignore the Palestinians and argued that they must be made part of the political solution to the Arab-Israeli conflict.[74] Indeed, by the end of the month, Paris had begun to refer to the Palestinians as a "political fact."[75]

It was precisely this political fact that King Hussein—under pressure from the White House—hoped to obliterate. On 25 September a delegation of visitors from the Arab states returned to Cairo from Amman with the disturbing news that Jordanian forces were seeking to annihilate the PLO in Jordan. The moderate Arab regime in Tunisia placed the blame for the violence on the Jordanian government. While the fedayeen, with minor exceptions, had respected a recent cease-fire, it appeared as if Jordanian forces had continued their efforts to accomplish the destruction of the fedayeen.[76] After hearing reports from the delegation, which left "absolutely no room for doubt," Nasser cabled King Hussein and expressed his anxiety over the continuing Jordanian offensive, his fear that King Hussein was trying to destroy the Palestinian resistance, and his concern that "a terrible massacre is in progress, in which all Arab and human values are being ignored."[77]

The war in Jordan would have far-reaching implications for the region. After considerable effort, the Arab states succeeded in achieving the September 27

Cairo Agreement, which brought an end to the fighting in Amman.[78] The following day, Nasser suffered a fatal heart attack, most likely brought on by exhaustion from his efforts to secure an end to the war in Jordan.[79] While the situation in the Arab world certainly had been transformed, a new page seemed to have been turned in the U.S.-Israeli relationship as well. In a telephone call to Ambassador Rabin thanking him for Israel's support during the crisis, Kissinger said that the United States was "fortunate in having an ally like Israel in the Middle East. These events will be taken into account in all future developments." Rabin interpreted it as "probably the most far-reaching statement ever made by a president [sic] of the U.S. on the mutuality of the alliance between the two countries."[80] The crisis would also give Kissinger a stronger hand in his ongoing struggle with the State Department for control of Middle East policy. Kissinger warned the president in the wake of the crisis that he still saw "no evidence of a disciplined adherence to a solid long-term strategy" in Washington.[81]

Meanwhile, Israeli policy makers judged the events in Jordan to be confirmation of their standing strategy of bringing pressure on the Arab states to crack down on the guerillas. Dayan would write that King Hussein's victory resulted in a "triple blessing to Israel." Attacks from the East Bank all but ceased, relations with Amman improved dramatically, and a working relationship between Israel, Jordan, and the Palestinians in the occupied territories emerged. Fedayeen attacks from Lebanon were, moreover, considerably less destructive than had been the incursions from Jordan. Indeed, Dayan credited the "suppression of terror inside Israel" to three main factors: the policies of the military government in the occupied territories (which included collective punishment in the form of the demolition of houses of suspected PLO collaborators), the actions of the IDF in increasing security along the frontiers, and King Hussein's crackdown on the PLO in Jordan. The last of these, moreover, was a credit to Israel's reprisal policies. "If Israel had not reacted so sharply to sabotage operations undertaken from Jordanian territory," Dayan explained, "the government of Jordan would have reached a *modus vivendi* with the terrorists. Hussein finally resolved to stamp out terrorism because the alternative would have been the destruction of ordered life in Jordan." The devastation throughout the Jordan Valley was "just the beginning."[82]

The guerillas had been dealt a serious blow. Amman's attacks had forced the PLO to accept an internationally brokered cease-fire and resulted in significant guerilla and civilian casualties. The struggle was not lost, however, according to Arafat. Despite the hardships of the war, the Palestinian people's resilience had "frustrated the colonialist conspiracy which... was closely interlocked with the base American conspiracy against the people of Indonesia and Vietnam. This endurance also convinced our people and our nation that this people is capable of engaging in a long struggle until victory is won."[83]

Not far away, Lebanese officials worried about the broader implications of King Hussein's crackdown on regional politics, particularly in their country. As the fedayeen suffered at the hands of the Jordanians, Lebanese officials feared that more and more Palestinian fighters would stream into Lebanon. Though the Soviets, the Egyptians, and the Syrians did not wish for this to happen, it remained a distinct possibility that the guerillas would regroup in Lebanon. Beirut hoped that the possibility of U.S. intervention against the fedayeen in Lebanon might discourage the guerillas from becoming too active in that country. State Department officials agreed with the Lebanese assessment that fedayeen activity would increase as a result of the recent events in Jordan. "Should the fedayeen however try to pull a Jordan in Lebanon," they noted, "we believe that the Lebanese would fight." Nevertheless, Beirut would most likely need more weapons if it hoped to confront the guerillas. Ultimately, should the "fedayeen desire to start trouble in Lebanon," the Americans predicted, Lebanese security would depend on Beirut's ability to defend itself, the desire of Moscow, Cairo, and Damascus to preserve security in Lebanon, and Beirut's confidence in Washington's support.[84]

In the wake of the Black September crisis, support for the creation of some sort of Palestinian entity became the norm in the world community. Paris was among the first Western governments to open contacts with the fedayeen and express public support for the idea of a Palestinian state. Beyond arguing that the Palestinians represented a political fact, the French government had discussed the Palestinian question with Moscow and suggested that Palestinian self-determination might serve as the basis for a potential political solution in the Middle East. Nevertheless, the French maintained that the question of a solution to the Palestinian problem must be viewed as a long-term issue.[85]

Algiers continued to pressure State Department officials to establish contact with the fedayeen and make provisions for the Palestinians in Rogers' diplomacy. Although they still endorsed the concept of a "de-Zionized" political entity in Israel, the Algerians also argued that recognition from the United States might give fedayeen leaders incentive to enter into negotiations with Israel. They dismissed Washington's search for a Palestinian silent majority, suggesting that even if such a majority existed, acceptance of a political settlement would ultimately fall on guerilla leaders. Staunch supporters of Fatah, the Algerians insisted that divisions among the fedayeen were the product of meddling by eastern Arab states. If their own history was any guide, the Algerians argued, Fatah would eliminate its rivals in the resistance movement and then continue the liberation struggle with the help of international support. While State Department officers remained skeptical about the benefits of opening contacts with Fatah, they suggested that by taking up a more serious engagement with the issue of Palestinian rights, Washington could win points with the Algerians and possibly bring Algiers on board with efforts to engineer a political solution to the conflict.[86]

Not everyone was convinced that Palestinian moderates could work toward a political settlement, however. American officials in Beirut warned that Fatah was becoming more radical. The failures of the guerilla war against Israel were forcing some fedayeen to conclude that an effective resistance must garner more support from neighboring Arab states. They warned that with this conclusion in mind, Fatah seemed to be coming around to a position embraced by radicals such as the PFLP, which called for confrontation with Arab governments.[87]

Regardless of the political direction it might take, the PLO had shown itself to be an important player in the region, one that might demand political engagement in the future. The crisis in Jordan had convinced the White House Senior Review Group (SRG) that the Palestinians were now a "force to be reckoned with in the Near East." The fedayeen's capacity to disrupt the peace negotiations, their influence in Jordan and Lebanon, their popularity in the Muslim world, and the emerging national awareness of the Palestinians in the wake of the June War had all transformed the Palestinian problem into a major concern. In short, the State Department argued, the Palestinians "cannot be ignored. At best they could become constructive partners in a peace settlement, and a fruitful U.S. relationship with them might contribute substantially to our position in the region." While guerilla groups had played a role in regional affairs, the PLO did not function as a centralized political structure in the same way as the Algerian FLN did. This disorganization allowed some officials to continue to insist that the guerillas represented only a small portion of the population and that strong sentiment in support of reconciliation with King Hussein existed among the population.[88] Such thinking would persist in the coming years.

To be sure, the emergence of the Palestinians represented a headache for U.S. policy makers in the Middle East. Some officials warned that while there was a possibility that bringing Palestinian leaders into the negotiating process might encourage moderation among the fedayeen and strengthen the Palestinian silent majority, it was also possible that such an action might further radicalize the movement. Moreover, these moves could make life significantly more dangerous for King Hussein. At the same time, substantial negotiations with the Palestinians were likely to force Washington to stand up to Israel. Israel's leadership would apply concerted pressure on the U.S. officials to prevent them "from working in a direction tending to raise the international standing of the Palestinians, especially fedayeen."[89]

The Soviets also took greater interest in Arafat and the PLO in the wake of Nasser's death. U.S. observers suggested that Moscow might be seeking to improve relations with moderates such as Arafat in an effort to isolate more-radical groups such as the PFLP.[90] An article in Moscow's *New Times* at the end of the month argued that Moscow's future support for the fedayeen might be dependent upon the latter's adoption of a moderate approach toward a potential peace settlement with Israel. The Jordanian crisis had forced a reconsideration of fedayeen extremism and energized moderate forces in the movement. Should the Palestinian fighters adopt a program leading toward a potential settlement, the article suggested, they would gain support from the international circles that favored such a settlement.[91]

Even the British seemed willing—if still somewhat reluctant—to engage with the Palestinians as a legitimate group. U.K. foreign secretary Alec Douglas-Home pointed out that the Arab desire to drive Israel from the territories occupied at the end of the war had fueled fedayeen activities since 1967, and he railed that the international community had condemned activities of the Palestinian guerillas and come to recognize "in stateless freedom-fighters a new threat to peace and security." As regional violence continued, the need for a just settlement became ever more pressing. While London could not endorse a political settlement calling for the dissolution of the state of Israel, any potential solution needed to win the support of all regional actors, including the Palestinians.[92]

Thus, while the conflict in Jordan represented a humanitarian and military disaster for the PLO, it functioned as something of a political victory in the international community. If nothing else, the clashes between Amman and the fedayeen demonstrated the dim prospects of any Palestine-as-Jordan solution. Although they might lack the power to establish the material trappings of a state or to overthrow the Jordanian government, Palestinian fighters had won the political influence necessary to survive as an independent movement. The PLO could no longer be ignored as a regional player.

Despite the military setback in Jordan, support for the Palestinian cause from radical governments and liberation groups around the world increased, a fact that the PLO leadership held up as evidence of the fedayeen's revolutionary credentials. Nongovernmental groups constituted an important source of support for the Palestinian fighters. The Ninth Conference of the Afro-Asian People's Solidarity Organization, held in Libya, reconfirmed its support for the "Arab Palestinian people, which is an inseparable part of the international liberation movement, [and] deserves the support of all honest forces in the world." Warning of imperialist plots against the resistance, the conference urged the resistance and the Arab states to continue their struggle to liberate all occupied Arab territory, and insisted on the right of the Palestinian people—and all peoples living under foreign rule—to engage in armed struggle for liberation and self-determination. Conference participants condemned U.S. military assistance to the IDF and Washington's support for Israel at the United Nations, and warned the peoples of Africa and Asia and their governments of the danger of Israel's increased attention to the two continents.[93]

Dissident groups in the West also mobilized in support of the PLO. The Association of Arab-American University Graduates denounced U.S.

"military and economic support to racist settler regimes, to colonial and Fascist regimes throughout the world." Washington's aid to Israel stood alongside support for struggling Portuguese colonial regimes in Mozambique and Angola and the policies that backed the settler regimes of South Africa and Rhodesia. Furthermore, the association warned that Washington's failure to suspend diplomatic relations with these regimes and "to pursue a policy based on the principles of justice, liberty and dignity invites definite alienation of free people throughout the world and may become a factor leading to certain world conflagration."[94]

In November, a group of African American leaders took out an advertisement in the *New York Times* condemning U.S. support for King Hussein during the war in Jordan. The ad stated that Washington's support for "King Hussein's slaughter of Palestinian refugees and freedom-fighters is consistent with its support of reactionary dictatorships throughout the world—from Cambodia and Vietnam to South Africa, Greece and Iran." The Palestinian revolution was the leading edge of the Arab revolution and was "part of the anti-colonial revolution which is going on in places such as Vietnam, Mozambique, Angola, Brazil, Laos, South Africa and Zimbabwe." The letter alleged collusion between the forces of Zionism and imperialism and called for an end to all military aid to Israel, citing Israeli support for U.S. policy in Vietnam, for French counterrevolutionaries in Algeria during the revolution, and for reactionary forces in Indonesia and southern Africa, plus South African support for Israeli foreign policy.[95] Historical parallels showed—in the eyes of the PLO's supporters—the bankruptcy of U.S.-Israeli efforts to contain Palestinian nationalism.

Beijing's support for the PLO was a key component of the latter's international success. In a cable to Beijing on the twenty-fifth anniversary of the establishment of the PRC, the PLO saluted China as the "mightiest citadel of freedom in the world—a citadel which has firmly and unyieldingly resisted all the forces of imperialism, headed by the United States of America, the first enemy of struggling peoples." The PLO also expressed its appreciation for Beijing's attitude toward the fedayeen and the PRC's long-standing aid to the resistance: "The Palestinian people have not forgotten their friends who have always stood by them, and first and foremost among these are the great people of China."[96]

Aging nonaligned heavyweights such as Tito pushed for their own visions of a just political solution in the Middle East. While he admitted that the Rogers formula was flawed, Tito suggested that it represented the first step toward a lasting political settlement. He called on governments who had influence over Israel to encourage the Jewish state to come on board with UN efforts. Tito also warned against any attempts to take advantage of the situation created by Nasser's death and pleaded for responsible efforts to achieve a peace in the region.

We are living at a time when every people and every country must think about the fate of other countries and peoples, regardless of geographical distance. All that is happening in any part of the world is reflected in one way or the other on the entire international community. It is not only the rights of the peoples of Indochina, Arab countries and the African south that have been brutally violated in Vietnam, the Middle East and South Africa, but also the basic principles of the Charter wherein certain irrevocable values of international relations are solemnly proclaimed.

The right to self-determination must be preserved by all "peace loving and progressive forces" unless the world is to suffer under the weight of "power politics and the right of the stronger."[97]

Israeli leaders remained steadfast, however, in the face of multilateral efforts to achieve a resolution. Prime Minister Golda Meir was adamant that the UN's effort to push her government into granting concessions to the Arab states and its opposition to Israeli attempts to consolidate new international boundaries had further eroded Israeli confidence in the institution, as had a recent General Assembly resolution calling on Israel to withdraw from the occupied territories and insisting that the rights of the Palestinians be incorporated into a peace settlement.[98]

Two Separate Political Entities in Jordan

On 2 October, NSC staff members Harold Saunders and Richard Kennedy prepared a memo for Kissinger's aide Alexander Haig assessing the aftermath of the Jordanian crisis. They wrote that there were now undeniably two separate political entities in Jordan: King Hussein's regime and the Palestinian nation. U.S. policy makers had to decide whether to continue to back Hussein exclusively or to open the door to an option in which the Palestinians would represent themselves.[99] State Department analysts explained that although recent negotiations had brought an end to the immediate crisis, they served as a temporary cease-fire rather than a lasting solution to the problem. Indeed, in the coming months, King Hussein's security forces would continue their assault on fedayeen strongholds in the north in an effort to crush the remaining pockets of guerilla power in Jordan. In the immediate aftermath of the war, however, the question of who would control Jordan remained unresolved. The king had increased his control over the military and strengthened his position with the Bedouin by uprooting the fedayeen in the south, but the guerillas continued to hold parts of Amman and significant territory in the north. Although much of the fedayeen leadership had fled, analysts warned, their political base in Jordan remained essentially intact.[100] The crisis had shown interested observers in Washington that despite King Hussein's crackdown, the Palestinians were now, as the French had described them, a political fact.

The new situation in the region presented dangers as well as opportunities. While he had weathered the initial showdown with the fedayeen, King Hussein's battle was not yet over. The situation was especially fluid given that Nasser's death on 28 September 1970 would reshape the dynamics of inter-Arab relations and lead Moscow to move to retain or strengthen its position in Cairo. The need to prevent the "further radicalization and alienation of the Palestinians, which has implications not only for Jordan but for Lebanon and for the whole course of future settlement prospects," was of paramount concern for the White House. While the events of September had hurt the guerillas, they would eventually rebuild. This resurgent, more radical fedayeen movement would likely move against moderate Arab regimes such as those in Amman and Beirut. Meanwhile, the greater part of the Palestinian population remained destitute. With Nasser dead, the "future trend of Palestinian opinion and loyalties will depend on who offers them the most hope of getting out of the squeeze they find themselves in and of helping them realize their national identity."[101]

U.S. officials were devoting more attention to the question of how to deal with the Palestinians and the PLO in the wake of the Jordanian crisis. In a June speech, Joseph Sisco, assistant secretary of state for Near Eastern and South Asian affairs, warned that time was not on the side of local governments, Arab or Israeli: "This is because the area is in ferment—the Palestinian movement which is committed to a solution by force is crystallizing into a much more formidable political movement centering on the idea of the need to satisfy the aspirations and the concerns of the Palestinians by means of some kind of a political entity."[102]

While they remained cautious, some State Department officials argued that Washington should consider recognizing the PLO. Ambassador Charles Yost wrote from the United Nations that the latest General Assembly debate had shown that the "Palestinian movement as a political entity has come to be recognized as an essential element in any peaceful settlement." However, like U.S. officers in the Arab world, the U.S. mission in New York believed—as did a number of Arab governments—that the movement was in turmoil, with no clear leader who could claim to represent the entire diaspora. Moreover, Yost suggested that a U.S. approach to the fedayeen could risk bestowing greater influence on the movement. Nevertheless, Washington "should move quickly to develop [a] new, forward-looking approach to [the] Palestinians." Such an approach could prompt them to begin working within the political process rather than trying to play a spoiling role. This development might also circumscribe the influence of the PRC and more-radical elements within the PLO itself as well as preempting potential Soviet moves to transfer support away from Arab governments and toward the fedayeen.[103]

Yost continued by noting that recent public statements by U.S. officials had given the impression that Washington's thinking was coming around to a more positive outlook on the Palestinian role: "We should not let [this] momentum die." Although it was probably too soon to approach Palestinian leaders, he said, Washington should consider opening a dialogue with those Arab governments that might exercise influence over the Palestinians. Ultimately, the Arab governments should be encouraged to develop proposals for a resolution to the Palestinian problem and to act as "political godparents for any contacts by the US and others of the four [powers] with the Palestinians." Cooperation between the Arab governments and the Palestinians toward a political settlement might open a path to an eventual solution.[104] According to journalist David Ignatius, the CIA had in fact attempted to establish just such a dialogue between Washington and the PLO as early as 1969, when Robert Ames made contact with one of Arafat's lieutenants, Ali Hassan Salameh, in Beirut. While this channel would be temporarily closed in late 1970, Salameh would emerge in later years as a key connection between the PLO and the CIA and a source of intelligence on more-radical Palestinian groups that might target U.S. officials.[105]

The question of who was actually in control of the PLO represented an ongoing dilemma for U.S. policy makers. Although no single organization could claim uncontested political leadership within the diaspora, some State Department analysts suggested that power within the fedayeen movement was being consolidated in the hands of larger groups. In particular, Fatah's relative influence in the movement seemed to have increased as smaller factions disappeared. The split between Arafat's Fatah and Habash's PFLP now seemed to represent the major fissure within the PLO. Analysts noted that the confrontation in Jordan had done little to alter the top leadership in the PLO, adding that Yasir Arafat was still the central figure. The struggle between moderate and extremist wings of both organizations would play out alongside the struggle between the Jordanian government and the fedayeen. Although the guerillas had now come to see King Hussein as the enemy, many had resolved to adopt a " 'low profile' policy instead of a collision course with the Jordanians. The next few months will tell whether they will proceed from this relatively passive stance to a more active one."[106]

Other State Department officers were more skeptical of the PLO's ability to function as a partner in peace. The U.S. embassy in Amman insisted that Fatah did not represent a majority of Palestinians, and it was skeptical about the prospect of the guerillas having a "responsible" role in peace negotiations. Indeed, the fedayeen had denounced the Rogers initiative and, only two weeks before, had been calling for the destruction of King Hussein's regime. Moreover, because the perception of a U.S. preference for Israel was so deeply ingrained, a dialogue between Washington and the guerillas might not bring any dividends in the realm of public opinion. Such a dialogue could in fact undermine Arab moderates in the region.[107]

Likewise, embassy officers in Amman warned that the fedayeen should be considered radicals even in the Arab world and were likely to drift leftward in the wake of the fighting in Jordan. "The overwhelming popular support among Palestinians on both banks for a peaceful solution," they suggested, "indicate that on this most important issue, [the] fedayeen speak basically for themselves." Moreover, the contested nature of leadership within the movement meant that any approach from Washington to leaders such as Arafat would be seen as a "potential kiss of death." Rather than seeking a formal approach—especially given the uncertain future of events in Jordan following a particularly bloody civil war—officials recommended that informal contacts with the fedayeen be expanded, adding a suggestion: officers should seek to establish ongoing contacts with Palestinian notables on both banks who had remained politically independent of the fedayeen. While these individuals were not to be regarded as an alternative to the regime in Amman and the PLO, some argued they enjoyed a degree of traditional respect that might be used to expand the power base of the Jordanian government.[108] The State Department's focus had begun to shift away from the antiquated view that the old urban notables might represent the emerging Palestinian nation.[109]

Officials in Washington remained wary of the PLO, informing U.S. embassies in mid-October 1970 that although informal contacts with the fedayeen were acceptable, officers should not appear to be in search of them. However, in light of recent events, the department believed that the time had come to take account of Washington's assets among the Palestinians and reassess the ways in which they might be used in hopes of forwarding the Arab-Israeli peace process. In particular, moderate Arab regimes such as those in Tunis, Rabat, or Amman might play a role in bringing the Palestinians into the peace process. Concerns remained, however, about whether a dialogue with the PLO might result in the radicalization of those moderate Arab governments that Washington hoped to use as intermediaries.[110] U.S. officers in the Gulf States were similarly wary of what they saw as the PLO's ability to foment internal subversion given the large number of Palestinians working in the region.[111]

The U.S. consulate in Jerusalem offered another perspective, arguing that the only practical solution would be the creation of a unified East and West Jordan in which the Palestinians would enjoy much greater political participation. Under this scheme, King Hussein should remain the head of state because the king—with Washington's support—had the best hopes of achieving a satisfactory settlement with Israel. However, the United States should avoid the appearance of giving more support to the Palestinians, for fear of undermining King Hussein in his struggle with the fedayeen and backing the still-disorganized and relatively amorphous idea of Palestinianism. Any effort to broaden Washington's contacts among the Palestinians was unlikely to result in significant short-term gains for the United States so long as American policy remained firmly behind Israel and Jordan.[112]

NSC staff also recognized the importance of finding some way to deal with the changing situation in the wake of September's events, but Kissinger was loath to consider active engagement with the guerillas. The SRG judged that, in light of the possibility that the PLO might declare itself a government in exile as well as Fatah's recent approaches to the United States, the time had come to make some sort of decision as to how to deal with the fedayeen. Noting that the king had declared his intention to resist the creation of a West Bank entity outside of his control, the group faced a key decision: "Should the U.S. go on putting all its bets on Hussein—to the tune of another $120 million or so in arms—or should we regard the Palestinians as the wave of the future and move very cautiously on arms aid to Hussein?" One perspective suggested that the creation of a Palestinian state would be in Washington's best interests if its leadership would make peace with Israel. However, participants were skeptical about the possibility of such moderation on the part of the Palestinians. In light of this uncertainty and the perception that the prospects for an Israeli-Palestinian settlement were ultimately unrealistic, the group resolved to follow Hussein's lead. "We should continue to operate on the assumption that Palestinian objectives can best be met—albeit only partially—through the current negotiating process in which King Hussein serves in effect as their spokesman." While the U.S. government should encourage the king to bring more Palestinians into the negotiations, King Hussein would retain Washington's favor. Meanwhile, policy makers would do their best to "make clear to the Palestinians that we have their best interests very much in mind."[113] In practical terms, however, keeping Palestinian interests "in mind" meant rearming the regime that was in the process of crushing the PLO, along with several thousand civilians who happened to be in the way.

A background paper for the decision to grant Jordan's request for U.S. weapons explained why Washington would continue to back Amman. As one of the "few Arab leaders who sincerely wants and is willing to take risks for a peace settlement with Israel," King Hussein sought a policy that complemented U.S. efforts to seek a negotiated peace in the region. However, the regime's ability to survive without U.S. support in the face of external pressure from Syria and Iraq as well as internal threats from the fedayeen remained doubtful. As part of his request, the king noted that Amman had ceased to look upon Israel as the primary threat to its security: "Jordan, today, is a battlefield of different ideologies and approaches, and Jordan could be used as a base that could alter the face of the Middle East." The paper thus recommended that Amman's principal arms requests be granted.[114]

In a memo to the president, Kissinger outlined his rationale. The crisis in Jordan had brought the Palestinian question "to the fore." Particularly noteworthy were reports that Arafat was seeking to establish a Palestinian state with the support of neighboring Arab governments. Nevertheless, he argued, it was impossible to know the extent of Palestinian support for this idea given that Fatah had no following among the leadership in the West Bank and that the Palestinians in the refugee camps were "captive to the fedayeen."

The substantial Palestinian populations in Kuwait and Saudi Arabia were, according to Kissinger, "more interested in making money than in organizing themselves politically." For his part, King Hussein—whose security apparatus was in the process of crushing the guerillas—preferred a solution in which the occupied territories would be returned to Jordanian sovereignty and then granted some autonomy under a federated system. While Kissinger noted that one could argue for the long-term logic of creating a Palestinian state, he warned that the most viable incarnation of such a state would include Jordan and the occupied territories under Palestinian leadership.[115]

Although events in Jordan might be leading to such an outcome in the future, the PLO's position vis-à-vis Israel remained a sticking point for the time being. Kissinger worried that a Palestinian state would not in fact support a peace with Israel. Thus, a move to support the creation of a Palestinian state "could be read as backing away from Hussein—who is prepared to make peace with Israel and give the Palestinians political autonomy—in favor of a political group dedicated so far as we know to changing the Jewish character of Israel." The only reasonable option, Kissinger concluded, was to continue working with Amman and strengthening the king's efforts to bring the Palestinians into the political process.[116] These were strong conclusions by a man who had claimed to know little about and have virtually no influence over U.S.-Middle East relations.

Ultimately, Kissinger's argument in support of the status quo would win out and the momentum in the State Department for some sort of concerted action on the Palestine issue was lost.[117] While it would be wrong to attribute uncontested leadership of the fedayeen to Arafat, Fatah was consistently cited by the State Department and various Arab officials as the dominant organization within the PLO—a position it would retain into the next century. Moreover, the PLO itself was clearly the most dynamic force of Palestinian nationalism following the 1967 war. In this light, Washington's concerns about not knowing which Palestinians to approach appear somewhat disingenuous. A more satisfying explanation can be found in Nixon and Kissinger's claims that the White House hoped to create a stalemate in the Arab-Israeli conflict that would eventually sway the Arab world away from Moscow. The administration's determination to craft global strategies had trumped the need to address the local dynamics of Palestinian nationalism and the changing political landscape of the Arab world.

"This Will Be Us, and That Will Be Israel"

For its part, in late 1970 the PLO was beginning to entertain the idea of a political solution to its liberation struggle. The various guerilla factions maintained their strong opposition to the creation of a Palestinian state in the occupied territories in the wake of the Jordanian war. Arafat warned, "We will oppose the establishment of this state to the last member of the Palestinian people for the day that such a state is established it will mean the end of the entire Palestinian cause." The fedayeen feared that a rump state, stripped of Jerusalem and Gaza, was likely to be a puppet of Israel and a bane to the PLO's already abysmal relationship with Amman. Moreover, because the PLO had been devastated in the recent showdown with King Hussein, it seemed highly unlikely that the organization would have control of such a state. Rather, it feared the leadership of a Palestinian state in the West Bank would be composed of collaborators with Jordan and Israel. The creation of a Palestinian ministate would thus entail a dual threat to the PLO: either the organization would be locked out of a leadership role in the new Palestine or it would run the risk of becoming trapped by the task of administering an economically and strategically unviable state that lived at the mercy of the PLO's two greatest enemies, Israel and Jordan. Such a scenario had little appeal for the fedayeen in late 1970. The PLO would have to rebuild its strength before entertaining the prospect of any political settlement.[118]

However, Arafat signaled privately that the prospect of creating of a Palestinian state alongside Israel was gaining traction among PLO moderates. "We need a change of tactics," he told Soviet intelligence officer Yevgeny Primakov in Damascus in mid-1971. "We cannot affect the outcome of the political settlement unless we participate in it." Palestinian interests would not be served by the restoration of Jordanian rule in the West Bank and Egyptian authority in Gaza. "We want to see a Palestinian state on these territories," he confessed. Arafat then drew a map of Palestine divided into Israeli and Palestinian sections, "This will be us and that will be Israel." On this he was clear, at least according to Primakov: "The Palestinians see the establishment of a Palestinian state as the way toward a political settlement, not the implementation of UN Security Council resolution 242."[119]

The UN stance on the Palestinian issue was also changing. While leaders in Washington resolved to boost their support for King Hussein's efforts both to crush the fedayeen and to stand as the international representative for the Palestinian people, the UN General Assembly passed a resolution on 30 November expressing its concern that "many peoples are still denied the right to self-determination and are still subject to colonial and alien domination," affirming the legitimacy of resistance struggles in Palestine and South Africa against foreign rule, and recognizing the right of said struggles to "receive all kinds of moral and material assistance." The resolution also condemned the South African and Israeli governments in particular for the denial of the right of self-determination to "the peoples of southern Africa and Palestine."[120] On 8 December, the General Assembly passed another resolution that reaffirmed the right to Palestinian self-determination and called on Israel to take immediate steps for the "return of the displaced persons.[121] Although they carried little material weight, these resolutions were evidence of Palestinian victories in the emerging global public sphere and the growing divide between the United States and the majority of the world community on issues such as Palestine and South Africa. For many observers around the world, Palestinian appeals for independence and sovereignty were more persuasive than U.S., Jordanian, and Israeli arguments about order and stability. Because they had adopted many of their ideas and much of their imagery from postcolonial struggles in other parts of the world, Palestinian guerillas managed to gain wide international support, which would play an important role in the years to come. The appeal of this revolution was, however, precisely what U.S. policy makers such as Nixon and Kissinger hoped to foil.

Although the clash with the guerillas forced a reconsideration of the Palestinian question in Washington, the episode resulted in a hardening of the administration's attitudes about the fedayeen rather than a fundamental change in U.S. policy. Despite signs that the Palestinian guerillas represented a new force in Arab affairs that was unlikely to disappear in the near future, the White House chose to reaffirm its support for King Hussein. Rather than deal with the new situation in the Middle East occasioned by the arrival of the fedayeen, policy makers opted to redouble their efforts to turn back the clock by recasting the Jordanians alongside the Israelis as important representatives of U.S. interests in the region and bulwarks against the sort of radicalism represented by the fedayeen.

The September showdown thus confirmed Kissinger's logic of treating Israel as a strategic asset in the region, serving to bind U.S. and Israeli security interests closer together. Israeli reprisals against the PLO might interfere with the State Department's diplomatic efforts, but they provided the type of aggressive approach that the White House seemed to be looking for. Israel was fast proving its value as a key strategic asset in the Middle East and a model regional policeman in the Third World. In this respect, Israel's active defense strategies fit remarkably well into Nixon and Kissinger's designs for the emerging post-Vietnam global order in which local allies would bear most of the responsibility for maintaining security and combating upheavals in the developing world. The men in the White House would have been hard pressed to find a state that was more deserving of Nixon Doctrine aid than Israel. In the coming years, U.S. aid to Israel reflected the expansion of this strategic relationship. While U.S. military aid to Israel had amounted to only $7 million in 1967, the Nixon administration managed to secure some $2.5 billion worth of military assistance for Israel in 1974, making that country the foremost recipient of U.S. foreign aid.[122]

Though an official alliance would not be created, the Nixon administration consummated Washington's "special relationship" with Israel in the years following the 1967 war. From 1971 onward, the Nixon White House would insist on the need to preserve what it called the "military balance" in the region, largely in response to Soviet arms shipments to Egypt and Syria. As was dramatically demonstrated by virtually every military engagement during the period, as well as by the statements of Israeli political and military leaders, however, the "military balance" in the region sat decisively in Israel's favor. Preservation of the status quo meant, in practical terms, maintaining IDF military supremacy over its neighbors. Israel must be understood as a core component of the Nixon administration's strategy in the Middle East.

Kissinger remained a key advocate for this strategic relationship with Israel, but other voices in Washington had begun to question the wisdom of the Nixon administration's posture in the Middle East. In October 1969, NSC aide Harold Saunders sent Kissinger what the former regarded as "perhaps the most important" memo he had written during Nixon's time in office. Saunders warned that Washington was on the verge of switching from an even-handed policy in the Middle East to a position in which regional strategy would be based "exclusively" on Israel. By channeling massive amounts of weaponry to Israel, yielding to Israeli nuclear capacities, and assenting to the continued occupation of Arab territories, the White House was on the brink of being committed to "Israel in a way that we have never before accepted."[123]

Saunders' voice was not the only one warning against this new approach. Secretary of Defense Melvin Laird sent a memo in 1971 warning Nixon that the glut of arms shipments to the Israeli government was ultimately not in Washington's best interests. Citing the Pentagon's intelligence analysis, Laird reiterated that Israel enjoyed "overwhelming military superiority" over the Arab forces. Indeed, given the large numbers of aircraft shipments from the United States, Israel currently had more warplanes than trained pilots. Moreover, the White House's strategy of channeling more arms to Israel had the effect of forcing the Arab states to allow greater Soviet penetration of their military and political institutions. An added concern was that while Moscow was arming the Arab states with primarily defensive weapons systems, Washington was outfitting the IDF with offensive armaments. Current policies associated the United States "dangerously with Israeli developments over which we have no control," Laird told the president. "Specifically, Israeli production of highly sophisticated and special-purpose weapons introduces a critical new factor in the Middle East military equation which will reflect on the USG most disadvantageously if and when the full story eventually surfaces." Ultimately, the strategy of arming Israel to the teeth robbed the United States of political leverage over the Jewish state, reduced its diplomatic flexibility in the region, and associated Washington with Israeli military and political positions that were not in the United States' best interests.[124]

Stapled to the cover of the NSC's copy was a dismissive note to Kissinger claiming that Laird's approach to Israel would "break all the crockery that is left. He would push the Israelis hard with no leverage left." Kissinger apparently agreed. In an NSC meeting with the president several days before,

Kissinger had stressed that, for the Israelis, military balance meant the ability to defeat its Arab neighbors quickly. In other words, for Kissinger and the Israeli government, balance meant superiority. Three weeks later, in a meeting with Ambassador Rabin, Kissinger dangled the issue of military aircraft in front of the ambassador as an incentive to proceed with interim agreements with Cairo. Kissinger had no intention of scaling back American arms shipments to Israel.[125]

This reality was not lost on contemporary observers. In early July 1971, one Israeli journalist asked Ambassador Rabin if the United States now considered "Israel to be part of the Western defence deployment." Rabin did not go so far as to agree, replying that Washington had made no "formal obligation to come to Israel's assistance with troops" and that the United States had extensive interests among the Arab states, not just Israel. However, he did say "that the United States recognizes the fact that a country called Israel, a strong democratic state, is capable of defending itself with its own forces in a localized dispute if it receives the necessary monetary, military and political aid." Moreover, U.S. leaders understood that Israel was "far closer to the US spirit and understanding of how a country should be run than probably any other country in the Middle East." Though they might disagree over the appropriate level of aid flowing from the United States to Israel, one thing was clear: Washington's diplomatic support was critical on the international stage. "In my opinion," Rabin revealed, "everything that takes place [at the United Nations] is meaningless.... As long as the United States does not support resolutions of the type passed at the 25th UN Assembly [in criticism of Israel and in support of Palestinian self-determination], these resolutions have no significance." Ultimately, he remarked, what "is more important is what concerns the United States, because we have not received a single dollar, a single bullet, a single aircraft, and no economic assistance from the United Nations." Thus the "hostility of the world as manifested at the United Nations" was, in Rabin's eyes, "useless and meaningless."[126]

Though it consummated the "special relationship" between the United States and Israel and bolstered the regime in Amman, the September war was no one-sided affair. The crackdown in Jordan would help transform the PLO and Arafat into archetypes of the global offensive, further internationalizing the resistance. The brutality of Hussein's crackdown as well as the amount of international attention it attracted won sympathy for the Palestinian cause in forums such as the Conference of Non-Aligned States and the UN General Assembly. Moreover, the conflict marked a split between King Hussein and the fedayeen that carried ambiguous results. Although the PLO was unquestionably hurt by their clash with King Hussein's army—a fact that would become more apparent in the coming months—the conflict demonstrated that the fedayeen problem could not be solved by military means alone. Though bloodied, the guerrillas had shown themselves to be a political force in both regional and international affairs. King Hussein's victory over the guerillas and his continuing counterinsurgency campaign in the north cut off their main field of cross-border operations and forced the fedayeen to shift their attention to Lebanon. The war in Jordan marked the boundary of Arab support for PLO and the upper limit of fedayeen guerilla capability and signaled the beginning of a new stage in the Palestinian resistance movement in which the primary task of the armed struggle would shift from liberation to defense of the revolution.[127]

Ultimately, the Black September crisis, like the massacre at Deir Yassin and the Battle of al-Karama, would come to symbolize a watershed in the Palestinian liberation narrative. This symbolic dimension was captured in the October 1970 edition of Fatah's newsletter, which carried on its cover a picture of a guerilla perched with a rifle atop a pile of wreckage overlooking a city street. The picture's caption was a quotation from Frantz Fanon: "In all armed struggles, there exists what we might call the point of no return. Almost always it is marked off by a huge and all inclusive repression."[128] Although their military strength lay buried in the ashes of Amman, the fragments of the guerilla movement would regroup to present a new and more radical threat to the regional and international status quo in the coming years. After its near-expulsion from Jordan, the PLO would move into Lebanon and begin to transform its tactics. The 1970 war and its repercussions set the stage for the next act in the story of the Palestinian struggle, which would transform the global arena into a battlefield in the PLO's war with Israel.

A Worldwide Interlocking Terrorist Network

In the early morning hours of 5 September 1972, five Palestinian guerillas from a shadowy group calling itself the Black September Organization scaled the fence surrounding the Olympic Village in Munich and made their way to a building that housed members of the Israeli Olympic team. At approximately 6:00 a.m., the guerillas stormed into the Israeli apartments, killing two and taking another nine hostage. German police and marksmen took positions in and around the building by seven-thirty, and a standoff ensued. The gunmen demanded the release of a group of fedayeen prisoners from Israeli jails. "We are not highwaymen or thieves," they insisted. "We are not killers or shedders of blood." At 10:00 p.m., after hours of negotiations, the guerillas and their hostages boarded a bus and then three military helicopters, which then took them to Fürstenfeldbruck Airport outside of Munich. Shortly after the group arrived, German police opened fire, initiating a firefight during which the fedayeen executed all nine hostages. In addition, one German policeman and four guerillas were killed in the exchange. After news of the killings broke, Black September announced that the guerillas who carried out the Munich operation had achieved their goals by terrifying the world, adding, "Long live the revolutionaries of the world who are fighting for freedom, justice and peace."[1]

Although they presented a defiant face to the outside world, the Palestinian guerilla movement was suffering from internal turmoil throughout 1972. On the day of the attack, the U.S. embassy in Beirut released a report describing the PLO as being in disarray. Arafat and the moderates in Fatah were being squeezed by internal schisms as well as outside pressures and heavy limitations imposed by the Arab governments. Extremists within the movement were "seemingly obsessed with the idea that the 'flame of the Palestinian revolution' be kept alive until it can provoke some future political conflagration through-out the Arab world." The result had been a sharp increase in external operations and a move into "what appears an increasingly nihilistic phase in order to show their feelings about the rest of the world, stepping-up collaboration with like-minded groups outside the Middle East in order to strike at selected targets in Western Europe and elsewhere." While outsiders could pressure the guerillas to curtail their terrorist activities, many Saudis, Kuwaitis, Syrians, and Egyptians "may also feel that a little 'protection money' is the best way to avoid appearing on some feda'i's assassination list." Thus, while the general military power of the guerilllas had been undercut, their ability to launch external attacks—fueled by a "burning desire...to strike out recklessly and almost blindly in order to show the world and their enemies that the Palestinian spark has not been extinguished and the Palestinians are a force which must be reckoned with"—remained intact. While they could not unify the movement or liberate Palestine, these external operations would preserve Palestinian power as a force in the Middle East.[2]

The Munich operation would be the most spectacular episode in the PLO's campaign of international violence in the early 1970s. As Palestinian fighters regrouped in Lebanon, they renewed their guerilla struggle through a combination of external operations and efforts to extend their networks of international support. However, Munich and Black September were emblematic of a deep crisis within the ranks of the fedayeen following their expulsion from Jordan. Factionalism within the embattled PLO threatened to pull the movement apart at the same time that Israel and the United States grappled with the challenge of responding to spectacular acts of violence such as Munich. These efforts were severely circumscribed, however, by the success of Palestinian diplomacy in forums such as the United Nations, particularly among African states. The rise of the Black September Organization would thus come to personify the fury of the PLO's global offensive in the 1970s.

Sanctuary in Lebanon

The war in Jordan had taken a heavy and extended toll on the PLO. In late October 1970, King Hussein instructed his newly appointed prime minister, Wasfi al-Tal, to begin purging Palestinians from the ranks of the Jordanian state. As Jordanian intelligence services stepped up covert operations against the PLO, the regime began construction in Amman of a citywide network of police stations designed to protect vital installations and enforce order throughout the capital. Meanwhile, Jordanian security forces—equipped with weapons recently acquired from the United States—began a new campaign to consolidate their control over Amman. In December, the army began a "creeping offensive" engineered to push the guerillas from their strongholds to the north and west of the capital and cut Palestinian fighters off from their sources of support in the refugee camps. As Jordanian troops closed the noose around the remaining guerillas, Arafat escaped to Syria to begin the difficult task of rebuilding the resistance. The climax of the offensive took place on 12 July when the king's forces besieged the fedayeen stronghold in 'Ajlun. After four days of fighting, the Jordanians achieved a complete victory, killing more than 200 guerillas and capturing 2,300 others.[3]

While the Jordanian authorities had reestablished control, the Lebanese government had good reason to be worried. As the guerillas were pushed out of Jordan in a long and bloody counterinsurgency campaign in the months following the clashes in Amman, they regrouped in Lebanon. The few U.S. officials who were paying close attention to the region saw this relocation as an indication of trouble on the horizon; the U.S.-backed Jordanian crackdown had stabilized Amman at the price of imperiling Beirut. As early as November 1970, Foreign Service officers were warning that the fedayeen were renting properties in strategic positions throughout the city, a clear sign that the guerillas were looking to increase their presence in Lebanon.[4]

Lebanon, which shared a significantly shorter and more defensible border with Israel, was cut off from the West Bank and less conducive to guerilla operations than Jordan. Nevertheless, as the guerillas moved to their new sanctuaries, fedayeen attacks on Israel increased, as did threats of reprisal from Israel. Israeli officials warned that if the government of Lebanon could not restrain the guerillas, it should expect IDF intervention.[5] The key problem, in the minds of U.S. officials, was that IDF retaliation put the Lebanese government in a dangerous position, caught between the need to show strength in the face of Israeli attacks and the need to reestablish control over the guerillas and its own territory.[6]

Although retaliatory operations might encourage Beirut to increase its efforts to control the fedayeen in the short term, they risked creating even greater problems in the future. As the situation spiraled further out of control, the IDF announced that it was considering moving its forces north into a permanent occupation of southern Lebanon. State Department officials in Lebanon warned that this might undermine Beirut's authority at the precise moment it had stepped up its efforts to control the fedayeen. U.S. government support for the governments of both Lebanon and Israel made the situation even more complicated. By failing to respond to Israeli threats, Washington gave the impression that it did not support the Lebanese. Reluctance to support Beirut against the Israeli attacks, they warned, might hurt Washington's position in Lebanon and lead to a change in Beirut's long-standing moderate policies. A narrow focus on Israeli interests, some argued, even when they jeopardized the stability of neighboring states, was not an effective strategy for maintaining U.S. influence in the region.[7]

The voice behind these dissenting cables belonged to William Buffum, a career Foreign Service officer who had spent most of the 1950s in West Germany and the greater part of the 1960s working with the United Nations.

Born in Binghamton, New York, the future diplomat attended Oneonta State Teachers College before earning a master's degree at the University of Pittsburgh, after which he joined the army and served in World War II. Appointed to the post of ambassador to Beirut on 21 September 1970, in the darkest hours of the conflict in Jordan, Buffum would be tasked with the job of watching Lebanon slide toward its own civil war. Like his predecessor, Dwight Porter, Buffum reminded his superiors that Lebanon remained a pivotal state in the Middle East, occupying a "position of strategic importance completely disproportionate to its size." The Soviets were making concerted efforts to increase their influence in Lebanon and the PRC had opened its first diplomatic mission. The Lebanese government was thus under increasing pressure from left-wing elements both at home and abroad. The ambassador argued that Washington should make some gesture to affirm its support of Beirut. Coming on the heels of recent Lebanese moves to bring pressure on the PLO, such a gesture would reiterate U.S. support for moderates in the Arab world.[8]

The situation grew worse in February 1972 when a fedayeen bazooka attack killed two Israeli civilians and the IDF retaliated by launching a four-day invasion of southern Lebanon designed to root out guerilla sanctuaries. Although the Israeli government assured Washington that the raid was nothing more than a quick search-and-destroy operation, IDF units remained in Lebanon for some time, prompting Beirut to take the matter—against U.S. wishes—to the Security Council.[9]

Despite a substantial outcry over the invasion, officials in Washington refused to demand a reduction in the scope of IDF reprisals, explaining that Israel faced significant domestic pressures when civilians were killed. At the same time, Washington pressured its Lebanese allies to keep the matter away from the United Nations. Should the Lebanese government choose to lodge a complaint with the Security Council, it would be faced with a no-win situation. Any resolution acceptable to the Lebanese would be predominantly critical of Israel, without extensive attention paid to the larger context of fedayeen attacks. While such a resolution would probably win a majority in the Security Council, it would exacerbate the differences between Lebanon and the United States. Thus, from Washington's perspective, a "Security Council debate on this incident could only be detrimental; it would provide [a] heyday for [the] Soviets, Chinese and Arab extremists, and we do not see how it could serve Lebanese interests in [the] long run or be other than harmful to US-[Lebanese] relations."[10] In essence, Washington advised Beirut to sit back and take whatever punishment Israel chose to offer.

Walworth Barbour, U.S. ambassador to Tel Aviv, further pushed this way of thinking, reporting that nothing within reason could be done to dissuade Israeli retaliations, and adding that international assurances of respect for Lebanese territorial integrity would, paradoxically, only encourage further violence from Israel. Because the threat of Israeli retaliation could lead the Lebanese to crack down on the guerillas, the removal of this threat was likely to prompt a decrease in efforts to control the fedayeen and a subsequent rise in guerilla operations. This rise would, in turn, lead to an intensification of violence from the IDF. It was therefore imperative for U.S. security interests in Lebanon to preserve the threat of Israeli retaliation.[11]

The Lebanese ambassador in Washington insisted that his government had done its best to comply with U.S. wishes to avoid a Security Council discussion of the present crisis in Lebanon. He warned, however, that Israeli attacks would force his government to appeal to the United Nations. State Department officers countered that the U.S. government could not insist on an end to Israeli retaliations while terrorist attacks continued. Rather, as it had done previously, the U.S. government would seek a more balanced resolution—which was unacceptable to the Lebanese because such a resolution would seem, in their view, to suggest Lebanese culpability for the present situation. The Lebanese ambassador offered the opinion that fedayeen operations would persist as long as the Palestine question remained unsolved, adding that it had not been Beirut that had created the problem of Palestinian refugees in Lebanon. The Lebanese government had done all it could to control the guerillas, but it could not grant the government of Israel the right to carry out military operations on Lebanese soil. Such recognition would open the door for Israeli incursions further north, into the heart of the country. The ambassador cautioned that U.S.-Lebanese relations were at a "possible turning point" if Washington could not find the means to support Lebanon in the Security Council on this matter.[12]

Watching events from Amman, Jordanian officials—recalling their own campaign against the fedayeen from the previous year—predicted that the Lebanese army could defeat the guerillas in a confrontation, but they feared that the "worst was yet to come." The fedayeen would gather in Lebanese cities, and, due to the open nature of those cities, bloody urban warfare was likely to break out.[13] Even so, some observers pointed to the Jordanian experience as a potential blueprint for what Lebanon might be able to accomplish with the fedayeen. Ambassador Buffum, however, attacked analogies between Beirut's current position and Amman's situation in September 1970, saying, "Lebanon is not Jordan." The smaller, less well-equipped Lebanese military would have a more difficult time with the guerillas than the Jordanian army. This relative weakness, coupled with sectarian tensions, the Lebanese system of democratic government, the vulnerability of Lebanese cities to terrorism, and the dual threats of foreign intervention and confessional strife, suggested that a confrontation with the guerillas would probably be "vicious, protracted and bloody."[14] The prescience of the ambassador's predictions would become apparent in the coming years.

Meanwhile, in Israel, the Palestinian question had become less urgent following Amman's crackdown. Public discussions of the PLO in statements by

Israeli officials declined during 1971, as did the number of fedayeen attacks. One reporter for Israel Defense Forces Radio went so far as to ask Chief of Staff Chaim Bar Lev whether he even considered them as a "tangible" military factor at all. Bar Lev responded that while the guerillas could not "be discounted altogether," they were "at present in a very low state." However, he warned that even in this diminished capacity the PLO was still a threat. Indeed, lacking the ability to launch a sustained guerilla campaign into Israel and the West Bank, Palestinian fighters might "direct their efforts at other vulnerable targets," such as civil aviation. Regardless, he was adamant that Israel should not "acquiesce in restoration of the situation on any spot along our border to what it was previously." Whatever might come, Israel must remain steadfast.[15] As late as August 1972, Deputy Prime Minister Allon remarked, "Terrorism has been eliminated all along the frontiers, stability has increased...the eastern front...[of] the Arab war against Israel has collapsed." At the same time, voices in Israel called upon the government to use the IDF to support settlement in the West Bank. In April, Moshe Dayan argued that Israel should begin preparations to establish permanent control over the occupied territories, particularly the West Bank. The majority of Israel's population, Dayan said, wanted Israelis to have the right to live anywhere they chose in the territory. Thus, he called upon the state to establish a "security line" that was "identical with the river Jordan."[16]

In the wake of the conflict in Jordan, U.S. officials also wondered about the larger prospects for order in the region and whether the PLO might be in retreat. For Secretary of State William Rogers, the fedayeen remained a concern—particularly in light of reports that they were receiving Soviet support—but he was skeptical about their potential resurgence. In February 1972, President Nixon warned Congress that the United States must remain committed to shaping "new patterns of order" in the Middle East, Asia, and Africa. In the Middle East, Nixon affirmed his commitment to maintain the present military balance in the face of Soviet efforts to rearm its Arab allies. Moscow sought to exploit regional tensions to "expand its own military position in Egypt...to gain the use of naval and air facilities." This move had "serious implications" for the current regional and global balance of power. He also explained that the Palestinian struggle was still a force that threatened to undermine stability and menaced friendly governments, with the help of outside support. Nixon would not permit the search for peace and a new regional order to be derailed by these forces.[17] In August, Assistant Secretary of State Joseph Sisco reiterated this determination to maintain the military balance in the region as well as the wider world. "It must continue to be bulwarked by a strong American presence in the Mediterranean," he told the Convention of Jewish War Veterans of the USA. "Diplomacy must have teeth to be credible in the area." However, he warned that current hostilities gave "continuing opportunity to our adversary for penetration in the area," and thus he insisted that diplomacy must move forward. Sisco reminded his audience that there were ongoing peace negotiations on the Korean peninsula, between the two Germanys, in South Asia, and between Washington and Beijing. "If we can talk to the Viet Cong every day in Paris—then the force of the argument that the Middle East must remain a unique exception in this regard is weak and unrealistic." This might not mean direct talks immediately, but progress must continue.[18]

Defending the Revolution

The months following their expulsion from Jordan found the various factions of the PLO in the midst of a vigorous debate over the lessons of the war and the challenge of creating guerilla sanctuaries inside sovereign states while remaining aloof from the internal political affairs of those states. The Popular Front groups insisted that defeat was the result of a failure to align with the forces of popular resistance in Jordan. The fedayeen had not devoted enough attention to the revolution in the Arab world and thus had not built enough support among the Jordanian population. Fatah, conversely, argued that the confrontation should have been avoided altogether. Citing the long-held principle of nonintervention in the domestic affairs of Arab governments, leaders including Arafat argued that the conflict with Jordanian authorities had sidetracked the real struggle against the Israeli occupation of Palestine. In the wake of the war in Jordan, Fatah became even more wary of dependence on any one Arab state for support. This debate between radicals and moderates in the PLO had clear implications for Lebanon as the focus of fedayeen power moved from Amman to Beirut.[19]

The U.S.- and Israeli-backed Jordanian offensive against the PLO that had pushed the organization into Lebanon and generated a crisis among the fedayeen had another unanticipated side effect: the rise in "external operations"— what critics would denounce as "international terrorism"—in late 1971 and 1972. While such operations had been undertaken primarily by the PFLP in earlier years, several factors led other elements in the PLO to turn to these tactics after 1970. From a practical standpoint, the new sanctuaries in Lebanon were less conducive to guerilla operations. Located farther from Israeli population centers and lying across a more easily defended frontier, fedayeen bases in Lebanon afforded fewer opportunities for traditional guerilla tactics. At the same time, the defeat at the hands of King Hussein's security forces had been a major blow to existing leadership structures within the PLO. In particular, Arafat's role as chairman had come into question, and power struggles soon emerged within the various groups. Both challengers and established authorities needed tangible success in the form of successful military operations to bolster their claims to leadership; external operations seemed to provide the best available options for such demonstrations.[20] At the same time, these external operations generated a movement toward what can be described as the globalization of the Palestinian armed struggle. While the PLO's political efforts had long taken place in the international sphere, 1972 saw the fedayeen launch an unprecedented number of guerilla operations abroad.

For many Palestinian fighters, the first order of business called for revenge against the architects of King Hussein's brutal crackdown in Jordan. Vengeance came on 28 November 1971 as Jordanian prime minister Wasfi al-Tal was visiting Cairo for a meeting of the Arab League. As he entered the lobby of the Sheraton Hotel on the banks of the Nile River, four men approached Tal and his entourage, firing four shots point-blank into the prime minister. As he lay dying on the floor, Tal gasped: "They have killed me. Murderers . . . they believe only in fire and destruction."[21] Conflicting reports of the PFLP's denial of responsibility for Tal's assassination led U.S. officials to focus their suspicions on Fatah. Arafat received news of Tal's death via telephone during a meeting with Palestinian students and was reportedly shaken. The following day, Fatah's newspaper, *Hisad al-'Asifa*, issued an official statement from an unknown group, the Black September Organization, claiming responsibility for Tal's death. The statement warned other Arab leaders not to interfere with Palestinian rights and praised the execution of Tal, "that digger of graves."[22]

The guerillas' ability to assassinate a leader of Tal's status in a foreign capital signaled a new direction in fedayeen violence. State Department officers in Beirut speculated that the operation had been carried out by radical elements within Fatah, most likely without Arafat's knowledge. One Lebanese journalist claimed that Black September was an unofficial faction within Fatah composed of a "suicide-band of some 400 commando fanatics" trained in China, Algeria, and Syria and set in opposition to more moderate mainstream elements within the organization. In addition to serving as a dangerous new element in the guerilla movement, the appearance of Black September hinted at the depth of the rift between radical and moderate elements in Fatah and the degree to which Arafat's control of the organization had slipped.[23] An article that appeared in *Le Monde* described Black September as an "autonomous clandestine organization" composed of Fatah dissidents "charged with dangerous missions in Arab states and abroad." Originally created to prevent more radical elements in the organization from splitting off and joining the PFLP, Black September had grown into a powerful faction within Fatah under the leadership of Salah Khalaf. Khalaf, who seems to have been the only senior member of Fatah who supported Black September, faced considerable opposition from mainstream leaders, who argued that assassinations would alienate the Arab governments. With clandestine cells placed in a number of different capitals and a list of spectacular attacks planned for the future, Black September represented a threat to the leadership of Fatah and to those Arab states accused of collaboration with Amman and Washington. Indeed, it is doubtful that Arafat exercised control over Black September. Although some accounts suggest that Arafat oversaw Black September's operations, they present no clear evidence.[24]

The more plausible interpretation is that Arafat was forced to tolerate Black September operations prior to early 1973 but had little knowledge of their details. Helena Cobban argues that it is "extremely doubtful" that the creation of Black September was the result of a unanimous or even majority decision among Fatah's leadership. Alan Hart, a BBC correspondent who wrote a controversial, highly sympathetic, semiauthorized biography of Arafat, notes that while Black September was able to exploit many of Fatah's communications and intelligence assets, it drew recruits from other guerilla groups and maintained its own leadership structure under Ali Hassan Salameh, Abu Yusuf, and Kamal Adwan. The organization also was the target of private criticism from Fatah's more moderate leaders. As one guerilla recalled, "Arafat could not afford to speak against us in public because he knew that what we were doing had the support of the majority in the rank and file. . . . But in our private meetings he took every opportunity to tell us we were wrong." Khaled Hassan, Fatah cofounder and so-called foreign minister of the PLO, told Hart that while he was opposed to Black September's operations, he understood the logic behind the violence.

> I have to say they were wrong, and I did so at the time, but I have also to understand them. In their view, and in this they were right, the world was saying to us Palestinians, "We don't give a damn about you, and we won't care at least until you are a threat to our interests." That doesn't justify what they did, but it does explain their thinking and their actions. Perhaps one day Third World action groups will turn to terror to make you Westerners care about the poverty that is killing many millions every year.

Arafat too recognized the value of Black September's attacks, but he remained wary of the stigma of being labeled "terrorists," the punishing Israeli reprisals that such operations invited, and the likelihood that Khalaf was emerging as a potential challenger for control of Fatah. After weighing its options, Fatah's leadership decided to try to establish some measure of control over Black September in an effort to scale back the violence. As Hassan told Hart, "We had to associate ourselves with what was happening in order to give ourselves the credibility to take control of the situation and then turn off what you would call the terror tap." Had Fatah's leadership opposed such operations from the beginning, Hassan commented, "we would have lost our credibility as leaders; nobody in the rank and file of our movement would have listened to us; and the terror operations would still have taken place. And some of us would have been assassinated."[25]

Tal's assassination was planned by Salameh, Khalaf's former lieutenant, who had gone rogue following the string of PLO recriminations in the wake of the Jordan crisis. Salameh envisioned Black September as a means to "rebirth the revolution." While his early involvement remains uncertain, Khalaf soon

FIGURE 5.1 *Cover of PFLP's newspaper* Al-Hadaf. *Courtesy of the Library of the Institute for Palestine Studies, Beirut.*

came to recognize the utility of Black September's external operations as a means of boosting Palestinian morale and gaining international prestige. He had been calling for the escalation of the PLO's international operations since 1971. The PLO's battle was with not only Israel but also the United States and the "reactionary" Arab states, he maintained.[26]

Khalaf outlined his thinking on the coming phase of the guerilla struggle in an interview in mid-October with *Jeune Afrique*. In particular, he appeared to argue in support of four key changes: the formulation of a defined revolutionary strategy, the implementation of tactics based on external guerilla operations, the creation of a unified fedayeen command, and alignment with other revolutionary forces in the wider world against what he described as American imperialism. Khalaf said that one of the key problems of the guerilla movement in the run-up to the war in Jordan had been a focus on tactics rather than on a clear strategy. The coming phase, he argued, would reverse these priorities. Second, he alluded to the failure to create a united front among the various resistance organizations in contrasting the Palestinian and Algerian experiences. "In Algeria you had one front," he remarked. "We tried through the P.L.O. to regroup all the other organizations, but this experiment has not yet succeeded, and I believe that the experience of the P.L.O. must be deepened in order to effectively unite." Third, Khalaf argued that a key component of the next phase of the armed struggle would consist of external operations. "This time, we expect attacks from the most unexpected of directions and places," he said. Finally, these rejuvenated guerilla forces would operate—in conjunction with revolutionary forces in the Arab and wider worlds—with clear strategic goals against the "counterrevolutionary front" spearheaded by "American imperialism."[27]

"A World-Wide Interlocking Terrorist Network"

Disturbing as the Tal assassination had been, Western governments' fears about the international reach of the fedayeen were soon to increase: Palestinian operatives were about to take their armed operations global. On 6 February 1972, two men armed with a pistol and submachine gun burst into a basement flat outside of Cologne, West Germany, and gunned down the five occupants. *Der Spiegel* identified the victims as Jordanian agents working with either West German or Israeli authorities and attempting to infiltrate Palestinian organizations in Europe.[28] That same morning, guerillas from Black September detonated bombs at an electronics factory and on a natural gas pipeline outside Hamburg and Ravenstein.[29] On 9 February, Fatah's newspaper published a statement by Black September claiming credit for the attacks on facilities belonging to the "imperialist establishments" that had underwritten Israeli military power.[30]

The Palestinian armed struggle was no longer merely a regional threat: it had emerged as the first global resistance movement, and the PLO would soon be labeled as the first group to employ international terror tactics. The U.S. embassy in Beirut warned that the recent operations in Europe might open the door for fedayeen attacks against U.S. interests in the Middle East and elsewhere. Petroleum installations were especially vulnerable, the report warned. Moreover, PLO director Shafiq al-Hut had claimed the latest attacks in Europe as evidence that the resistance had found new battlefields, noting the benefits of attacking remote targets and warning that striking American assets was the only alternative to direct attacks on Israel. As the Arab governments stepped up their efforts to restrict guerilla attack against Israel, al-Hut warned that the fedayeen would increasingly turn to "sabotage and terrorism directed against American interests, particularly oil installations in [the Middle East]." Years later, Khalaf explained that because they had lost their sanctuary in Jordan, the young men in Fatah had chosen to carry out "a revolutionary violence of another kind, commonly known elsewhere as 'terrorism.'"[31] Ambassador Buffum also warned of rumors that guerilla groups were planning a major operation to coincide with Nixon's trip to Moscow, which he compared to similar operations launched by Vietnamese communists—the 1972 Easter Offensive—that were designed to grab world attention.[32]

On 22 February, the guerillas struck again, hijacking a German Lufthansa 747 and its 174 passengers forty-five minutes after it took off from Delhi. They demanded that the pilots fly to Aden. After releasing the passengers, the guerillas wired the aircraft with explosives and announced their intention to hold the crew as hostages to be exchanged for five Palestinian commandos being detained by the West German government. The crew was eventually freed after the West German Ministry of Transportation agreed to pay more than $5 million in ransom—delivered in a suitcase by a man wearing a black coat and carrying a copy of *Newsweek* to a car parked in the Beirut airport.[33]

While Washington and Bonn sought a more delicate approach to the problem of international terrorism, Israeli leaders had their own ideas. On 8 May, four guerillas from the Black September Organization—two women and two men armed with guns, hand grenades, and explosives—hijacked a Belgian Sabena airliner in Vienna on its way to Tel Aviv and demanded the release of approximately one hundred Israeli-held Palestinian prisoners in exchange for the hostages. After landing in Tel Aviv, the plane was surrounded by heavily armed Israeli security officers—a number of whom disabled the jet by deflating its tires and emptying its fuel tanks—and a twenty-three-hour standoff ensued. The following afternoon, Israeli commandos posing as technicians made their way onto the aircraft's wings and then burst into the cabin through the plane's emergency exits. In the ensuing firefight, the two male hijackers were killed, six passengers were wounded—one mortally—and the two female guerillas were captured.[34]

The Sabena operation did little to discourage Palestinian fighters, who remained defiant in the face of Israeli success; these counterterrorism efforts might even have contributed to an escalation in fedayeen violence. Black September announced the death of one of the hijackers in what had been a "battle of wills" between the Palestinian fighters and the Zionist authorities.[35] The organization took a defiant tone in the wake of the Israeli operation, promising that the revolution would survive intact through "blood sacrifice."[36] Fatah leaders insisted that the operation had been part of the ongoing battle against the Zionist enemy. Moreover, the incident had shown the brutality of the Israeli government and its cavalier disregard for civilian casualties.[37]

Meanwhile, the Israeli representative at the United Nations circulated a letter in New York announcing the success of the Israeli commando operation and attacking Egyptian and Lebanese media that had praised the hijackers. Because of the moral, material, and political support the Egyptian, Syrian, Lebanese, and Algerian governments had given to the Palestinian guerillas, the letter insisted, the incident reflected "not only the criminality of the activities of Arab terror organizations, but also the involvement and responsibilit[y] of the Arab governments.... The international community cannot permit the continuation of such activities."[38]

An editorial in the *Times* of London following the dramatic Israeli special forces operation commented that the hijackers' bluff had been called. "A logical assessment of the situation," the author suggested, "may lead the guerilla movement to the obvious conclusion that innocent bystanders cannot by used as political pawns." On the other hand, "the injury to Arab pride could lead to the greater extremes of the type that gave birth to the Black September organization."[39] It would not be long before this second conclusion would be proven true.

Far from being cowed by the spectacular Israeli counterterrorist operation, the PFLP rose to the challenge, engineering its own bloody reprisal at Israel's Lod International Airport in Tel Aviv. On the evening of 30 May, three men entered the airport terminal, pulled AK-47s and grenades out of their bags, and began firing at the nearly three hundred people inside. After killing twenty-six and wounding another seventy-eight, one of the attackers committed suicide using a grenade, another was killed by security officials, and the third was severely wounded and apprehended. "This is one of the worst bloodbaths in the history of civil aviation," announced Minister of Transportation Shimon Peres.[40] As the details of the operation became public, the attackers were identified as members of the Japanese Red Army, a Maoist group working with the Popular Front for the Liberation of Palestine (PFLP). The transnational scope of the Lod attack was startling: here were Japanese citizens working in conjunction with a Palestinian resistance organization to attack one of the key points of Israeli contact on a global transportation grid; moreover, most of the victims in the attack would turn out to be American citizens, Puerto Ricans on a pilgrimage to the Holy Land.

FIGURE 5.2 *Cover of PFLP's newspaper* Al-Hadaf, *"Lod Airport Operation: The Single Battle Against the United Imperialist Enemy." Courtesy of the Library of the Institute for Palestine Studies, Beirut.*

Conversations among the fedayeen reveal the importance attached to the Lod attack's international scope. To be sure, the Marxist orientation of the Popular Front contributed to the group's global focus, but the inclusion of Japanese Maoists in an attack inside Israel demonstrated the wider appeal of the fedayeen message. The cover for the 3 June issue of the PFLP's *Al-Hadaf* showed four raised arms, each brandishing a Kalashnikov assault rifle, beneath PFLP logos in English and Japanese. The caption, written in Arabic, captured the group's message: "The Lod Airport Operation: The Single Battle Against the Common Imperialist Enemy."[41] The group touted the attack as evidence of a unified global network of revolutionary fighters struggling for the cause of liberation.[42]

This effort to frame its battle as part of a worldwide struggle against imperialism was a running theme for the PFLP. As George Habash insisted in a March press conference:

> The reinforcement of our revolutionary alliances at [the] world level with all the socialist countries, national liberation movements and workers' forces throughout the world will enable us to confront the world imperialist camp and all its plans to strike at the movement of the peoples of the world.[43]

In line with these efforts, the PFLP stressed the global dimensions of the Lod operation in its public discussions of the attack. The three Japanese gunmen were, according to the group, part of a joint struggle against imperialism and racist colonialism. Zionism's collusion with global imperialism and colonialism would be met by an alliance of revolutionary forces from around the world; the PFLP thus cast its struggle as one part of a global contest between the forces of imperialism and world revolution.[44] The Japanese cadres who had carried out the assault shared these sentiments. Upon his conviction and sentencing to life imprisonment by an Israeli court, the lone surviving participant in the Lod attack, Kozo Okamoto, confirmed his faith in the ultimate justice of the Palestinian fight and the historical inevitability of victory of liberation struggles around the world. He insisted that this was a people's war, a just struggle, and recalled the crimes of the "imperialists in Vietnam and in several regions of the globe and expressed his faith in the victorious march of the revolution."[45]

Given these global dimensions, the problem for the Israeli leaders was one of choosing whom to retaliate against. For lack of a more convenient target, the government of Israel identified Lebanon—the "home" of the PFLP—as the party responsible for the attack. Beirut's ambassador to the United States immediately approached the State Department out of concern over Israel's threat to retaliate, explaining that his government was "deploring [the] Lod attack and disclaiming any connection with it," and insisting that Beirut could not be held responsible for the incident, adding that if Israel wanted to be consistent with its attack on Beirut's airport in December 1968, it should launch a strike on Rome's airport, since that had been the terrorists' point of departure. He argued that Lebanon's weakness made the state an easy scapegoat for Israeli leaders under pressure to give the appearance of taking some action against terrorism. State Department officials suggested that Beirut send a letter to the Security Council denouncing the attack and crack down on the PFLP in hopes of bolstering the position of the moderates in the Israeli government.[46]

Groups such as Black September did not fit cleanly into traditional frameworks of international relations designed to function on a state-to-state basis; as the global playing field widened to include nonstate actors, the situation was bound to become more volatile and less predictable. The Department of State privately warned Ambassador Buffum that the fact that the PFLP had claimed responsibility for the attack from Beirut presented obvious dangers for the Lebanese government. The extremely violent nature of the incident, the killing of a number of American citizens, and the fact that the attack jeopardized international travel were all cause for serious concern.[47]

The transnational scope of the operation presented another troubling reality. Though the PFLP claimed credit for the attack, the Beirut newspaper *Daily Star* noted that the attackers were part of a larger contingent of Japanese Red Army members, including fighters and medical personnel as well as lines of supply, working with the PFLP. This link was itself part of a larger exchange program that included other groups in West Germany (likely the Baader-Meinhof Gang), Latin America, and the Weathermen in the United States.[48]

Lebanese president Suleiman Franjieh condemned the attack but argued that his country could not be held accountable for the actions of Palestinian organizations that took advantage of the relative freedom of Lebanese society and its position at a geographic crossroads to coordinate their operations. Rather, as the latest attack demonstrated, the problem was international in scope and demanded coordinated international action similar to what Interpol had accomplished with narcotics. Ambassador Buffum urged the government to establish some sort of distinction between the PFLP and Fatah based on the fact that the "former is publicly committed to such actions as hijacking, is intimately linked to international left-wing extremist groups and is committed to [the] ultimate overthrow of conservative govts in [the] area, including Lebanon."[49]

State Department officials warned the White House to expect a major Israeli reprisal against Lebanon in the near future, which was likely to complicate the U.S. strategy in the region. An Israeli attack would have a destabilizing effect, both within Lebanon and on the U.S.-Lebanese relationship; it would likely unify the fedayeen behind the PFLP, while a crackdown by the Lebanese government would have the same effect, in addition to forcing Beirut to request more military aid from Washington. They pointed out that Lebanon's relatively open, democratic society made the task of controlling the fedayeen considerably more difficult than had been the case in Jordan. The deeper question of malaise in the peace process with Israel would continue to fuel extremism in the region and make it increasingly difficult for moderate governments such as Lebanon's to rein in militant groups. "The prospect of more terrorism looms ahead," they forecast.[50]

The logic behind the potential Israeli retaliation for the Lod massacre confounded U.S. officials in Beirut. Buffum objected to Israeli foreign minister Abba Eban's statement, which seemed to blame Lebanon for Israel's current troubles. Rather, the latest attack had revealed, in addition to the persistent instability in the region, the "dangers of [a] world-wide interlocking terrorist net[work]." Indeed, the threat of an Israeli attack was now coupled with the disturbing realization by the Lebanese government of how great a danger terrorism represented to internal stability. The brutality of the Lod attack and the organization's links to international guerilla networks were a "frightening revelation to Lebanese leaders." Nonetheless, Israeli leaders had to recognize that there was only so much that Beirut could achieve in its efforts to restrain an organization with financial and arms ties to "such wide-spread countries as Algeria and Iraq, [the] USSR and China, and...direct links with Japanese, Turks, Libyans and other terrorist/nihilist organizations around the world." Moreover, Buffum insisted, "we are dealing with [a] type of terror which is striking with increasing frequency around the world, including Israel proper and [the] occupied territories, Iran, [the] United States, West Germany, Japan, Italy and other countries whose governments can hardly be accused of complicity or complaisance where terrorists are concerned." "It also must not be forgotten," he added, "that terrorism is a manifestation of the basic area problem and not the problem itself." While the Lebanese could impose stricter controls on PFLP cadres in Beirut, such measures must be coupled with a long-term global campaign against groups such as the PLO.[51]

This would not be simple. The U.S. ambassador to the United Nations, George H. W. Bush, saw some merit in Beirut's proposal for international action but expressed caution regarding the potential difficulties that Washington would face at the United Nations. Bush was certain that neither the Soviets, the People's Republic of China, Sudan, India, nor the African countries would accept a resolution condemning the Lod attack. Moreover, any effort to pass such a resolution would be met by Arab calls for the implementation of UN 242. Thus he warned that bringing the matter to the United Nations was likely to result in a bitter Middle East debate, which would serve no one's interests and likely would defy U.S. efforts to limit discussion to the specific issue of terrorism.[52]

These discussions glossed over the internal complexities of the guerilla organizations, however. Tensions within Fatah had led to an apparent coup attempt against Arafat and the more moderate leaders of the organization. Fighting broke out in June between rival guerilla factions in several refugee camps; while it was quickly put down, tensions remained high between the moderate leadership and the radical supporters of Black September.[53] U.S. officials speculated that the current dissent was likely to lead to a drift toward radicalization within the organization. The "young wolves"—who had more in common with the PFLP than with Fatah's moderates—had apparently won the latest contest for power with the guerilla "establishment" in the refugee camps. Arafat would likely now be forced to "back off and trim his sails in order to maintain his own position, and—most important—accelerate radicalization within Fatah and [the] fedayeen movement in general."[54]

The Lebanese government was working to exploit this schism in an effort to overhaul its relations with the fedayeen, starting with Fatah. Specifically, Beirut hoped to compel Fatah to accept a new arrangement that would require the guerillas to curtail cross-border operations, evacuate positions near the Israeli frontier, and accept the authority of the Lebanese military. The key, so far as Beirut was concerned, lay in targeting the more moderate resistance fighters in Fatah, separating the mainstream fedayeen from the more-radical factions such as the PFLP and Black September, and avoiding a general confrontation between the government and the guerillas. The delicate negotiations would require Arafat's acceptance and would be encouraged by pressure from Fatah's principal sources of financial support, Saudi Arabia and Kuwait.[55]

Meanwhile, by 1972, Israel had settled into what Avi Shlaim describes as a strategy of diplomatic attrition toward its Arab neighbors. As Abba Eban said, "The Israeli defense strategy was frankly attritional.... [I]f the Arabs were unable to get their territories back by war or by Great Power pressure, they would have to seek negotiation and to satisfy some of Israel's security interests." The creation of the Nixon Doctrine in Washington bolstered the Meir government's conviction that, as a regional police power working in conjunction with a U.S. government that wished to decrease its direct involvement around the Third World, Israel could operate with a free hand in the Middle East. This approach dovetailed with Kissinger's strategy, which aimed at driving a wedge between the Arab states and Moscow.[56]

Israeli decision makers were apparently convinced—after the experience with Jordan—that military strikes against Lebanon offered the best hope of inducing its government to crack down on the Palestinian guerillas. Moreover, they seem to have concluded that the summer of 1972 was an opportune time, due to regional and international factors, to move against Beirut. Soviet unwillingness to "go to the mat for the Arabs" combined with the upcoming U.S. election and the general horror over the Lod massacre had apparently cleared away any potential superpower-imposed impediments to retaliation. These calculations, along with intense public pressure for action, seemed to be pushing the Israeli government toward an increasingly aggressive posture vis-à-vis Beirut. The general sense of exasperation with the international community and the United Nations was, according to State Department officials, leading Israel to take matters into its own hands.[57]

Whether efforts to split Arafat and the moderate guerillas off from the more radical factions within the fedayeen might have succeeded remains a matter of speculation. Even as negotiations between Beirut and the moderate guerillas were under way, the Israeli cabinet authorized a strike against Lebanese and Syrian targets in retaliation for the Lod massacre. On 21 June eyewitnesses reported the appearance of Israeli jets just after noon over the Lebanese provincial capital of Hasabaya. In the course of the attack, Israeli Skyhawk warplanes struck the guerilla camps as well as the town, turning the central marketplace into "a virtual cauldron" and causing significant civilian casualties.[58]

Far from breaking the will of the PLO and the Lebanese, the attacks seemed to unify opinion against Israel. Even the conservative newspapers in Beirut were, by the next day, referring to the attack as a massacre. Left-wing papers pointed to the U.S. relationship with Israel—specifically the delivery of American-made Skyhawk jets to the IDF—as evidence of Israeli ties to U.S. imperialist policy. The pro-Cairo paper *Sawt al-Uruba* attacked Israeli hypocrisy in seeking international sympathy after the Lod massacre, then "carrying out yesterday's savage attack at Hasabaya village and earlier massacres at Deir Yassin, Bahr al Baqar, Abi Zabal and elsewhere," adding that "Israel has proved its nature, which is void of any human or international concept... it is nothing but a Nazi monster."[59]

Some argued that the attacks were designed to punish the Lebanese rather than the guerillas. Yigal Allon issued a statement insisting that Beirut was as capable of controlling the fedayeen as Jordan had been. He added, "Between what the [IDF] did in South Lebanon and the air bombardments of the U.S. Air Force in North Vietnam there is not even a coincidental similarity. If Lebanon knows what's good for her she will remove the saboteurs or at least dissociate herself from them."[60] U.S. officials observed that Israel's primary targets seemed to be the Lebanese and Syrian militaries, but the nearby town of Hasabaya suffered significant civilian casualties.[61]

Washington was doing little to help its allies in Beirut. On 22 June, the Lebanese ambassador to the United States approached Joseph Sisco at the State Department about his country's desire to bring the matter of the recent border incidents with Israel to the Security Council. The ambassador complained that Israel was using the upcoming U.S. election to attack Lebanon under the assumption that American leaders would be unwilling to criticize the Jewish state. Sisco tried to dissuade the Lebanese ambassador from going to New York, expressing his fear that a Security Council meeting would only complicate the situation. A Security Council "meeting would doubtless open up [a] long drawn-out debate which would not be helpful in overall [Middle East] problem and which would focus on general security problem[s] in [the] area," placing Washington in a difficult position.[62]

Indeed, because it had associated itself with liberation movements around the Third World and established a degree of credibility among African and

Asian countries, the PLO received a measure of protection in international forums such as the United Nations. While a multilateral approach to the Lod massacre and the Israeli retaliations seemed to be the most reasonable response, Washington recognized that its efforts in the international arena would be hamstrung by world support for the Palestinians, a lack of sympathy for Israel in the international community, and a general hostility to U.S. foreign policy in the non-Western world. U.S. efforts encountered immediate problems in Africa, which, like Europe, was being transformed into a sort of sideshow in the Israel-Palestine conflict. Many of the African states focused on the underlying tensions of the Arab-Israeli conflict and continued to support increased pressure on Israel to withdraw from the occupied territories and accept the provisions of UN 242.[63] Further, U.S. policy toward the Arab-Israeli conflict had negative repercussions on the African continent. A Tanzanian editorial from February denounced an administration policy report as "leaving countries outside [the] direct sphere of American imperialism breathless" with its "amazing hypocrisy and arrogance." Nixon's Cold War saber-rattling and "defense of 'little' Israel" was working against the cause of peace in the region. Drawing parallels to the African states' refusal to negotiate with the South African regime, the editorial rejected American proposals to encourage talks between the Arab states and Israel.[64]

Cold War tensions presented another obstacle: the Soviets were unlikely to support a Security Council resolution on international terrorism. The U.S. embassy in Moscow warned that although the Kremlin deplored the Lod attack, Soviet officials were reluctant to jeopardize the USSR's broader relationship with the Arab world. Furthermore, Moscow was wary about losing face in the propaganda struggle with Beijing over the Palestinian issue.[65] European governments were similarly reluctant to join Washington in these antiterrorism efforts at the United Nations, albeit for different reasons. Aside from a hesitation to jeopardize oil interests in the Arab world and a general skepticism regarding the utility of antiterror initiatives, governments in France, West Germany, and the Netherlands shied away from what they saw as a pro-Israeli bias in the U.S.-backed proposals.[66] For the time being, the PLO's popularity in the world community was wreaking havoc on U.S. efforts at the United Nations. Meanwhile, in Europe, Black September's war had just begun.

The Munich Massacre

In September 1972, the Palestinian armed struggle went prime-time as television audiences around the world followed the horror of the Munich Olympics massacre. The shock waves from the attack swept across the Atlantic, hitting Washington with full force. While State Department officials had been monitoring the fedayeen for some time, the spectacular nature of the attack captured the attention of the White House. President Nixon's initial alarm upon learning of the deaths of the Israeli athletes soon gave way to a grim realism. He told Deputy Assistant for National Security Affairs Alexander Haig that Israel was sure to retaliate but its target was not yet clear. Within minutes, an irate Nixon decided—at least temporarily—that Washington must sever relations with nations that "harbor any sort of terrorist groups. Hell what do we care about Lebanon. Think we have to be awfully tough." In a telling display of the White House's priorities on the Middle East, Lebanon and Jordan both made the president's short list of states that would be cut off from U.S. economic support. Haig warned Nixon that "we may have some Chinese problem on this." "Screw the Chinese on this one," Nixon snarled. "Be very tough." While Nixon blew off steam in private, larger concerns loomed.[67]

The most immediate question was whether to cancel the Olympic Games in light of the tragedy. While the Israeli government was calling for such a response, Nixon thought differently, explaining that the suspension of the Olympic events would constitute a small victory for Black September. "They want to make it appear that they've stopped the games," he told Kissinger, adding, in reference to American hippies, "It's like those assholes that tried to stop us running the government." "That's right," the national security advisor agreed. "If we'd have stopped like some of the softheads around here [wanted] or gone over and prayed at the Lincoln Memorial," the president continued, "that's what they want."[68] Neither Palestinian guerillas nor hippies would intimidate the Nixon White House.

On the larger issue of international terrorism, Nixon and Kissinger decided to approach the United Nations immediately. The president ordered Kissinger to tell the Israeli ambassador, Yitzhak Rabin, that "it will be good to put the goddamn UN on the spot. We want to put them on the spot on this issue, because we think we got them by the balls here." Ultimately, Nixon insisted, it must be stressed to Israeli leaders "that now that they're in this good position, don't blow it ... You've got to remember that the President is their friend. Now we've got some world opinion for them. But don't [squander it]—these things can turn very fast."[69] Other observers in Washington warned that the United States might not have quite so much leverage at the United Nations as the president seemed to think, noting that only a handful of countries, including the United States, the United Kingdom, Japan, and Argentina, were likely to vote for a strong resolution. Indeed, even if the French could be persuaded to go along with this bloc, opposing votes could come from the USSR, the PRC, Yugoslavia, Somalia, Sudan, and Guinea. "Afro-Asian support for liberation movements in general" made the matter even more difficult in the General Assembly. It was therefore quite conceivable that an approach to the United Nations, after the expected failure of a U.S.-sponsored Security Council resolution, might actually end up heartening the PLO and embittering Israel.[70]

No one was surprised by the Israeli retaliation on the afternoon of 8 September, with waves of Israeli warplanes attacking fedayeen bases in Syria and Lebanon. State Department telegrams warned of dozens of Lebanese casualties.

> We presume Israelis know as well as we do that [the] fedayeen bases or camps [that were attacked] are not bases in usual military sense of that word, but are simply areas in which commandos have established themselves in [the] midst of or, or in close proximity to, Palestinian refugee camps and Lebanese settlements. No matter how careful and elaborate the aerial reconnaissance and other preparations that precede such attacks, they invariabl[y] produce [a] large number of innocent civilian casualties among Palestinians and Lebanese alike.[71]

U.S. officials noted the disparity between Israeli intelligence and their own sources, which suggested that fedayeen casualties were negligible. While Israeli reconnaissance showed a guerilla base at one of the bombing sites, U.S. intelligence suggested that site was actually a playground. Indeed, guerillas throughout Syria and Lebanon apparently had expected Israeli raids in the wake of the Munich attack and retreated from their forward positions. Moreover, the view that the latest reprisals were driven by a desire for vengeance seemed to have made Israel, rather than the guerillas, the primary target of Lebanese resentment. On the whole, State Department officials judged that recent events were "likely to generate (rather than discourage) increased fedayeen enthusiasm for further terrorist operations."[72]

Intelligence reports argued that, far from hurting the guerillas, Israeli reprisals were making them stronger. From the guerillas' perspective, the Munich attacks had paid off. The massacre had garnered international attention and goaded the Israeli government into a harsh retaliation that would benefit the position of extremists in the Arab world. On the whole, Munich had "set back the international peace effort...and it has reinvigorated the terrorist cult in the Arab world." Meanwhile, Kissinger's NSC worried that Israel's new "war of attrition on the fedayeen" might spark an escalation in violence between Israel and Syria, and expressed the desire to avoid another disagreement with Israel over the "time-worn issue" of retaliatory strikes.[73]

The air strikes were not, however, the end of the attack. An armed incursion came on 16 September when IDF units occupied sixteen villages in southern Lebanon. The thirty-two-hour invasion encountered stiff resistance from guerilla fighters, leaving behind "a trail of destruction and opening the way to what could be a major clash between the Lebanese authorities and the Palestinian guerillas." The invasion killed an estimated eighty people, seven of whom—including a woman and an eight-year old boy—were found in a taxi that had been crushed by an IDF tank. A British correspondent in Beirut reported seeing "at least a dozen private cars which had been partly or wholly crushed. All bore the marks of tank tracks."[74]

This type of disproportionate response damaged many of the moral arguments that the government of Israel might put forward in the wake of the Munich murders, at least in the eyes of much of the world community. The Saudi press argued that the Western world seemed more concerned with Israeli casualties than Arab ones. State Department officials commented that the "repugnance felt by Western nations" after the Munich massacre was "not wholly shared by Saudis who have no particular emotional attachment to [the] Olympics and who argue [that] there [is] no difference between personal violence of terrorists and impersonal violence of bombing Lebanese and Egyptian civilians."[75] In some eyes, the Western "double standard to violence committed by Arabs and Israelis ever since 1948" combined with a long list of atrocities, from the Holocaust and the atomic bomb to Deir Yassin and Vietnam.[76] Further, military reprisals would only fan the flames of resistance and bolster the positions of radicals within the PLO: "Just as Black September was born at Wahdat Refugee Camp (attacked by Jordanian Army) in Jordan in 1970, new phoenixes will emerge from Israel[i] attacks on refugee camps in Lebanon and Syria."[77] Another editorial warned ominously that the Arab world had the power to strike at U.S. interests in the Middle East: "We do not believe [that U.S. Secretary of State William] Rogers is ignorant of the fact that those who are able to strike in Munich, Trieste, Rotterdam and Hamburg will be [able] to strike in areas of American imperialism."[78]

State Department intelligence analysts also cautioned that Israel's reprisal policies could bolster Moscow's position in the Arab world. Recent intelligence suggested that the Israeli government was turning toward Syria as a principal target for its retaliatory strikes. Because potential targets for guerilla attacks were so numerous and difficult to defend and because the fedayeen were themselves so difficult to attack—being "strewn across the map from Algeria to China"—Israeli decision makers had come to rely on the strategy of reprisal raids. As Israel turned its attention toward Damascus, it was likely to push the regime in Syria into a closer relationship with Moscow, thereby giving Soviet leaders a chance to regain some of the ground lost after their recent fallout with Cairo.[79]

The moral ambiguity of a conflict that took such a heavy toll on civilians hindered U.S. efforts at the United Nations to cast the coming war on terrorism as a righteous endeavor undertaken by Israel in self-defense. Secretary Rogers cabled Ambassador Bush, explaining that Washington hoped to avoid a Security Council resolution on recent events, since the majority position was likely to focus on the carnage wrought by Israeli reprisals. In contrast, the most desirable outcome would probably be a discussion that focused on fighting terrorism but fell short of passing any resolutions. Washington would support only a resolution that condemned terrorism and called on the Arab states to do more to fight it.[80]

Third World solidarity and enthusiasm for liberation struggles would hold out against condemnations from the U.S. government, however. As predicted, the debate in the Security Council was primarily focused on the Israeli attacks on Lebanon and Syria. The basic problem revolved around the question of whether one sovereign state had the right to attack another sovereign state in retaliation for the actions of individuals; specifically, was Israel justified in attacking Lebanon in retaliation for Black September attacks on German soil? India, Guinea, and the Soviet Union all deplored the murder of the Israeli athletes in Munich but were insistent that Syria and Lebanon bore no responsibility for that tragedy. The Indian delegation argued that the "chain of responsibility" for violence in the Arab-Israeli conflict stretched back to the days of the British Mandate, and they were adamant that some sort of distinction be made between the actions of sovereign governments and the deeds of individuals. The U.S. draft resolution was, according to the Indians, "unbalanced and entirely silent on the recent Israeli attacks." The Soviets went even further in this regard, calling on the Security Council to remove all reference to the Munich tragedy because its inclusion would give the appearance of condoning the recent Israeli attacks: "To draw a parallel between acts of terror committed by persons in a desperate situation and those of a State that had become an aggressor would remove from that State the responsibility for the murder of hundreds of innocent people."[81]

Other states also rejected U.S. attempts to equate the recent Israeli attacks with the Munich massacre, arguing that much of the violence in recent years had come as the direct result of Israel's ongoing refusal to abide by Security Council resolutions. In this context, Guinea, Sudan, and Yugoslavia argued that the Security Council was required to reject Israeli attempts to claim the right of military retaliation against its neighbors. The Munich tragedy, according to the representative from Beijing, was being used as a pretext for Israel to continue the aggressive expansionist policies it had employed since the end of World War II.[82]

The final vote for the Security Council resolution condemning the Israeli air strikes was thirteen to one; the United States opposed the resolution. This was the first time that Washington had issued a lone veto—a previous veto on Rhodesia had, at the very least, been seconded by the British delegation. British papers reported with some concern that the "American veto marks a distinct shift towards Israel in the United States posture at the United Nations."[83] The U.S. embassy in Tel Aviv cabled that the Israeli prime minister and foreign minister were pleased with the U.S. veto and hoped that Washington would "continue to block what [they] consider[ed] to be one-sided Security Resolutions." Israeli leaders suggested that U.S. willingness to exercise its veto might help to transform the United Nations into a "more effective organization."[84]

Washington's veto would indeed have a significant impact on the international diplomacy of the Arab-Israeli conflict, allowing Israel to continue to dismiss the rising political and diplomatic influence of the PLO. As long as the United States continued to shield the government of Israel from the effects of successful PLO diplomacy, the Jewish state could continue to argue that Palestinian fighters were nothing more than "terrorists" who had no right to participate in regional diplomacy. Standing Israeli policies for dealing with the PLO as a military rather than political threat would thus remain in place with the help of U.S. veto power at the United Nations.

While Israeli leaders were pleased with Washington's support in the Security Council, many in the world community were not. Reactions to Washington's veto in the Security Council were strident. Moscow said that the entire world should be amazed at the U.S. decision to block the latest resolution and insisted that by doing so, Washington now assumed a great deal of responsibility for future violence in the region. Sudanese and Somali officials worried that the veto would grant Israel carte blanche to continue its aggression against the Arab world.[85]

News of the veto received extensive coverage in the Yugoslav press, which compared Washington's expressions of shock following the Munich massacre to its reaction to the Israeli reprisal. The press noted that despite the deaths of hundreds of civilians in the Israeli attack, the U.S. response contained a complete absence of "blame for that act or commiseration with victims." The Belgrade press also noted comparisons to the situation in Vietnam, quoting the *Washington Post* on the matter of the "moral difference between throwing [a] hand grenade into [a] helicopter with Israeli athletes and dropping 30 tons of bombs on [a] half square mile of Vietnamese peasant land."[86] Sudanese officials complained about what they perceived to be a "distressing change in the U.S. position," which seemed to entail unflinching support of Israel. While the Munich massacre was reprehensible, Khartoum pointed out that the Security Council was not qualified to issue resolutions on acts of nongovernmental bodies. Moreover, in response to U.S. pressure for cooperation on antihijacking legislation, the Sudanese insisted that no Arab government could afford to sever ties to the Palestinian fighters.[87]

The moderate, relatively pro-U.S. government in Tunisia was likewise deeply concerned about the impact of Washington's veto. The U.S. ambassador in Tunis observed that Tunisian leaders were concerned for the plight of Arab moderates and the U.S. position in the region so long as Washington continued with its pro-Israel policies. President Bourguiba said that he found this current U.S. approach difficult to understand and impossible to defend. The veto had "especially astonished him." The Tunisian population was deeply wedded to the concept of Arab solidarity, the president explained, and so he could not take a critical position vis-à-vis the Palestinian guerillas. Although he understood that Nixon was facing an election in the coming months, Bourguiba insisted that action must be taken to rein in the rising levels of violence in the Middle East.[88]

Though it was a failure in practical terms, the symbolism of this early Security Council debate on terrorism had deep repercussions. The U.S. veto served as hard evidence of Washington's tilt toward Israel and an indication of its growing isolation from mainstream sentiment on the issues of national liberation and decolonization. The paradox rested in the likelihood that this rhetorical isolation would render ineffective multilateral efforts to deal with the substantive issue of international terrorism. American leaders needed the cooperation of the international community in order to create effective global policy, but the U.S. stance regarding the Palestine question and national liberation alienated potential partners. Ultimately, Washington's willingness to veto the resolution pointed to fundamental differences between how the Americans perceived the Arab-Israeli conflict and how the global mainstream saw it. While the prevailing mood in the United States tended to treat Israel as a special case—worthy of singular consideration up to and including the abrogation of international law—the apparent majority in the world community saw Israel as a state like any other. This basic difference in perceptions would have far-reaching consequences.

Terror or National Liberation

The United States was not the only actor in the international arena troubled by this new form of transnational violence. The Munich incident led UN secretary-general Kurt Waldheim to take the unprecedented move of placing the issue of terrorism on the agenda of the General Assembly's twenty-seventh session. This first official attempt to address the issue of terrorism though the official channels of international governance proved highly controversial. The Arab world was especially apprehensive. The Algerian daily *Moudjahid* attacked Waldheim's call for a General Assembly "plan of action against terrorism as pro-Israeli and tied it to [the] West's 'new crusades' against [the] Arabs."[89] The power of the nonaligned nations at the United Nations would again prove a major obstacle to antiterror resolutions.

U.S. decision makers recognized that any potential antiterrorism policy in the Middle East would have to operate with some degree of cooperation from the Arab governments. Efforts to encourage such cooperation were hindered, however, by the essentially universal perception in the Arab world of the United States as a supporter of Israel. The State Department thus recommended approaching other friendly capitals in an effort to gain the support of U.S. allies in trying to convince the Arab world to take action to combat terrorism.[90] British officials agreed that it would not be sufficient to win the support of only a few Western governments on this matter.[91]

A crucial difficulty in the wider world lay with the definitional tension between "terrorism" and "resistance" that had confounded U.S. and Israeli anti-fedayeen policies at the United Nations and served as a key component of the guerillas' global diplomacy. As they approached Third World governments, U.S. officials found sympathy for Munich's victims, but also an unwillingness to support antiterrorism conventions. Officials from Ghana asserted their government's desire to look to the future:

> As a supporter of various African Liberation movements, [the government of Ghana] may one day be faced with a hijacking carried out by one of these organizations. It is not a question of Ghanaian connivance in such a hijacking...but Ghana would certainly have problems if, for example one of the Liberation groups were to force a hijacked plane (e.g., South African) to land in Ghana.

The government would have great difficulty both with its neighbors and its own public should it surrender hijackers from an African liberation group to South African, Rhodesian, or Portuguese officials. By approaching Accra on such matters, Washington was asking Ghanaian officials to put themselves in the impossible position of turning their backs on ongoing national liberation movements in Africa.[92]

In an effort to address these types of concerns, Secretary Waldheim suggested that the United States should include a special provision excluding southern Africa from this antiterrorism initiative. The South African government was obviously unhappy with Waldheim's statement and its "blatant double standard" on the problem of terrorism. The Johannesburg *Star* argued that "by specifically excluding Southern African 'freedom fighters' (or 'terrorists') from proposed international action against terrorism he (Waldheim) immediately makes a mockery of any campaign. He cannot fight violence with one hand," the editorial continued in a criticism that reached beyond the immediate South African situation, "and support it with the other."[93]

Ambassador Bush warned that strong opposition to the terrorism item was likely to emerge not only from Arab member states but also from African delegates. Bush's sources predicted that the debates would once again, contrary to U.S. wishes, focus on the definition of terrorism. Moreover, Bush expected the debate to quickly move to charges of U.S. terrorism in Vietnam, although he suggested that Washington might even make use of such an opening to draw attention to "Viet Cong terrorism in South Vietnam."[94] All parties recognized that the question of "terrorism" was an intensely politicized one.

For this reason, the approaching debate threatened to arouse major dissension within the General Assembly. French discussions with the Chinese delegation shed light on Beijing's belief in the existence of two types of terrorism: "international brigandage and 'legitimate' national liberation struggles." While its position on the latter was clear, the PRC "believed [that the] former category merited businesslike discussion" at the United Nations. As predicted, the

African delegations continued to focus on the need to distinguish between the notions of terrorism and national liberation. Furthermore, contacts with the delegations from the nonaligned nations suggested that they believed Washington to be behind Waldheim's terrorism initiative.[95]

The French government was adamant that "terrorist" acts and Israel's reprisal policy ought to be condemned equally as actions that resulted in significant civilian deaths. Paris also warned State Department officials against presenting the problem of international terrorism within a narrow Arab-Israeli focus. Furthermore, the UN debate on terrorism was likely to pit the Western powers against much of the Third World. French officials warned that this "polarization between [the] Europeans and [the] Third World would not be desirable and would only serve to diminish [the] possibilities of [a] constructive Western role." Paris therefore intended to approach the question of international action with caution due to its extreme complexity and in hopes of avoiding further division within the organization.[96]

In conversations with the State Department, French officials stressed their continuing concerns that without substantive moves toward a political settlement in the Arab-Israeli conflict, the Middle East was likely to become even more radical. One official predicted the rise of "Qadhafi-ism" in the region unless Egyptian president Anwar Sadat received some sort of Western assistance. Paris also saw Israel as the "main factor in whether there would be political movement" in the peace process, explaining that while "terrorism was horrible, [its] cause must be attacked at [the] root." The threat would remain "until [the] Palestinians were given [the] possibility of political expression."[97]

The range of views in the global community on the issue of terrorism made progress tremendously difficult, especially as long as officials in Washington refused to compromise. Sources at the United Nations indicated that the African and Asian bloc had resolved to oppose Waldheim's initiative, while Moscow would push the line that two forms of "terrorism" existed—official and unofficial—and make the argument that the former generated the latter. Moreover, the Soviets would "allude to US actions in Vietnam and Israeli acts in [the] Middle East as examples" of this process at work.[98]

The fact that many U.S. policy makers tended to look with condescension upon the question of African and Asian solidarity and Third World sympathy with national liberation movements did not help matters. Because the initiative could be defeated by a coalition of African and Arab votes, State Department officials hoped that the African states would behave according to "their enlightened interest rather than artificial bloc solidarity." U.S. officials warned that the "top levels of our government will be looking at [the] vote, how individual countries voted, and what efforts were made to make sure they are aware of [the] significance of their vote." The African states had been influenced by concerns such as the fear that terrorism resolutions might endanger the African liberation movements—terrorism having been closely associated

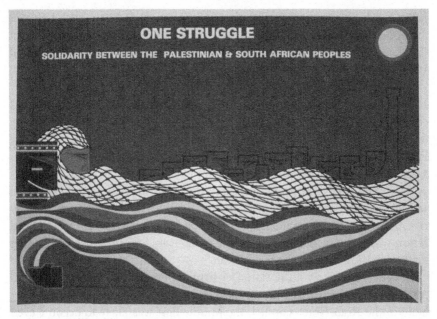

FIGURE 5.3 *PLO Poster, Nadir Tharani, "One Struggle," c. 1978. Courtesy of the Palestinian Poster Project Archives.*

with the language of South Africa's apartheid policies—and the hope of maintaining solidarity with the Arab world. Washington was therefore compelled to engage in the debate over the difference between terrorism and national liberation movements.[99]

Despite this opposition, State Department officials seemed unanimous in their view that the issue of terrorism ought to receive priority at the United Nations; the struggle might be difficult, but a genuine resolution would be worth the effort. On one hand, the General Assembly's failure to consider the issue—a major concern of the world community—would represent a blow to the organization's credibility as a body that was relevant to world affairs. The State Department understood the issue of terrorism, insofar as it related to the Middle East, as a product of the Arab-Israeli conflict. Hence, a lasting solution to the problem was ultimately tied to the resolution of this larger conflict, which could only be accomplished along the lines set out by UN 242. The "Palestinian Arabs from whose ranks terrorist movement draws its principal participants, have legitimate grievances," but external operations ultimately harmed the Palestinian cause and replaced international sympathy with "universal abhorrence of terrorist acts." Nevertheless, they said, it was a mistake to expect that progress toward UN 242 would result in an end to terrorism. Rather, the opposite was true: "It is necessary to make progress toward ending terrorism in order to make progress toward settlement based on Res 242."[100] Aside from the fact that external operations had not destroyed the majority of the international community's sympathy for the PLO—not to mention the general lack of U.S. effort to deal with the Palestine question prior to the appearance of the fedayeen violence—the larger problem concerned the reality that, however the State Department saw UN 242, the White House had effectively abandoned it.

In any event, the uproar over the terrorism-versus-national-liberation debate was so strong that Washington issued a statement on its intention to limit the debate over "terrorism" to attacks on commercial aircraft, the kidnapping of diplomats, the transport of explosives through the international mail, and the killing of civilians in a third country. A State Department spokesman remarked that the "question of the so-called liberation movements and their activities is in our view separate." The terrorism debate at the United Nations should concern itself with political violence that affected "international transportation, communications, and what you would have to call more generally civil order throughout the world."[101]

Washington hoped to establish mechanisms at the United Nations that might function to contain transnational guerilla violence, preventing its spread to third-party states. The convention would "cover only the most dangerous threats to international order and fundamental human rights," such as the Lod and Munich attacks and the recent wave of letter bombings. The convention would apply only to violence in which third countries became involved and therefore would not address the acts of the Irish Republican Army in the United Kingdom, resistance groups in Rhodesia or Angola, or Palestinian fighters in Israel so long as those acts did not knowingly target non-nationals.[102]

While much of the nonaligned world approached the question of international terrorism from the perspective that violence was a symptom of deeper problems, the roots of which must be addressed, the United States and Israel continued to push their understanding of "terrorism" as a "challenge to the world social order."[103] Israeli officials, for example, blamed the rise in external operations not on the absence of a political solution in the Middle East conflict but on the support of the Arab states for the PLO and on the failure of Western governments to move against it. The Israeli ambassador to Greece compared the problem of "international terrorism" to that of maritime piracy in past centuries, explaining, "In the past the civilized world fought as one against and 'defanged' piracy; it would be able today to do the same thing." He likened "terrorism" to a communicable disease that demanded the active engagement of every government.[104]

By refusing to compromise, the U.S. and Israeli governments were making the prospect of multilateral efforts to curtail external operations increasingly unlikely; unilateral action seemed the only option in the absence of a global response to this international problem. Thus, the government of Israel announced that it had "decided to work in every possible direction throughout the world where terrorist activity is taking place to its detriment, because this constitutes a matter of Israeli defense and security." The only way to fight the epidemic was to attack its roots in Damascus, Cairo, Tripoli, and Beirut. At the same time, the Arab "Mafia" living in the United States and Europe, "whose only aim is to murder the unsuspecting," would "meet the same fate.[105] Statements such as these supported arguments that those behind the recent antiterrorism initiatives were more interested in attacking the Palestinians and their supporters than in actually addressing a problem of global concern.

While brutal transnational attacks paid dividends for Palestinian fighters, external operations such as the one in Munich also had the effect of thrusting the Palestinian question back into the spotlight and dispelling any notion that war in Jordan had rendered the PLO irrelevant. Even Israeli officials—despite their shock and anger over Munich—began once again to discuss the place of the Palestinians in the region. "There is a Palestinian people who are part of the Arab people," Eban stated in late September, but this did not mean that they "should be allowed self-determination one hundred percent." Rather, Palestinian self-determination must not interfere with Israeli sovereignty. Because there were sixteen Arab nations and only one Jewish state, "Israeli self-determination takes moral and historical precedence over Palestinian self-determination, though it does not rule it out entirely." In a speech before the United Nations six days later, Eban insisted the best interests of the Palestinian people lay in a regional peace settlement, which would allow the question of their civic and political identity to be settled. It was thus paradoxical that the PLO should be the most stubborn opponent of such a settlement. "The problem of curbing the terrorists is now our most urgent preoccupation," he argued. "We are resolved to resist and weaken them in our region. We believe that national, regional, and international action against Arab terrorism is an indispensable prelude to the fruitful exploration of peaceful prospects for the Middle East."[106] Although these were far from ringing endorsements of Palestinian self-determination—and they were outright condemnations of the PLO—Eban's statements were an indication of renewed Israeli recognition of the importance of the Palestinian issue.

Ironically, the heyday of fedayeen external operations was brief. The first signs that Fatah's leaders were working to halt Black September's activities came in the wake of Munich. "Munich," explains one historian, "marked the turning point for the Palestinian leadership, as it catapulted Khalaf to the fore in Fatah politics and threatened any diplomatic gains made by the PLO. The genie had to be put back in the bottle." If Fatah's attempts to rein in the organization were successful, Munich would be Black September's last operation. It would prove difficult to deactivate this international violence, however. Despite Fatah's efforts, Black September would pull off one last major operation after Munich, which—in conjunction with the Olympics massacre—would unleash decades of controversy.[107] Fatah and Black September were not the only groups moving away from external operations. In March 1972, George Habash announced an end to the PFLP's hijacking operations. While he still insisted that Israel's El Al fleet represented a legitimate military target, since the state had been known to use its airliners to transport military supplies during wartime, he pointed out that the PFLP's supporters in the revolutionary and socialist world who did not follow this logic opposed such as attacks. Because these international alliances were so important to the organization, Habash said, the PFLP had decided in November 1970 to halt these hijackings.[108]

Ending external operations sparked an exodus from both Fatah and the PFLP. The architect of the PFLP's external tactics, Wadi Haddad, split off from Habash's group to create his own group, the External Operations branch (PFLP-EO), with support from Iraq in 1970. Following Arafat's decision to halt external operations, Fatah's liaison to Libya, Ahmed Abdel-Ghaffar, defected to Tripoli, and the organization's agent in Baghdad, Sabri al-Banna, defected to Iraq. Al-Banna, aka Abu Nidal, would go on to create the Abu Nidal Organization, one of the most violent and feared transnational militant groups of the 1970s and 1980s. Both defectors later received death sentences from Fatah's moderate leadership.[109]

Still, Black September's spectacular campaign of transnational violence had brought the issue of "international terrorism" into focus as an urgent matter for the world community. Earlier hijackings by groups such as the PFLP had garnered a great deal of attention but had failed to draw widespread condemnation; travelers had been delayed and a few injuries and the occasional fatality had occurred, but these actions hardly seemed like a major threat to the global order. The Lod and Munich incidents, however, provided a chilling demonstration of how deadly such attacks could be. In response, the U.S. government launched what could be understood as a sort of first "war on terrorism" in which American policy makers sought to construct at the United Nations an international response to the problem of transnational violence. Ironically, this counterterrorism push came after the PLO's mainstream leadership had made the decision to halt external operations.

Making matters worse, the U.S. approach to the issue was clumsy and failed to win support on a number of levels. Perceptions that Washington's conception of antiterrorism was designed to protect Israel alienated many states that sympathized with the Palestinian cause. Likewise, the U.S. tendency to frame fedayeen violence as a black-and-white issue clashed with the opinions of many in the world community who saw a great deal of ambiguity in the actions of groups such as the PFLP and Black September. The image of the desperate guerilla standing up to the imperialist military machine had become familiar in the postcolonial era. For many international observers, especially in the Third World, Palestinian actions seemed to fit this picture. The debates at the United Nations headquarters in New York clarified the difficulty of assigning labels such as "freedom fighter" or "terrorist" to nonstate groups that used violence to achieve political objectives.

Similarly, aggressive Israeli reprisals also stymied U.S. attempts to build political support for antiterrorism: while few in the world community praised the murder of innocents at the hands of Palestinian militants, many argued that the slaughter of Lebanese and Syrian civilians by the state of Israel was even more reprehensible. The disproportionate level of bloodshed, with Arabs and Palestinians making up the overwhelming majority of the casualties, led many observers in the nonaligned world to question whether the United States placed a higher value on the lives of Israelis than on those of Arabs. The net effect of these factors exposed the isolated position of the United States in the world community in regard to the Israel-Palestine issue, especially after Washington's unprecedented lone veto in the Security Council. Regardless of the logic behind the veto itself, the incident poisoned subsequent U.S. attempts to put together multilateral support for antiterrorism efforts at the United Nations and provided further ammunition for those who accused Washington of unquestioned support for Israel.

Furthermore, the U.S. response in 1972 to the emergence of the PLO's external operations proved unsuited to the realities of the Palestinian liberation movement. Despite ample information from Foreign Service officers and area experts, who indicated that transnational attacks were the result of power struggles within the PLO and that the mainstream leadership of Fatah and the PFLP was working to deactivate their groups' external operations wings, the Nixon administration failed to take full account of changing political structures within the Palestinian movement. Rather than recognizing these power struggles and adjusting their approach to the PLO accordingly, leaders in Washington continued to treat the organization as a monolithic entity, making subsequent attempts to engage with the Palestinians increasingly difficult and less effective.

The lumbering approach to the issue of terrorism and national liberation, the refusal to account for the internal complexities of the PLO, and an uncompromising position vis-à-vis the issue of Palestinian nationalism resulted in woefully inadequate U.S. policy in the region and at the United Nations and the failure of any substantive progress on dealing with the problem of transnational guerilla violence. As the situation grew bloodier, Washington's popularity in the Arab world continued to decline. Meanwhile, the fragile nation of Lebanon, a longtime U.S. ally, was pulled deeper into the Israel-Palestine conflict.

"The Torch Has Been Passed from Vietnam to Us"

Between 28 July and 5 August 1973, hundreds of thousands of students and young people filled the streets of East Berlin as part of the Tenth World Festival of Youth and Students. Organized with considerable support from the communist bloc, the event had the feel of a large American rock festival as the city's central district was transformed into a giant pedestrian zone and vendors selling everything from German pilsner to fried chicken and bitter lemon took positions along street corners. As part of the celebration, Yasir Arafat, Angela Davis, and representatives from the Vietnamese NLF, the PRC, Warsaw Pact states, and African liberation movements were presented to the thousands in attendance. Arafat's visit coincided with the opening of a PLO office in East Berlin (making East Germany only the second socialist country after the PRC to allow the opening of such a facility) and marked a general warming in the organization's relationship with Moscow and the socialist bloc. It also demonstrated that operations such as those at Lod and Munich had not undermined international support for the PLO and the Palestinian cause. After the event's conclusion, Arafat announced that in East Berlin the PLO had been invited to take up "the banner of the global struggle" from the Vietnamese revolution.[1] Palestinian poet Mahmoud Darwish described the significance of the visit as the final transformation of the Palestinians from refugees to resistance fighters:

> There was a time when the world had a well-defined role to play towards us; namely to send us parcels of cheese, bread and clothing, parcels which became the motif or our nation. We were well behaved children....The world came to us—we were not allowed to go to the world....Our duty was to be refugees....We have changed a great deal and so has the world....What sustains us vis à vis the world is that we are fighting a battle for national liberty which has a progressive intellectual foundation....The world is

neither a single integrated unit, nor is it true that East is East and West is West. But we are part of an international revolutionary movement which has branches in both East and West. Crawling on our knees so as to gain the sympathy of official Western quarters will do nothing to diminish our alienation from the world....Palestine is no longer a pawn in anyone's hands....A cause may have justice on its side but remain struggling in thin air until it provides itself with muscle.

Echoing Arafat, Darwish proclaimed: "In the conscience of the peoples of the world, the torch has been passed from Vietnam to us." A question remained, however: "Can we live up to that heavy responsibility?"[2]

Events such as the World Festival of Youth belied arguments that external operations and international violence had undermined worldwide support for the PLO. Rather, operations such as the Munich attack had a more complex impact on the fate of the fedayeen, exposing both the horrors of "international terrorism" and the plight of the Palestinian people. Debates in forums such as the United Nations demonstrated a growing divide between the proponents of "national liberation" and the enemies of "international terrorism." Away from the spotlight, however, the attacks would contribute to a series of political transformations within the PLO itself and an opening of sorts in the organization's political program. Black September's fury peaked in the months following Munich, and a new moderation appeared among the PLO's leadership. Notably, Arafat would move to curtail the activity of Black September, put an end to external operations, and bring the more radical factions of the movement under his control. At the same time, elements in the PLO began sending signals regarding the prospect of a political approach to the conflict with Israel in the form of a two-state solution. The Nixon administration's anger over

FIGURE 6.1 *Yasir Arafat with Angela Davis at the World Youth Festival in East Berlin, 1973, from PLO newspaper* Filastine al-Thawra. *Courtesy of the Library of the Institute for Palestine Studies, Beirut.*

Palestinian attacks coupled with Kissinger's grand strategy for the region ensured that these tentative gestures would be ignored, however. The result, ultimately, would be more bloodshed.

Moscow, the PLO, and a Political Solution

The PLO's invitation to East Berlin and mounting support for the Palestinian cause in the communist world were indications of the organization's improving relationship with Moscow as well as evolving attitudes among the Palestinians regarding a political settlement to the conflict with Israel. PLO relations with the Soviet Union had improved gradually through the early years of the decade. A key turning point, however, came on 8 July 1972, when President Sadat expelled nearly 20,000 Soviet advisors from Egypt. In reaction to this major setback, the Kremlin moved to shore up its position in the Arab world, in part by directing support to PLO through Syria.[3] Arafat made official visits to Moscow in October 1971 and in 1972, both of which came on the heels of Soviet setbacks in the Muslim world. The first of these occurred in Sudan with the purge of communists in that nation; the second, more worrisome development took place in Egypt with Sadat's decision to expel Soviet advisors. Thus Arafat's visits were more a reflection of Moscow's need to bolster its prestige and radical credentials in the Arab world than a major reorientation of its stance vis-à-vis the PLO. The PLO was quick to trumpet the importance of the visits, however, arguing that they signified deepening ties between the organization and Moscow and the forces of revolution in the wider world. In any event, Moscow made good on its promised arms shipments to the PLO, which began arriving in Syrian ports soon after.[4]

Warmer relations between the Soviet Union and the PLO were also connected to evolving attitudes among the Palestinians regarding a political settlement to the conflict with Israel. From its earliest contacts with the fedayeen, the Kremlin had argued in favor of a two-state solution and urged the guerillas to abandon their calls for destruction of Israel. This pressure on PLO to accept Israel and compromise solution made only creeping progress at first, but by 1972—especially in light of the Kremlin's closer relationship with the guerillas—moderate leaders such as Arafat were entertaining such ideas.[5] Tunisian president Habib Bourguiba also advocated in favor of a two-state solution. Bourguiba had gone on record as early as 1965 suggesting that the 1947 partition of Palestine represented a "lesser evil" that might be the basis of a lasting regional peace. In a series of interviews in the spring and summer of 1973, Bourguiba again stepped forward with a call for the creation of a Palestinian state in the West Bank and Jordan. He insisted that the Arab states would never make peace with Israel without Palestinian support; "therefore a Palestinian state must be created."[6]

Debate between maximalist and incremental strategies had taken off inside the ranks of the Palestinian leadership in the wake of the 1970 disaster in Jordan. Whereas the maximalist strategy embraced by more radical elements such as the PFLP still called for the one-state solution of a secular democratic state in Palestine, more moderate groups including Fatah had begun to discuss the prospect of a ministate in the West Bank and Gaza Strip. This development marked a fundamental shift in the fedayeen's position and a critical departure from the notion that a solution to the conflict could come about only through military means. Indeed, by mid-1972, influential voices in the Palestinian guerilla movement were advocating an intermediate solution, a settlement to be based on the acquisition of only a part of historic Palestine. The most important of these early calls came from Nayaf Hawatmeh's PDFLP. While it had initially called for the overthrow of King Hussein's regime in Amman and the creation of revolutionary soviets in the Arab world, the group had begun to moderate in the early 1970s. In place of this more radical agenda, the leadership of the PDFLP suggested the implementation of a national authority scheme: the Palestinians would establish a government over the West Bank and Gaza following an anticipated Israeli withdrawal. From this position, an independent Palestinian national authority would begin working to reunify the whole of Palestine under a single democratic regime. Although this proposal was cast as an intermediate plan, it drew strong opposition from more radical groups such as the PFLP, which argued that such a strategy was likely to culminate in the creation of a rump Palestinian state and the recognition of the state of Israel. The PDFLP countered with the example of the Democratic Republic of Vietnam (North Vietnam), which served as a rear base for the Vietnamese National Liberation Front in the struggle to reunify the nation after 1954.[7]

As of mid-1973, however, these national authority schemes had not been openly embraced by leading factions of the PLO. Fatah did not make its position on the national authority proposal clear, although its newspapers did join the PFLP in criticizing the scheme. In spite of this, Fatah and the mainstream factions of the PLO were willing to entertain the idea of a Palestinian ministate, at least in theory, during the 1972–73 period. A potential political solution would ultimately need to bring the United States and Israel into dialogue with the PLO. Accomplishing such a feat would not be easy.[8]

A Paradigm Shift in Global Politics

Israeli leaders were only too aware that they were sitting on the wrong side of prevailing opinion at the United Nations. Abba Eban expressed his concern in a letter to Secretary Rogers in November 1972: though it supported international efforts to deal with the problem of terrorism, the Israeli government condemned the UN's decision to focus on the underlying causes of terrorism rather than its prevention. The most worrisome news, Israeli officials warned, concerned Washington's desire to exempt national liberation movements from the antiterrorism initiative. Citing the secretary's statement in an earlier debate, they asserted that the issue was not one of liberation struggles but a question of the safety of international air travel, postal exchange, diplomatic service, and participation in international events such as the Olympic Games. The Israeli government was adamant that the notion of struggle for self-determination must not be used as a justification for types of criminal violence being perpetrated by the PLO and its supporters.[9]

State Department officials responded that the reference to liberation movements was necessary in order to secure the support of key African states that would not otherwise accept a resolution. Thus far, Washington had spoken only to the African delegations about the self-determination issue, believing "it would be [a] mistake to arouse Arab interest in [the] issue to point where they link up with [the] Africans and insist on self-determination language to cover Arab interests as well."[10] The implicit argument was that in the eyes of Israel and its supporters, liberation was a legitimate aspiration for African groups but not for the Palestinians.

While they might grant a degree of recognition to liberation struggles—and would be forced to at least put forward the appearance of doing so in the interest of winning African support at the United Nations—U.S. officials could not endorse a resolution that condoned the use of force by liberation groups.[11] This prohibition on violence was, in turn, unacceptable to various Third World delegations from Africa and elsewhere as violence formed the only catalyst for change in oppressive political systems. As the Sudanese delegation said, "Some forms of terrorism are [a] necessary evil in [the] struggle for sometimes glorious goals." The United States, the Sudanese suggested, ought to remember its own colonial past, which had been violently resisted, as well as its domestic racial strife and civil disorder. Rather than simply condoning the ambition of self-determination, Washington should aid in its realization. Because "violence moves people to respond to correct unjust situations, it in fact is [a] useful and valuable tool." Just as the United States was attempting to address the problem of increasing violence by its own citizens by focusing on its source, the international community should seek to address the underlying causes of terrorism rather than seeking to punish the victims of social injustice.[12]

Thus the greater part of the international community insisted on the legitimacy of violence in the global struggle against oppression. The subsequent nonaligned nations' draft on the question of terrorism expressed deep concern for international violence but reaffirmed the "inalienable right to self determination and independence of all peoples under colonial and racist regimes and other forms of alien domination" and upheld the "legitimacy of their struggle, in particular the struggle of national liberation movements." The draft went on to condemn the continued repression and terrorism by colonial, racist, and alien regimes in their efforts to deny the independence and basic human rights of subject peoples.[13] This was not what the U.S. government had in mind when it expressed hope for a UN discussion on the problem of international terrorism.

The United States and Israel were confronting a paradigm shift in global politics: Third World nations now had the clout to push their own agenda in international forums such as the United Nations. Even U.S. allies such as Indonesia—ruled by pro-American strongman Suharto—were reluctant to vote in support of antiterrorist legislation that did not include special provisions for liberation movements. The U.S. ambassador to Indonesia, Francis Galbraith, reported, "We have made repeated representations over past several weeks and I have done my best to appeal to [the] Indonesian sense of order and decency to persuade them of common interest in finding effective way to stem international terrorism, hijacking, etc." However, he noted that it would be unrealistic to expect the Indonesians to take a stand against the rest of the Muslim world. Moreover, memories of their own violent liberation struggle against the Dutch were still fresh in the minds of Indonesian leaders.[14]

Thus, the State Department fulminated over the nonaligned countries' proposed resolution, which was not likely to result in substantial action to curb international terrorism. The resolution was unbalanced because it condemned the "repressive and terrorist acts of colonial, racist, and alien regimes [while overlooking the] spread of terrorism to third countries not party to the conflict concerned or condemning injury to innocent persons." Washington instructed its embassies to push their host governments on the issue, making the case that the failure of the United Nations to take action on this issue would damage its reputation and ability to act as an effective institution in the future. The U.S. government therefore hoped for a decisive no vote on the nonaligned countries' resolution so that the way might be opened for a resolution more in keeping with U.S. goals.[15]

UN General Assembly Resolution 3034 came to a general discussion and vote on 18 December 1972. It expressed the General Assembly's concern over "international terrorism" and stressed the need for international cooperation in bringing it under control. However, its third clause reaffirmed "the inalienable right to self-determination and independence of all peoples under colonial and racist regimes and other forms of alien domination" and upheld the rights of said peoples to struggle for national liberation. The fourth clause, moreover, condemned "the continuation of repressive and terrorist acts by colonial, racist, and alien regimes in denying peoples their legitimate right to self determination and independence and other human rights and fundamental freedoms."[16] UN 3034 thus acknowledged the issue of international terrorism, but it insisted that this problem could not be removed from the political context from which it had been born. Moreover, the resolution placed primacy not on condemning or prosecuting the purveyors of "terrorist" attacks but rather on protecting the rights of oppressed peoples struggling for national liberation. Finally, it made no special distinction between "terrorism" exercised by governments and that committed by nonstate groups. Thus, far from attacking acts of violence by nonstate groups, the resolution reaffirmed the legitimacy of national liberation struggles.[17]

As expected, the General Assembly's discussion of the resolution to prevent international terrorism was explosive, with delegates split between those who wanted a strong condemnation of "international terrorism" and those who argued that the United Nations' priority must be on protecting the cause of national liberation struggles around the Third World. The Cuban delegate expressed "categorical opposition" to the inclusion of the discussion on "terrorism" because it was obviously, in his eyes, designed by the "imperialist" powers as an "instrument against the national liberation movements." Likewise, the ambassador from Guyana quoted Arnold Toynbee, who insisted that there was "only one radical solution to the problem of terrorism. We have to eliminate the cause of terrorism . . . injustice. Injustice breeds violence, violence breeds counter-violence . . . a vicious circle and process which can only be stopped when injustice is eliminated." The French ambassador argued that "terrorism" could not ultimately be separated from its causes, "whose origin is to be found in situations which, without justifying them, explain the action of men who are prepared to risk their own lives in order to draw the attention of the international community to their aspirations or to the injustices of which they consider themselves to be the victims." The Iraqi delegate announced that he would support the measure because it respected the right to self-determination: "It gives us an assurance that the measures which will be adopted can in no way jeopardize the right to self-determination, the right to national liberation."[18]

Those opposing the resolution decried its failure to condemn "terrorism" as brutal, uncivilized, and a threat to the international order. U.S. ambassador George Bush warned that

> international terrorism poses a threat to all mankind . . . to the delicately interwoven network of modern transportation and communication facilities on which every single country is dependent . . . to the passenger who travels on an airplane, and to the innocent passer-by on the street.

Attacks had taken place on "every continent of the world and the islands in between . . . No one of us is immune from this scourge of violence." He said that the United States could not vote in favor of a resolution that did not condemn "random acts of violence which threaten the security of the individual," such as those that had taken place at the Munich Olympics. The Israeli ambassador blasted the United Nations for its failure to formulate an adequate condemnation of international terrorism: "The United Nations can no longer pretend to be what it is not. In the present circumstances our Organization cannot claim to represent international law and morality." Rather than honest consideration of issues of justice and morality, the United Nations had been reduced to a "numbers game." Ultimately, he warned, Israel would not rely on any international body for guidance in responding to "terrorism." The "collapse of the United Nations effort to deal with international terrorism will make Member States more conscious than ever of the need for measures of a national and regional scale." He insisted that "the plague of terrorist barbarism must be halted.... The carriers of this plague must be eradicated with all strength and tenacity."[19]

The proponents of national liberation would win the day, however. The assembly voted to adopt the resolution by a vote of 76 to 35, with 17 abstentions. Among those nations voting against the resolution were the United States, Israel, the United Kingdom, and a number of other European and Latin American nations. Those votes in favor included a strong showing from African and Middle Eastern states.[20] As the passage of UN 3034 showed, U.S. and Israeli priorities ran counter to the prevailing currents in the international community. While the former sought security in regard to the specific issue of international terrorism, the latter group was more concerned with rolling back what it saw as the vestiges of an oppressive system of colonialism that had held sway for centuries.

The transnational political connections between states and resistance groups around the Third World had outflanked Washington's efforts to build political support at the United Nations. Bush believed that U.S. efforts were doomed almost from the start: the Arab states had, according to the ambassador, convinced the African delegations that the resolution might be used to target national liberation movements. U.S. efforts to persuade the African states to the contrary were "unavailing and Non-Aligned solidarity carried the day against any meaningful expressions of community views on international terrorism or steps to carry the matter forward." Bush lamented the failure of efforts to split the Arab and African bloc despite indications that some African delegations did not agree with the direction in which the Arabs were pushing them. Likewise, the Soviets sided with the nonaligned states. Moreover, the failure of European states such as France and Sweden to push against this momentum also contributed to the nonaligned victory.

Ambassador Bush was vexed by the outcome of the vote: rather than the strong statement against terrorism that the U.S. government had hoped for, the General Assembly passed a "weak expression of community attitudes toward international terrorism" that might eventually cause harm by focusing international attention on problems in southern Africa. In his final assessment, Bush concluded that the solidarity generated among nonaligned nations from a combination of Arab pressure and Third World distrust of U.S. motives had prevailed.[21] This notion that the nonaligned world, rather than the Soviets, was in the driver's seat on such issues pointed to the evolving nature of international politics in the postcolonial world and the growing independence of the Third World vis-à-vis the great powers in the 1970s. At the same time, the U.S. rejection of the political power of Third World governments at the United Nations would carry repercussions beyond the Security Council and ultimately dovetail with Nixon and Kissinger's ideas about refashioning Washington's strategic position in the developing world.

A Symbolic Revolution

While officials in Washington grumbled about the UN's failure to draft acceptable antiterrorism resolutions, the reality of the situation was more complex. Indeed, even participants in a conference on terrorism sponsored by the State Department's Bureau of Intelligence and Research and attended by officials from the FBI, the CIA, and the Departments of Defense, Justice, and Transportation failed to arrive at a concrete definition of terrorism. Nor were they able to distinguish the phenomenon from guerilla warfare. Indeed, the commentators concluded that "almost any group, under sufficient stress of unresolved grievances, will resort to terrorism," and seemed to agree with conclusions from supposed terrorist sympathizers that the best means of combating the phenomenon lay in addressing the underlying grievances that drove terrorist actions. Compounding the difficulties of dealing with terrorist threats, they argued, regimes that resorted to repression to fight terrorism often defeated themselves and thus lost legitimacy.[22]

Moreover, the tactical challenge of preventing terrorism was virtually insurmountable. Even the former Israeli chief of intelligence admitted that the vaunted war on terrorism had not come about, because it was impossible to prevent attacks by an organization that could strike anywhere at any time. Beyond the prospect of international antiterrorism measures, the best Israel could hope for was to continue using the same methods—ineffective as they might be—of striking at suspected fedayeen bases in order to address domestic demands for retaliation in the wake of major terrorist incidents. Even so, "terrorism was not a strategic danger to Israel," the chief admitted. "It cannot affect basic issues of peace and security."[23] Rather, the challenge posed by terrorism was of a primarily political nature.

Another troubling dimension of the terrorist dilemma concerned the impact of events on the broader Arab world. Writing from his post in Beirut, U.S. ambassador Buffum asserted that the no-war, no-peace situation was undermining the stability of the entire Arab world as well as the fedayeen movement. A growing sense of hopelessness was setting in, prompting many Arab states to accept the necessity of maintaining the cease-fire with Israel and waiting for U.S. intervention in regional negotiations. This acceptance also entailed efforts to restrain the fedayeen's action, thereby creating tensions between the regimes and the Palestinian fighters and prompting concerns among the latter of a repeat of the Jordanian trap of September 1970. The guerillas had "reached [a] point of near-paralysis where guerilla action against Israel is concerned and have no present plans for resuming" operations from Lebanon. The resistance was demoralized.[24]

Making matters more complicated, officials confronted a fluid rather than static social milieu in the region. In a conversation with State Department officials, Palestinian-American professor Walid Khalidi warned of a widening generational divide inside the diaspora. While the older generation was motivated by more practical concerns, the younger generation of Palestinians—fostered by years of frustration and hopelessness—was increasingly driven by Marxist-Leninist ideology. This movement would gain momentum as long as the basic problem of Palestinian exile remained. While the older leadership might settle for "half a loaf...they see that they are only being offered crumbs."[25]

Despite the fact that guerilla operations had sunk to a dismal state, the PLO remained actively engaged in international diplomacy, which was becoming more sophisticated with time. This type of effort was evident in the PLO's distribution of a lengthy memorandum to UN member states laying out its views on the Middle East problem. The authors argued that the state of Israel was a colonial force built upon a politico-religious movement that claimed divine right to substantial parts of Lebanon, Syria, Iraq, Jordan, Saudi Arabia, and Egypt. By using a two-pronged strategy of military expansion and creeping settlement, the government of Israel was seeking to create a state stretching from the Nile to the Euphrates. The current international environment favored Israel insofar as the Arab world was disunited, Moscow was unable to assist the Arabs, and Washington was unwilling to put more pressure on the Jewish state.[26]

The Nixon administration had, according to the PLO, sought to guarantee Israeli military superiority over the Arab states through the supply of aircraft, missiles, and electronic weapons systems to the Israeli military. The authors called upon the United States to adopt a neutral position vis-à-vis the Arab-Israeli conflict and to cut off all arms shipments and financial support to Israel. Should it fail to do this, "the moderates in the Arab world will lose to the extremists." Without a solution to the Palestinian problem that provided justice for the Palestinian people, peace in the region would be impossible. Partial settlements between Israel and Egypt or Israel and Jordan could not provide the basis for a lasting order in the region. Rather, such settlements would only bring more violence and bloodshed to the Middle East.[27]

At the meeting of the Palestinian National Council in January, discussions focused on the continuing challenge of uniting the fedayeen movement and dealing with the challenges of coordinated action. U.S. officials warned that while the current fragmentation of the movement decreased its ability to launch guerilla operations, the PLO might increasingly turn toward external operations as the only means to strike at Israel and demonstrate its continued relevance in the Arab world.[28] Meanwhile, PNC resolutions called for the creation of more links to national liberation movements, the opening of offices in Asia, Africa, and Latin America, and the establishment of closer relations with Moscow and Beijing.[29]

Intelligence assessments warned that the current disorder within the PLO was threatening its very survival. In light of the current crisis, the fedayeen had been swept by a "tide toward leftism and terrorism" that had brought the ultimate purpose and leadership of the PLO into question. The apparent reality that no combination of Arab military powers could present a challenge or even a deterrent to Israel had "forced the fedayeen into the straitjacket of 'symbolic' revolution, which consists of token guerilla activity from Syria and international terrorism against Israel and pro-Israeli targets." While its guerilla capabilities had been virtually neutralized, the PLO maintained the capacity for external operations in the international sphere: "We consider every spot in the world a natural place to exercise the various forms of struggle against imperialism and zionism," remarked one Fatah official. In a substantial sense, however, "logic dictates that the Palestinians will never be strong enough in their own right to exert significant influence on Middle East affairs," as State Department analysts put it.[30] In this regard, the weakness of the PLO and its allies threatened to encourage more acts of "terrorism."

Even as officials in Washington predicted the imminent stagnation of the guerilla movement, Fatah officials announced their plans for continuing their armed struggle in order to reinvigorate their revolution. On a visit to Baghdad in early February, Arafat reiterated the PLO's intention to attack imperialism in the Middle East in the "same way [that the] people of Vietnam smashed American imperialism." Coming on the heels of the signing of the Paris peace accords, such a close identification with the Vietnamese could not have been welcomed by U.S. leaders.[31] Indeed, the PLO and various guerilla organizations heralded Hanoi's "victory" in the wake of the Paris accords with congratulatory cover stories such as "People's War: Victory in Vietnam…and the Coming Victory in Palestine."[32]

The need to demonstrate the continued potency of fedayeen action grew stronger in April 1973, when Moshe Dayan called for Israeli settlers to "create facts on the ground," seizing Palestinian territory in the West Bank in order to lay the literal groundwork for annexation. He called for "a new State of Israel with broad frontiers…extending from the Jordan to the Suez Canal." In July, he told *Time* magazine, "There is no more Palestine. Finished." While he was no moderate, Dayan represented a strong segment of Israeli society eager to expand into Arab territory.[33]

Salah Khalaf, the leader of the more militant wing of Fatah responsible for Black September's operations, insisted that the struggle would continue despite

FIGURE 6.2 *Cover of PLO newspaper* Filastine al-Thawra, *"People's War: Victory in Vietnam and the Coming Victory in Palestine." Courtesy of the Library of the Institute for Palestine Studies, Beirut.*

current hardships. Although the current fedayeen leadership recognized that it could not presently achieve its objectives, Khalaf said, it was intent on laying the foundations for the next generation of guerilla fighters that would make its predecessors appear tame by comparison. Acknowledging that the fedayeen's primary objective was the liberation of the occupied territories, Khalaf announced his intention to wage war on Israel in every corner of the world. Because they had been deprived of the "right to struggle on our own land, it is normal to enlarge [the] field of battle." For that reason, the resistance must move underground in order to operate in clandestine networks in areas around the world. "The Americans must understand [that] we are basically a revolutionary people and that, by our action, we will continue [to] create problems in this area, giving rise to instability that will contribute to fragility of established regimes," he said. It was not, ultimately, the PLO that refused to negotiate with Washington, but vice versa.[34]

These statements were more than just empty threats. Black September had shown its ability to strike at targets around the world, beginning with the Tal assassination in Cairo and climaxing dramatically at the Munich Olympics. In late December 1972, the organization struck again, this time in Bangkok. On 28 December, four gunmen took control of the Israeli embassy, hung a Palestinian flag out the window, and took six Israeli hostages. The compound was soon surrounded by Thai police, who received the militants' demands for the release of thirty-six Palestinian prisoners held by Israel. While they refused to concede to the gunmen's demands, the police and the Israeli government agreed to grant the militants safe passage out of Thailand in exchange for the hostages' release. After an hour of negotiations, the gunmen agreed, and were put on a plane to Cairo.[35] The next hostage crisis would not end so peacefully.

Sinai and Khartoum

Regional tensions erupted in tragedy in the skies over the Israeli-occupied Sinai Desert when, on 21 February 1973, Israeli fighter jets shot down a Libyan airliner that had strayed over Sinai airspace, killing approximately 105 of the 111 people aboard. Israeli foreign minister Yitzhak Rabin told Joseph Sisco, assistant secretary of state for Near Eastern and South Asian affairs, that Israeli warplanes had fired on the Libyan jet. The two men discussed their concern over the possibility of Arab counteraction against civilian planes, and Sisco worried about the possible effect of the incident on the cease-fire between Israel and Egypt.[36]

It was becoming apparent that the tide of international opinion was turning against Israel, as delegations at the United Nations reacted with shocked disbelief. Many delegates predicted violent reprisals from the fedayeen and worried that the attack would destroy any atmosphere for negotiating in the region.

The Soviets told U.S. ambassador John Scali that they considered such a brutal action to be unnecessary and warned that it was likely to obstruct further peace negotiations in the region. The British likewise blasted the "Israeli action as brutal and stupid." The government of Israel would not be able to "explain to world opinion why it was necessary to shoot down [a] clearly identifiable commercial aircraft."[37]

The French press and government sharply criticized the Israeli attack on the Libyan airliner as well as the IDF's recent strikes on suspected guerilla bases in the refugee camps of southern Lebanon. Paris condemned all acts of terrorism, citing any violent actions that threatened to aggravate the regional situation by killing innocent civilians. Meanwhile, French newspapers condemned the downing of the aircraft; recent events had demonstrated the "pitiless policy" undertaken in the atmosphere of "total Israeli intransigence and vigilance."[38] *Time* called the action, in which Israel "carried aggression to new heights," an "unpardonable breach...of international decency."[39]

The initial response from the Israeli government was obstinate. Defense Minister Moshe Dayan reiterated that the decision to down the civilian aircraft "had no political significance whatsoever." In his eyes there was no reason Israel should expect a reprisal from the Arab world, nor should it offer any sort of compensation to the families of the slain passengers, since blame lay solely on the shoulders of the Libyan pilots. The Israeli press was more troubled by the incident, one commentator suggesting that Israel, with its relatively secure military situation, might be prepared to accept the risk that the Libyan jet represented. Furthermore, unlike the defense minister, editorialists worried about the impact of attempts to exploit the incident in the court of world opinion.[40] Though the government of Israel insisted that its actions over the Sinai were justified, it privately expressed doubts about recent events, particularly in light of the scale of human tragedy. U.S. officials wondered if the fallout from the attack might shake Israeli policy makers out of the view that the regional status quo could continue without significant repercussions.[41]

Indeed, attitudes in Israel quickly softened as the reality of the tragedy sank in. Israeli leaders signaled their willingness to make reparations to the families of the slain passengers and proposed the idea of creating a hotline between Israel and its neighbors to prevent future incidents of this sort. Israeli newspaper editorialists questioned whether a corner had been turned whereby reliance on force and the mind-set of judging "actions solely according to intentions" were no longer sufficient. Perhaps the nation had become too settled in a "frightening acquiescence in a situation of constant war with all means: of a distorted relationship of 'the whole world is against us and we are against the whole world,' of regarding force as the exclusive value and reliance on the sword as the only way of life." *Haaretz* decried the notion that international criticism of the incident stemmed from anti-Semitism or hatred of Israel. Other writers suggested that the tragedy might serve to open the door to peace: "Sometimes a single act is likely to illuminate like a flash the abyss." The Sinai disaster had shown the "necessity to close at last the file which is soaked in blood and to start an effort to make peace."[42] Questions of whether the stream of international sympathy toward the Arab world and dismay over Israel's aggressive defense strategy might have generated a new chapter in Arab-Israeli peace negotiations in the wake of the Sinai disaster were about to become moot, however.

At around 7:00 p.m. on 1 March, U.S. ambassador Cleo Noel and Foreign Service officer George Curtis Moore were leaving an informal get-together at the Saudi embassy in Khartoum when a pair of Land Rovers appeared at the front gate, and one rammed the limousine waiting for Noel. Seven gunmen emerged from the vehicles and began firing automatic weapons. While some of the guests managed to escape, Noel and Belgian diplomat Guy Eid received minor wounds and the attackers forced them, along with the remaining guests, back into the embassy building. The attackers identified themselves as guerillas from the Black September Organization, picked out the two American diplomats, Eid, the Jordanian chargé d'affaires, and the Saudi host, and allowed the rest of the hostages to leave. Responding to the crisis, Sudanese security forces sealed off the embassy and received the gunmen's demands for the release of Palestinian leader Abu Daoud, who was being held in Jordan; two West German prisoners; all Palestinian women in Israeli jails; and Sirhan Sirhan, Robert Kennedy's deranged assassin.[43]

U.S. officials considered the option of a frontal assault but concluded that the best course of action would be to wait the attackers out in hopes that they would tire and agree to release the hostages in exchange for safe conduct out of the country—a scenario similar to the one that had played out in Bangkok. They reasoned that concessions could only encourage terrorism in the future. President Nixon later speculated that had Washington caved in to the "blackmail," Noel and Moore might have been released. But he was convinced that such an act would only serve to encourage future attacks.[44] Two of the attackers' deadlines passed without any concessions or actions being taken. As the third deadline passed, Noel made a call to the U.S. embassy and was informed that an American negotiator would arrive in an hour. "That will be too late," he said, and hung up the phone. At 9:39 p.m. police heard a series of gunshots inside the embassy. At midnight, a Sudanese official called the U.S. embassy to inform officers that Noel, Moore, and Eid had been executed and the killers apprehended.[45]

As the shock of the murders set in, officials in the State Department began confronting Arab governments. The crucial matter concerned the question of how to react to this latest tragedy, which hit U.S. diplomats particularly hard. The typical public reaction from the Arab states was to argue that the real lesson of Khartoum, much like that of Munich, was that the Palestinian people must not be ignored. Much like the nonaligned nations' sentiment expressed at the United Nations, these arguments focused on the underlying causes of terrorism rather than the acts of violence themselves. Lebanese editorials written during the hostage crisis but before the killings generally voiced support for the fedayeen's actions. The resistance, having been "shackled" in Jordan, Lebanon, and Syria, was left little choice but to resort to such attacks, they argued. The Arab states were working toward a political solution that would effectively abandon the Palestinian cause, a process that was fueling desperate terrorist operations such as the one in Khartoum. "Why should we blame [Black September] men," asked the independent newspaper *An Nahar*. "They hear nothing from us but sweet words…. [H]ad we been in their position, we would have done the same." The left-wing *Al Muharrir* agreed, arguing that leaders in Washington, Amman, Riyadh, and other conservative Arab states "had rendered such operations inevitable because of their 'collusion' against [the] Palestinians." Regardless of how they might be seen by outsiders, the Black September gunmen were "viewed as heroes by [the] Arab peoples, 'who love them.'"[46]

The proximity of Khartoum to the Sinai tragedy did not help Washington's position. Joseph Greene, head of the U.S. interests section in Cairo, pressed the Egyptian government, demanding that those responsible for the Khartoum murders be apprehended rather than given an easy escape through Egypt. Washington warned that it would come down on any local government that might choose to give asylum to the attackers. Undersecretary Ismail Fahmy said, off the record, that his government deplored the murders and expressed Egyptian hopes that Washington would finally "understand that there is a difference between people and governments like Egypt, on one hand, and fanatic misguided and criminal types such as those involved in the Khartoum tragedy." Greene warned Fahmy that if the gunmen were transferred from the Sudan to Cairo and then allowed to escape, Cairo would face consequences with the United States. When Fahmy began drawing parallels between the Khartoum killings and the recent downing of the Libyan jetliner over the Sinai, Greene objected and walked out of the meeting.[47]

Although few cheered the execution of the Western diplomats, there was no mistaking the reality that many in the Arab world viewed the Sinai massacre as a direct provocation for the murders in Khartoum. Noting President Nixon's public demand that the Khartoum killers be brought to justice, Cairo's *Al Ahram* asked why a similar call had not been issued regarding the individuals responsible for the downing of the Libyan airliner. "Why didn't this crime shake the White House and why didn't it consider this crime an act of international terrorism whose perpetrators should be brought to justice?" *Al Akhbar* argued that the United States had not heeded the "message of Munich," that Washington had contributed to the regional tensions, and that Palestinian desperation had reached a boiling point. Ultimately, the paper argued, violence was the only way of forcing a change in Israel's position.[48] Algerian sentiments were similar, drawing parallels between the Sinai and Khartoum incidents and calling on the world press to recognize the injustices, perpetrated by Israel and the great powers, that had forced the Palestinians to such desperate acts.[49] Embassy officials in Abu Dhabi captured the true tragedy of the situation:

> [The] broad based international sympathy and goodwill that [the] Arabs engendered as [the] result [of] the Israeli downing of [the] Libyan plane has been completely eradicated by this act of lunatic criminal fringe of [the] Palestinian resistance movement. [The m]ovement now finds itself even further discredited in [the] eyes of [the] responsible Arab leadership and especially among those westerners, who out of conviction have championed justice of [the] Palestinian cause. [The t]iming could not have been more unfortunate in playing perfectly into Israeli hands and deliberately alienating American public opinion.[50]

World reactions to the Khartoum killings were almost universally critical. Moscow condemned the murders and sought to distance itself and the PLO from the incident, suggesting that extremist groups outside Palestinian circles might in fact be responsible for Black September's actions.[51] The Yugoslav press condemned Black September's actions, insisting that the killings hurt the Palestinian cause and distracted the world's attention from the downing of the Libyan jetliner. One editorialist argued that Middle East diplomacy stood little chance as long as terrorist attacks continued. Nevertheless, just as terror "'cannot liberate [the] world from either great or small injustices," the world could not "be liberated from increasing terror as long as it remains blind toward injustice, wherever it appears." Still, U.S. officials noted that Belgrade continued to refer to Black September as "commandos" rather than "terrorists" and refrained from blanket condemnations of the fedayeen.[52]

There was no hesitation in Washington regarding the question of whether to begin treating Fatah as a "terrorist" threat. Indeed, the U.S. government had been calling the fedayeen terrorists all along. Nevertheless, Ambassador Buffum informed the Lebanese government that, as far as Washington was concerned, Fatah was now a terrorist organization whose leaders were nothing more than criminals. The government of Lebanon should seek the arrest of criminals such as Salah Khalaf.[53] This push to criminalize the issue of terrorism ran throughout the State Department's cable traffic and seems to have been related to Washington's efforts to push antiterrorism legislation at the United Nations. At the same time, the State Department was well aware that questions of a political settlement in the Middle East and Lebanon's internal stability were linked closely to the terrorism matter as well.[54]

The exact level of involvement by mainstream Fatah leaders such as Arafat remains a highly contested issue among scholars. However, the weight of evidence—uncovered by myself and other scholars including Helena Cobban, Alan Hart, Yezid Sayigh, Tony Walker, and Andrew Gowers—suggests that

Black September operated outside of Arafat's control. Indeed, with the exception of one summary of a U.S. State Department intelligence report, which claims simply that Arafat oversaw the 1973 killing of U.S. officials in Khartoum and does not provide any more information, there seems to be little evidence to support these accusations. Furthermore, most of these claims have not held up under sustained scrutiny. Most notably, the Israeli government accused Arafat of having overseen the Khartoum killings, citing a series of recordings made by Israeli intelligence services that reportedly contain Arafat's verbal instructions to execute the American hostages. When asked to produce these recordings by a group of U.S. congressmen in 1986 seeking to bring charges of terrorism against Arafat, however, Israeli intelligence was unable to do so. Based on insufficient evidence—the CIA, which was monitoring events in the embassy, also failed to collect evidence linking Arafat to the operation—the congressional effort was abandoned.[55]

Likewise, such allegations appear to be at odds with the much better-documented efforts of moderate Fatah leaders to rein in Black September's external operations. While some of Black September's autonomy was by design, much of it was a result of the fact that Arafat's leadership was under attack from radical factions within Fatah who were using Black September as a weapon against Arafat and other more moderate leaders. Indeed, the period witnessed a fragmenting of the Palestinian liberation movement, with the appearance of a number of splinter factions and PLO challengers such as Black September, the Popular Front for the Liberation of Palestine—General Command (PFLP-GC), the Democratic Front for the Liberation of Palestine (DFLP; formerly the PDFLP), the Palestinian Liberation Front, and the Abu Nidal Organization. Arafat was moving away from violence during this period in hopes of solidifying the PLO's diplomatic influence on the world stage. He had, however, failed to consolidate his hold over the various guerilla organizations, including wayward factions of Fatah involved with Black September. Ultimately, Arafat and other mainstream fedayeen leaders hoped to suspend external operations not so much because they considered them repugnant but because they recognized that acts such as the incident in Khartoum were interfering with their efforts to legitimize the PLO in the international arena.

Ultimately, the Khartoum killings represented the last straw for Arafat and the moderate Fatah leadership. The events in Khartoum convinced Arafat that this type of violence did more harm than good to the Palestinian cause. Throughout the second half of 1973, the moderate Fatah leadership moved to distance itself from external operations, culminating in a meeting in Damascus in February 1974 in which Arafat and the Fatah leadership concluded that the phase of external operations had run its course; the next phase, characterized by international diplomacy, would now begin. "The desperation waned because of the change in situation," Khalaf pointed out. "The leadership could assert its control." Signaling the beginning of this new chapter in Fatah's armed struggle and the reassertion of his power over the organization, Arafat announced that guerilla operations would focus on territories within—not outside of—occupied Palestine.[56]

Although low- and midlevel U.S. officials recognized this pragmatic dimension within the PLO, senior officials were more interested in putting anti- and counterterrorism measures in place. The U.S. government, in addition to criminalizing terrorism, also sought to exert political pressure to combat it. "Unless the criminals are punished," Sisco claimed, "there will be no deterrent to such violent actions. We have tried to underscore...that no country is safe from terrorism."[57] The State Department thus instructed its embassies in the Arab world to make a demarche regarding the global problem of terrorism. "We believe recent events however," State's message went, "have clearly demonstrated that rationalizing [the] existence of terrorist organizations by linking them with [the] Palestine cause serves only to give them [a] wider scope to [the] detriment of all and of [the] Arab cause." Nowhere would this be truer than in the eyes of the American public.[58]

Many other governments argued, however, that groups such as Black September were acting not out of some deranged bloodlust but in defense of the Palestinian cause. Washington's efforts to claim otherwise made little progress with foreign governments. Tunisia's president, for example, countered that the extremists staged their actions in hopes of derailing peace efforts; if Washington truly hoped to achieve lasting stability in the region, it ought to open a dialogue with moderates in the movement—including Fatah—in hopes of isolating extremists and moving toward a lasting political settlement. Arafat exercised only loose control over the organization and therefore could not be held accountable for the actions of rogue factions such as Black September.[59]

Meanwhile, Ambassador Buffum presented a similar argument to Lebanese officials. Khartoum had demonstrated the terrorists' intentions to spread violence throughout the Arab world and rendered it impossible to make a distinction between Fatah and terrorist factions such as Black September. The U.S. government thus hoped that Beirut would arrest or expel Palestinian leaders who were directly linked to these actions. "The measures taken by Arab governments will be seen as an indication," the ambassador warned, "of whether or not they desire to maintain normal international standards in government to government dealing." Like the Tunisians, however, Lebanese officials argued that Arafat could not be held responsible for the actions of extremist factions within Fatah who were seeking to challenge his leadership. Aside from being unrealistic, Washington's demand that Palestinian leaders suspected of terrorist activities be apprehended would do little to change the present course of events. The only response to the radicalization of the Palestinian movement that had any hope of contributing to long-term stability would be the achievement of progress toward a peaceful settlement of the Middle East dispute.[60] However, because Washington saw Black September as an adjunct of Fatah, which in turn enjoyed a dominant position within the PLO, prospects for a political solution remained dim. Moreover, Kissinger's strategy for the Middle East precluded any progress toward a broad regional peace. In this respect, Kissinger's vision was antithetical to the goal of eliminating the root causes of PLO violence.

Some voices in the Arab world also argued for a more nuanced U.S. approach to the problem of international violence. The Tunisians decried Washington's tendency to equate terrorism with the Palestinians; terrorist groups were active in Northern Ireland, Latin America, and Vietnam. Moreover, revolutionary violence should not be used as an argument against opening a dialogue with resistance movements. Indeed, London was talking to representatives of the Irish Republican Army, and the United States itself was dealing with the Viet Cong. Thus there was little reason why recent attacks should preclude exchanges between Washington and Arafat.[61]

The question of whether states could be guilty of "terrorism" also surfaced. Habib Chatti, director of the Tunisian president's cabinet, was quick to point out that his government made no excuses for the Khartoum murders, nor did it condone terrorism from any source, including the Munich killings, the Israeli downing of the Libyan plane, and Israeli attacks on Lebanese civilians; indeed, the Israeli actions were all the more reprehensible because they were undertaken by a government. Nevertheless, he argued, Palestinian actions should not be seen as taking place in a vacuum:

> As long as [the] Palestinians are given no option—as long as they see no hope for resolution of their grievances along constructive lines— extremist elements will turn to terrorism. In [the] absence of alterna- tive, [the] fedayeen feel they have nothing to lose thereby. At least they believe they are keeping [the] issue alive and forcing world attention on their problems.

This was not a justification of violence, he asserted, but merely an attempt "to explain facts of life. These cannot be swept under the rug." Such attacks were likely to continue until Palestinian grievances were addressed, regardless of U.S. efforts to counter the violence through increased "global security."[62]

U.S. foreign service officer Joseph Zurhellen, writing from the U.S. embassy in Tel Aviv, took a similar line of reasoning, though his conclusions were quite different. He pointed out that such violence had, in fact, been instrumental in the creation of the Israeli state. The "terrorists" of the 1948–49 period were honored in Israeli society. Analogous situations existed in Northern Ireland and in Basque territories in Spain. Moreover, Zurhellen was highly skeptical of the "premise that terrorist activities are so evil in themselves that they cannot be justified by any cause in which they might be employed" and of the concept that a blanket condemnation of terrorism should be the position of "any right-thinking person." He reasoned that any group that was truly committed to its cause would resort to such acts if put in a desperate enough situation. He added:

> In this age of the wholesale destruction of civilian population which has come since 1914, and especially since the advent of nuclear warfare and other modern weapons, there are many people who see less to condemn in the assassination of a few people from time to time than they do in oppression. This is not to say, by any means, that we condone terrorism, but that if we are going to fight it effectively we must understand what it is, and what it is not.

Much of the world did not believe that terrorist actions such as those in Khartoum, Munich, and Lod were so evil that they must be condemned "regardless of one's feelings towards the cause in which they were employed." The key difference was between the view that "the terrorists must be stopped at all costs" and the argument that justice must be done for the Palestinians so that these types of attacks would stop. If Washington hoped to secure the assistance of the Arab states in controlling revolutionary violence, it must present an argument that would resonate in the Arab world.[63]

At the same time, Zurhellen argued, the United States must understand the basic objectives of the PLO. Attacks such as those in Lod, Munich, and Khartoum were designed first to "alarm the world" in hopes of prompting the intervention of the great powers in the Arab-Israeli dispute; second, to prevent a political solution on terms unacceptable to the Palestinians; and third, to radicalize the Arab world, overthrowing conservative rulers. All other considerations were secondary. The fedayeen had been largely successful in these first two objectives. Furthermore, recent external operations had forced Washington to take measures against the fedayeen that were counterproductive to broader efforts to achieve a regional peace and had alienated a great deal of Arab sentiment. In this situation, officials in Tel Aviv agreed with Greene's earlier observations from Cairo that "too much rhetoric might cause more rather than less terrorism." At the same time, Washington should seek to pinpoint the issue of terrorism by focusing on fedayeen operations against the United States, rather than seeking to universalize the issue. This latter approach would become linked to the "problems of African liberation movements, the Irish, US domestic plane hijackings [and] other extraneous considerations."[64]

This questionable practice of issuing threats to friendly Arab regimes suspected of supporting the PLO would further undermine U.S. credibility in the Middle East. Riyadh's support—especially controversial considering that the Khartoum murders had taken place in the Saudi embassy—would ultimately continue no matter how upset the king was with Arafat or how stern Washington's warnings to the regime. When all was said and done, Zurhellen wondered, would the United States really "move strongly against Saudi Arabia...without cutting off our noses to spite our faces"? The Lebanese situation presented a similar dilemma. Rather than bringing pressure on the Arab states to fall into step by condemning such attacks and embracing Washington's core objectives, Zurhellen argued, U.S. policy should "concentrate on intelligence-police operations of [a] low-key non-political nature that have already proved so efficacious in causing [a] number of planned terrorist operations to fail." It was on this tactical—not strategic—level that international action might effectively work against such operations. Shocking as events such as those in Munich and Khartoum might be, the people of the region had "endured terrible levels of terror, death and destruction over the past 25 years rather than compromise what they think are their rights and interests." The idea that the murder of two American diplomats could itself function as a catalyst for an overarching solution was simply naive.[65]

Zurhellen's cable was representative of an important shift in U.S. strategy toward the region. Namely, Zurhellen seemed to have come to terms with the idea that Washington could not win the political battle against the PLO, at least not where it counted, in the Arab world and the United Nations. Thus, Washington's efforts, insofar as they sought to combat "terrorism," should focus on tactical and police operations, rather than seeking to achieve some sort of universal political victory. This second implication was representative of deeper changes in U.S. strategy toward the Third World typified by post-Vietnam policies such as the Nixon Doctrine. In this view, the battle for hearts and minds may have been lost, but Washington's war for the Middle East, not to mention the developing world, was far from over.

"The Price We Pay for the Abandonment of Even-handedness"

World opinion continued to represent a major obstacle for Washington's efforts to formulate effective international antiterrorism policies, however, particularly in sites such as the United Nations, where the PLO enjoyed strong political support. To be sure, the Khartoum murders were seen as particularly heinous, especially by established powers. The Soviet ambassador to Khartoum volunteered both personal and official condemnation of the killings. As a fellow ambassador from a superpower, the official conveyed his concerns that the guerillas might attack Soviet interests next. He also confided that recent information suggested that Black September had prepared to attack a Soviet target, most likely an aircraft. The Soviets believed that the organization was not representative of the PLO and the Arab cause, but rather served Libyan interests, and they expressed some willingness to share intelligence information with Washington in hopes of containing future violence.[66] East German authorities were at similar pains to voice their disapproval of the Khartoum slayings while still embracing the notion of national liberation struggles against imperialism. Operations such as those carried out by Black September were unwelcome forms of resistance, so far as Berlin was concerned. One East German newspaper article that sought to link "terrorism" with Western students made the point that recent attacks were spectacular but held no promise of actually destroying the capitalist system.[67]

Meanwhile, the Kuwaiti government was in the process of reassessing its relationship with the PLO in the wake of recent Black September operations. As U.S. officials emphasized, Kuwait was small, wealthy, and vulnerable: "It walks [a] tight rope 24 hours a day and must live by its wits." Kuwaitis supported the Palestine and Arab causes not only out of genuine identification but also out of fear of retribution. For this reason, the state could not take a public stand against terrorism. The U.S. ambassador to Kuwait also added his opinion that terrorism would continue as long as there was no peace in the region. Moreover, progress toward peace was likely to result in more violence; it would thus be folly for Washington to allow recent attacks to derail peace efforts because this would ultimately play into the hands of the guerillas. Rather, even if violence increased, American efforts in pursuit of a political settlement in the region must continue.[68] The ambassador also pressed the point with the Kuwaiti government that there was a

> critical difference between guerillas who fought [a] nationalistic fight against [a] recognized foe in [a] recognized area of dispute and guerillas whose targets were indiscriminate and methods pure terror. USG was asking for cooperation of Arab govts against [the] latter type, such as BSO [Black September] in particular. Unfortunately Fatah was now exposed as associated with BSO, and therefore, it had to assume money and other support for Fatah from Kuwait found its way to BSO at least in part. Americans had proven to be target of BSO operations, and Kuwaitis would be very unwise to assume that [the] terrorists [were] not capable of turning their attention to them as well sooner or later.

He warned that, ultimately, "no one was safe from such people."[69]

As had previously been the case, French sentiment seemed to settle into a position in the middle ground. In addition to fearing that Western pressure on Arab governments to crack down on terrorists could be counterproductive, French officials were skeptical of U.S. claims that the moderate leadership in Fatah was responsible for decision making within Black September; they also pointed out that if France had a terrorist problem, it came from Israeli attacks against Palestinians rather than vice versa. The recent murder of PLO representative Mahmoud Hamchari and the bombing of the Palestinian Library, both of which took place in Paris, were almost certainly the work of Israeli intelligence services; "there had been nothing comparable in France on the Arab side."[70]

Subsequent State Department discussions with the deputy director at the French Ministry of Foreign Affairs at the Quai d'Orsay revealed a shared distaste for the problem of terrorism but diverging ideas as to how to address it. The French stated a position not so different from that articulated in the UN General Assembly: terrorism was a "global problem, which should be dealt with in [a] global context." Paris would not participate in demarches that could be seen as being anti-Arab in character, nor was it willing to mark the fedayeen leadership as criminals. While the French sympathized with the U.S. position, the Foreign Ministry repeated its belief that pressure on Arab states to crack down on fedayeen groups would be counterproductive. Furthermore, the director added that it "would be desirable" to say something to Israel regarding its "terrorist" activities in France (i.e., the Hamchari assassination).[71]

Though many U.S. officials saw the PLO's attempts to cast Black September fighters as revolutionary fighters as ludicrous, such arguments resonated elsewhere.[72] The government of Tanzania, for example, refused to issue an outright condemnation of the killers, owing to what State Department officials described as genuine sympathy for the Palestinian cause and the "belief that the fortunes of the Palestinian guerilla movement are linked to those liberation groups seeking the overthrow of minority regimes in southern Africa." A state-owned newspaper ran an editorial arguing that terrorism could be stopped only by addressing those political grievances that lay at its root: "displacement, homelessness, oppression and exploitation." Another paper commented on the disparity between the international shock over the execution of the three diplomats and the worldwide reaction to the deaths of the passengers on the Libyan jetliner. The Tanzanians were not willing to condemn liberation organizations—be they African or Arab—even though they objected to the means employed by one of the organizations. Moreover, U.S. officials warned that Washington's apparent sympathy with minority regimes in southern Africa was bolstering support among Third World regimes for liberation groups.[73] When Washington did find support for anti-fedayeen measures in Africa, it often appeared as the result of other factors. Such was the case with the government of Ivory Coast, which condemned the Khartoum incident and issued a public warning to other African governments against groups such as Fatah. A U.S. diplomat in Abidjan remarked that the condemnation was "probably drawn in part from...[the] concern of late that radical Arabs [were] attempting to make inroads in West Africa through Islam."[74]

American officials were, at the same time, pushing governments in Western Europe to join U.S. efforts to pressure the Arab states to crack down on the guerillas. Although the foreign minister's office in Bonn had no objections to approaching Arab governments regarding the issue, West German officials doubted that such action would be sufficient to address what they described as the most difficult aspect of the Middle East conflict. Fedayeen violence was rooted in deep problems that were unlikely to be affected by such approaches. Moreover, the demonstrated ability of commandos from the PFLP and Black September to mount operations in Europe made the issue even more complicated for Western governments. If, for example, a representative of its government were being held hostage, Bonn would face tremendous public pressure to engage in some sort of clandestine negotiations to secure his or her release.[75]

U.S. officials failed to account for the array of interests that different governments around the world had in fighting such violence. Indeed, while the governments of Israel, France, Sudan, the Soviet Union, South Africa, and Kuwait all had an interest in reducing violence, the situation was far more complex than the American approach allowed for. Thus U.S. efforts to push for a multilateral response to "terrorism" at the United Nations faltered.

The Palestine question and the issue of terrorism exposed the deepening fault lines between the United States and a large part of the world community. In a circular to its embassies in the region, the State Department put forth the idea that because external operations threatened to undermine the internationally recognized framework of UN 242, the Arab states ought to join Washington in opposition to Palestinian extremists. Washington warned that if "BSO/Fatah operations are allowed to continue, and if Arab governments adopt [an] acquiescent attitude toward them, it will drive [a] wedge between [the] Arab states and, not only the US, but [the] entire civilized community which considers such methods anathema." Others might argue that if the UN debates were any indication, the wedge was being driven between the United States and Israel, on one hand, and the rest of the world, on the other. The United States would not "allow actions by [a] handful of criminals to alter our view that [the] Palestinians have legitimate grievances and aspirations that must be taken into account in any peace settlement."[76]

U.S. support for Israel—a country that continued to buck UN resolutions—compounded Washington's public relations problem in the Middle East and the wider Third World. As this conversation continued, the U.S. mission in Yemen sent Washington a cable that Secretary Rogers saw fit to distribute to other U.S. embassies in the region. While they agreed with the gist of recent U.S. observations regarding the issue of terrorism, embassy officials pointed out that part of the problem lay in Washington's retreat from what could be seen as an even-handed approach to the Arab-Israeli conflict. "If [the U.S. government] truly searches its soul on this matter," they argued, "we will have to recognize that since 1967 there has been a change in U.S. Middle East policy." Prior to the June War, Washington had rejected the prospect of any forceful alteration to the 1949 armistice frontiers. After 1967, however, the United States had appeared to accept Israeli territorial gains secured through a preemptive attack upon its neighbors.[77]

Likewise, officials continued, pre-1967 U.S. arms sales to Israel had been controlled. Subsequently, however, the U.S. government had appeared to remove all limits on the flow of weapons to Israel. The cable concluded that the "Arabs and Palestinians may be inept, reckless and often mistaken but they are not blind to this shift in the American approach. Terrorism and loss of American lives are the price we pay for the abandonment of even-handedness. Terrorism will continue until we convince the Arabs that we are willing to back with U.S. action and the full exercise of our influence our stated interest in a just peace in this area."[78] This suggestion that recent attacks might be the result of a reaction to U.S. policy—rather than barbaric fanaticism—stands out in the documentary record.

The U.S. embassy in Morocco agreed with other American diplomats that any progress toward peace in the Arab-Israeli conflict was likely to carry with it the prospect of an escalation in terrorist violence, possibly directed against U.S. officials. Although the process was likely to be difficult and perhaps dangerous, embassy officials were of the view that "if we must die for our country, [we] would rather do so as result of policy [that is] moving us towards peace rather than one which appears [to] acquiesce in Israeli territorial expansion. Israeli possession of [the] Sinai and [the] West Bank may be worth [the] lives of Israelis, but not those of American diplomats." Furthermore, they argued that if U.S. officials hoped to convince Arab governments of substantial links between Black September and the Fatah leaders, including Arafat, they would have to provide hard evidence rather than just strong assertions or confessions that had been extracted through torture from captured guerillas. In any event, the issue was largely academic so far as local governments were concerned; existing arguments would still justify many terrorist operations, distasteful as they might be. Finally, U.S. officials suggested that Washington should consider Moroccan suggestions that the United States establish contacts with Arafat: "I realize how repugnant this idea has been, and have no illusions about Arafat, but we have been in touch with worse characters in the past. He and [Fatah] are factors to be reckoned with."[79] Ambassador Buffum voiced his reservations about the post-Khartoum situation as viewed from his post in Beirut. Citing evidence of increased cooperation between Fatah and the PFLP, Buffum warned that the killings had energized the movement in addition to making external operations appear more attractive. In particular, the recent attack had demonstrated the PLO's capability to directly strike the United States—which, Buffum noted, was in the process of increasing arms shipments to Israel.[80]

An Impossible Task

While Foreign Service officers argued that the best course for U.S. policy was one of moderation and continued effort to achieve a peace that might address Palestinian grievances, U.S. decision makers chose to follow another route. Ongoing difficulties in dealing with the political clout of the PLO helped shift the focus of Washington's efforts away from antiterrorism legislation and toward more direct means of countering such actions. Having concluded that they could not win a political battle, U.S. policy makers began to focus on attacking "terrorism" rather than winning arguments. Earlier suggestions that antiterrorism ought to emphasize clandestine intelligence and police activity were coming to seem like the best available option until a more lasting resolution to the Arab-Israeli conflict could be achieved.[81]

Indeed, it appeared doubtful that any Arab government besides Amman would be willing or able publicly to support the U.S.-backed initiative against the fedayeen. However, all of Israel's Arab neighbors had their private quarrels with the PLO, reservations about Khartoum-style operations, and reasons to fear extremists such as those from Black September. Thus, although public support for U.S. antiterrorist efforts was off the table, private cooperation in covert counterterrorist measures might be conceivable. It was with this reasoning in mind that the U.S. mission to the United Nations suggested that Arab governments might be willing to implement clandestine counterterrorist measures.[82]

Along these same lines, U.S. officials in Beirut suggested the possibility of strengthening intelligence ties between U.S., European, and Arab governments in an effort to make counterterrorist operations more effective.[83] Likewise, the U.S. embassy in Rome raised the prospect of bringing the Italian government on board regarding international counterterrorist efforts. The Italians, like other Western European governments, had been pulled into the conflict by the extension of Black September, PFLP, and Mossad operations into Europe in recent months. Although the typical response involved the simple expulsion of militants rather than their prolonged incarceration—most European governments had no wish to become targets of Palestinian attacks seeking to liberate imprisoned cadres—pressure from Washington might lead to a change in policy.[84]

More aggressive operations in the Middle East might also contribute to the struggle against this type of violence. The U.S. embassy in Amman argued that actions at the United Nations would ultimately be unsuccessful in fighting Palestinian guerilla organizations. Rather, the Lebanese government must launch a Jordanian-style clampdown on the PLO. Jordan was not the only example of such an action: while the Khartoum attacks had demonstrated the vulnerability of U.S. assets in the Third World, they had been accompanied by a strong response from the Sudanese government. The murders in Khartoum introduced a new level of tension between the fedayeen and the Sudanese and marked the first time since the Jordanian civil war that an Arab government had moved against the PLO. The authors went on to suggest that the reactions of the other Arab governments signaled the existence of a growing rift in the Arab world.[85]

Nonetheless, American officials in Beirut insisted that a Jordanian-style attack against the fedayeen would not be so easy in Lebanon. A full-scale assault on the fedayeen in Lebanon would be impossible given that

Beirut's "mediocre army [was] about one-fifth the size" of Jordan's, there were approximately 300,000 Palestinians living in the country, and the government was "delicately balanced between Christian and Moslem." They went on to add, "We delude ourselves if we proceed on the assumption that we can get the Lebanese govt to 'move against [the] fedayeen' as Amman appears to envisage." If a confrontation was to come, it would come at the initiative of the PLO rather than the Lebanese government, which was wary of sparking a civil war in the country. Moreover, officials pointed out the hypocrisy of demanding that PLO offices in Beirut be shut down while their counterparts in New York and various European capitals remained open. Indeed, even if a large-scale crackdown against the PLO in Lebanon could be achieved, officials believed, the violence would probably continue: the "bitter experience in Viet-Nam and elsewhere reveals the difficulties in eliminating" clandestine operations in any foreign country.[86]

State Department experts hinted to Secretary Rogers the difficulty of addressing the problem of terrorism within the framework of U.S.-Arab relations. While it hoped to create some strategy that would effectively reduce the Arab states' support for terrorist organizations, Washington should be careful not to take any action that was likely to unify the Arab world against long-term American interests in the region. A "scatter-gun approach" was likely to drive the Arab governments into closer relationships with the PLO; thus the best policy was to exploit existing inter-Arab tensions by targeting specific governments. "We believe Lebanon, a country with which we have some leverage and which occupies a key position in any effort to crack down on the terrorists[,] should be the focus of our strategy."[87]

This strategy might function in the following manner: The U.S. government should select two or three Arab states such as Libya and Kuwait that were known to provide substantial support to the fedayeen. Washington could adopt a carrot-and-stick approach to the Lebanese while using these states as a backdrop. Beirut would watch as the U.S. government instituted punitive measures against Libya and Kuwait, thus adding to the weight of American arguments. This would allow Washington to avoid a public confrontation with Beirut while at the same time making it clear to the Lebanese government that some action must be taken if it hoped to maintain good relations with the United States. In this formulation, Beirut would "be forced to choose between a conflict with the USG and serious domestic disturbances the consequences of which cannot be foreseen." Indeed, the authors warned that "punitive action by the USG would risk driving Beirut into a closer relationship with the Palestinians and a more acquiescent policy toward [the] terrorists." Moreover, they argued that Washington must give careful consideration to the idea that this strategy could "in fact play into the hands of the fedayeen, by depicting them in confrontation with the world's greatest power, by allowing them to drive a wedge between the US and the Arab governments, and by having elicited from us a reaction which will further exacerbate the atmosphere in terms of peace negotiations."[88]

The U.S. ambassador to Kuwait—a country that was one of the potential targets of this new counterterrorism policy—put forth a very different argument. He insisted that the real means of fighting terrorism lay not with the Arab states but with the Palestinians themselves. Although he agreed with others that Washington must adopt a more activist approach in dealing with terrorism, especially in the wake of Khartoum, he dismissed the notion that a crackdown in Lebanon was the best way to do this. Such a move was, in the ambassador's eyes, likely to increase Black September–style attacks and push Lebanon into a civil war, which could itself carry major repercussions in the region. Moreover, with their "mobility and international contacts," Black September and the PFLP could launch operations from Kuwait, Bahrain, the United Arab Emirates, Oman, Yemen, or locations outside the region. It was unreasonable to expect crackdowns against the PLO in all of these places. The ambassador promoted the view that the best means of addressing the problem of terrorism lay in dealing with the Palestinian problem itself:

> It seems to me that in order to successfully combat Arab Palestinian terrorism we have to come to grips with the problem of what is to be done with [the] Palestinians as a whole. [The] chief reason Arab govts are so spineless about openly declaring themselves against [the] fedayeen terrorists is because they all feel tremendous guilt about how they have treated [the] Palestinians ever since 1948. Nobody wants [the] Palestinians: they are discriminated against everywhere. They are lost souls. [The] Arab govts' excuse for 25 years has been that [the] Palestinians must be returned to their lands in Palestine, knowing perfectly well (as virtually all Palestinians themselves know) that this will never happen. It has been a charade that all Arabs have played, but [the] losers are [the] Palestinians. And [now the] Palestinians have "had it," and [the] lunatic fringe of [the] Palestinians has taken matters i[n]to its own hands.

The only real solution lay in convincing mainstream Palestinians to reject extremists such as Black September and work toward a peaceful solution to the Middle East crisis. To do this, however, the Palestinians must be given some incentive. Washington should bring concerted pressure on all sides to develop a just and fair solution to the Palestinian question, which lay at the heart of tensions in the region. Moreover, U.S. leaders should signal that they were prepared to help in solving this urgent problem and willing to talk to moderate Palestinian leaders. Although it should not be allowed to control events or American actions, recent violence was a "clear symptom of how far [the] rats are into [the] cheese. Seems to me," the ambassador concluded, "USG has some very good reasons to tell both sides in [the region that we are] not prepared to see [the] situation drift on any longer."[89] Despite the reservations of a number of embassies in the region, friendly Arab governments, and the State Department's intelligence section, Washington's sights remained on Lebanon. In April, Secretary Rogers cabled President Nixon explaining the need to continue placing pressure on Beirut to crack down on the fedayeen in spite of the risk of civil war in Lebanon.[90]

Ambassador Buffum insisted, once again, that Washington's focus on Beirut was not only dangerous but also ineffective. Citing operational information obtained from Abu Daoud—a fedayeen leader being held in Jordan whose confession was extracted through torture—Buffum laid out the series of events that had led up to two Black September operations (Munich and an aborted action in Amman). Abu Daoud had traveled to Kuwait via Beirut and then Baghdad, meeting various fedayeen leaders, before returning to Beirut. He established contacts with Eritrean rebels; purchased in Kuwait operational vehicles that were sent to Beirut to be loaded with arms before being sent on to Baghdad; and secured Bahraini, Saudi, Jordanian, and Omani passports for himself and other operatives, some of whom he met in Baghdad. "Abu Daud then trekked to Kuwait, Baghdad, Damascus (to meet [Salah] Khalaf who came from Cairo), Kuwait and Baghdad from whence he departed for Amman via Saudi Arabia on Feb 7. Members of his group were divided into four bunches, each of which was to enter Jordan separately from Saudi Arabia." Meanwhile, the first planning session for the Munich operation was held in Sofia, Bulgaria; Rome and Belgrade were used as bases for preparation for the attack, which made use of Iraqi, Libyan, and Algerian passports. The attackers themselves came from Libya.[91]

This dizzying list of locales attested to the difficulty of trying to "identify any single center where [Black September] planning and training [was] taking place." Thus, a move against any one location would do little to disrupt the long-term capabilities of guerilla groups. The only meaningful way for Washington to address fedayeen violence lay in eliciting the help of Arab governments in controlling passports and financial resources, limiting diplomatic access, and increasing state-to-state intelligence exchange in hopes of restricting fedayeen ability to move across borders. While these measures would help in the short term—though governments such as those in Libya, Iraq, South Yemen, and probably Algeria would find ways around them—the only long-term solution lay in changing the current state of affairs in the region and creating a "counter pole of attraction for Palestinians, including those among [the] fedayeen movement who retain [the] ability to think rationally." The Palestinians must be given an incentive—in the form of a political solution (Buffum here suggested enlisting Amman)—to abandon guerilla warfare. "Unfortunately," he concluded, "Israel does not seem disposed to make minimal concessions essential for this plan to be implemented, despite its professed concern over fedayeen terrorism abroad and within [the] occupied territories."[92]

The ambassador was not alone in these types of conclusions. Even in the wake of the Khartoum murders—which were in some respects more upsetting for Washington than the Munich attack was—voices in the State Department cautioned against a policy that would continue to ignore the political influence of the PLO. In early April 1973 the Bureau of Intelligence and Research released a report on the evolution of fedayeen strategy suggesting that terrorist incidents were likely to increase. Palestinian fighters had committed themselves to a military solution because they were unwilling "to play a toothless political role in the waiting rooms of foreign ministries, the Arab League, and the UN." Recent violence was due, paradoxically, to the success of Israeli counterinsurgency efforts against Palestinian guerilla fighters. The IDF's policy of exacting heavy reprisals on neighboring Arab states had pressured those states into imposing restrictions on fedayeen activity and left external operations as the only outlet for the Palestinian grievances. Since 1970, the report noted, "Palestinian terrorism has assumed the scope and character that make it a major international problem." In part, this was because terrorist operations had paid off for the fedayeen in financial, political, and diplomatic terms. In addition to prisoner releases and payoffs, large operations had damaged the credibility of the PLO's enemies in the Arab world (such as Jordan), radicalized the region, slowed the peace process, bolstered the PLO's credibility, and brought pressure on the great powers.[93]

Ultimately, organized Palestinian nationalism was likely to result in violence if not given some avenue of legitimate political expression. State intelligence analysts saw that as Israel's protector, Washington remained a primary adversary of the PLO, and its actions had seriously damaged U.S.-Arab relations. Because Palestinian violence was rooted in a sense of mass injustice, it was unlikely to be stopped by reprisals and retaliatory military attacks. Rather, the best hope for a long-term solution lay in the resolution of the deeper Arab-Israeli dispute and the Palestine question itself. Efforts to restrain less violent actions such as hijacking and hostage taking might actually lead to an increase in the bloodier type of attacks seen in recent months. External operations would be a major threat so long as they remained the Palestinians' only option. "Whatever materializes," the report concluded, "it is unlikely that the PLO can be ignored. However savage and unruly, it speaks for a large bloc of Arab opinion, and it may well be a progenitor of the Arab leadership of the next generation." Ultimately, the authors added, the PLO was "only agency that can speak for the Palestinians *en masse*."[94]

Furthermore, Palestinian external operations were as much a product of internal division as of outside pressure. U.S. officials in Beirut argued that the Khartoum operation and other recent terrorist attacks had created "considerable ferment" within the PLO among leaders who had hoped to steer the movement away from these attacks and back toward guerilla operations or, at worst, achieve a compromise that would allow for the continued survival of fedayeen moderates. A major component of this disquiet was rooted in concerns that tighter border controls in Lebanon might in fact force the fedayeen to turn to external operations as the only outlet for their armed struggle. Despite these efforts to reinvigorate fedayeen guerilla activities, U.S. ambassador to Lebanon William Buffum argued, officials were likely to see more attacks in the future. In lieu of alternatives, PLO leaders who wished to scale back "terrorism" were left "with no argument strong enough to withstand [the] demagogic appeal of radicals" and no means of quelling the "frustrations and bitterness of the many Palestinians who see no future for themselves or their families, no sense of identity as Palestinians, and no hope of retaining influence (even negative influence) with Arab govts except by [a Black September]-type action." However, he noted that if there was a genuine possibility of the creation of a Palestinian state, the hand of the moderates might be strengthened.[95]

Other observers echoed this notion that Palestinian hopelessness was fueling external operations. Indeed, as debates at the United Nations had shown, many Western European governments were skeptical of U.S. efforts to fight "terrorism" through international action. West German officials insisted that violence was rooted in the basic tensions of the region and was thus likely to continue until a comprehensive peace settlement appeared. Thus, the only real hope for reducing violence lay in combined superpower action to achieve a solution to the Arab-Israeli conflict. Prospects for such a solution remained dim, however, as the cycle of attacks and reprisals continued.[96]

Israel's War on "Terror"

Shortly after midnight on 10 April 1973, approximately sixty Israeli naval commandos and paratroopers armed with machine guns and eight hundred pounds of explosives landed small boats on several beaches and wharves in Beirut. The soldiers were picked up by undercover Mossad agents in rented cars and driven to two different destinations. One group went to Rue Khaled Ben al-Walid, to a pair of apartment buildings housing PLO leaders Abu Yusuf, Kamal Adwan, and Kamal Nasser. The Israelis burst into the apartments, machine-gunning the three men along with Abu Yusuf's wife. A number of fedayeen guards, two Lebanese policemen, and an Italian woman were killed in firefights as the commandos made their escape. A second group of soldiers drove to the PFLP's headquarters, where they planted the explosives, destroying three floors of the building. Meanwhile, more Israelis attacked the village of Ouzai and a nearby arms factory, and commandos attacked a machine shop in the Doura neighborhood. Twenty-five miles south, in the city of Sidon, Israeli commandos blew up a fedayeen garage.[97] This bold operation—dubbed "Spring of Youth"—would once again highlight the gulf between international opinion and the United States and its Israeli allies, raise the prospect of another

U.S. veto at the United Nations in defense of Israel, and arouse a new wave of anti-U.S. sentiment in the Middle East.

The IDF's attack on Beirut on 10 April 1973 demonstrated the precision and the ferocity of Israel's counterterrorism capabilities. Lebanese, Palestinian, and Arab reactions to news of the attack were a mixture of shock and outrage. The Lebanese government insisted that Operation Spring of Youth represented a brazen violation of its sovereignty by a neighboring state that amounted to "state terrorism" engineered to "either to exterminate the Palestinian people, or to force them to surrender their legitimate rights." Accusations of U.S. assistance soon appeared alongside fedayeen denunciations of the raid. Rumors that Mossad agents had used U.S. passports and cars circulated throughout Lebanon, as did reports that some of the Israeli attackers had taken refuge at the U.S. embassy following the attack. The embassy compounds, said Ambassador Buffum, had become a convenient target for those who were angry in the wake of this latest reprisal.[98]

While they were less inclined to engage in conspiracy theories than the general population, Lebanese officials were furious. Ambassador Najati Kabbani warned Assistant Secretary Sisco that these repeated attacks represented a direct threat to Lebanese sovereignty. Kabbani argued that, rather than a reprisal for a recent fedayeen attack in Cyprus, the raid represented Israel's active defense strategy, whereby the IDF would attack the PLO at will, effectively opening Lebanon to Israeli strikes. The distraught ambassador signaled that Beirut was considering approaching the Security Council to demand some sort of action against Israel. Sisco cautioned against such an approach and advised that it would not receive Washington's support.[99]

Rather, the only solution—so far as the U.S. decision makers were concerned—envisioned tighter Lebanese controls over the guerillas, something for which Washington had been calling for some time. The only way for Lebanon to ensure its own security would be to rein in the guerillas. Ignoring for the moment the demonstrated inability of the Lebanese government to accomplish this task, Kabbani argued that a distinction must be made between fedayeen political organization and tactical planning in Lebanon and the actual execution of attacks elsewhere. While cross-border attacks could and indeed were being controlled by the Lebanese government, the type of counterterrorism operations against the fedayeen organizations that the United States and Israel were demanding could only be carried out using authoritarian measures. The "fedayeen enjoy [the] same freedoms that all Lebanese citizens have," Kabbani said. "These freedoms, which are rooted in [the] Lebanese political system, should not be considered as constituting [a] violation of [the] ceasefire and armistice agreements." Lebanon was not a police state.[100] The liberal nature of Lebanese society had allowed the fedayeen to operate outside of the government's control; it also made the nation a prime target for Israeli reprisals.

In contrast to Lebanon's relatively open society, the authoritarian monarchy in Amman had managed to crush the PLO's organizational structure. Jordanian officials were "positively gleeful" upon learning of the raid and had begun plotting black propaganda designed to forge a rhetorical link between the moderate Yasir Arafat and the more radical Abu Iyad, who had not been killed in the strike. Even Amman, however, did not consider it advisable for the Lebanese government to confront the fedayeen directly. Nevertheless, the government should do everything in its power short of a showdown to keep Beirut from becoming a battlefield between the PLO and the IDF.[101]

Dirty tricks and stepped-up police operations would not, however, generate a comprehensive solution to the problem of organized Palestinian nationalism. As Secretary Rogers explained in a memo to President Nixon, the biggest sticking point may have been the close relationship between Washington and Beirut and the array of shared U.S.-Lebanese interests. American leaders, in confronting Lebanon on the issue of the PLO, were approaching friends who had good reason to be worried. The relatively large number of Palestinians living in Lebanon (approximately 10 percent of the population), the small and comparatively weak Lebanese military, and the fear that Muslim extremists and left-wing elements might unite with the PLO in the event of a crackdown raised the very real prospect of a civil war. In spite of these concerns, Rogers argued that Beirut *had* managed to place significant limits on fedayeen action in Lebanon, most notably by pushing the guerillas away from the Israeli border and thereby almost eliminating guerilla attacks from Lebanese soil.[102] Now Washington was insisting that Beirut embark on the tremendously difficult and dangerous task of moving against Palestinian organizations based in Lebanon that might be involved in planning terrorist attacks elsewhere.

Indeed, recent Israeli reprisals were pushing Beirut toward a confrontation with the PLO in a sort of repeat of the scenario that had played out in Jordan in the run-up to the September 1970 war. As pressure for a confrontation mounted, Rogers maintained that Washington must reassure the government of Lebanon of its position as an ally. If they were confident of Washington's support, Lebanese leaders would be more likely to crack down on the commandos. For this reason, the Pentagon should begin making more arms and communications equipment available to the Lebanese military; plans should also be made for U.S. action to shield Beirut from a possible Syrian intervention in the event of a showdown between the PLO and the Lebanese forces. With this in mind, Rogers proposed continued efforts to push Beirut to take measures to deal with Black September and Fatah.[103]

Meanwhile, voices in the Arab world continued to accuse the United States of having a hand in the Beirut raid. Indeed, Arab shock at the IDF's ability to orchestrate such an operation fed conspiracy theories about American involvement in the attack. West Bank Palestinians were dismayed and "intensely embarrassed that [the] IDF could waltz into an Arab capital and gun down leading resistance leaders in their bedrooms." The Israeli intention with the raid had been to drive home the reality that the PLO's struggle was hopeless, editorials in local newspapers suggested. In addition to accusations of U.S. and Jordanian assistance, one writer argued that the raid demonstrated that Israel's presence was "no longer confined to Palestine and has become [a] thorn in [the] side of [the] entire Arab nation." Indeed, far from concluding that the struggle was futile and must be abandoned, one writer argued that the operation, in conjunction with long-standing U.S. support for Israel, was a lesson to Arab leaders about the fundamental futility of seeking aid from Washington.[104] While impressive, the Beirut raid, like other reprisals before it, generated defiance rather than submission.

The raid did have one unanticipated effect on the PLO's external operations, however. In response to the attack, in which several key Fatah officials were assassinated, Fatah reorganized its command structure. Most notably, the attack prompted a reconciliation between Arafat and Khalaf, whose falling-out had come as a result of Black September's rise. The Israeli attack on Beirut ultimately helped Arafat reconsolidate his control over Fatah's more militant factions.[105]

Reactions at the United Nations were largely critical of Israel. As expected, Moscow criticized Israeli aggression and reminded the assembly of Washington's earlier veto in defense of the post-Munich reprisals, while Syria and Sudan both charged Israel with crimes of genocide for its attempts to silence and eradicate the nation of Palestine. The more moderate Yugoslav representative criticized Israel for the latest raid: "Superior force was used against [a] small peaceful country whose only protection is [the] UN." He insisted that the Security Council address the Beirut operation, arguing that it was unacceptable to place the actions of governments such as Israel alongside those of individuals such as the fedayeen.[106] The Algerian ambassador accused Washington of encouraging Israeli belligerence, noting that it was "curious that the U.S. should recognize no responsibility for the use that is made of the arms and financial aid that it furnishes Israel, or that it should express astonishment at the suspicion shown toward it when events such as those in Lebanon take place." In the end, Washington was able to avoid using its veto by abstaining from a resolution condemning the Beirut raid and deploring all recent acts of violence.[107]

Israeli discussions with U.S. officials make clear just how estranged the Jewish state had become from the majority at the Security Council. Foreign Minister Abba Eban laid out his government's concerns that a joint British-French resolution resembled Arab drafts. He was nevertheless confident that Washington would use its veto if the final resolution received supporting votes from the rest of the Security Council. Of course, if the resolution was acceptable to Israel, it would never receive enough votes to pass. Eban argued that Washington should announce its intention to veto any resolution that it did not deem balanced. Prime Minister Meir, he emphasized, was adamant that "there be no weakening on [the] part of [the] US. Any abstention by US would be taken as a change in policy" from Ambassador Bush's earlier veto. Indeed, Kissinger's "instinct" was to use the United States' veto, although he understood the need to merely abstain, considering London's involvement in the resolution.[108] The stark divisions between the U.S. and Israeli positions and the position of much of the international community could hardly have been clearer.

The Israeli government remained defiant in the face of international criticism. In an interview, Eban explained that the attack had discouraged the fedayeen and, importantly, drawn little criticism from the United States.[109] In an earlier piece of analysis, U.S. ambassador Zurhellen commented on this phenomenon, observing that the "Israelis are growing accustomed to standing alone in the world and are learning to live with the fact that the world often does not agree with their decisions." They were disturbed, however, that despite their history of oppression, they had been cast in the role of oppressor vis-à-vis the Palestinians. Israeli leaders saw this as an unjust image, he added, which "rankles them far more than any fear that the country is heading down a one-way road toward militarism or any suggestion that their credo of overwhelming might in defense of a secure existence might have a corrosive effect on Israeli society."[110]

While the Beirut raid grabbed headlines, an ongoing assassination campaign in Europe represented a quieter, if potentially more disturbing, example of Israeli counterterrorism. Following the murder of Israeli athletes at the Munich Olympics, the Israeli cabinet convened to devise a strategy of joint Mossad, Shin Bet, and military intelligence operations against Black September operatives in Europe that would function side by side with the IDF's punitive strikes in the Arab world.[111] Meir appointed Major General Aharon Yariv to head up the operation. "The policy was to go for the leaders, and also to create circumstances under which it would make it very difficult for [Palestinian agents] to operate," Yariv said. "Maybe there were other defensive ways, and we also understood that it was risky. What we could do, they could do as well." Indeed, Palestinian operatives were eager to join the fight. Salah Khalaf, head of Black September, argued that because guerilla attacks from Lebanon, Jordan, and Egypt were now impossible, the fedayeen had begun to "fight the enemy anywhere in the world because every country bears the guilt for Palestine." *Time* magazine warned in 1973 that the Israeli operation, nicknamed "Wrath of God," was turning Europe into a battlefield.[112]

While it had monitored fedayeen activity, the Mossad did not treat the PLO as a priority until after the 1970 war in Jordan. The Mossad's involvement increased, however, as the scope of the PLO's external operations increased from an estimated 3 percent of total activities in 1971 to approximately 30 percent by 1973. Western Europe would be a key theater of operations for both

Palestinian and Israeli intelligence. Many of the Israeli activities in Western Europe would be coordinated by Baruch Cohen, a native of Haifa who had served with the Shin Bet in the West Bank and Gaza before being transferred to the Mossad. The Munich massacre was the trigger for this escalation of the Mossad's anti-fedayeen activities.[113]

In what reporters began calling a "war of the spooks," Mossad agents began assassinating suspected Palestinian leaders in Europe. Wail Zwaiter, the Palestinian translator of *One Thousand and One Nights* whom Israel accused of plotting attacks on the El Al aircraft, was gunned down the lobby of his Rome apartment building in October; Mahmoud Hamchari, publisher of Fatah's French-language newsletter, died from injuries from a bomb hidden in a telephone in his Paris apartment; Hussein Bashir was killed by a bomb placed under his bed in a hotel room in Cyprus. This was a dangerous business, however. The day after Bashir's assassination, Baruch Cohen was shot while walking along a crowded street in Madrid. Ami Shachori, an official in the Israeli embassy in London, was killed by a letter bomb, and Khodr Kanou, a Syrian suspected of working as a double agent for Israeli intelligence, was shot outside his apartment in Paris.[114]

The operation took an embarrassing turn for Israel when one of its hit squads made the mistake of murdering Ahmed Bouchiki, a Moroccan waiter they mistook for a PLO operative, in Lillehammer, Norway, in front of his pregnant wife. Local officials apprehended six Israeli agents in connection with the killing, setting off an international scandal over the ongoing assassination program.[115] From Beirut, Ambassador Buffum fumed that such events were ultimately hurting efforts to fight violence associated with the conflict both in the Middle East and elsewhere:

> Recent arbitrary Israeli assertion of its court jurisdiction over [the] fedayeen captured in Lebanon, Mrs. Meir's statement on [Israel's] obligation and justification [in striking] "terrorists" wherever they might be, and [the] incident in Norway are grist for [the] mill of [the] fedayeen and their supporters. These events enable [the] fedayeen to reinforce their longstanding argument that they are justified in using terrorism since it was [the] Israelis who introduced it into [the] area in [the] first place, [the] Israelis have never stopped using it against Palestinians and other Arabs, and [the] latter must therefore protect themselves by using similar methods. It will be interesting to see if some of these arguments emerge during [the] current United Nations consideration of terrorism.[116]

According to Black and Morris, the Lillehammer debacle—and Baruch Cohen's assassination, if Salah Khalaf is to be believed—dealt a devastating blow to the Mossad's operations in Europe. The prosecution of the assassination squad in Norway revealed the extent of Israel's clandestine mission in Europe: "Agents who had been exposed had to be recalled, safe houses abandoned, phone numbers changed and operational methods modified." Nevertheless, Mossad hit squads continued to hunt PLO operatives throughout the following decades, albeit at a less frenetic pace.[117]

Meanwhile, Israeli military leaders remained confident in their superiority in the Middle East itself. Although its increased dependence on the United States for arms represented a potential point of vulnerability—especially as voices in Washington began calling for the channel of arms to be used as leverage to pressure Israel to grant concessions in the peace process—much of the military establishment was convinced both of its ultimate supremacy in the region and of Washington's continued support. "Israel is a military superpower," General Ariel Sharon announced in July.

> Nothing will happen if America stops sending [Phantom warplanes]. But it is a mistake to think that America will apply sanctions against us. For the Americans there is nothing more important than a strong Israel. All the forces of European countries are weaker than we are. Israel can conquer in one week the area from Khartoum to Baghdad and Algeria. But there is no need for that.

In the coming months, the IDF would be put to the test in the Sinai Peninsula and the Golan Heights, but Sharon's statements proved largely correct.[118] Throughout 1973, Washington remained committed, as Kissinger remarked in October, to "maintaining the military balance in the Middle East in order to bring about a negotiated settlement that we had sought."[119] The Nixon administration would preserve Israel's military superiority as part of its larger effort to achieve a regional settlement that was favorable to U.S. interests.

Ultimately, Israeli counterterrorist operations such as Spring of Youth and Wrath of God blurred the lines between "terrorism" and response as counterterrorist agents adopted many of the tactics used by the supposed terrorists. This practice bolstered outside assertions that Israel's state-sponsored attacks were even more deplorable than similar actions undertaken by nonstate groups. The Lebanese government insisted that there was a crucial difference between acts of terrorism by individuals and attacks on civilians by the armed forces of a government.[120] This transnational war of the spooks had sweeping political implications. As an Israeli intelligence chief would observe decades later, "[The Palestinians] think in strategic terms much better than we do. They analyze our strategy. They do not always draw the right conclusions, but they understand that the aim of any military operation is political, and that the success of such operations should be measured in political terms."[121] Indeed, the Israeli-PLO war of the spooks diluted American arguments about good versus evil, and thereby the situation's ambiguity, which was not lost on the international community.

The strains of military counterterrorism could also threaten regional stability. The aftershocks from Israel's attack on Beirut continued through the spring of 1973. In late April, Arafat's moderate leadership appeared to be slipping and the fedayeen seemed to be moving toward a confrontation with the government.[122] On April 27, Lebanese police arrested three men—who turned out to be members of Fatah—attempting to board an Air France flight with ten kilograms of dynamite. Concerned about the volatility of the situation, security forces blocked the road to the airport and set up barricades around the Sabra and Shatilla refugee camps in Beirut. The following day, Black September issued bomb threats and demanded the prisoners' release as authorities increased security around the airport.[123]

Fighting between the guerillas and government forces broke out on 2 May around the Beirut camps, apparently encouraged by intra-fedayeen competition between the PDFLP and Arafat's more moderate leadership. The PLO accused the Lebanese government of seeking to paralyze the resistance and attacking the PLO's civilian supporters in Lebanon. While they insisted they had no intention of interfering with Lebanese self-rule, they also said they would defend themselves against attacks by Lebanese security forces.[124]

Fedayeen snipers took positions atop apartment buildings while Lebanese artillery and tanks fired on the camps and the roads leading into them, destroying a number of buildings. Negotiations between Arafat and left-wing Lebanese leaders such as Druze leader Kamal Jumblatt secured the release of three captured soldiers and led to a cease-fire, which put an end to the immediate crisis, but the underlying tensions remained unresolved. On 20 May, fedayeen elements captured two more Lebanese army officers, precipitating a minor confrontation with the government in which security forces again laid siege to a number of the camps. As the siege continued, Lebanese tanks began shelling the camps, setting a number of buildings ablaze as the guerillas returned fire.[125]

Beirut's problems with the fedayeen were only the beginning, however; the mounting crisis in Lebanon was proving to be immensely complex. The influence of regional powers made the situation more volatile. The U.S. embassy in Beirut cabled Washington, warning

> that [the government of Israel] wishes [to] force a Jordanian-type confrontation between [the] Lebanese and [the] Palestinians, tactically to further deter cross-border and terrorist operations by [the] fedayeen but strategically to eliminate [the] Palestinians as a political force which [the government of Israel] must factor into its dealing with Arab govts.

Robert Houghton, the U.S. chargé d'affaires in Beirut, repeated his and his colleagues' conviction that "Lebanon is not Jordan" and that Beirut would seek to avoid a direct confrontation with the PLO while still trying to impose tighter controls over the guerillas. He was adamant that the Israeli leaders not assume they had the right to strike targets in Lebanon at will. The apparent belief that Israel could force confrontations in Lebanon could by no means be construed as self-defense. Moreover, he warned that Israeli actions might very well impinge on U.S. interests and the safety of American citizens around the Arab world. Washington should make it clear to Israel that provocations would complicate Beirut's efforts to rein in the fedayeen and make the situation more dangerous for Americans throughout the region.[126] Houghton insisted that Beirut currently needed all the help it could get in its effort to control the guerillas, and Israeli statements had the effect of inflaming sentiments among all competing factions. While the fedayeen saw Israeli statements as justification for why they must remain armed in order to defend themselves against foreign attacks, pro-government factions interpreted it as another "tightening of [the] screw by Israel on Lebanon in [an] effort [to] provoke [a] full scale fight and [a] possible civil war."[127]

The threat of civil war was growing dire. The small Lebanese army was internally divided and unlikely to be able to keep the peace in the event of a major sectarian conflict. While left-wing forces in Lebanon might seek to leverage a crisis to gain power, both Syria and Israel might use a crisis in Lebanon as an excuse to launch a major armed intervention.[128] The danger of the conflict in Lebanon turning into a regional conflagration was potentially greater than had been the case in Jordan in September 1970 due to Beirut's extensive economic and political links with other Arab nations, the probability that Lebanese security forces would have a more difficult fight against the fedayeen, and the near certainty of Syrian meddling in any prospective conflict. A further reservation, voiced by the government of Kuwait, was that the PLO not be pushed out of Lebanon and into the Gulf states. Were this to happen, the fedayeen would be farther from Israel but much closer to oil facilities, which could become targets in the PLO's global war. U.S. officials insisted that forcing the PLO out of Lebanon would not put an end to fedayeen and terrorist violence.[129] The following year, Israel would launch a new initiative to fortify the Lebanese border by supporting a Lebanese Christian militia led by Sa'ad Haddad, who would later form the infamous South Lebanon Army.[130] There seemed to be no reasonable solution to the mounting problems in the small republic.

Meanwhile, the Jordanians had begun channeling arms into Lebanon through Saudi Arabia, Iran, and Turkey. While King Hussein was pessimistic about Beirut's ability to crack down on the guerillas as effectively as had been the case in Jordan, he agreed to work with the United States in building up Lebanese forces to the point where they might triumph in a confrontation with the PLO. The other question posed by U.S. officials concerned what Amman would do if the Syrians intervened in Lebanon. Noting that he had already moved his army to the Syrian border and placed it on high alert, the king replied that he would be willing to attack Syria if asked to do so by Washington. The United States, however, must "be prepared to help him out when the rest of the Arabs fall on him like a ton of bricks. I don't think we need to charge up King Hussein any more on this issue," Ambassador L. Dean Brown added.[131]

U.S. officials were keen on the notion of using Jordan as an example for dealing with the coming crisis in Lebanon. Ambassador Brown argued that the Jordanian model should be used as a means of dealing with the PLO in Lebanon. As had been the case in Jordan, the ambassador believed, the government should move slowly, since a showdown was likely to destroy Beirut. While the fedayeen would certainly recognize a military buildup, any attempt to take preemptive action against the Lebanese government would provide the pretext for a large-scale crackdown on the PLO in Beirut. The ambassador expounded upon "the squeeze: systematic, house by house clean-out of strongpoints in Beirut; harassment below the level of showdown. Above all," he added, the Lebanese government should drive a "wedge between camp-dwellers and fedayeen on one hand and between fedayeen and Sunni Moslems on the other." He even suggested that UN aid might be disrupted in such a way as to put the PLO's credibility in doubt. Such actions might serve to preoccupy the fedayeen, redirecting their energies away from terrorism.[132]

This plan to crush the PLO between the Israeli hammer and the Lebanese anvil overestimated the strength of the Lebanese political system. As embassy officials in Beirut pointed out, the fedayeen outnumbered the Lebanese security forces. Although the army had greater firepower, urban warfare would diminish this advantage. State Department officials warned that despite U.S. efforts to shore up the regime, the overall position of the Lebanese government vis-à-vis the fedayeen was not improving and might well be deteriorating. The biggest danger, however, lay in the nation's deep confessional divisions between Sunni, Shi'a, and Christian minorities, sectarian rifts that the U.S. government should not be trying to manipulate. In light of these mounting difficulties and potential hazards, embassy officials warned that the government of Lebanon might "eventually be forced [to] make compromises that could produce far-reaching changes not only in [the] Lebanese power structure, but in [the] balance between radical and 'moderate' forces in [the] Arab world."[133]

The U.S. embassy in Beirut was not alone in its fears about the risk of sparking a sectarian conflict in Lebanon. Former Lebanese president Camille Chamoun warned that the state could not survive a clash with the fedayeen. Indeed, Beirut would need at least three more army divisions merely to survive. A confrontation with the guerillas would likely be disastrous.[134] Meanwhile, the PFLP had begun to refer to the recent fighting with Lebanese forces as "Black May," an ominous reference to the 1970 crackdown in Jordan. Radical fedayeen leaders called on Palestinians in Lebanon to strengthen fortifications in their camps using the "'Vietnamese example,' to make their camps 'impregnable' against forces, led by the US and Israel, who are still trying to 'liquidate' the fedayeen through a repetition in Lebanon of the September 1970 events in Jordan. 'History will not repeat itself—the events of Jordan will not recur here.'"[135]

The events of late 1972 through 1973 illustrated the complexity of the issue of international "terrorism," largely as a result of the diffusion of power in forums such as the United Nations that had given more influence to nonaligned states. As much as U.S. officials detested the argument made by Third World governments at the United Nations that the underlying causes beneath terrorism—rather than the acts of violence themselves—must be addressed, they could no longer ignore them. The following months and years would show that police and military actions could not suppress Palestinian nationalism. Indeed, the U.S. officials with the most exposure to the Arab world—the Foreign Service officers serving in places such as Cairo and Beirut—were suggesting that the PLO, as a political movement, was not going to go away no matter how many times the IDF bombed Beirut. As long as Palestinian grievances remained unanswered, they would continue to fuel violence regardless of any action taken by U.S. or Israeli officials. Ironically however, the heyday of the PLO's external operations had already passed by late March 1973. These spectacular acts of violence had helped rebuild the PLO's credibility as a regional force and kept the Palestinian issue alive in the international forums as the guerillas struggled to recover from the disaster in Jordan. In doing so, events such as those in Lod, Munich, and even Khartoum allowed PLO moderates to move toward the prospect of a political solution rather than a purely military one.

Even as segments of the PLO began to discuss a diplomatic solution, Israel and the United States redoubled their efforts to contain Palestinian influence. Operation Spring of Youth marked the spectacular culmination of a larger process unfolding in Israel and Washington circa 1973: the turn away from antiterrorism initiatives at the United Nations and, in Israel's case, toward counterterrorism policies on the ground. This transition stemmed in large part from the failure of earlier efforts on the part of the United States and Israel to persuade the international community to support antiterrorism legislation. Far from sanctioning U.S. and Israeli efforts to criminalize the PLO, UN debates on the problem of international terrorism showcased the political influence of emerging Third World nations in the international community. Although the United Nations lacked direct military power, its influence as the only institution of global governance was increasingly important in a globalized world order. Thus, while U.S. officials held a certain degree of contempt for nonaligned power in the United Nations, they were now inclined to take it more seriously, if not more sympathetically. Although a U.S. veto in the Security Council had struck down the resolution that came out of Secretary Waldheim's initiative, debates on the issue of terrorism continued in the General Assembly. As had been the case before, these discussions pointed to the gulf between the U.S. and Israeli position on the question of terrorism and national liberation and the position of much of the nonaligned world.

In retrospect, the bloody events of early 1973—Sinai, Khartoum, Spring of Youth—might have led to a change in policy on the part of the U.S. and Israeli governments, the actors with the most power to alter the course of events in the region. Unfortunately, the opposite proved to be the case. While the Sinai disaster resulted in widespread shock and introspection in Israel, this reaction was quickly overshadowed by the horror of the Khartoum murders. Likewise, U.S. attitudes hardened in the second half of the year. Fury over the killing of its diplomats combined with a growing sense of alienation at the United Nations to push U.S. policy further in favor of Israel and its active defense strategies. U.S. leaders seemed resolved to continue the global campaign against terrorism with or without the support of the world community, the approval of its allies, or the endorsement of its many of its Foreign Service officers. Meanwhile, the Israeli government became more entrenched in its counterterrorist strategies, which were designed to advance a robust military response to terrorist threats. Tragically, this narrowing of options came only months before another tremendous opportunity for progress in the Arab-Israeli conflict and the question of Palestine.

The Diplomatic Struggle

On 13 November 1974 the United Nations General Assembly invited Yasir Arafat to address the assembled representatives shortly after the United Nations recognized the PLO. "We live in a time of glorious change," Arafat observed, when "an old world order is crumbling before our eyes, as imperialism, colonialism, neo-colonialism and racism...ineluctably perish." The chairman expressed his faith in the future and his hope for a world in which "just causes will triumph," but he condemned those nations—citing the United States in particular—that stood in the way of those causes. "All this is done not only at our expense," he continued, "but at the expense of the American people, and of the friendship we continue to hope can be cemented between us and this great people, whose history of struggle for the sake of freedom we honour and salute." As he neared the end of his address, he issued a warning to the assembled representatives: "Today I have come bearing an olive branch and a freedom fighter's gun. Do not let the olive branch fall from my hand. I repeat: do not let the olive branch fall from my hand." He concluded on a hopeful note: "Wars flare up in Palestine, and yet it is in Palestine that peace will be born."[1]

Arafat's speech signaled the beginning of what the PLO hoped would be a new chapter in its struggle, when diplomacy would replace international guerilla operations. Spectacular attacks such as those in Lod, Munich, and Khartoum had paved the way for Arafat's appearance in front of the General Assembly; now the PLO's leadership had shifted its global offensive to the diplomatic phase. The impetus for this transition had been building within the ranks of the fedayeen for several years, but the principal catalyst came in the form of the 1973 Arab-Israeli War. In the wake of the conflict, the PLO leadership began hinting at its willingness to negotiate for a two-state solution as part of the postwar peace process and to establish open relations with the United States. These gestures would be given the cold shoulder by Henry Kissinger and Israeli leaders, however. As Arafat and the PLO gained ground in the international arena—at the Rabat meeting of the Arab League and in the UN General Assembly—the United States and Israel moved to lock the Palestinians out of the formal peace process, ensuring that violence would continue for the foreseeable future.

The October 1973 War

On 6 October 1973 Egyptian forces, using water cannons and Soviet bridging equipment, breached the Israeli Bar-Lev line, a supposedly impenetrable network of defenses along the east bank of the Suez Canal. At the same time, Syrian forces attacked Israeli positions in the Golan Heights. The new leaders in Cairo and Damascus, Anwar al-Sadat and Hafiz al-Assad, had launched a surprise attack on Israeli positions in the Sinai and the Golan Heights that would dramatically reshape the diplomatic terrain of the Arab-Israeli conflict and help to restore a measure of Arab pride lost in the 1967 war. While the Syrian assault threatened to break IDF lines in the north, Egyptian forces deployed shoulder-launched antitank missiles against Israeli armor while remaining under the cover of Egypt's Soviet-supplied surface-to-air missile system along the canal. Sadat halted the Egyptian offensive after crossing the canal, however; his goal had never been to attack Israel itself, nor had it been to conquer the Sinai. Meanwhile, as the IDF regrouped and began to pound at Assad's forces in the Golan Heights, Damascus pleaded for Cairo to continue its push across the Sinai. Sadat's fateful decision to abandon the protection of his missile defense network and move into the desert left his forces open to IDF counterattack and chipped away at the achievements made early in the war. In the United States, Henry Kissinger recognized the opportunity created by the conflict. Here was a chance to break the current stalemate and achieve diplomatic progress. The key, however, was that neither side must achieve total victory, as had been the case in the 1967 war. Kissinger thus stalled Soviet attempts to put a cease-fire in place, allowing time for Israel's counteroffensive to push Syrian and Egyptian forces back. Soviet threats to intervene in order to stop the fighting prompted Kissinger to place U.S. nuclear forces in an elevated state of readiness, DEFCON 3, the highest alert since the Cuban Missile Crisis in 1962.[2]

By the time the war came to an end on 25 October, the diplomatic landscape in the region had been transformed. The coordinated Syrian and Egyptian offensives caught Israeli forces off guard and achieved surprising early gains. While these were largely reversed by the Israeli counterattack, which succeeded in pushing back Egyptian and Syrian forces and completely encircling the Egyptian Third Army, Damascus and Cairo managed to force a new round of diplomacy in the Arab-Israeli dispute. The war also diverted attention away from the immediate issue of fedayeen action. The guerillas' initial excitement at the prospect of the long-anticipated combined Arab effort to liberate Palestine gave way to disappointment as cease-fires were announced first on the Egyptian front and then on the Syrian front.

The sweeping diplomatic changes that appeared in the war's aftermath affected the fedayeen as well as the Arab states. The early success of the Egyptian and Syrian armies in the October War had destroyed the myth of Israeli invincibility and dramatically strengthened the Arabs' bargaining position in the diplomatic arena. The PLO Executive Committee moved quickly to announce that the cease-fires did not apply to the Palestinian revolution.[3] Reactions against the U.S. decision to resupply the Israeli military after its losses of equipment in the war without first demanding the withdrawal of Israeli forces from occupied Arab territory drew criticism, even from pro-Western Arabs. Left-wing papers in Beirut went so far as to argue that the real fight was not with Israel but with the Americans who furnished its weapons. Denouncing Washington's support for Israel, one paper argued that just "as the heroic Vietnamese people defeated the US...[the] Arabs, who defeated Israel in less than 15 days, know how to defeat [the] US with [the] help of [the] Afro-Asian people, Soviets, Chinese and free people everywhere."[4] The October War also marked a possible opportunity for the guerilla organizations to consolidate a number of diplomatic gains. To this end, moderate groups in the PLO began to consider the idea of declaring a Palestinian provisional government that could participate in the peace negotiations. U.S. officials believed that the loss of prestige that had accompanied the war had created a greater pragmatism among Palestinian leaders, who had come to recognize their weakness vis-à-vis Cairo, Damascus, and the Gulf states that had mobilized the oil weapon, imposing an embargo on petroleum shipments to the United States in retaliation for Washington's perceived one-sided support for Israel in the recent war.

The architects of the conflict had anticipated possible consequences for the PLO. In the run-up to the war, while Sadat and Assad laid plans to attack Israeli positions in the Sinai and the Golan Heights, they were aware of implications of their actions for the PLO. In August, Sadat had informed senior Fatah members of his intention to launch a war in the fall of 1973. On 9 September, with the surprise attack still weeks away, President Sadat summoned Arafat and his lieutenants. There he told Fatah leaders of his plans for a postwar peace conference and said that he expected the PLO to participate. In late October, several days after the war had come to an end, Sadat called Khalaf and Faruq al-Qaddumi to his palace. "Well now," he asked the two Palestinians, "will you agree to participate in the Geneva Peace Conference?" Khalaf replied that Sadat had put the PLO in a nearly "impossible" situation. While the Palestinians did not want to "reject the principle of a peace conference out of hand," they were reluctant to embrace the idea. Such a conference, Khalaf pointed out, would be convened on the basis of UN 242, which did not acknowledge

Palestinian national aspirations. "So we decided not to reply either way until we received a formal invitation," he recalled. "It was only then that we would be in a position to define our position in a clear and precise manner."[5]

Moscow was also eager to bring the PLO into the post-1973 peace process. The Kremlin's precondition would be high, however: if it hoped to gain a seat in Geneva, the PLO must accept the principle of a Palestinian ministate, which itself would represent an implicit recognition of Israel. Such a move would also entail the creation of the united front that had eluded PLO leaders.[6] In November 1973, the Soviet Union invited the major factions of the PLO to come to Moscow for talks about the new diplomatic situation in the Middle East. The Kremlin's representative told the visiting Palestinians that a final settlement to the Arab-Israeli dispute was inevitable and that the PLO must make preparations for a coming Palestinian ministate. The Soviets stressed the need for the Palestinians to be flexible and politically pragmatic in the coming negotiations. Otherwise, they explained, the Palestinians ran the risk of being left out of a final settlement, which might isolate the PLO as the lone Arab actor still contesting Israel.[7] Thus, in addition to offering arms and training to Fatah, Soviet leaders told the group that there was "no revolution in the world that does not have a program for each phase. You must phase your struggle."[8] Moscow would be disappointed by the PLO's response. Fatah was still unable to advance a clear position in favor of negotiations; the DFLP was skeptical about Geneva's prospects. Even worse, the PFLP flatly rejected Moscow's appeals, judging correctly that the Soviet diplomatic plan entailed recognition of Israel. This public break resulted in a collapse of the PFLP's relations with Moscow that lasted the rest of the decade.[9]

Geneva and a National Authority

Thus, the changed regional and international situation following the war—particularly the widely accepted conviction that a settlement to the regional conflict must grow out of the latest round of hostilities—presented two key questions to the PLO: Was it time for the guerillas to form some sort of national authority? Should they participate in the postwar peace conference in Geneva at the end of the year?[10] Each of these questions raised an array of ancillary issues. Perhaps the most pressing matter concerned the fate of the occupied territories. Although the government of Israel was in no rush to evacuate the territories, few observers accepted the proposition that the West Bank and Gaza should remain under Israeli occupation. Nevertheless, fedayeen commanders lacked a clear plan for what should be done with them. King Hussein, for his part, argued that the liberated West Bank ought to be returned to Jordanian sovereignty, as had been the case prior to the 1967 war. At that point, he explained, the residents of the West Bank would be allowed to decide on the issue of their own autonomy and self-determination.[11] It was in this regard that growing political mobilization of the West Bank Palestinians would play an important role.

Sentiment on the West Bank was by no means monolithic or fixed, but prevailing public opinion rejected King Hussein and embraced the PLO.[12] Palestinian notables on the West Bank—whose influence was waning as younger generations began to turn to the PLO as the new force of political leadership in Palestinian society—had also begun to urge the PLO to participate at Geneva. Following the war, fearing that the absence of a Palestinian voice in the political process was likely to leave the "occupied territories to become plaything[s] between Jordan and Israel," a coalition of West Bank leaders organized as the Palestinian National Front (PNF) announced its support for the PLO as the sole representative of the Palestinian people.[13] While they had been wary of Fatah's initial fedayeen operations in the late 1960s, six years of military occupation had convinced many West Bank Palestinians of the need to establish an independent political authority over their territory. Citing the Algerian, Yemeni, and Vietnamese examples, the PNF's political program echoed the PLO's attempts to link its struggle with revolutionary struggles in the Third World, proclaiming, "Ours is the era of people's liberation . . . and the defeat of colonialism." The PNF was largely representative of popular sentiment in the West Bank, according to a public opinion poll conducted by an Israeli institute, which showed that only 19 percent of residents favored the return of Jordanian sovereignty and 44 percent hoped to be part of an independent Palestinian state. Along with this strong support for independence, the PNF insisted that the PLO was the *only* viable political body that could claim to represent the Palestinians.[14]

In December, the PNF released a statement expressing solidarity "under the banner of the PLO" and outlining its appraisal of the Palestinian situation in the wake of the October War. Earlier in the month, the organization had sent a letter to the PLO in which it repeated its desire to end the Israeli occupation and to set up a Palestinian national authority under the leadership of the PLO, which would be independent from Amman. It also expressed the desire to take advantage of the present regional and international circumstances, and it discussed the prospect of the PLO's participation at Geneva. The PNF warned that if the conference was held without the PLO, the only force representing the Palestinians would be King Hussein. This circumstance would, according to the organization, be disastrous. The PNF was calling on the PLO to go to Geneva with the intention of creating a Palestinian ministate. This organized expression of grassroots West Bank support reinforced the new pragmatism growing in the guerilla leadership.[15]

Jordanian designs on the West Bank also put pressure on the guerillas to develop some sort of counterproposal for the area. In March 1972, King Hussein outlined his plan for a United Arab Kingdom on the East and West Banks.

Amman, which had maintained jurisdiction over the West Bank from 1948 to 1967, hoped to regain the territory after Israeli forces evacuated. In response, Nayaf Hawatmeh's DFLP called upon the PLO to produce an alternative plan, a challenge to King Hussein's attempts to lay claim to the West Bank. By the end of the following year, the October War had made the question of whether to establish a Palestinian state even more urgent. Hawatmeh proposed the creation of a Palestinian national authority in any part of the occupied territories that Israel vacated, as an intermediate phase in the Palestinian struggle. Criticizing what he described as the joint U.S.-Israeli-Hashemite scheme, he insisted that the revolution must offer some counterproposal. "We will not permit the return of any Palestinian land to King Hussein, nor annexation by Israel," he proclaimed. "We must build an independent Palestinian national authority." The DFLP would thus emerge as the loudest and most persistent voice in the resistance calling for a pragmatic and incremental approach to the question of Palestinian liberation. These calls marked the genesis of what would become the PLO's Ten-Point Program. By the end of 1973, larger guerilla groups such as Fatah and Saiqa were beginning to consider the possibility of just such a move.[16]

Scant Palestinian contributions to the war effort had pushed leaders such as Arafat to consider engagement in the coming peace talks as a means of regaining political influence in the Arab world. Although the conflict represented something of a crisis for the PLO, it also presented an opportunity whereby the majority of the key actors in the region seemed to recognize that prospects for long-term peace would be dim so long as Palestinian interests remained unaddressed. A major hurdle would be achieving fedayeen unity, a goal that had eluded the PLO for nearly a decade. U.S. officials feared that tensions unleashed by these new developments likely would result in violence from more extremist elements.[17] Indeed, the PFLP and other radical organizations warned that they would not accept any sort of compromise settlement in the wake of the latest war.[18]

Nevertheless, by late 1973, under pressure from Cairo and Moscow, the mainstream leadership of the PLO had chosen to pursue an intermediate solution, but it was not willing to demand a seat at the table in Geneva. The reason was tactical, as Arafat explained in late November: "The interests of our cause requires that we should be the last to speak." It was vital, he added, that the PLO not "show its cards" until it had "something definite to reply to." The PLO would come to Geneva if invited, but it would not request an invitation for fear of sacrificing its negotiating position; it would not negotiate for the opportunity to negotiate. Khalaf reiterated this argument, explaining that because the PLO had not yet been invited to Geneva, he did not want to commit to a position. "If I did talk about it and rejected it, my rejection would be weak," he told reporters, "and if I accepted I should lose a political card without its having been shown to me."[19]

If granted a place at Geneva, the PLO would push for the creation of a national authority. Fatah had discussed the creation of a Palestinian ministate intermittently since 1967, but the idea gained wide support in the aftermath of the 1973 war. Moderate Palestinian leaders concluded that in the event of a comprehensive peace settlement—which looked to be a genuine possibility in the months following the war—the Palestinian struggle ran the risk of being isolated as the sole remaining belligerent in the Arab-Israeli conflict. Senior Fatah member Khaled al-Hassan remarked that Fatah's leadership "came to the decision that the best for us is that the West Bank and Gaza should be a Palestinian state."[20] As Arafat noted, "We also knew the Arab states would make peace without us if we did not express our demands in a realistic way...I mean if we did not produce a political programme which the Arab regimes could support." In the months following the war, however, Fatah had declined to issue an explicit endorsement of the national authority concept. Fatah's leadership, beyond being internally divided, was intent on maintaining the unity of the PLO. Thus, the organization quietly encouraged the DFLP and the PNF to put the question of a national authority on the table, allowing Fatah to set itself in the position of being a potential future broker. By January 1974, Fatah had moved into a position where it could begin issuing public calls for the creation of a Palestinian state in the occupied territories.[21]

During this same time, however, Fatah began floating what scholar Alain Gresh describes as "trial balloons that showed a real desire to compromise" with Israel on the issue of an eventual Palestinian state. In mid-November 1973, an article written by Said Hammami, the PLO representative to the United Kingdom, appeared in the London *Times*. Hammami made several main arguments, two of which marked a radical departure from the PLO's position in late 1973. The first was a demand that the PLO be invited to participate as a full member in the post–October War peace conference; the second was a call for the creation of a Palestinian state. While the pre-1967 period had been characterized by a "flagrant disregard of the human and national rights" of the Palestinian people, recent years had witnessed a growing recognition of these rights within the world community, as shown by UN General Assembly resolutions. As this trend continued, the possibility of the Palestinian people taking the "first step toward reconciliation for the sake of a just peace" was in sight. Hammami's article contained the basis for a compromise solution to the Israel-Palestine conflict, suggesting that while it still hoped for the eventual creation of a secular democratic state in the whole of Palestine, the PLO accepted the reality that this was a long-term prospect that could be achieved only with the cooperation of the population of Israel. In the meantime, the creation of a Palestinian state was the sole feasible option. Hammami's declaration marked a historic shift:

> The Israeli Jews and the Palestinian Arabs should recognize one another as peoples, with all the rights to which a people is entitled. This recognition should be followed by the realization of the Palestinian Arab entity

through a Palestinian state, an independent fully-fledged member state of the United Nations.

Hammami concluded by stating that if an invitation to Geneva based on the dual recognition of Palestinian national rights and the legitimacy of the PLO's leadership was offered to the organization, he was "sure the Palestinian leadership would accept." The chairman of the PLO's Foreign Relations Committee, Khaled al-Hassan, later said, "In the leadership we were committed to an accommodation with Israel.... It is true that we could not afford to declare our real hand in public.... [But] if the Israeli Government of Yitzhak Rabin had responded to the signals we were sending through Hammami, we could have had a just peace in a very few years."[22]

This new pragmatism among the moderate leadership of the PLO set off a wave of protest from the hard-line guerilla groups. The PFLP announced its opposition to the national authority scheme in late 1973. The organization accepted the prospect of a "revolutionary authority" in the West Bank and Gaza, but it refused to accept the idea of a ministate, arguing that such an arrangement would be tantamount to recognition of Israel.[23] George Habash insisted that a national authority would ultimately exist at the mercy of Israel and Jordan, meaning that a Palestinian entity would function as an instrument for the containment of Palestinian self-determination rather than for its realization. The result, he said, would be a partial victory that would spell the end of the larger aspiration of creating a secular democratic state in Palestine.[24]

The Road to Geneva Runs Through Washington

State Department officials explained that although the war had whipped up resentment over the issue of U.S. support for Israel, it had also demonstrated Washington's preeminence in the region—a key goal of Nixon and Kissinger's Middle East strategy. Thus, while the PLO remained skeptical of Washington's ability to resolve the regional conflict, the organization was well aware of the crucial role the United States played there. The Europeans had given the Palestinians verbal support, the Soviets had provided weapons, but only the United States could create the political momentum for a return of Arab territory. While a number of issues still had to be worked out, the prospect of concerted Palestinian engagement in the planned peace talks in Geneva appeared as if it might be within reach.[25]

Fatah leaders realized that the PLO's road to Geneva must run, sooner or later, through Washington. With this in mind, Arafat began reaching out to United States in hopes of signaling the organization's willingness to enter negotiations with Israel. Arafat adopted a somewhat ambiguous position, hedging on the issue of forming a provisional government—which would allow the PLO to go to Geneva—and still claiming to embrace a vision of a secular democratic state in all of Palestine. However, he left the door open to the possibility of participating in the peace conference, stating that he was waiting for a formal invitation before he could commit to any position. At the same time, he promised that the PLO would not hesitate to follow the Vietnamese example of waging its armed struggle in the midst of negotiations—talking while fighting—if forced to do so.[26]

These messages made their way to Kissinger's inner circle in Washington. Voices in the State Department and on the NSC staff advocated in support of substantive negotiations on the Palestine issue. In November 1973, NSC staffer William Quandt prepared a study on the question of Palestine and the postwar negotiations. Quandt laid out several different options for dealing with the issue of the Palestinians within the framework of a broader Middle East settlement. While the Palestinian political situation was relatively fluid, the PLO represented the only "organized body of Palestinian leadership that has any legitimacy within the Arab world and among Palestinians." Moreover, Fatah leaders such as Arafat and Khalaf were fundamentally pragmatic rather than ideological and could be expected to adapt to the changing political situation in the wake of the October War. Ultimately, Quandt wrote, the United States found itself in the "position of being able to help legitimize the PLO...while probably not being able to do much to undercut the PLO or to build up King Hussein as an alternative to the PLO." He added that the prospect of Washington finding a Palestinian leader capable of competing with Arafat and the PLO was "extremely doubtful." The best Kissinger could hope for was to be able to postpone the issue of the Palestinian participation—perhaps by using King Hussein as the initial intermediary—in the peace process until the second round of negotiations.[27]

Kissinger would focus on using Jordan to keep the PLO out of the peace process. The secretary recognized that the "PLO had a high potential for causing trouble all over the Arab world" and hoped that it would not interfere with U.S. diplomatic efforts in the Arab-Israeli conflict. To this end, Kissinger dispatched General Vernon Walters, deputy director of the CIA— and a participant in the secret channel to the North Vietnamese—to meet with PLO representatives in Rabat. His first order of business was to issue a threat: "I must tell you quite clearly that this killing of Americans has got to stop—or else it will come to a situation where torrents of blood will flow, and not all of it will be American." Walters went on to make the case that Washington would look on the Palestine question as an inter-Arab problem rather than an international one; the United States would not back away from King Hussein. The PLO made it clear that it would never accept Hashemite authority, and it remained evasive on the question of Israeli recognition.[28] The PLO's envoy expressed anger over the lack of U.S. recognition and reiterated the organization's conviction that it was they and not King Hussein who represented the

Palestinian people. The problem with this idea, however, rested in the fact that the Washington was aligned with the PLO's two greatest enemies: Israel and Jordan. "There were two fundamental foundations to our policy," Walters informed Palestinian officials. "The existence and security of Israel, and our strong friendship for Jordan and King Hussein. These were the bedrocks of our policy."[29] Neither Jordan nor Israel was eager to see Arafat at Geneva.

Thus, Washington remained opposed to bringing Palestinian organizations into the peace process. As Kissinger wrote in his memoirs, negotiation on the Palestinian issue was a "no-win proposition for the United States." Such a diplomatic exchange would present Moscow as the "lawyer for the Arab side," while the United States would be forced into an isolated position as Israel's advocate or be forced to "deliver Israeli acquiescence to a program incompatible with its long-term survival." The United States would either receive the blame for failing to bring Israel on board or be compelled to force Israel into surrendering a measure of security and diplomatic leverage.[30] Hence, Kissinger worked to obstruct any diplomatic progress on the PLO's front: "The beginning of our dialogue with the PLO was also its end.... This was no accident. At this stage, involving the PLO was incompatible with the interests of any of the parties to the Middle East conflict." Indeed, even if the PLO were to accept a modified version of UN Resolution 242 and recognize Israel's right to exist— something that some State Department officials thought likely—Kissinger was skeptical about the organization's potential for moderation. Thus, rather than an earnest attempt to connect with the Palestinians, the meeting was a ploy to buy time for Kissinger's negotiations and "prevent radical assaults on the early peace process."[31]

While his memoirs indicate that the secretary never had any intention of bringing the PLO into the peace process, other sources suggest otherwise. Journalists Tony Walker and Anthony Gowers cite an unnamed State Department source—probably Talcott Seelye—who suggests that Kissinger came very close to opening a covert channel with the PLO in early 1974. "The 1973 war had opened up possibilities that had not existed before, and it had become clear that the PLO could not be ignored if we were to solve this problem," the official explained. "Kissinger had become aware of this.... And he was frustrated at having to talk to the PLO through intermediaries." Although Kissinger had made promises to Israel that the United States would not negotiate with or recognize the PLO, Seelye recalled that the secretary had tried to leave a loophole—which was later closed—that would have allowed a dialogue.[32]

Despite Washington's tepid response, international momentum built toward the creation of a Palestinian state. On 15 November 1973, Moscow issued its first public pronouncement of support for a Palestinian state. While the Soviets had been quietly pushing the PLO toward creating a government in exile, the official announcement of Kremlin support for the legitimate national rights of the Palestinian people marked an important development in the organization's struggle for international recognition.[33] The Kremlin embraced the position that lasting peace would be impossible without the recognition of Palestinian national rights. With the isolation of Israel in the international community, Moscow argued, the moment for such recognition was at hand. Privately, the Soviets sent signals to Washington that the PLO's participation in the peace negotiations in Geneva was inevitable.[34]

The Arab summit held in Algiers later in the month called for the "restoration of the full national rights of the Palestinian people" and recognized the PLO as their representative. This decision restricted Amman's power in speaking for the Palestinians, although, in an effort to appease Amman and Washington, it did not mention recognition of the PLO in official documents. Despite this deliberate ambiguity, the Algiers meeting suggested a possible opening for the PLO at the Geneva conference. Likewise, the summit and subsequent statements by PLO leaders left open the issue of a provisional Palestinian government.[35] Arafat hinted at the possibility of joining the peace negotiations as well.[36] Salah Khalaf, too, was striking an increasingly moderate, pragmatic tone. Khalaf argued that the PLO must put itself in a position to gain a place at Geneva so as not to be excluded, pointing out that an "absolute 'No' is not always the hallmark of the absolute revolutionary."[37] The PLO had come to recognize a provisional government as a potential tactical gain given the set of new realities that appeared in the wake of the October War. This more pragmatic and moderate approach, however, was woven together with more traditional calls for the liberation of Palestine. Acceptance of a Palestinian entity on the West Bank and Gaza might function as a first step on the road to a larger Palestine.

While this argument did not sit well with Israeli leadership, Ambassador Buffum opined that it ought to be taken with a grain of salt. Leaders such as Arafat understood popular discontent with the notion of a government in exile and thus would be careful in their public statements. Nonetheless, Buffum believed that a number of fedayeen groups including Fatah were prepared to participate in peace talks leading toward the creation of some sort of Palestinian entity.[38] The announcement of support for a Palestinian state by DFLP leader Nayaf Hawatmeh represented the "clearest public indication to date that [the] bulk of fedayeen leadership is moving more and more out of its protective shell in preparation for what it hopes will be PLO peace talks at Geneva and [an] eventual independent Palestinian state."[39]

Both Jordan and Israel stood in the way of this momentum for PLO participation in the political process. Israeli officials were of the opinion that King Hussein—with clandestine Israeli assistance—hoped to manipulate a proposed postsettlement plebiscite on the West Bank to ensure that pro-Hashemite elements would emerge victorious, thus granting Amman continued sovereignty in the area. Thus, the proposal that the West Bank be turned over to King Hussein temporarily, after its evacuation by Israeli forces, could in reality amount to the return of the pre-1967 status quo. The Algiers summit, however, had become a direct challenge to Hussein in this regard. Cairo was also throwing its weight behind the PLO in this contest with Amman. Israeli officials warned that the creation of an "independent Palestinian entity in [the] West Bank and Gaza Strip would lead automatically to [a] fedayeen takeover because no moderate leadership exists among [the] Palestinians."[40]

Much of the Israeli leadership still refused to come to terms with the notion of a Palestinian people. U.S. officials suggested that rigid Israeli opposition to a Palestinian entity stemmed from a fear that such an entity would strengthen Palestinian nationalism. While pragmatism was pushing many Israeli officials toward the idea of some sort of Jordanian-Palestinian confederation, they would demand a "firm Hashemite hand behind [the] scenes on [the] West Bank... and they may insist," State Department officers said, "on having [a] clandestine role themselves."[41]

Meanwhile, Fatah pushed its moderate position forward. In January 1974, *Filastine al-Thawra* announced that the Palestinian people would enjoy full sovereignty over any parts of the occupied territories vacated by Israeli forces. Arafat said that the West Bank and Gaza could either return to Jordanian control or fall under the rule of "a Palestinian authority." The 1973 war would "give us parts of Palestine," and the next war "will give us Tel Aviv."[42] The next month, Fatah and Saiqa joined the DFLP in its calls to create a national authority.[43] In February 1974, the three guerilla groups submitted to the PLO a working paper calling for the organization to adopt what was in essence an incremental approach to the question of liberation. Although the PLO would continue the struggle for the whole of Palestine, the organization should seek to establish control—and thereby reject Jordanian sovereignty—over any territories that Israel evacuated.[44] While the PLO's official goal remained the total liberation of Palestine, pragmatists in the organization who favored the phased approach understood that the creation of a secular democratic state in the whole of Palestine in the foreseeable future was unlikely.[45] As Arafat later described, Fatah was caught between the need to operate within the boundaries of what was possible for the PLO to achieve and domestic pressures from the Palestinian people. "When a people is claiming the return of 100 per cent of its land, it's not so easy for leadership to say, 'No you can take only thirty per cent.'" These dual constrictions forced Arafat to put forth an ambiguous position regarding a ministate, at least in public. "But I must also tell you," he told journalist Alan Hart, "that our real position was always known to the governments of the world, including the governments of Israel.... From 1974, even from the end of 1973, certain of our people were officially authorized to maintain secret contacts with Israelis and with important people in the West. Their responsibility was to say in secret what at the time we could not say in public."[46]

A major force of opposition to the PLO's participation in the Geneva conference and a Palestinian government in exile came from radical guerilla organizations such as the PFLP. While leaders such as Arafat saw the peace negotiations as an opportunity for incremental progress, George Habash and the PFLP denounced the political process as a betrayal of the Palestinian cause that would grant legal recognition to Israeli aggression.[47] The creation of a rump Palestinian state required concessions that would be tantamount to surrender. Habash called on his fellow guerilla leaders to reject the prospect of participation in the political process.[48] Extreme elements in the fedayeen hoped to poison the atmosphere of the Geneva conference when, on 17 December 1973, they launched an attack on the Rome airport. The incident, which killed thirty-two people, drew widespread condemnation from Arab leaders including Arafat, who expressed his contempt for the attack. Salah Khalaf denounced the violence for taking innocent lives and harming the Palestinian cause. Official PLO condemnations sought to distance the organization from the Rome attack, calling the incident a "conspiratorial act aimed at distorting [the] true picture of [the] Palestinian revolution." The DFLP criticized the attack as a "dirty, criminal and unjustified act which constitutes [a] grave injury to [the] Palestinian cause." Ambassador Buffum noted that, despite wide and apparently sincere fedayeen condemnation, the PFLP remained silent.[49]

PLO moderates suffered another blow later in the month when the Syrian-backed guerilla group Saiqa—under pressure from Damascus—rejected the notion of fedayeen participation at Geneva.[50] U.S. officials argued that the continuing tensions between moderates and rejectionists seemed to be heading toward a showdown. In particular, a series of recent attacks had led to speculation that the PLO might expel the PFLP. PFLP leaders accused PLO moderates of being willing to surrender. American officials expected tensions within the PLO to increase as Damascus and Amman moved toward disengagement agreements with Israel. They warned that a showdown between PLO moderates and rejectionists seemed inevitable.[51]

Representatives from the Arab League approached U.S. officials in March 1974, saying that the complex set of difficulties facing the prospect of Palestinian participation at Geneva required Moscow and Washington to articulate a clear position on the question of a Palestinian government in exile. In essence, hopes for a durable peace in the region hinged on the inclusion of the Palestinians in the current political process as a national group rather than simply as refugees. In order for this to happen, however, the PLO would have to form a provisional government, which it would do only if it was assured that such a government would be taken seriously by both the United States and the Soviet Union. This support from Washington and Moscow would encourage Palestinian leaders in the occupied territories to throw their support behind the PLO, thereby creating the legitimacy necessary for the PLO provisional government to come to Geneva.[52]

Indeed, the time appeared ripe for the creation of a lasting solution to the Arab-Israeli conflict. A former Lebanese prime minister—described as the most pessimistic official that Rogers and Sisco had met on an earlier tour of the region—approached Ambassador Buffum to voice his change of heart. "I was wrong," he said. "A revolution has taken place in [the] Arab mentality." The Saudis, the Kuwaitis, the Egyptians, and most notably the fedayeen were "now ready to settle for peace with Israel." Arab honor had been vindicated by the Egyptian and Syrian performance in the October War, and an entirely different mood now prevailed in the region. The current moment represented a "unique opportunity for America to bring durable peace to [the] area." However, should this moment be lost and

> Sadat's gamble on American willingness to press Israel to make [a] rea-
> sonable settlement fail, there will be [a] serious backlash effect. [The]
> Arab states, including Saudi Arabia, would then perforce proceed down
> [a] more militant path. He believed that [the] newly found unity of [the]
> Arab world would prevail and in a matter of time there would be further
> recourse to Arms which he doubted Israel could survive.

"In short," Buffum wrote, seeking to sum up the former prime minister's thoughts, "this is the one last big chance for peace in the Middle East and it is all riding on Dr. Kissinger."[53]

Unfortunately, Dr. Kissinger had other plans.

Kissinger, Shuttle Diplomacy, and the PLO

In the aftermath of the October War, all eyes looked to Kissinger to play the crucial role of third party in negotiations between Israel and its Arab neighbors. While he was eager to fulfill this function, Kissinger's basic goal of shielding Israel from pressure to withdraw from those territories occupied after the 1967 war remained intact. As historian Salim Yaqub recounts, "Kissinger needed some mechanism that created the illusion of progress toward the 1967 borders while ensuring that those borders would never actually be restored."[54] Shuttle diplomacy became that mechanism. In essence, Kissinger would refuse to pressure Israel to enter into comprehensive negotiations with the Arab states as a group; rather, he would establish a series of bilateral exchanges facilitated by his high-profile visits or shuttles between Israel and various Arab capitals. The latter approach would, in time, open the door to bilateral agreements between the Arab states and Israel, thus splitting the bloc of left-wing Arab states. It was through this shuttle diplomacy that Kissinger was able to lay the foundation for peace agreements between Egypt and Israel that would effectively take Cairo out of the Arab-Israeli conflict, preventing another large-scale war between the state of Israel and its neighbors.

This approach was at odds with the prevailing sentiment in the world community that looked to a comprehensive settlement of the conflict, presumably at an international conference to be held in Geneva. This Geneva approach envisioned key roles for the Soviet Union and the United Nations alongside the United States and would aim at creating an all-embracing peace settlement between Israel and its Arab neighbors. Kissinger was not enthusiastic about Geneva. Beyond practical considerations regarding the difficulty of achieving diplomatic progress in such an unwieldy forum, he recognized that Geneva would undermine his goal of pushing Moscow's influence out of the Middle East; it would also give a stronger voice to the United Nations, an organization that had not proved amenable to Washington's interests in recent years. Furthermore, efforts to achieve a comprehensive peace settlement would put Israel in the position of having to negotiate with the assembled Arab states. In contrast, Kissinger's shuttle diplomacy would avoid these complications, opening secret one-on-one negotiations between Israel and the various Arab states, with Kissinger himself acting as mediator. Bilateral diplomacy strengthened both the U.S. and Israeli positions in the post-1973 peace process.[55] It would also help render moot the increasing pragmatism and moderation in the PLO. Kissinger's framework excluded the PLO and the Palestinian question from bilateral negotiations between Israel and the Arab states.

The PLO's refusal to recognize Israel's right to exist served as one of the key justifications for keeping the organization out of the peace process. Some would argue, however, that this refusal was a rhetorical sticking point and was of only debatable importance. State Department officials in the Arab world, for example, rejected Israeli fears that a Palestinian state would merely represent a new sanctuary for irredentist fedayeen. Officers in the Beirut embassy argued that moderate fedayeen were ultimately more pragmatic than radical leaders such as Habash and were thus likely to be amenable to an eventual political settlement. The fact that fedayeen leaders continued to espouse the goal of creating a secular democratic state in Palestine did not mean that they saw such a goal as realistic. The U.S. chargé d'affaires in Beirut, Robert Houghton, insisted that such calls merely reflected the reality that a majority of Palestinians would not immediately accept the concept of a rump Palestinian state in the West Bank and Gaza. If the PLO leadership had any hope of selling the concept of a smaller state in part of Palestine to their followers, they must continue to advocate the larger goal. U.S. and Israeli leaders should not be fooled, however, because moderate leaders such as Khalaf and Arafat would participate in the peace process in hopes of "obtaining whatever can realistically be salvaged in [the] way of Palestinian nationalist aspirations" as actions by the key Arab states transformed the regional diplomatic landscape. Washington needed to recognize that there was a difference between rhetoric and policy.[56]

In the face of these reports, however, Kissinger appeared willing to concede to Israeli demands that the PLO be excluded from direct negotiations. Going against the tide of regional and international opinion, Kissinger insisted that King Hussein should serve in its place as the spokesman for the West

Bank. Meanwhile, Israeli officials announced their intention to maintain their military positions in West Bank settlements. Minister Dayan held that Amman's position must be strengthened to counter the current "Palestine for the Palestinians" mood in the international community. Kissinger agreed: "What-ever strengthens the Government of Jordan is in our interests." Responding to Prime Minister Meir's insistence that the PLO be barred from the conference, Kissinger said, "I give you our judgment that it is not desirable for Arafat to be negotiating at the Conference for a Palestinian state to emerge from the Conference. Our considered opinion is worth more than memoranda of understanding. It is in no way in our interest."[57] At a meeting with his staff, Kissinger congratulated himself on the success of his earlier stalemate diplo-macy in pushing Cairo toward recognition of the United States as the preemi-nent great power in the Middle East. Sadat had recognized the "basic fact that has produced a stalemate in the Middle East for twenty-five years, some of which we deliberately contributed to...that no settlement in the Middle East was possible against the United States...whether they liked us or hated us, the fact of the matter was that the route to any progress led through us."[58]

A number of complications remained, however, and time for Kissinger's plans appeared to be running out. Notably, Kissinger saw Israeli reluctance to embark on negotiations with the Jordanians as inexplicable. Israel's apparent goal of maintaining control over the entire West Bank was untenable, and Israel must open talks with Hussein as soon as possible or be forced to deal with an internationally recognized PLO under Arafat's authority. The biggest danger for Israeli leaders would be for King Hussein to "tell them to go to hell...in that case Arafat is the inevitable successor, unblockable by anybody." Kissinger was adamant that "if Hussein isn't re-established in some way on the West Bank, we are going to face one hell of a problem with the Palestinians. And we will have it," he added, "as a U.S.-Palestinian problem, or an Israeli-Palestinian problem, while otherwise it will be an internal problem, at least as much as an Israeli-Arab problem." Ultimately, he emphasized, it was "abso-lutely not in the American interests to surface the Palestinian issue."[59] Kissing-er's strategy, however, did not square with realities on the ground. U.S. officials in Jerusalem had already made the argument that King Hussein no longer appeared to be an adequate representative of Palestinian interests. The rise of the PNF and its alignment with the PLO—and subsequent rejection of a Jordanian administration—dampened the prospects for a return of the West Bank to King Hussein. It was becoming exceedingly difficult to argue that the PLO did not represent Palestinians in the West Bank.

Kissinger's NSC staff sent a new paper to the secretary in February urging him to push for some sort of rapprochement between King Hussein and the PLO. Saunders suggested that Washington might even approach the PLO directly in an effort to cajole the organization into accepting the king as its negotiator during the preliminary round of peace talks. By bolstering the influence of moderates such as Arafat, the United States might have its best shot at a genuine settlement to the Israel-Palestine question with both the PLO and the government of Israel. "If moderate political leadership emerges on the West Bank," Saunders noted, "Israel will have to think more seriously about jeopardizing a settlement by refusing to compromise on key issues. Israel has no reason to compromise now," he concluded, "but if a favorable settlement seemed possible, Israel would have to think twice before killing it."[60]

Although he clearly had access to these types of reports noting that large segments of the Palestinian population had come to embrace the PLO and rejected the notion of Jordanian rule, Secretary Kissinger made it clear to the king that the White House had no desire to see the creation of a Palestinian state. Responding to King Hussein's fears that the United States might be working toward the creation of such an entity—which the king judged to be the choice of the Arab world and the international community—Kissinger assured the monarch that he had Washington's total support. The United States would not open any negotiations with the PLO unless they had first been discussed and agreed with Amman. Kissinger grumbled that Israeli leaders, however, were "extremely parochial," driven primarily by domestic issues, namely, a fear of the National Religious Party, which demanded the whole of biblical Palestine. Israel should have engaged with the king earlier, Kissinger thought, when his claims to speak for the Palestinians were largely unquestioned. In any case, the king need not worry about continued support from the United States, Kissinger said, insisting that "we cannot see any possible acceptable solution unless Your Majesty is the spokesman for the West Bank. This is our policy."[61]

Kissinger was still betting on the monarch. He made it clear to King Hussein that both Israel and Washington preferred that "Your Majesty remain the negotiator... [Y]our presence in the West Bank would give Your Majesty an important presence vis à vis the PLO. Once you are on the West Bank, the option of turning over principal responsibility is still open." Moreover, while it was evident that Moscow and the other Arab states would recognize a Palestinian government in exile, Washington could not do so due to its close relationship with and domestic political support for Israel. It would be a good idea to delay the creation of a Palestinian government in exile, which might be done, Kissinger suggested, through the establishment of a devious dialogue with the PLO. "I was serious," he elaborated. "It might be a good idea for Your Majesty to open contact with the PLO just to waste time." The conversation then turned to other matters, such as Kissinger making jokes about perpetuating war in Cambodia so as to channel more weapons to Amman.[62] Despite the tremendous opportunity in the wake of the 1973 war, Kissinger was more interested in his larger strategic design for U.S. supremacy in the Middle East, even if that meant that the Arab world would, in the secretary's words, "hate us."[63]

Israel also continued to figure prominently in that design. In April, Nixon issued a presidential determination forgiving a $1 billion Israeli debt for military equipment. The following month, the White House authorized Golda Meir to read the contents of its private message to the Israeli government before the Knesset. In the message was a pledge of U.S. "political support" for any defensive or preventative military measures that Israel might take against Syria in the event of further guerilla attacks and a stipulation that Washington would not regard such measures as violations of cease-fire agreements with Damascus.[64] At the same time that it sought to arbitrate the Arab-Israeli dispute, the Nixon administration was using U.S. military aid to reinforce Israel's military position along the cease-fire lines in both defensive and preventative capacities.

Talking While Fighting

In the Palestinian camp, the split between the moderates and the rejectionists remained a key obstacle to the PLO's entry into the political process. The most obvious outward sign of these internecine tensions was a number of guerilla operations launched by extremists in the hopes of derailing progress toward a negotiated settlement. Moderates in the PLO such as Arafat were opposed to external operations as long as the prospect of a political solution to the Palestine question seemed within reach. PLO news sources argued that external operations—such as a recent attack on the Japanese embassy in Kuwait—hurt the Palestinian cause in international forums and were a direct threat to fedayeen unity. The PLO's news agency wrote that the "leadership considers this operation will create nothing but [a] negative impression on international opinion which [the] Zionists will exploit to taint our just struggle with [the] terrorist image."[65] For rejectionist leaders, however, such attacks represented the best means of sabotaging a political process that they feared might result in the destruction of the Palestinian cause. Larger and more violent operations were in the works.

Early in the morning of 11 April 1974 three guerillas from the Popular Front for the Liberation of Palestine–General Command slipped into the northern Israeli town of Kiryat Shmona and entered an apartment building. Once inside, they began moving room to room and firing at the men, women, and children within. Four hours later, after a clash with Israeli troops, the three guerillas and eighteen civilians were dead, with another fifteen wounded. A spokesman for the PFLP-GC—a splinter group from the PFLP that placed an emphasis on tactical operations rather than political mobilization—promised more suicide attacks against Israel as part of a campaign to spoil peace negotiations.[66]

The new U.S. ambassador in Beirut, McMurtrie Godley, was of the opinion that the massacre at Kiryat Shmona had been designed to foil peace negotiations, bolster the influence of the rejectionist fedayeen organizations, and signal to moderates that "their adherence to some kind of fedayeen role in [the] settlement process will only result in their isolation, repudiation, and eventual downfall." Under this increased pressure, moderate fedayeen leaders and Arab governments had been compelled to praise the guerillas responsible for the operation as heroes and martyrs. In all, Godley warned, the attack had given the rejectionists a much-needed boost. The question for moderates such as Arafat was whether the recent violence would drag them into a more confrontational posture in the Arab-Israeli dispute. He explained that moderate leaders such as Arafat hoped for encouragement from Washington in this struggle against radical fedayeen elements. Godley concluded that the PFLP and the PFLP-GC would continue such operations in hopes of increasing their influence in the PLO and disrupting the peace process. Meanwhile, the Lebanese government was watching anxiously and preparing for the all but inevitable Israeli reprisal.[67] Washington should expect additional spoiling operations from fedayeen extremists so long as the political process continued to show negligible results.[68]

A second suicide operation occurred a month later when, in the early morning hours of 15 May 1974, three guerillas from the DFLP moved into the Israeli town of Ma'alot, where they managed to seize control of a school and take some eighty-five children and several adults hostage. After separating the students by sex, the guerillas sent Israeli authorities a list of ten political prisoners to be released. In addition to eight Palestinians, the list included Kozo Okamoto, one of the Japanese attackers in the 1972 Lod massacre. The guerillas wired the building with explosives and waited as Israeli officials—who made the unprecedented decision to concede to the terrorists' demands—scrambled to satisfy the list's complex protocols. As the guerillas' deadline approached, Israeli forces pleaded for an extension, which they failed to get. Thirty-three minutes before the deadline, the Israeli commander ordered an assault on the school. When the smoke from the firefight cleared, all three Palestinians lay dead, along with seventeen students. Some seventy other Israelis in the school were wounded; five more would eventually die from their injuries.[69]

Ambassador Godley identified two trends exemplified by the Kiryat Shmona and Ma'alot attacks that were, in his judgment, "even more upsetting than the loss of young lives." The latest incident confirmed fears that moderate fedayeen organizations—in this case Hawatmeh's DFLP, which had previously endorsed the idea of Palestinian participation in peace negotiations—were turning back toward violence out of frustration with the political process. The moment of opportunity to bring moderate fedayeen into peace negotiations was slipping away. Godley warned that moderate fedayeen were adopting the North Vietnamese motto of "talk[ing while] fight[ing]" as they continued their diplomatic efforts. At the same time, operations such as those in Kiryat Shmona and Ma'alot represented a new type of violence that focused on targets inside Israel rather than in the international system and, as had been the case in the most recent attack, was launched by West Bankers. While the Israeli government had retaliated against Lebanon, it now appeared that more and more Palestinians in the occupied territories were joining the fight. As these types of attacks mounted, Godley cautioned, the only remaining hope in addressing the root problem of Palestinian violence seemed to lie in efforts to bring the fedayeen to the negotiating table.[70]

The following day, as the funerals for the slain students were taking place, thirty-six Israeli warplanes loaded with 250 tons of bombs struck Palestinian refugee camps in Beirut and Sidon. The string of crushing reprisals unleashed by an incensed Israeli government were the most severe since the post-Munich attacks. Commenting in the wake of Israeli naval attacks on Palestinian refugee camps in Lebanon, U.S. officials noted an apparent return to the post-Munich strategy of active defense whereby the IDF would attack fedayeen targets wherever and whenever it chose. As had been the case with previous Israeli strikes, the attacks increased militancy among both radical and moderate fedayeen leaders. Moreover, Lebanese officials had begun calling for the acquisition and deployment of Soviet surface-to-air missile systems in order to protect the country against Israeli warplanes. American observers judged that the Israeli policy of attacking Lebanon was at best ineffective and was probably leading to an increase in terrorist operations.[71]

While PFLP newspapers continued to denounce the peace negotiations as treasonous accommodations of U.S. imperialism, the pro-Soviet *Al Akhbar* accused the United States of seeking to delay substantive peace negotiations at the Geneva conference in favor of bilateral negotiations between Israel and individual Arab governments. In doing so, Washington would buy time for Israeli attacks designed to weaken the PLO, give King Hussein an opportunity to restore his influence in the West Bank and Gaza Strip, and move Cairo out of play in the Arab-Israeli conflict.[72] Judging from the content of Kissinger's secret conversations with Israeli leaders and King Hussein, Moscow's analysis was surprisingly accurate.

Even as radical guerilla groups launched attacks aimed at spoiling peace negotiations, Arafat continued to push a more moderate line. In April 1974, Arafat told the Egyptian magazine *Ruz Al-Yusuf* that PLO sovereignty would be "established immediately over every inch of Palestinian territory evacuated by the enemy." He insisted that Palestinian self-rule over their territory was inevitable. Arafat believed that the October War had opened a new phase in the Arab and Palestinian history: the Palestinian revolution, which had been absorbed in the negative aspects of the post-1967 situation, must turn its efforts to dealing with the positive aspects of the latest war. He went on to point out that the positions of Fatah and Hawatmeh's DFLP—which advocated a dialogue between Palestinian and Israeli representatives—differed in their specifics but not in their substance.[73] Although he still spoke of the total liberation of

Palestine, Arafat had signaled his willingness to establish a government in the West Bank and Gaza.

In the run-up to the twelfth PNC, Fatah and the DFLP worked feverishly to reach some sort of compromise solution with the rejectionists. The compromise came in the form of the Ten-Point Program, which established the PLO's official position on the subject of the post-1973 peace process. The program insisted that lasting peace would never come to the Middle East without the restoration of Palestinian national rights and reaffirmed the right to armed struggle for the liberation of the Palestinian homeland. The document rejected the prospect of participation in the Geneva conference so long as the latter sought the implementation of UN Resolution 242—because it made no mention of the national rights of the Palestinian people—as its basis. The amendment of UN 242 to include such a stipulation, however, might open the door to attendance. Indeed, point ten allowed for the prospect of a special meeting of the PNC to deal with extraordinary developments should they arise, such as an invitation to Geneva or the opportunity to establish a national authority in the West Bank. Ultimately, the program's most radical innovation was its acceptance of the prospect of a political solution that was *not* based on the liberation of the whole of Palestine. It marked the first official PLO document that suggested the feasibility of a two-state solution. Although the terms of the program were still far from anything that the government of Israel might accept, the document represented a historic first step toward a compromise solution.[74] The twelfth PNC represented, according to scholar Shaul Mishal, "a real shift in the PLO position towards the occupied territories; unequivocal support for military struggle has ever since been supplemented by a willingness to consider political means as well."[75]

On the same day it released the Ten-Point Program, the PNC also issued a recommendation to the PLO executive committee on the question of participation at Geneva. The PNC reiterated its rejection of UN 242 but went on to say "at the same time that the Palestinian people shall not be excluded from the international political moves" surrounding the postwar peace process. Rather, the PLO must engage the process in a "framework other than that of resolution 242." Citing the UN charter on the primacy of equality and national self-determination, the PNC called upon the PLO to "take part in the conference as being the sole legitimate representative of the Palestinian people." The PNC was urging the PLO to go to Geneva.[76]

Fatah's failure to create a united front would once again become an issue in the wake of the twelfth PNC, however. Almost as soon as the meeting had ended, factions inside the PFLP began agitating against the Ten-Point Program. The more radical elements in the group concluded that the program amounted to a slippery slope toward an "imperialist solution" and a "liquidationist settlement" to the Palestinian question. In a series of communiqués issued in the coming months, the PFLP outlined its opposition to the PLO's national authority scheme and to participation at Geneva. In a clear break between the PFLP and Fatah, Habash's group insisted that the Palestinian resistance must issue an explicit rejection of the conference.[77] The existence of the Rejectionist Front—composed of the more radical guerilla groups including the PFLP and the Arab Liberation Front—provided ammunition for the argument that the PLO did not speak for the whole of the Palestinian resistance movement and thus should not participate at Geneva. Although the overwhelming support for the PLO among the Palestinian population—Gresh notes that some 80 percent of the population would vote for pro-PLO candidates in municipal elections held in 1976—as evidence of the Rejectionist Front's weakness, the group's challenge to the moderate leadership of the PLO had repercussions at the international level.[78]

"Arafat Clearly Wishes to Move Toward a Political Settlement"

Although Israel dismissed the proposal—citing the PLO's continued goal of liberating Israeli territory—it provided a crucial measure of diplomatic legitimacy to the PLO in the international realm.[79] As President Sadat told Kissinger, the program amounted to a "Palestinian state with the West Bank, Gaza, and a corridor. [Israel's leaders] should consider this. Because it will mean coexistence with them...and no army, only an administration. This will solve the whole problem for us."[80] Indeed, if Arafat and the PLO could make the transition from guerilla group to recognized government, it might solve a host of problems.

Despite lingering obstacles to official U.S. recognition of the PLO, Egyptian and Syrian pressure made the logic of such a move more appealing. Nixon and Kissinger discussed the issue of contacting the PLO with Syrian president Hafiz al-Assad in mid-June. Assad insisted that Arafat had the support of at least 90 percent of Palestinians and encouraged the Americans to consider talking to the PLO. Kissinger claimed—disingenuously—that in order for such a move to be considered, Palestinian terrorism must be halted for several months. Otherwise, he said, Israel could use the media attention from the attacks to argue that all Palestinians were terrorists and thereby pressure Washington to backpedal.[81] In truth, Kissinger was aware that leaders such as Arafat had suspended external operations and were pushing other fedayeen to do the same. Kissinger's reservations in this regard were merely a cover for his strategy to isolate the Palestinians.[82]

This isolation clashed with the advice from the Middle East analysts on Kissinger's NSC staff. NSC staffer William Quandt maintained that the Ten-Point Program amounted to a statement by the PLO, "in heavily qualified language...that it was prepared to settle for a Palestinian state consisting only of the West Bank and Gaza." In effect, this was recognition of Israel coupled with a warning that the Palestinian aspirations would not be "adequately represented by King Hussein." With this in mind, Quandt pushed for the opening of a U.S.-PLO dialogue in August 1974 in hopes of encouraging a working relationship between Arafat and King Hussein with an eye toward the creation of a distinct Palestinian political entity. Beyond forcing the king to carve out an official role for the Palestinians, the move might serve to moderate the PLO leadership. If the organization was locked out of a settlement, he added, the result would almost certainly be more terrorism in Israel and Jordan. "The Palestinians cannot be crushed and will not acquiesce in their exclusion from the peace-making process," he cautioned. The door to bring the PLO into the negotiating process must be left open. Quandt and his fellow NSC staffer Robert Oakley argued that, while the PLO still had to "cover its tracks" with verbal bluster and threats against Israel, "Arafat clearly wishes to move toward a political settlement recognizing, at least implicitly, Israel's right to peaceful existence." Current guerilla operations—based on the North Vietnamese strategy of "talking while fighting"—were designed to preserve the PLO's negotiating position. "[Arafat] is anxiously awaiting some indication of the attitude of the United States toward the Palestinians." Ultimately, Washington must decide whether the moment was right to open a dialogue with the PLO.[83]

That same summer, Joseph Sisco forwarded a paper from Alfred Atherton Jr. at the State Department's Near Eastern affairs desk that argued that Washington must find some means of dealing with the PLO without provoking a backlash from Israel. Atherton said that to date, the United States had relied on the concept of postponing PLO participation in the peace talks, looking instead to use King Hussein as the negotiator. He questioned this approach, however, suggesting that a better option might involve the creation of a U.S.-PLO dialogue with the intention of establishing an informal position for the organization in the Israel-Jordan negotiations. This latter approach seemed to be gaining ground with Arafat, Cairo, Damascus, and Amman.[84] In the end, Washington could play a positive role in bringing the PLO into the political process, but it would require opening links with Arafat and other moderate leaders.

The prospect of building direct links with the PLO—extending even to the government of Israel itself—seemed less far-fetched when a modest opening appeared in Israel's position. On 12 July 1974, an unnamed State Department official—probably Joseph Sisco—announced that high-level contacts between Washington and the Palestinians would be desirable at some point in the future, presumably after the particulars of the Geneva conference had been sorted out. The PLO's calls for the destruction of Israel remained a stumbling block, but the possibility of U.S. engagement with the organization was under consideration.[85] Soon after, Israeli minister of information Aharon Yaariv declared, "Should the Palestinian Liberation Organization announce that its covenant was no longer valid and declare its readiness to enter into negotiations while acknowledging the existence of a Jewish state here in Israel, and should this organization announce the cessation of all hostile acts against Israel and indeed terminate these activities, then it would be possible to start negotiating."[86] The following week, however, the Israeli cabinet changed direction, refusing to consider disengagement from its positions along the Jordan River. Kissinger's efforts to persuade the Rabin government to reconsider and remain flexible ran into a brick wall: in accordance with earlier pledges, any effort to withdraw from the West Bank would need Israeli public approval in the form of a national election. Given the democratic nature of the Israeli political system, Rabin could not move forward.[87]

Israeli journalist Matti Golan writes that the June 1974 opening was part of a larger struggle between Washington and the Rabin government over Kissinger's efforts to achieve progress on the Jordanian front. Sisco's announcement that the United States was considering an opening to the PLO was designed to pressure Rabin to push forward with King Hussein in hopes of achieving a bilateral agreement between Israel and Jordan before the PLO achieved recognition as the sole representative of the Palestinians. The message thus contained a threat: while Washington had not yet recognized the PLO, "it was not inconceivable that the United States would shift in the future if Israel persisted in its refusal to negotiate" with Jordan.[88] Although it did not develop into official relations, the U.S. and Israeli declarations of June 1974 signaled that a future opening to the PLO—in the event that Arafat's organization recognized Israel and was willing to abandon violence—was not beyond the realm of possibility. This path would not be taken, however.

The possibility of establishing diplomatic relations with the PLO ran counter to standing Israeli policies, although the structure of leadership in the Jewish state was changing. The failure of Israeli intelligence to predict the beginning of the 1973 war resulted in significant political changes in Israel. The older generation of Israeli leaders such as Meir and Dayan—some of them already preparing to retire from political life—was replaced by a younger group including Yitzhak Rabin and Shimon Peres. Rabin's ascension to the prime ministership thus marked the transition to a new generation of Israeli leadership. Born in Jerusalem, Rabin joined the Palmach, the elite warfare unit of the Haganah, in 1941. Imprisoned for six months in 1946, he would become deputy to Yigal Allon, commander of the Palmach, upon his release. Two years later, during the 1948 war, Rabin commanded IDF attacks on the Palestinian towns of Lydda and Ramla. His recollection of the operations sparked controversy in 1979 when an Israeli review board voted to censor the section of his memoirs in which he described the forced expulsion of some 50,000 Palestinian civilians from the towns. The account was subsequently published in the *New York Times*. Rabin continued to rise through the ranks of the IDF until 1964, when he became chief of staff. His conduct in the 1967 received much praise throughout Israel. When he retired from the military the following year, he was appointed ambassador to the United States. In the coming years and decades, Rabin would become a central figure in the peace process.[89]

Rabin was more amenable to UN 242's land-for-peace formula than his pre-decessor. He understood that any peace would require the return of most of the Arab territory occupied since 1967. "Areas with dense Arab population in the West Bank and Gaza Strip could not remain under our rule forever," remarked an official in the Foreign Ministry under Rabin. However, like Meir, Rabin looked to Jordan rather than the Palestinians as the appropriate negoti-ating partner in any eventual exchange. Indeed, the Rabin government cate-gorically rejected the prospect of direct negotiations with the PLO. He was also unwilling to consider the creation of a Palestinian state. Such an entity, he argued, "would be the beginning of the end of the State of Israel." Likewise, Rabin was determined to rebuild Israel's strength so as to avoid withdrawal from any territories "in the shadow of the Yom Kippur War and under the pres-sure of Arab oil power." The Arab states must not be given any reason to believe that the 1973 war had been a diplomatic success.[90] Further, he told the Tel Aviv daily *Haaretz* that the PLO was simply "an instrument in the inter-Arab strug-gle" that

> would not exist if certain Arab states decided that it was no longer serv-ing their interests. We must prove that we have nothing to discuss with the PLO and that we do not intend to talk with it. Such an attitude might, during the coming year, bring Hussein back as a partner in a positive process of progress in negotiations.

Like his predecessor, Rabin rejected the concept of an independent Palestinian entity and called upon a solution to be mediated through Amman.[91]

Rabin's cabinet was wary of the PLO's Ten-Point Program, which it saw as an incremental strategy for continuing the Palestinian war with Israel. In the face of minority opposition within his cabinet—which argued that Israel should engage with any Palestinians who were willing to recognize the Jewish state's right to exist—Rabin opted to keep the question of Palestine "in the refrigerator." Historian Avi Shlaim comments that this amounted to a con-tinuation of Meir's earlier policy of rejecting outright the notion of negotia-tions with the PLO. Meir "denied the existence of a Palestinian people," Shlaim writes. "Although [Rabin] recognized that a Palestinian people existed and that there was a Palestinian problem, he was not prepared to do anything about it."[92]

Two months after Meir's departure, another key player would leave the scene. On 9 August 1974, Richard Nixon resigned rather than face impeach-ment for his role in covering up the Watergate affair. His successor, Gerald Ford, lacked Nixon's interest in foreign affairs and relied on Kissinger, who had survived the scandal relatively untouched, to coordinate White House policy. Would the new president continue the step-by-step process pioneered by

Kissinger, or would he seek a comprehensive, Geneva-type approach? As William Quandt explained later, Kissinger's shuttle diplomacy did not develop a means of addressing the "core issues of peace, security, and the Palestinians." However, it would have taken a very strong president, Quandt contends, to carry out the transition from Kissinger's shuttle diplomacy to a comprehensive settlement of the regional conflict. Ford simply was not that president, having come into office without being elected to the position in the midst of one of the greatest crises in the history of the American executive.[93]

Not surprisingly, Kissinger continued to oppose the notion of a comprehensive approach, although he acknowledged that it was "intellectually" tempting and that it "had the support of most academic experts" and the State Department prior to his tenure as secretary of state. He was wary of this comprehensive approach, however, because it would give more power to parties such as Syria and the PLO, it would involve the Soviet Union, and it threatened to isolate the United States. As Kissinger told Rabin on his first visit to Washington as prime minister,

> [The choice is] either [a] total settlement or a series of partial settlements. A total settlement would lump all the issues together and its failure would lead to great pressures. Secondly, it would raise the issue of the 1967 borders prematurely. Thirdly, it would raise Jerusalem and the Palestinians.... [For all these reasons] there must be some alternative framework to prevent the Palestinian issue from overwhelming all else.... It is essential that the Geneva conference meet as late as possible and hopefully to ratify something already done.

Kissinger thus stuck to his guns. With his step-by-step approach, he had established the parameters for the peace process, and he refused to embark on any diplomacy that might result in the compromise on three fundamental points. First, the United States would not agree to any course that would allow Soviet participation in the peace process. Second, the United States would not increase pressure on Israel to make concessions to the Arab states. Third, Washington would not seek to address the Palestinian issue outside of the Jordan framework. On this third point, he informed Rabin that the United States agreed that a prospective Palestinian state would likely seek the "destruction of both Jordan and Israel." Moreover, he told the prime minister that for the time being, Washington had "no incentive to feature the Palestinians." Rather, the White House would continue to push the Jordan option as the only means of addressing the Palestinian question.[94]

While Kissinger justified each of these points on the grounds of potential complications at a hypothetical peace conference, his basic position was clear: the United States was not acting as a neutral arbiter in the Arab-Israeli dispute. Rather, Kissinger was using the peace process as a means of pushing Soviet influence out of the region and bolstering Washington's position in the Middle

East. His primary objective was not to secure long-term peace or a final settlement to the Arab-Israeli dispute but rather to further U.S. interests in the Middle East. A militarily preponderant Israel contributed to this larger strategy by securing Washington's position as intermediary between the Jewish state and the rest of the Arab world—one of the few services that Moscow could not provide. Furthermore, Kissinger would work to ensure that no other player—particularly the Soviet Union or the United Nations—would challenge Washington's preeminent position as mediator in the Arab-Israeli dispute. The Palestinians and the PLO simply did not fit into Kissinger's framework, and its victories, symbolic though they might be, served only to complicate the process whereby disillusionment would bring the Arab states into alignment with Washington.

"At the Moment When We Palestinians Desire Peace, the Israelis Will Be the Ones Who Refuse"

Meanwhile, the Soviet Union continued to advocate for the PLO's inclusion in a comprehensive settlement to the regional conflict. In July 1974, the PLO's news agency announced that the Kremlin had declared its support for the PLO's participation at Geneva on equal footing with the other parties at the conference during Arafat's visit to the Soviet Union. This declaration increased the pressure on the PLO emanating from Moscow to engage in a political process that would lead to a two-state solution.[95] In the same month, an article in the Moscow daily *Izvestia* encouraged the PLO to adopt an even more moderate position under a unified leadership. Likewise, in September, Moscow announced its official support for the creation of a Palestinian state and reaffirmed its conviction that the question of Palestine remained at the heart of the Arab-Israeli dispute. By November, the Kremlin had shifted to a position of full support for the creation of a Palestinian state. Soviet efforts to promote a Palestinian state—along with the PLO's own political and military operations—would represent a thorn in the side of Kissinger's initiatives to achieve bilateral agreements between Israel and its neighbors. The Soviet-PLO offensive thus would function to push the alternative vision of a comprehensive settlement to the Arab-Israeli dispute. This comprehensive strategy would demand a joint effort by the superpowers, rather than Kissinger's unilateral approach.[96] In October, Soviet premier Leonid Brezhnev called for the resumption of the Geneva conference with the inclusion of the Palestinians. Soviet leaders recognized that Kissinger had pushed Moscow to the sidelines of the peace process.[97]

While the White House equivocated on the question of PLO recognition in hopes of salvaging the Amman-as-negotiator option and Israeli leaders rejected both the idea of negotiations and the notion of a Palestinian state, other actors in the world community moved to grant increased recognition to the PLO.

The heads of state of the Organization of African Unity expressed their official support for the PLO and their condemnation of Israel in mid-June 1974. Using language lifted from PLO declarations, the OAU declared its "full support for the struggle of the Palestine Liberation Organization in its capacity as the sole legitimate representative of the Palestinian people and for its heroic struggle against Zionism and racialism."[98]

In September, Cairo, Damascus, and the PLO issued the Tripartite Declaration, announcing that the PLO was the sole legitimate representative of the Palestinian people: the Palestinians would speak for themselves through the institution of the PLO. The organization could no longer be dismissed as a fringe group, unrepresentative of broader Palestinian society. Meanwhile, revelations of a Jordanian–South African arms deal served as a further blow to Amman's credibility in international forums such as the United Nations. In response to growing evidence of its political isolation on the issue of Palestinian representation, Jordanian officials declared a diplomatic freeze whereby Amman's participation in the peace process would be temporarily suspended. King Hussein found himself in the difficult situation of fighting his own "battles with the PLO while avoiding an open break with [the] Arab 'consensus.'" As the Rabat summit of Arab leaders approached, however, the king had begun seeking to resume negotiations with Israel in hopes of reestablishing his credibility with other Arab regimes as a representative of the West Bank. Nonetheless, officials in Amman worried that the king's time was running out.[99]

King Hussein's credibility was clearly waning. Algerian president Boumedienne insisted that the Palestine issue remained at the heart of the Middle East crisis. Moreover, the Jordanian government was playing a dangerous game. Given the choice between the monarch and the Palestinians, "without hesitation and without any reservations we choose the Palestine revolution." Algiers would thus recognize the PLO as the sole legitimate representative of the Palestinian people and endorse the organization's participation in the anticipated Middle East peace conference in Geneva.[100]

When the Rabat summit convened, Amman found itself in an isolated position on the issue of Palestinian representation. PLO Executive Committee member Abu Lutf warned that Israel and the United States were seeking to undermine Arab gains made during the October 1973 war and restore the IDF's regional military supremacy. Washington and Israel wanted to destroy the Palestine revolution by installing the Jordanian government as the spokesman of the Palestinian cause. These efforts, he argued, ignored the success of Palestinian suicide operations in Ma'alot, Nahariya, Jerusalem, and Tel Aviv and the PLO's political victories in sites such as the United Nations. With these victories in mind, Abu Lutf asserted the PLO's right to represent any state that might be established in the Palestinian territories. Moreover, the PLO would reach out to Europe and Africa in hopes of gaining further support for its armed struggle in the region and its political struggle at the United Nations.[101]

Still hoping to divert the momentum toward recognition of the PLO, Amman insisted that the current attempts to find a "suitable definition of a Palestinian National Authority... [did] not necessarily mean the authority of the PLO," and furthermore that the recognition "by some Arab countries of the PLO as sole representative of the Palestinians has no practical operational effect and hence does not prohibit [the] exercise of [the] Jordanian role in negotiations."[102] State Department analysts pointed out that Amman's main negotiating position focused on the idea that Jordan was the only representative of the West Bank that Israel and the United States were likely to accept.[103] Despite these arguments, the Arab League, in recognition of the PNC's Ten-Point Program, declared the PLO the sole legitimate representative of the Palestinian people on 28 October 1974. King Hussein, in journalist Helen Cobban's words, "was now formally out of the diplomatic ballgame, and the PLO was seeking a way to get in."[104] Arafat thus left the Rabat summit with a unanimous endorsement of the PLO as the sole legitimate representative of the Palestinian people, of the organization's right to establish a national authority in "all liberated Palestinian territory," and of its right to speak on behalf of the Palestinian people.[105]

While the Americans, Israelis, and Jordanians mourned the news from Rabat, the greater part of the Arab world was delighted. Lebanese opinion interpreted the Rabat summit as a major victory for Arafat and the moderates in the PLO and hoped that this latest diplomatic success might lead to a resolution of the PLO's conflict with Amman and an opening for a broader Middle East peace settlement. Arafat and the PLO were already looking ahead to the coming UN General Assembly discussions of the Palestine question, where they were expecting to achieve yet another diplomatic victory. Ambassador Godley speculated that Arafat might use momentum from Rabat to declare a PLO-led government-in-exile prior to the UN debate in hopes of solidifying "Arab and Third-World support for [the] PLO initiative in New York" and encourage the French government—which was had already issued de facto recognition of the PLO—into rallying European support for it." The Rejectionist Front, however, had begun to attack Arafat for bowing to the United States and to the Egyptian, Saudi, and Syrian designs for a Middle East peace. Godley reasoned that Arafat might be seeking to consolidate his strength through his efforts in places such as Rabat in the expectation of a showdown with the more extreme guerilla organizations.[106]

American officials in Beirut picked up indications that Arafat and the PLO were adopting a more moderate, pragmatic, and constructive stance in the wake of Rabat and in anticipation of the coming General Assembly debates. A member of the PLO delegation to the UN General Assembly announced that with the organization's participation in the proceedings, "we are going to demonstrate that at [the] moment when we Palestinians desire peace, [the] Israelis will be [the] ones who refuse." Likewise, although official

PLO rhetoric maintained that the creation of a National Authority was "merely a stepping-stone toward [the] achievement of [a] 'secular, democratic state' in all of Palestine," State Department officials argued that "this kind of talk is calculated... for internal Palestinian consumption and is really not taken seriously by PLO 'moderates.'" Nevertheless, they emphasized, such rhetoric stoked Israeli fears. In the end, they suggested that the litmus test that might indicate whether this PLO moderation was indeed legitimate would be Arafat's reaction to Security Council Resolution 242; if confronted with this, the PLO delegation "would be forced to show its true colors regarding "Israel's existence."[107]

Building on this diplomatic momentum, the PLO took its case to the UN General Assembly. Arafat delivered his dramatic gun and olive branch address to the assembly on 13 November to wide acclaim. The following week, the assembly passed, by a vote of 89 to 7, resolution 3236, which reaffirmed the "inalienable rights of the Palestinian people in Palestine, including:... the right to self-determination...The right to national independence and sovereignty.... [and] the inalienable right of the Palestinians to return to their homes and property...and calls for their return." Resolution 3237 granted the PLO official observer status.[108] In anticipation of Arafat's appearance, the PLO's newspaper ran a cover shot of an arm, upraised and grasping an AK-47, superimposed over a photo of the UN General Assembly above a caption announcing that the armed struggle had arrived. Another newspaper heralded the PLO's actions in New York, cheering, "Palestine has re-entered History."[109] His "gun and olive branch" speech at the UN proposed a potential compromise with to Israel, according to Arafat. "I had to send my signals in... [an] ambiguous way....But really I was not so ambiguous....I said enough for people of goodwill, even Israelis of goodwill, to understand that I was offering a very big compromise in the name of my Palestinian people."[110]

In addition to being a tremendous public relations coup, Arafat's visit to the United Nations generated two General Assembly resolutions that would have a critical impact on the PLO's position in the peace process. Resolution 3237 offered the PLO official observer status in the UN General Assembly, granting the Palestinians an official role at the United Nations. The other resolution, UN 3236, acknowledged the "inalienable rights of the Palestinian people, including" the right to national self-determination, independence, and sovereignty, and recognized the Palestinian people as "a principal party in the establishment of a just and desirable peace in the Middle East." This was a monumental victory for the PLO, one that the guerillas had been struggling for since the end of the 1967 war. Resolution 3236 effectively neutralized Resolution 242 as a longstanding obstacle to Palestinian participation in the peace process. In the PLO's formulation, UN 3236 would provide a legal basis for participation at Geneva. In the eyes of the United Nations, the Palestinians were no longer merely Arab refugees. The Palestinians were a nation.[111]

FIGURE 7.1 *PLO, "105 Nations Stand with Us," c. 1974. Courtesy of the Palestinian Poster Project Archives.*

FIGURE 7.2 *Cartoon, Arafat at the United Nations, PLO newspaper* Filastine al-Thawra. *Courtesy of the Library of the Institute for Palestine Studies, Beirut.*

Even as he presented the Palestinian case to the General Assembly, Arafat continued his efforts to court Washington, telling *Time* magazine that "the US holds the key to Israel" and calling upon the United States to recognize that "friendship with our Arab nation is more important, lasting, and beneficial" than an alliance with Israel.[112] While in New York City for his trip to the United Nations, Arafat and several PLO officers held a secret meeting with CIA officials at the Waldorf-Astoria hotel. There they hammered out an agreement whereby the PLO would suspend its armed operations outside of Israel in exchange for U.S. recognition of Palestinian rights. Arafat—who added that he could not be held responsible for the actions of Palestinian fighters outside of his organization—apparently understood this to mean U.S. recognition of the PLO, but on this he would be disappointed. Kissinger made such recognition contingent on the PLO's acceptance of UN Resolutions 242 and 338 and recognition of Israel.[113] By December 1974, Arafat was publicly criticizing Kissinger's bilateral diplomacy as a plot to undermine the talks at Geneva—implicit evidence of the guerilla leader's support for a comprehensive peace settlement through political channels.[114]

Secretary Kissinger was not charmed by Arafat's overtures, nor was he pleased with the PLO's new diplomatic position. In an off-the-record conversation with a group of American media executives, the secretary explained that the Rabat decision—and Arafat's subsequent appearance in New York—had essentially closed negotiations on the prospect of a Palestinian state. Ignoring the analysis of State Department Arabists, Kissinger seemed to take the PLO's irredentist rhetoric at face value: "What Arafat said makes it, of course, impossible to negotiate for Israel, because within the context of a unified Palestinian state, in which they would have to give up their identity, there is no possible basis for negotiation for Israel." Rather than push Israel's leaders toward pragmatic compromises with PLO moderates—who, in the judgment of U.S. ambassadors in the region, were merely trying to placate the Palestinian population—the secretary concluded that a solution to the West Bank problem was unachievable short of a change in PLO attitude or the reappearance of the Jordan-option. Kissinger still held out a sliver of hope that King Hussein might represent the Palestinians.[115]

Behind closed doors, Kissinger fumed over Arafat's reception in New York, explaining that the United States now faced a massive problem with the PLO. Buffum remarked that the "reception given Arafat was just incredible," to which the secretary responded, "It is really intolerable. This is what I object to with South Africa, with Arafat. This Assembly is no longer an international body; it's a forum for an anti-Western" sentiment. "I mean it's likely to turn to a massive onslaught on us in another year or two," he warned, seeming almost personally insulted at the PLO's popularity. "That is totally wrong of the United Nations to treat the head of the liberation movement with so much respect."[116]

While Kissinger remained frustrated in Washington, PLO leaders continued to follow a more moderate path, voicing strong opposition to the hijacking of a British jetliner in late November. In private Robert Houghton praised their statements, calling them an indication of the PLO's determination to follow a more moderate course now that it had been accepted by the world community as a national liberation movement. Leaders such as Arafat were aware that future external attacks were likely to damage the cause. This most recent condemnation, Houghton predicted, "foreshadows PLO determination [to] behave more 'responsibly' in Arab and international context."[117] Here was the solution to the problem of Palestinian violence that the State Department and the international community had been looking for. It was not, however, a solution that the White House or the government of Israel was willing to consider.

A key question remains, however: if Arafat was sincere about his intentions to bring the PLO into a comprehensive framework for peace in the Arab-Israeli conflict, why did he choose not to declare a government-in-exile? Indeed, such a move almost certainly would have facilitated the organization's path to Geneva. The South Vietnamese NLF, for example, had created just such an organization with the Provisional Revolutionary Government of the Republic of South Vietnam (PRG) in 1969. The PRG achieved had achieved diplomatic victory—which the PLO would celebrate—only months before, when it became one of the signatories of the Paris peace accords that ended the U.S. war in Vietnam. Although Arafat hinted at his willingness to create such an institution if doing so was necessary to participate at Geneva—"If the proclamation of this government will lead to disengagement and acquisition of a territory," he told *Al-Ahram*, "we shall hasten to do so"—he did not take the initiative of forming one. There are a number of reasons for this refusal. The creation of such a body could be interpreted as another step toward recognition of Israel. It would thus constitute a concession, which bore no guarantee of being reciprocated. Indeed, if recognition was the PLO's trump card in its negotiations with Israel, the organization had no desire to play that card merely as a condition for gaining a seat at the table. Thus, as Fatah announced in early November, its opposition to the creation of a provisional government concerned timing, not principle. Moreover, PLO leaders expressed the fear that if they were to form a government-in-exile, it risked being forced to negotiate under unfavorable conditions. Such an institution might make it easier for Soviets and Egyptians to bring pressure on the PLO to make concessions.[118]

The refusal to create a provisional government must be understood as yet another of the repercussions of Fatah's failure to craft a united front. Arafat's decision not to bring the various guerilla groups under Fatah's command in 1968 would ultimately play a role in keeping the PLO from consolidating the gains from its armed struggle and political action in the following decade. In short, the absence of a united front prevented the PLO from translating its popularity into political realities in the post-1973 diplomatic landscape. The creation of a government-in-exile would risk splitting the PLO between its mainstream elements and the Rejectionist Front at an extremely inopportune time. Moreover, the moderate leadership of the PLO was almost certain that if it did take the step of declaring itself a government-in-exile and then the negotiations at Geneva failed, it would suffer a severe political blow inside the movement. Such a scenario would undermine the moderates' base of support within the PLO and vindicate the Rejectionist Front's more militant position.[119]

Even so, the PLO continued to move toward acceptance of the prospect of a political solution to its dispute with Israel, solidifying its position on international diplomacy and the peace process in the early weeks of 1975. In January, Arafat answered his critics in the Rejectionist Front, telling *Le Monde* that the inclusion of the PLO in "every international assembly" was a victory for the people of Palestine. The PLO, like other national liberation movements, would continue to push its global offensive into the diplomatic arena. Further, Arafat declared his willingness to speak with Kissinger or, presumably, the government of Israel. "Personally," he announced, "I have no objection against meeting anyone who would allow me to clarify or advance the cause of our people." The chairman chastised Kissinger's shuttle diplomacy, however, as a brazen attempt to "torpedo the Geneva conference, to conduct negotiations 'step by step' outside of any international control, and to eliminate" the Soviet Union from the peace process. If these efforts should succeed in pulling Egypt out of the dispute with Israel, he added, "the situation in the Middle East would notably deteriorate.... Under those conditions one has to expect that the vital interests of the United States and the West in general will be hard hit."[120]

Over this same stretch of time, Moscow continued to lobby for the incorporation of the PLO into a comprehensive framework for peace. In February, Leonid Brezhnev called once more for reconvening the Geneva conference with the inclusion of the PLO, explaining that "its postponement is inadmissible unless complete indifference is to be shown to the destinies of the countries and peoples of the Middle East...and to the fate of world peace." Arafat responded with a message of thanks for the Soviet premier. In early April, the PLO called for

> an early meeting of the Geneva Conference, so as to discuss and iron out all aspects of the Middle East crisis and in particular the Palestinian problem, on the basis of Resolution 3236...participation by the PLO with full rights in the Geneva Conference is an essential condition for its success.

In August, Arafat announced that the PLO was prepared to "participate in any meeting, any international conference convened to respond to the aspirations of the Palestinian people, such as they have been laid down in UN General Assembly Resolution 3236...This is the only condition we make."[121] As they were at pains to make clear to any who were willing to listen, Arafat and the PLO were prepared to sit down at the negotiating table with Israel in 1975.

Sinai II and the End of the Road

For a brief moment, it appeared as if the Americans might be prepared to meet them there. Kissinger's shuttle diplomacy had hit a roadblock in March 1975 with an impasse over negotiations for Israeli withdrawal from the Sinai. With talks at a standstill, Gerald Ford began considering "a reassessment of our whole Middle Eastern policy," namely, whether to scrap Kissinger's step-by-step approach and take the peace process back to Geneva. The president admitted that this latter path would provide a sounding board for Palestinian demands. "I don't mean to infer that we have made any decision," he said. "But the Palestinians have to be examined as part of the overall Middle East situation." The inclusion of the PLO would be impossible, however, so long as the organization refused to deal with—and most likely recognize—Israel.[122] Bringing Israel to Geneva, especially if Arafat was sitting at the table, would require the White House to exert a great deal of pressure on the Jewish state. While many policy advisors, analysts, and area specialists argued for such action, support for the idea largely stopped there.[123]

On 21 May, seventy-six senators sent a letter to President Ford criticizing attempts to place more pressure on Israel and calling for a "reiteration of our nation's long-standing commitment to Israel's security 'by a policy of continued military supplies and diplomatic and economic support.'" "Recent events," the letter said, in a reference to Vietnam and Watergate, "underscore America's need for reliable allies and the desirability of greater participation by the Congress in the formulation of American foreign policy." The United States should bolster its commitments to "nations which share our democratic traditions." Further, a powerful Israel constituted the "most reliable barrier to domination of [the Middle East] by outside parties." Any decision to withhold military equipment—Washington's best means of pressuring Israel—would threaten to undermine the "military balance" in the region and thereby risk renewed hostilities. It was becoming clear, according to William Quandt, that "continued pressure on Israel would be politically counterproductive. Ford and Kissinger realized that the only viable strategy...was to resume step-by-step diplomacy."[124]

Five days later, the White House confirmed this new direction when Secretary of Defense James Schlesinger announced that "the military balance [in the Middle East] is far more favorable from Israel's standpoint than it was in October, 1973." Moreover, in the event of another broad conflict, Washington would be able to begin military resupply operations to Israel in about thirty-six hours. Far from preserving the "military balance" in the region, the United States had helped increase IDF superiority. The United States must be resolved,

Schlesinger concluded, "to hold the ring in the Middle East. There's just nobody else who can stand up in the Soviet Union. Some Americans want to go off in a sulk for five years. But if we do, we'll wake up some bright day and discover that the Soviets have achieved paramount power in the Eastern Hemisphere. We are just not in a position to indulge in that luxury."[125] Rather, Washington must be ready, in the wake of defeat in Vietnam, to maintain its position in the Middle East. In July, Kissinger told reporters that the Washington must remain active in world affairs, but some "parts of the world have now developed some strength and self-confidence and can assume larger responsibilities." As he noted, the United States was "reluctant to undertake new commitments for the long-term stationing of military forces abroad and looks rather for the local capacity to defend itself if necessary and, if we think it is in our own interests, with our support." Then Kissinger reminded his audience, "We are the country that has been the major source of support for Israel." Ultimately, Washington's "role is changing. It is less direct than it was in the past, and it is less military than it has been in the past. But it still has to be significant." Kissinger was effectively linking the Nixon Doctrine to Israel.[126]

Kissinger's efforts achieved a major breakthrough in September 1975 with the signing of the Sinai Interim Agreement—also known as Sinai II—which secured a pledge of nonbelligerency between Egypt and Israel. Henceforth, disputes between the two regional powers would be solved through diplomacy rather than military means. Although few acknowledged it at the time, Sinai II would all but complete Egypt's diplomatic shift away from Moscow and bring it into alignment with Washington and, by extension, Israel. Cairo's shift transformed the geostrategic map of the region, removing the largest and most powerful Arab state from the Arab-Israeli conflict, undercutting Soviet influence in the area, and leaving players such as Syria and the PLO out in the cold. This major achievement for Kissinger's shuttle diplomacy would be a crushing defeat for the PLO's efforts to secure statehood. Kissinger's bilateral approach established a precedent for later peace efforts that proved surprisingly hard to overturn. After Sinai II, Israeli leaders would not again face the serious prospect of having to negotiate a comprehensive settlement with its Arab neighbors. With Egypt out of the equation, the pressure on Israel to come to terms with the PLO and states such as Syria was dramatically reduced.

Moreover, in the run-up to Sinai II, Washington bound itself to a position on the PLO. In a memorandum of agreement with Israel in preparation for the signing of the agreement at Geneva, Kissinger pledged not to recognize the PLO as long as the organization refused to accept UN 242 and Israel's right to exist. Moreover, Kissinger pledged that the United States would "consult fully and seek to concert its position and strategy with Israel with regard to the participation of any other additional states" at the Geneva conference and that the inclusion of any "additional state, group, or organization" in any future phase of the conference would "require the agreement of all the initial participants."

Kissinger effectively locked the United States into a position whereby it would need official Israeli consent to bring the PLO into the peace process. In an addendum to the memorandum released the same day, Washington committed to "continue to maintain Israel's defensive strength through the supply of advanced types of equipment, such as the F-16 aircraft," and to begin a joint study with Israel of "high technology and sophisticated items, including the Pershing ground-to-ground missiles with conventional warheads." Henceforth, the administration would work with Congress to allocate "military and economic assistance in order to help meet Israel's economic and military needs." Thus, as part of the Sinai II agreements, the White House would provide the IDF with the latest generation of American-made jet fighters, and it would also consider Israeli requests for medium-range ballistic missiles designed to carry conventional or nuclear warheads.[127]

Israeli leaders made it clear that they had no plans for political accommodations with the PLO. One day after the signing of Sinai II, Israeli defense minister Shimon Peres reiterated Israel's stance on its "war against the terrorists" based on the active-defense model of striking at the "terrorists while they are still in their bases and camps, before they move." Two months later, the Knesset reacted to the UN General Assembly's passage of Resolution 3376, which reaffirmed the assembly's support for Palestinian self-determination and lamented the lack of progress toward this end—by passing its own resolution that pledged never "to negotiate with the terrorist organizations in any forum," and to boycott the Geneva conference if forced to do so. The PLO, argued the Knesset, "is a framework for organizations of murderers whose declared aim is to destroy the state of Israel."[128]

Perhaps the most dramatic break between Israel and the United Nations came soon after, with the passage of UN 3379 on 10 November by a vote of 72 for, 35 against, and 32 abstentions. The resolution—which cited the 1963 UN Declaration on the Elimination of All Forms of Racial Discrimination, the World Conference of the International Women's Year, and the OAU—determined that "Zionism is a form of racism and racial discrimination," affirming many of the arguments that the PLO had been making for years. The PLO's representative, Faruq Qaddumi, praised the resolution and characterized the last two UN General Assembly sessions as "a turning point in the history of" the United Nations; "its universality and credibility have increased. The results are a reflection of the international march against imperialism and colonialism and backward racist beliefs, foremost among which is Zionism." The two most vocal opponents of the resolution, Daniel Patrick Moynihan of the United States and Chaim Herzog of Israel, denounced the resolution as "infamous" and driven by "hatred, falsehood, and arrogance" respectively. While Herzog announced that the United Nations was "on its way to becoming the world centre of anti-semitism," Moynihan warned that "a great evil has been loosed upon the world."[129] Though the debates over UN 3379 carried little practical weight in and of themselves, they showcased the dramatic polarization in the international arena over the question of Palestine, the strong support that the Palestinians had gained by the mid-1970s, and the acrimonious relationship between Israel and the United Nations.

The following month, Peres said on American television, in terms that Washington was sure to understand, that the creation of some sort of Palestinian state between Jordan and Israel was unthinkable. "Such as state will be oriented upon Soviet Russia," he insisted. "We'll have Russian arms, their missiles, their guns will menace our parliament, our populated areas, and in addition to that, they may transfer the Fatah bases from Lebanon to the West Bank."[130] As 1975 came to an end, Prime Minister Rabin made clear that the PLO's victories at the United Nations would not be enough to compel Israel to seek terms with the organization. Meanwhile, Rabin said, the United States had not placed any pressure on Israel to deal with the PLO. The Palestinian issue was not "the key to a Mideast solution," he insisted. "We will flatly refuse any attempt to detach the Palestinian problem from Jordan." Even if the PLO were to renounce "terrorism" and recognize Israel,

> we will never negotiate with the so-called PLO. Admittedly we are quite isolated. But . . . we must stick to what we believe regardless of what others might think. The purpose of our enemies is our destruction and we will have to conduct policy knowing that we are still at war after 27 years and that this war might last another 27 years.

It was clear that, left to itself, the Rabin government was not interested in establishing any sort of political relationship with the PLO that might lead to Palestinian self-determination, nor would pressure from international organizations such as the United Nations encourage Israel to do so.[131]

Thus, while Israel sought to complete the military encirclement of the PLO with the help of large amounts of U.S. aid, Kissinger worked to achieve diplomatic containment. Rather than accepting PLO moderates' de facto recognition of Israel and attempts to begin negotiations aimed at producing a political solution to the Israel-Palestine dispute—and encouraging the Israeli government to do the same—Kissinger stonewalled. Unlike much of the rest of the international community, the United States refused to acknowledge the legitimacy of the PLO and instead pushed the idea that Amman would function as the best negotiator for the Palestinians. This approach supported U.S. Cold War strategic interests in the Middle East, but it did not serve the prospects of achieving a long-term peace. By sidelining the PLO and the Palestinians—at the very moment when the PLO was moving toward a more moderate political stance—this diplomatic approach ensured that low-intensity warfare would continue in the region for the foreseeable future.

Conclusion

Standing at the podium of the cavernous main hall of the UN General Assembly, the chairman of the PLO announced, "The time has come for my courageous and proud people, after decades of displacement and colonial occupation and ceaseless suffering, to live like other peoples of the earth, free in a sovereign and independent homeland." The chairman was greeted by "thunderous applause" from the ranks of the nearly two hundred member states represented in the hall. In the days before the chairman's speech, a former Saudi ambassador to the United States explained its significance to Washington: "The United States must support the Palestinian bid for statehood at the United Nations...or risk losing the little credibility it has in the Arab world." Following the speech, an American journalist observed, "The United States and Israel now look trapped together, weakened and dangerously isolated during a period of deep transformation."[1] This drama played out not in 1974 but in 2011. Indeed, nearly thirty-seven years after Arafat presented his "gun and olive branch" speech to the United Nations, the question of Palestinian statehood remained at the forefront of world attention; so too did the question of what Washington's role toward such a state should be. The cast of characters had changed, but many of the issues remained the same, leaving the question of Palestine as a sort of Cold War relic, one of the key international concerns of the bygone era that remained unresolved in the second decade of the twenty-first century.

From 1967 to 1975, Palestinian fighters waged a global offensive that they hoped would culminate in the liberation of their homelands west of the Jordan River. Their armed struggle was embraced by revolutionaries on every continent. Their international diplomacy won the support of a commanding majority of states at the United Nations, which hailed the Palestinian struggle as a leading front in the global movement for national liberation. Writing nearly twenty-five years later, the dean of Middle East studies, Edward Said, observed, "With the rise of the PLO in the late 1960s came...an unusual new cosmopolitanism in which figures such as Fanon, Mao, and Guevara entered the Arab political idiom." "Some day," he continued, "the history of exchange and support between the PLO and such groups as the African National Congress, SWAPO, the Sandinistas, as well as the anti-Shah revolutionary Iranian groups will describe an extraordinary chapter in the twentieth-century struggle against various forms of tyranny and injustice."[2] Most histories of the twentieth century do not, however, include the Palestinians among the ranks of the Algerians, Cubans, Vietnamese, and South Africans. Instead, the PLO's story has been isolated from this international narrative, consigned to a sub-plot in the Arab-Israeli conflict, or, more recently, written as the first chapter in the rise of "international terrorism." This study has endeavored to recover the original cosmopolitan dimensions of the Palestinian liberation struggle of the 1960s and 1970s by locating the PLO within the historical context from which it emerged as part of the global wave of national liberation movements that developed in the 1950s and 1960s.

In the eight years following the 1967 war, Palestinian fighters pioneered an innovative strategy of revolutionary struggle designed to exploit the transnational terrain of the emerging global order. These connections with the wider world would play a central role in shaping the Palestinian liberation struggle, arming the PLO with the weapons it would need to launch a guerilla war against Israel and with the concepts of national liberation that it would use to push its agenda onto the world stage. On the conceptual level, Palestinian fighters embraced the cause of revolutionary groups from around the Third Word, imagining their own movement as the spiritual successor to the Chinese, Algerian, Cuban, and Vietnamese examples. In their military capacity, Palestinian fighters built upon earlier models of guerilla warfare, engineering a set of tactics designed to project their armed struggle into an increasingly interconnected world order. The PLO's greatest victories would come not on the battlefield, however, but in the political arena. As it continued this diplomatic campaign, the PLO emerged as the world's first globalized insurgency and became a seminal influence for rebellions in the post–Cold War era.

As they intensified their armed struggle, Palestinian fighters clashed with the world's greatest superpower, which was seeking to revamp its global security strategies in the midst of a collapsing counterinsurgency taking place in Vietnam. Just as the Palestinian revolution should not be studied in isolation from global events, the U.S. response must be placed in its wider context. U.S. policy makers feared that the revolutionary fires that had engulfed Cuba, Algeria, and Vietnam might spread through much of the rest of the global South. The PLO's global offensive—like other revolutionary movements throughout the Third World—threatened to undermine friendly regimes and create opportunities for Soviet advances in the region. The Nixon administration thus resolved to shore up its position in the eastern Mediterranean as part of an integrated response to Cold War challenges throughout the global South.

The administration would do this through a combination of military aid to its allies—Israel and Jordan—and diplomacy designed to drive a wedge between Moscow and the Arab powers. At the same time, the White House worked to isolate the PLO from the Arab-Israeli peace process and blunt the impact of Palestinian victories on the international stage.

The PLO thus sat at the junction between the worldwide struggle for national liberation, the Cold War, and the Arab-Israeli conflict and marked the beginning of a new chapter in twentieth-century international history. Palestinian victories came at the climax of Third Worldism as the nations of the postcolonial world lined up to express their support for groups such as the PLO, the African National Congress, and the Vietnamese NLF. Debates over issues such as international terrorism, self-determination, and the ongoing violence surrounding decolonization exposed vast fissures in world opinion between North and South, between East and West, and even within societies. Observers cast guerillas such as Arafat as heroic liberation fighters struggling against the vestiges of imperialism or as savage "terrorists" threatening to destroy the foundations of the modern world order. The PLO's story thrust these divisions into the spotlight, but it also revealed the limits of cosmopolitan visions of national liberation.

Tales of heroic guerillas, popular demonstrations, and pledges of Third World solidarity in forums such as the United Nations and the Conference of Non-Aligned States could only do so much. While it appeared to many as if the 1970s would witness the triumph of the forces of Third World revolution and the retreat of U.S. power from the postcolonial world, the military might of the superpowers remained unrivaled during the decade. Although they might lose arguments on the floor of the General Assembly, U.S. leaders had other means to achieve their goals. The Nixon administration found one of these means in the doctrine that would bear its name. The Nixon Doctrine's defense of the Cold War periphery—which looked to a network of regional allies to carry out police operations and wage low-intensity conflicts around the developing world—forestalled revolutionary victories but prolonged bloody civil wars by funneling military aid to pro-Western regimes. This support for regional policemen played upon local tensions, exacerbating preexisting conflicts in what appeared to many observers a classic colonial technique. While the White House sought stability and order among the great powers, it endeavored to push conflicts into the Third World and the frontiers of the Cold War system. Thus, while images of the fall of Saigon flashed across television screens around the world, the age of postcolonial revolutions quietly came to an end. If the victory of Vietnamese communist forces in 1975 was the greatest triumph of a broader wave of postcolonial wars of national liberation, the story of the PLO's armed struggle during the same period can be seen as one of its first great defeats.

In this regard, the PLO's armed struggle must be understood as a forerunner of the conflicts of the post–Cold War era. Unlike the other national liberation struggles of the 1950s and 1960s, the Palestinian experience of the 1970s was not an immediate consequence of imperial collapse; the British had abandoned Palestine in 1948. Similarly, the Palestinian struggle was not a direct result of the Cold War rivalry between Moscow and Washington. Like the conflicts of the post–Cold War era, the war for Palestine grew out of the legacy of the decolonization and superpower rivalry but was the direct consequence of neither. As such, it retained a certain moral ambiguity, being neither a war against colonial oppression nor a theater in the contest between communism and democratic capitalism.

This ambiguity was amplified by the PLO's innovations in revolutionary warfare, external operations. For leaders such as Habash and Arafat, so-called terrorist tactics represented a new form of guerilla warfare. Like the Algerians, Cubans, and Vietnamese before them, Palestinian fighters adapted Mao's theories of guerilla revolution to the set of challenges presented by their unique situation. Thus, while the Cubans had relied on elite cadres to sow the seeds of revolution among the populace, the Algerians had moved their struggle from the countryside to the cities, and the Vietnamese had sought to foment a general offensive and mass uprising, groups such as Fatah and the PFLP launched a string of external operations designed to exploit the transnational networks of exchange that proliferated in the global era. More than any previous group, the PLO demonstrated the power of nonstate actors in the new global order. In the final years of the Cold War and the decades that followed, other militant groups with vastly different agendas—from the ANC to Hamas—would adopt the tactics pioneered by the fedayeen.

The increasing global interconnections that opened the international system to violence perpetrated by nonstate groups also signaled the beginning of a new era of security interdependence. The PLO's ability to coordinate operations across state frontiers and continents and to function in the space between nation-states presented a new set of challenges in the arena of international affairs. As threats, interests, and actors began to operate outside of the nation-state framework, the effectiveness of traditional modes of state-to-state diplomacy diminished. Efforts to control problems such as "international terrorism" demanded methods of multilateral cooperation and underscored the importance of international organizations such as the United Nations. While many governments recognized the necessity of building broad coalitions to deal with the new challenges of a global system, others expanded their capacity for unilateral action. The Israeli government had little patience for the challenges of building multilateral coalitions among postcolonial states with a broad set of interests and sympathetic positions vis-à-vis the PLO. While UN member states debated the best course of action to take in response to the emergence of the Palestinian guerilla organizations, Israeli leaders developed an active-defense strategy based on counterterrorist tactics, disproportionate reprisals, and preventative strikes that integrated military and intelligence operations in the occupied territories, the Arab world, and the international system. Although these methods proved effective at limiting fedayeen guerilla capabilities, they did little to stem the rising tide of revolutionary Palestinian nationalism.

Other governments followed the Israeli example of focusing on the military dimensions of revolutionary violence rather than the political ones. Most notably, the United States emerged as a staunch proponent of military containment. In this way, Israeli counterterrorism tactics would provide the prototype for Washington's efforts to respond to the new threat of transnational guerilla violence.[3] Both of these priorities dovetailed with the Nixon administration's determination to develop the capacity to respond to challenges to American authority around the globe and, in particular, in the global South. This theme, which first surfaced in Kissinger's calls to defend "gray areas" during the 1950s, was codified with the Nixon Doctrine. Ultimately, this new mode of conflict foreshadowed the wars of the post–Cold War era. As such, the PLO's global offensive was one of the first military conflicts in what some have termed the era of globalization, and served as an indication of challenges to come.

The PLO's story during this period thus marked an important chapter in the wider story of globalization, which would be characterized by tension between small states and groups with newfound diplomatic muscle and larger states that maintained a near monopoly over conventional forms of global power. The fact that the United States found itself in a shrinking minority on the question of Palestine in global forums such as the United Nations pointed to a deeper shift in the international system whereby the voices of the Third World would speak with greater authority and autonomy; the character of the global era would be defined not only by the East and West but also by the global South. As U.S. leaders struggled to adjust to the demands of an increasingly interconnected global environment and new transnational challenges, the importance of American "soft power" became more apparent.

These dynamics reflected the reality that the process of globalization was taking place not only from the top down, so to speak, but also from the bottom up. Ultimately, the emergence of a global system was not only a process whereby leaders in Western capitals projected their great-power influence onto the peoples of the world or the ways in which the international economy created a global system. It was simultaneously a story about how guerilla fighters, student activists, and revolutionary states created a world of relations unto themselves in an effort to push their own visions of global order. The Palestinians and other liberation fighters around the world did not look to Western actors to save them or wait for Western reformers to effect change. As the PLO's story shows, they drew upon the strength and experiences of other groups around the global South in hopes of achieving their own salvation. The ascendance of this Third World community in international affairs, which began with Bandung in the 1950s and reached full force by the 1970s, was a key component of the diffusion of power that would mark the new era of globalization.

By the mid-1970s, the PLO could point to an array of international supporters and list a host of radical groups around the world that celebrated its struggle, but it was no closer to its goal of creating a Palestinian homeland. U.S. support for regional allies such as Israel and Jordan was stronger than ever, and the republic of Lebanon was in the process of collapsing into a civil war that would pull the fedayeen into further conflict with Lebanese militias, the Syrian army, and Israeli military forces. In the end, the PLO would remain locked out of statehood into the twenty-first century. In the months following the signing of Sinai II, the momentum for a wider peace in the region would be lost. While Cairo and Amman concluded lasting peace agreements with the Jewish state—much to the chagrin of increasingly powerful religious elements in Egypt—Syria, Lebanon, and the PLO remained in a state of conflict with Israel. By the time agreements for the creation of the type of Palestinian ministate envisioned in 1973 were put forward some twenty years later, the PLO had lost much of its dynamism.

In the intervening years, Lebanon would be transformed into a new battleground in the Arab-Israeli conflict that helped radicalize the Arab world. The Lebanese civil war combined elements of a regional conflict with the sectarian violence between Maronite, Shi'a, Druze, and Sunni. Syria's intervention in that war—for a time against the PLO—provided a measure of authoritarian stability but deepened the divisions in the Arab sphere. Meanwhile, IDF interventions—most notably 1982's Operation Peace for Galilee, the siege of Beirut, and the Sabra and Shatilla massacres—served to further catalyze international opinion and local resentment against Israel. The war would also help to give birth to a new force in the region: Hezbollah, the armed Shi'a resistance movement in Lebanon.

As war raged in Lebanon, a new generation of Palestinians would grow up under Israeli military occupation, watching the PLO's struggles, failures, and retreat to Tunis. While leaders such as Arafat and Habash continued their fight from exile, local forces in the occupied territories managed day-to-day affairs. As the failures of secular nationalism mounted, the influence of traditional sources of social authority such as the Muslim Brotherhood grew. The 1987 Intifada against the Israeli occupation provided the catalyst for the emergence of a new resistance movement, Hamas, which drew its inspiration from radical religious clerics rather than secular postcolonial nationalists. Hamas would combine the PLO's guerilla tactics with religious conservatism and extensive grassroots social networks in the West Bank and Gaza.[4]

Thus, by the time Arafat accepted the prospect of a two-state solution in 1988, the PLO faced a new set of rivals for leadership of the Palestinian revolution. Making matters worse, the much-anticipated engagement with the United States was slow to pay dividends, as was the peace process of the 1990s. In the first decade of the twenty-first century, the PLO found itself assailed by its rival, Hamas, as the Second Intifada turned Israel and the occupied territories into a war zone. Arafat's death in 2004 was followed by significant victories for Hamas in the 2006 Palestinian legislative elections, which led to a civil war between that group and Fatah that left the former in control of Gaza and the latter in control of the West Bank. At the same time, international attention focused not on the Israel-Palestine dispute but on the U.S.-led global war on terrorism in countries such as Iraq and Afghanistan. As the construction of Israeli settlements on the West Bank ate away at the proposed territory for a Palestinian state, the prospects for peace and statehood still seemed far away. In September 2011, PLO chairman Mahmoud Abbas officially requested UN recognition of Palestinian statehood, which prompted threats from U.S. congressmen and the Israeli government to cut off aid to the Palestinian territories. While the United States vowed to veto any resolution in the Security Council recognizing Palestinian statehood, observers warned that Palestinian support in the UN General Assembly—which could only elevate the Palestinians' status to that of a nonmember observer state, similar to the Vatican—was overwhelming. Though it was Abbas who stood at the podium, the scene was strikingly reminiscent of Arafat's appearance in 1974.

It has been almost half a century since the PLO emerged as a force in the Middle East. Few observers in 1967 would have guessed that in the second decade of the twenty-first century the dispute over Palestine would still be unresolved or that it would outlive Arafat. Indeed, since the summer of 1967, the basic outlines of a peaceful resolution to the Arab-Israeli dispute have appeared fairly clear, with one exception—what was to be done with the Palestinians? The PLO's global offensive played a central role in answering that question, establishing the Palestinians as a "political fact" and winning widespread international recognition by the early 1970s. Two critical and related goals eluded Arafat and the PLO during this period, however: recognition by the United States and the creation of a Palestinian state. Was there an opportunity to have secured one or both of these goals during the pivotal decade of the 1970s when the peace process and the PLO were still in their prime?

The most common response to this question is no. The PLO never fielded a force powerful enough to seriously challenge the IDF. The U.S.-Israeli "special relationship" was too strong. The United States had no incentive to recognize an organization that menaced its principal allies in the region, rejected the proposition of a two-state solution, and attacked civilians and U.S. diplomats. The PLO was too divided by internal conflicts to warrant serious engagement in the peace process of the 1970s. These are simple answers that gloss over the complexity and contingency of the past. History is not so simple, nor is it so clean; it is the product of structures and agents, choices and mistakes, irresistible forces and fateful accidents. So it was with the PLO.

Like many liberation movements—and nation-states—the PLO hoped to achieve through diplomacy what was not possible by force. While its guerilla operations never presented a grave challenge to Israeli national security, Palestinian fighters marshaled an impressive array of diplomatic supporters. Diplomatic power was in fact more important than military capabilities, which leads to the real stumbling block: Washington's decision not to engage the PLO in the peace process. Here, too, denial of recognition was not inevitable. At every stage of the struggle, U.S. officials contemplated whether to engage elements in the PLO. In the wake of the 1973 war, when the peace process fell under Kissinger's control, the opportunity for engagement presented itself. The Nixon administration had established the precedent of negotiating with guerillas in Vietnam when it sat down with the NLF—a group that had shed far more blood, American or otherwise, than the PLO—at the Paris peace conference. Moreover, a diverse set of voices from Moscow to the United Nations to officials in the U.S. government called upon Kissinger to bring the PLO into the peace process. Kissinger chose not to do so, but his choice was made easier by a number of factors.

The Cold War itself played a central role. Palestinian fighters were not the first group of Third World revolutionaries that the United States had opposed, and they would not be the last. While the United States presented itself as a neutral arbiter in the Arab-Israeli conflict, in reality leaders such as Nixon and Kissinger chose to treat negotiations as an opportunity to advance U.S. Cold War interests and influence in the Middle East at the expense of the Soviet Union. This need not have been the case, particularly if the administration had defined U.S. interests as resting in a peaceful resolution to the regional conflict rather than the advancement of the superpower rivalry. While the PLO presented a wrinkle in Kissinger's standstill diplomacy prior to 1973 and in his step-by-step diplomacy afterward, the organization was understood to be central to the long-term prospects of peace in the Arab-Israeli conflict. In subordinating the peace process to its Cold War priorities, the Nixon administration chose a path that demanded the diplomatic isolation of the PLO.

The U.S. relationship with Israel also presented an obstacle to engagement with the PLO, but it was a manageable one. While it may be tempting to draw a straight line of constant support between Harry Truman's recognition of Israel in 1948 and the consummation of the "special relationship" in the 1970s and 1980s, in fact U.S. and Israeli policy makers frequently and acrimoniously disagreed. Although public support for Israel was strong in the United States, the Nixon White House was experienced in insulating its foreign policies from domestic pressures. Likewise, a strong case existed—and still exists—that Israel's best interests lay in a lasting peace in which the PLO must inevitably play a part, rather than perpetual conflict with its neighbors. That is not to say that engagement with the PLO would have been the easiest move, but it is certain that the Rabin government would have been unable to sever its relationship with its only superpower patron over the latter's engagement with the PLO. Indeed, many Israeli officials expected Washington to open a dialogue with Arafat, and some U.S. officials hinted that they were preparing to do so.

Such a move might have borne fruit. Israeli society has always been characterized by a wide range of views and spirited debates over policy. As is the case in any democratic system, however, Israeli leaders were accountable to public opinion and to myriad outside pressures. A key difficulty that the government of Israel faced during these critical years was the absence of effective pressure to make concessions to the Palestinians and the wider Arab world. This lack of pressure deprived the Israeli leadership of much-needed domestic cover to make the controversial moves necessary to begin negotiations for a comprehensive peace during the pivotal decade after 1967. As later administrations in both Israel and the United States would find, the Israeli government was best equipped to engage in the peace process when it could point to outside pressures forcing some progress in peace negotiations. Indeed, the most significant achievements of the subsequent peace process—such as the 1979 Egypt-Israel peace treaty and the 1993 Oslo accords, both of which, most commentators argue, served the long-term interests of Israel—would be made under U.S. presidential administrations that were willing to pressure the Jewish state to move toward peace.

The U.S. government during this period, then, did a double disservice to Israel: first, by failing to push the Jewish state to engage more fully in the quest for peace, and second, by shielding Israeli leaders from the negative repercussions of condemnation at the United Nations. Washington's actions thus helped to deflect the fallout from the Israeli occupation of Arab territories during these critical years, depriving Israel's democratically chosen leaders of the justifications they needed to sell the peace process to the Israeli public. U.S. policy enabled the government of Israel to maintain the illusion that it held all the cards in the region and was thus entitled to set the terms of a peace settlement. In short, U.S. policies made it easier for Israeli leaders to forgo the difficult path toward a long-term peace in favor of protecting short-term political and security interests. They made it possible for the Israeli government to indulge its fantasy that a military solution existed to the political challenge of Palestinian nationalism.

In the end, the Nixon administration chose to deny recognition to the PLO, isolating it from the 1970s peace process and placing the Palestinian question on the back burner. This decision seems to have been made in the months following the 1973 war, precisely when the mainstream PLO leadership was embracing a more moderate, pragmatic approach. It is in this light that the lack of an official dialogue between Washington and the PLO—which might have encouraged greater pragmatism on the part of Arafat and his comrades—appears even more unfortunate. Ironically, U.S. officials had substantial clandestine contact with the PLO through intelligence channels and, later, on matters of security during the Lebanese civil war. That such contacts were barred from the diplomatic realm seems especially regrettable.

The PLO was responsible for its share of missteps as well. For all its achievements, the organization was unable to make the moves necessary to become a fully recognized player in the diplomacy of the Arab-Israeli conflict during the 1970s. In particular, the guerillas fell short of making a clear statement announcing their willingness to recognize Israel's right to exist within the pre-1967 borders. Although mainstream leaders such as Arafat quietly acknowledged that their professed goal of a secular democratic state in all of historic Palestine could not be achieved through guerilla action, they failed to craft an unambiguous position on the creation in the West Bank and Gaza of a Palestinian state that could peacefully coexist alongside Israel. By clinging to the rhetoric of complete victory and refusing to declare a government in exile, Arafat and his fellow leaders gave the PLO's opponents—namely, the United States and Israel—the justification they needed to withhold recognition. By the time Arafat renounced "terrorism" and accepted Israel's right to exist in 1988, the PLO had spent thirteen years on the sidelines of the peace process, had been battered in the Lebanese civil war, and had been exiled to Tunisia. Arafat's PLO had achieved little in the intervening years; it had lost much of its dynamism and credibility and was in the midst of being upstaged by the first Intifada and the rise of Hamas.

Why, then, did Arafat and his comrades decline to take these steps in the critical years following 1973? The first and most perhaps most fateful factor was Fatah's inability to create a united front among the Palestinian guerillas. By allowing a diverse set of political leaders to function within the resistance movement, Fatah permitted its rivals to become entrenched in the PLO. When the time came, after 1973, for the PLO to make the difficult political concessions necessary to secure an official place in the peace negotiations, Arafat lacked complete control over the organization. Fear of internal dissent kept Arafat from declaring an unambiguous position on the peace process. Thus, instead of moving forward, he was forced to guard against attacks from an array of competing guerilla groups, none of which had the power to unseat Fatah but all of which had the ability to launch political and military sabotage operations against the peace process.

The PLO's second failure lay in its inability to develop a clear strategy for its armed struggle. While Palestinian fighters created an effective set of guerilla tactics that established their credibility as a force in the region and secured recognition of the PLO on the international stage, larger goals remained elusive. Part of the reason for this rests in Fatah's failure to unify the fedayeen, but the issue merits further discussion. The PLO's guerilla tactics—both conventional and external—were never sufficient to match the strategic goals of the movement.

Although their private conversations and vague public pronouncements suggested that they understood this strategic deficiency, PLO leaders clung to the rhetoric of total victory through popular revolution. Thus, when the opportunity for diplomacy opened in the wake of the 1973 war, the PLO was unable to commit to a political solution. Rather than demanding a place at Geneva and possibly securing a position in the larger peace process, Arafat and the PLO vacillated. The inability at every stage of the armed struggle to define a clear and realistic strategy—and then to revise that strategy to account for the changing situation on the ground—represented a significant failure on the part of the PLO's leadership.

Ultimately, the leadership of both Israel and the PLO sought military solutions to what were primarily diplomatic and political problems. In hindsight, it is doubtful that any amount of action by the Israeli security services could have prevented the politicization of the Palestinian diaspora and the rise of groups such as Fatah and the PFLP, especially after the Battle of al-Karama. At the same time, it is difficult to imagine that any combination of guerilla operations—conventional or external—could have achieved the PLO's goal of bringing down the Israeli government and creating a secular democratic state in Palestine. In lieu of a military solution, political and diplomatic engagement provided the only avenue toward a resolution of the Israel-Palestine conflict. However, both parties chose to indulge in their respective fantasies that a military solution might exist rather than take the very difficult steps necessary to begin political and diplomatic engagement. The costs of these failures to find peace would be borne not by the leaders themselves but by generations of Israelis and Palestinians who would be forced to wage a seemingly endless war for the land alternatively called Israel or Palestine.

A critical period of possibility came to an end after 1975. The failures of the U.S.-led peace process of the 1970s left the IDF and the Palestinian guerillas to batter each other in Israeli towns and cities and across the hillsides of southern Lebanon. Israel and the PLO would square off at the United Nations and amid the ruins of downtown Beirut, but neither side was able to achieve its political goals. The case of the PLO highlighted both the possibilities and the dangers of an increasingly interconnected world order; it revealed the potential for globalized revolution and the limited ability of these cosmopolitan visions to reshape local realities. Even as the rise of the PLO returned the Palestinian question to the center of the Arab-Israeli dispute, it marked the end of the age of the triumphant national liberation fighter and heralded the beginning of a new era. During the Cold War, a series of guerilla campaigns swept across Asia, Africa, and Latin America, sparking a string of revolutions throughout the developing world. Many nations gained independence as part of this global offensive. Palestine did not.

{ NOTES }

Abbreviations Used in the Notes

AAD Access to Archival Databases (National Archives)
FRUS *Foreign Relations of the United States*
IDP *International Documents on Palestine*
IPS Library of the Institute of Palestine Studies
NARA National Archives and Records Administration
NPMP Nixon Presidential Materials Project
UKNA National Archives of the United Kingdom
UNISPAL United Nations Information System on Palestine
WFA *Al-Watha'iq al-Filastiniyyah al-Arabiyah* (Palestinian-Arab Documents)

Introduction

1. "Fateh Men in China, Vietnam," *Fateh* 2, 6 (2 April 1970), IPS; Abu Iyad, *My Home, My Land*, 67–69; Terence Smith, "Enemy in Vietnam Opens Wide Drive, Ending Long Lull," *New York Times*, 2 April 1970.

2. Nixon's exact words were as follows: "Whoever would think that there would be somebody more radical than the Syrians, within the radical Arab states, fedayeen that are more radical, the super-radicals—when we think of all these factors, we can see what a very difficult situation it is." "A Conversation with the President About Foreign Policy," 1 July 1970, *Public Papers of the Presidents: Richard Nixon*, 208.

3. Hoffman, *Inside Terrorism*, 65.

4. It should be noted that the PLO's global insurgency was at most a precursor to the activities of groups such as Al-Qaeda insofar as it comprised a series of international networks working toward a political goal and willing to exercise violence. Unlike Al-Qaeda, however, the PLO was avowedly secular, embraced a localized cause, and was open to pragmatic solutions. Any attempts to equate the PLO to groups such as Al-Qaeda should be seen as highly suspect.

5. I use the term "Third World" to refer to the widespread notion in the second half of the twentieth century that Africa, Latin America, Asia, and the Middle East constituted a sociopolitical unit on the order of the First and Second Worlds of the Cold War. In this sense, the Third World functioned as a concept rather than a clearly delineated geographical region. Unlike some scholars, I do not see the term as pejorative, largely because leaders in the so-called Third World embraced the idea and used it for their own ends, at least in the Palestinian case, as this book hopes to show. The term itself first appeared in an article by Alfred Sauvy in *L'Observateur* in 1952 and carried deliberate connotations linking it to the notion of the French Third Estate under the ancien régime: an underrepresented majority destined to seize power and influence. For the sake of literary style, I use the term interchangeably with "developing world" and "nonaligned world."

6. "Hadith Sahafi khas Sayyid Yasir Arafat, Rayiss al-Lajanah al-Tanafithiyah al-Munathamah al-Tahrir al-Filastiniyah Huwal Qadaya al-Saʿah," 28 November 1973, *WFA*, 473 (see also *IDP* 1973, 53).

7. Hämäläinen, *The Comanche Empire*.

8. See, for instance, Awet Weldemichael's study of the Eritrean and East Timorese liberation movements, "Grand Strategies of Liberation in Eritrea and East Timor," *Africa* LXV, 1–2 (2010).

9. Examples of works that seek to move beyond focus on the great powers to assess the impact of other actors on the international system include Tony Smith, "New Bottles for New Wine: A Pericentric Framework for the Study of the Cold War," *Diplomatic History* 24, 4 (Fall 2000); Manela, *The Wilsonian Moment*; Westad, *The Global Cold War*; Gleijeses, *Conflicting Missions*; Connelly, *A Diplomatic Revolution* and *Fatal Misconception*; Suri, *Power and Protest*; Nguyen, *Hanoi's War*.

10. Hämäläinen, *The Comanche Empire*.

11. A short list includes state newspapers such as *Al-Ahram*, *Al-Baʿath*, and *Al-Thawra*, which provide a window into the official workings of the Arab governments; the collections of organizations such as the Institute for Palestine Studies, which together have assembled millions of pages of documents from Middle Eastern governments, guerilla organizations, and NGOs; and published series devoted to regional affairs and thousands of reels of microfilm sitting virtually unused in library collections. Even more materials wait on the shelves of small bookstores scattered throughout the Arab world. All of these resources are open and waiting for any scholars interested in using them—provided that they can read Arabic.

12. See note 9.

13. Some of the most important works include Sayigh, *Armed Struggle and the Search for State*; Cobban, *The Palestine Liberation Organization*; Smith, *Palestine and the Arab-Israeli Conflict*; Quandt, Jabber, and Lesch, *The Politics of Palestinian Nationalism*; Gresh, *The PLO*; Picaudou, *Le Mouvement national palestinien: Genèse et structures*; Khalidi, *The Iron Cage*; Khalidi, *Palestinian Identity*; Kimmerling and Migdal, *The Palestinian People*; Norton and Greenberg, eds., *The International Relations of the Palestine Liberation Organization*; Rubin, *Revolution Until Victory?*; Hirst, *The Gun and the Olive Branch*; Cooley, *Green March, Black September*; Seale, *Asad*; Walker and Gowers, *Arafat: The Biography*.

14. See, for instance, Little, *American Orientalism*; Hahn, *Caught in the Middle East*; Morris, *Righteous Victims*; Shlaim, *The Iron Wall*; Oren, *Six Days of War*; Quandt, *Peace Process*; Neff, *Warriors Against Israel*. Two recent books on U.S.–Middle East relations notable for their focus on Arab players are Yaqub, *Containing Arab Nationalism* and Citino, *From Arab Nationalism to OPEC*.

15. Fisk, *Pity the Nation*, 441.

16. Tessler, *A History of the Israeli-Palestinian Conflict*, xii.

17. Dowty, *Israel/Palestine*, 83–87.

Chapter 1: The Struggle Against Oppression Everywhere

1. Hart, *Arafat*, 235.

2. Mattar, ed., *Encyclopedia of the Palestinians*, 47–49.

3. On Palestinian society, see Khalidi, *The Iron Cage*; on Syrian and Iraqi society, see Batatu's *Syria's Peasantry* and *The Old Social Classes and the Revolutionary Movements of Iraq*.

4. Mattar, ed., *Encyclopedia of the Palestinians*, 154–55.

5. I will refer to Jarring's efforts to arrive at a formula for the implementation of UN 242 throughout this book as the "Jarring Mission." Smith, *Palestine and the Arab-Israeli Conflict*, 309.

6. See Walker and Gowers, *Arafat*, 49. The numbers on Palestinians in Israel and the occupied territories are based on an Israeli census cited in Kimmerling and Migdal, *The Palestinian People*, 240–41. The estimates of Palestinians living in the Arab world and abroad come from Ya'acob Caroz, "The Palestinians: Who They Are," in Curtis et al., *The Palestinians*, 78.

7. Abu Iyad, *My Home, My Land*, 52.

8. See Suri, *Power and Protest*; Fink, Gassert, and Junker, eds., *1968*; Prashad, *Darker Nations*, xv–xix.

9. John M. Gates, "Toward a History of Revolution," *Comparative Studies in Society and History* 28, 3 (July 1986): 542–43.

10. Walker and Gowers, *Arafat*, 49; Aburish, *Arafat*.

11. *Dirasat wa-Tajarib Thawriya*, August 1967; "Interview with a Leader of the Palestine National Liberation Movement," *Al-Usba' al-Arabi*, 22 January 1968, *IDP* 1968, 298; "'Alaqat al-Thawrah al-Filastiniyyah bi-l-Thawrah al-'Arabiyah wa al-Thawrah al-'Alamiyah" [Relations Between the Palestinian Revolution, the Arab Revolution, and the World Revolution], *Dirasat wa-Tajarib Thawriya*, August 1967.

12. According to Yezid Sayigh, these documents were translated more or less verbatim from original sources by Hani al-Hasan. In his comments on this manuscript, Sayigh has expressed some doubt as to how much senior fedayeen leaders regarded these theories as practical outlines for action. Rather, their use was largely instrumental, designed to highlight the guerilla's association with other liberation movements around the globe. This philosophy can be seen generally in, for example, *Dirasat wa-Tajarib Thawriya*. See also "Munaqashah Huwal al-'Amaliyyat al-Harajiyyah" [Discussion of External Operations], *Al-Hadaf* 2, 106 (26 June 1971).

13. "Munaqashah Huwal al-'Amaliyyat al-Harajiyyah," 106.

14. Lufti al-Khuli, "Interview with Abu Iyad," June 1969, *IDP* 1969, 729.

15. "Interview with Mr. Yasir Arafat, Chairman of the Executive Committee at the Palestine Liberation Organisation and Official Spokesman of the Palestine National Liberation Movement Fatah," August 1969, IPS.

16. PFLP, "The Political Strategy of the Popular Front for the Liberation of Palestine," February 1969, *IDP* 1969, 622–24.

17. Fatah, *Dialogue with Fateh* (Beirut: Al-Fateh, 1969), 51.

18. *Hisad al-'Asifa* 9 (17 February 1969).

19. Fatah, "Address by Al-Fateh Delegation to the Second Conference in Support of the Arab Peoples," Cairo, January 1969.

20. Fatah, *Dialogue with Fateh*, 91.

21. Fatah, *Notre lutte politique et armée* (Beirut: Palestine National Liberation Movement, Al-Fateh, 1969), IPS.

22. See the periodic articles in guerilla newspapers such as Fatah's *Hisad al-Asifa* and *Al-Thawra al-Filastiniyya* and the PFLP's *Al-Hadaf*.

23. Fatah, *The Palestinian Freedom Fighters and the World Press* (Beirut: Al-Fateh, 1969), IPS.

24. Fatah, "Statement by the Palestine National Liberation Movement 'Fateh' to the United Nations on the Legality and Objectives of the Palestinian Resistance," 17 October 1968, *IDP* 1968, 451.

25. Fatah, "The Heroic Challenge Against Neo-Nazism," Address to the United Nations Conference on Human Rights, 27 April 1968, IPS.

26. Fatah, "Press Release No. 1," *IDP* 1968, 303.

27. "Taqarir al-Tharwra fi-Nisf Shahr" [Reports of Revolution in the Last Half Month], *Al-Thawra Al-Filastiniyya* 1, 12 (6 October 1968), IPS.

28. "Al-'Afaf al-'Alamiyya" [Global Horizons], *Al-Thawra Al-Filastiniyya* 1, 22 (January 1970), IPS.

29. Fatah, "News Conference Statement and Remarks by a Spokesman of the Palestine National Liberation Movement 'Fatah' on the Peaceful Settlement of the 'Middle East Crisis,'" October 1968, *IDP* 1968, 453–56.

30. "Taqarir al-Thawra fi Nisf Shahar," *Filastine al-Thawra* 1, 11 (6 September 1968); Fatah, *Revolution Until Victory* (Amman: Palestine National Liberation Movement, Al-Fateh, 1970), IPS; "Interview with Mr. Yasir Arafat," August 1969, *IDP* 1969, 774.

31. See "Al-Thawra Al-Jaza'ariya wa-Istratijiyataha" [The Algerian Revolution and Its Strategies]," *Filastine al-Thawra* 1, 11 (6 September 1968).

32. Lufti al-Khuli, "Interview with Abu Iyad," June 1969, *IDP* 1969, 699–733.

33. Habash, *Nous Vaincrons*, 10.

34. PFLP, "Palestine Resistance Rejects Settlement," *Al-Tali'ah* (Kuwait), 30 October 1968, reproduced and translated in *Selected Arab Documents on the Palestinian Fedayeen, July 1968–February 1969* (Beirut: IPS, 1969).

35. PFLP, *Military Strategy of the P.F.L.P.* (Beirut: Information Department, PFLP, 1970), 65.

36. "M-Day, Vietnam and Palestine," *Fateh* (Beirut) 1, 3 (24 October 1969).

37. "Vietnam Has Its Deir Yassin," *Fateh* (Beirut) 1, 55 (5 December 1969). I use the term "Zionist" here, instead of "Israeli," because the massacre occurred just over a month before the founding of Israel.

38. Lufti al-Khuli, "Interview with Abu Iyad," June 1969, *IDP* 1969, 731.

39. See, for instance, *Filastine al-Thawra* 1, 7 (Early June 1968).

40. "Min Al-Tajraba Al-Viytnamiyya" [From the Vietnamese Experience], *Al-Thawra al-Falastinia*, 15 August 1969, IPS.

41. See, for instance, Fatah, "Al-Tajariba Al-Kubiyya [The Cuban Experience]," *Dirasat wa-Tajarib Thawriya*, August 1967; "Fateh Invites Castro to Tour," *Fateh* (Beirut) 2, 12 (5 August 1970).

42. Lufti al-Khuli, "Interview with Abu Iyad," June 1969, *IDP* 1969, 729.

43. Fatah, "News Conference Statement and Remarks by a Spokesman of the Palestine National Liberation Movement 'Fatah' on the Peaceful Settlement of the 'Middle East Crisis,'" October 1968, *IDP* 1968, 453–56.

44. "Interview with Dwight J. Porter," 5 November 1990, Foreign Affairs Oral History Collection of the Association for Diplomatic Studies and Training, Library of Congress, http://memory.loc.gov/ammem/collections/diplomacy (accessed July 2009).

45. CIA, "World Trends and Contingencies Affecting U.S. Interests," National Intelligence Estimate, 6 June 1968, www.foia.cia.gov.

46. Ibid.

47. Ibid.

48. Dannreuther, *The Soviet Union and the PLO*, 34.

49. CIA, "Growth of Chinese Influence Among World Communists," National Intelligence Estimate, 17 May 1963, www.foia.cia.gov.

50. Cobban, *The Palestinian Liberation Organization*, 218.

51. CIA, "Restless Youth," September 1968, Declassified Document Reference System database; CIA, "Dissident Youth: The Dynamics of Protest," National Intelligence Estimate, 1 December 1964, www.foia.cia.gov. See also Suri, *Power and Protest*.

52. CIA, "World Trends and Contingencies," National Intelligence Estimate, 6 June 1968, www.foia.cia.gov

53. Ibid.

54. On the role of oil as a strategic commodity, see Yergin, *The Prize*. For U.S. interest in the region and the decline of the British Empire during the early Cold War, see Kuniholm, *The Origins of the Cold War in the Near East*; Hahn, *The United States, Great Britain, and Egypt*; and Louis, *British Empire in the Middle East*; on the Eisenhower Doctrine, see Yaqub, *Containing Arab Nationalism*; CIA, "Soviet and Chinese Communist Strategy and Tactics in North Africa, the Middle East, and South Asia," National Intelligence Estimate, 15 July 1965, www.foia.cia.gov; CIA, "Soviet Strategy and Intentions in the Mediterranean Basin," National Intelligence Estimate, 1 June 1967, www.foia.cia.gov; Westad, *The Global Cold War*.

55. See Little, *American Orientalism*, 94–96; Bass, *Support Any Friend*.

56. Little, *American Orientalism*, 31, 96–99, 277–79; Quandt, *Peace Process*.

57. See Ajami, *The Arab Predicament*; Kepel, *Jihad*.

58. Dayan, *Moshe Dayan*, 32, 276–84; Fred Skolnik et al., eds., *Encyclopedia Judaica*, 2nd ed., vol. 13 (Detroit: Macmillan Reference, 2007).

59. Ashton, *King Hussein of Jordan*, 138.

60. Dayan, *Moshe Dayan*, 412–14, 422.

61. Black and Morris, *Israel's Secret Wars*, 345.

62. Shlaim, *The Iron Wall*, 255.

63. Ibid., 255, 261, 264.

64. Black and Morris, *Israel's Secret Wars*, 236–42. Ami Pedahzur also argues that, throughout most of its history, Israel focused on terrorism as a military rather than political problem; see Pedahzur, *Israeli Secret Services and the Struggle Against Terrorism*, 3.

65. Quandt, *Peace Process*; Little, *American Orientalism*, 101; Shlaim, *The Iron Wall*.

66. Memorandum to Thomas Hughes from Bureau of Intelligence and Research staff member Oliver Troxel Jr., "African Reactions to the Middle East Crisis," Department of State, 7 August 7, 1967, Declassified Document Reference System database.

67. Rostow meeting with Majid Khadduri, 21 January 1968, RG 59, Records Relating to Iraq, Jordan, Lebanon, and Syria, 1966–72, Box 2, NARA.

68. Saunders to Rostow, "Lack of U.S.-Arab Understanding," 14 March 1968, RG 59, Records Relating to Iraq, Jordan, Lebanon, and Syria 1966–72, Box 1, NARA.

69. Beirut to DOS, "Some Observations on the Nature and Implications of the Fedayeen Movement," 30 September 1968, RG 59, Central Files 1967–69, POL 27 ARAB-ISR, Box 1813, NARA.

70. Mak to DOS, Memorandum of Conversation with Dr. Charles Rizk, 17 September 1968, RG 59, Records Relating to Iraq, Jordan, Lebanon, and Syria 1966–1972, Box 2, NARA.

71. CIA, "The Effect of the International Political Climate on Vietnamese," National Intelligence Estimate, 31 December 1966, www.foia.cia.gov. For more on Algeria, see Connelly, *A Diplomatic Revolution*.

72. INR–Thomas Hughes, "Changing Image of the Arab *Fedayeen*," 17 April 1968, RG 59, Central Files 1967–69, POL 27 ARAB-ISR, Box 1809, NARA.

73. Rodinson, *Israel*, 9–15, 90–91, 94–96.

74. "Jerusalem: Les nouveaux Palestiniens," *Jeune Afrique* 366 (14 January 1968): 23.

75. "Al Fath Parle," *Jeune Afrique* 383 (12 May 1968): 13, 50.

76. Bertrand Russell, "How Much More Aggression Will the World Tolerate," advertisement paid for by the Arab States Delegation, *New York Times*, 23 February 1970.

77. See Edward Said, "Chomsky and the Question of Palestine," *Journal of Palestine Studies* 4, 3 (Spring 1975): 91–104. A similar argument is made in McAlister, *Epic Encounters*.

78. "Statement from the Editorial Collective," *Jewish Radical* 7, 2 (February 1976). I am indebted to my colleague Jeremy Popkin (one of the authors of this piece) for sharing it with me.

79. Joe Stork, "The American New Left and Palestine," *Journal of Palestine Studies* 2, 1 (Autumn 1972): 64–69. For the cartoon, see Linda Charlton, "Jews Fear Anti-Zionism of New Left," *New York Times*, 14 August 1970.

80. Lewis Young, "American Blacks and the Arab-Israeli Conflict," *Journal of Palestine Studies* 2, 1 (Autumn 1972): 70–85.

81. Stork, "The American New Left and Palestine," 67.

82. Young, "American Blacks and the Arab-Israeli Conflict," 79.

83. Quoted in ibid., 79–80.

84. State Contribution to National Intelligence Estimate 30-2-68, "The Eastern Arab World," n.d., RG 59, Records Relating to Iraq, Jordan, Lebanon, and Syria, 1966–72, Box 3, NARA.

Chapter 2: The Storm

1. Abu Iyad, *My Home, My Land*, 57–60; Walker and Gowers, *Arafat*, 56–57.

2. Walker and Gowers, *Arafat*, 56–57.

3. Ibid., 51.

4. Abu Iyad, *My Home, My Land*, 57.

5. Memcon with Rabin, State 133284, 20 March 1968, RG 59, POL 27 ARAB-ISR, Box 1807, NARA; Shlaim, *Iron Wall*, 330.

6. Morris, *Righteous Victims*, 366–68.

7. Black and Morris, *Israel's Secret Wars*, 253.

8. Ibid.

9. U.S. Embassy Tel Aviv to Secstate, "Eshkol Knesset Statement," 21 March 1968, RG 59, POL 27 ARAB-ISR, Box 1807, NARA; "Ma'arkah al-Karamah Muna'ataf Tarikhi fi Musiratna al-Nidaliyah," *Hisad al-'Asifa* 13 (21 March 1969), IPS; Walker and Gowers, *Arafat*, 57.

10. Ma'an Abu Nuwar, *Ma'arakat al-Karamah: 21 Adhar 1968* (Amman: Mudiriyat al-Matabi al-'Askariyah, 1982).

11. Walker and Gowers, *Arafat*, 59.

12. Henry Tanner, "Algerians Advise Al-Fatah on Winning International Support," *New York Times*, reproduced in *Selected Documents on the Palestinian Fedayeen, July 1968 to February 1969* (n.p.: Universal Bureau of Applied Languages, 1969), IPS.

13. "Note Verbale Dated 10 March 1968 from the Minister for Foreign Affairs of Jordan to the Secretary-General," 13 March 1968, UNISPAL, http://unispal.org (accessed June

2008); Amman to DOS, Amman 3936, 21 March 1968, RG 59, POL 27 ARAB-ISR, Box 1807, NARA.

14. UNSC Official Records, Meeting 1402, 21 March 1968. http://domino.un.org; Battle Memcon with Sharaf, "March 21 Fighting," 21 March 1968, RG 59, POL 27 ARAB-ISR, Box 1807, NARA.

15. UNSC Official Records, Meeting 1402, 21 March 1968, domino.un.org; Battle Memcon with Sharaf, "March 21 Fighting," 21 March 1968, RG 59, POL 27 ARAB-ISR, Box 1807, NARA; Eilts Memcon with Saqqaf, "Israeli Raid on Jordan," Jidda 3302, 23 March 1968, RG 59, POL 27 ARAB-ISR, Box 1807, NARA.

16. USDAO to DIA, 0569, 28 March 1968, RG 59, Central Files 1967–69, POL 27 ARAB-ISR, Box 1807, NARA; Barbour, "Political Commentary and Chronology—March 1968," 2 April 1968, RG 59, Central Files 1967–69, POL 27 ARAB-ISR, Box 1809, NARA.

17. Campbell, "Terrorism," Jerusalem 1139, 2 April 1968, RG 59, Central Files 1967–69, POL 27 ARAB-ISR, Box 1809, NARA; Lucius Battle, "Objectives and Directions of U.S. Policy in the Near East," 16 May 1968, *IDP* 1968, 65–66.

18. Dannreuther, *The Soviet Union and the PLO*, 33.

19. "Report by the Bulgarian Foreign Minister on the Ministerial Meeting in Warsaw Regarding the Situation in the Middle East," 19–21 December 1967, Cold War International History Project, www.wilsoncenter.org; Soviet speech in UAR, January 1968, *IDP* 1968, 5.

20. *Pravda*, 23 March 1968, reprinted in *Current Digest of the Soviet Press* 20, 12 (10 April 1968), 17; INR-Hughes, "Soviet Attitudes Toward Arab Terrorism and Resistance Against Occupation," 22 April 1968, RG 59, POL 27 ARAB-ISR, Box 1809, NARA.

21. Dannreuther, *The Soviet Union and the PLO*, 40–42.

22. Cobban, *The Palestinian Liberation Organization*, 46.

23. Dannreuther, *The Soviet Union and the PLO*, 42–43.

24. CIA, "Soviet Interests and Activities in the Arab States," NIE 11-9-69, 18 January 1968, Digital National Security Archive; Saunders Memcon with Khammash, 29 January 1968, RG 59 Records Relating to Iraq, Jordan, Lebanon and Syria 1966–72, Box 4, NARA. See also Douglas Little, "A Puppet in Search of a Puppeteer," *International History Review* 17, 3 (August 1995): 539.

25. INR, Denney, "Financial Support to Fatah from Saudi Arabia, Kuwait, Libya, and the Persian Gulf Shaikhdoms," 18 October 1969, RG 59, Central Files 1967–69, POL 27 ARAB-ISR, Box 1814, NARA; U.S. Embassy Jidda to DOS, "Conservative Saudi Views on the Palestinine Question," 31 October 1968, RG 59, Central Files 1967–69, POL 27 ARAB-ISR, Box 1814, NARA; Eilts to DOS, "Saqqaf's Views on Fatah Activities," Jidda 6107, 26 November 1968, RG 59, Central Files 1967–69, POL 27 ARAB-ISR, Box 1815, NARA.

26. "Al-Thawrah al-Jaza'iriyah wa Istratjiyataha," *Al-Thawrah al-Filastiniyah* 11 (6 September 1968), IPS; Hoffacker to DOS, "Fatah Spokesman Arafat in Algiers," Algiers 168, 3 February 1969, RG 59, Central Files 1967–69, POL 27 ARAB-ISR, Box 1818, NARA; DOS to AmEmbassy Algiers, 31 December 1968, RG 59, Central Files 1967–69, ARAB POL 13-10, Box 1786, NARA.

27. Newsom to DOS, "Fatah Leader's Statement," 29 November 1968, RG 59, Central Files 1967–69, ARAB POL 13-10, Box 1786, NARA.

28. "Speech by the Algerian President of the Revolutionary Council Boumedienne," *Ahdath wa Watha'eq*, 19 June 1968, *IDP* 1968, 381; Algerian Front de Libération Nationale, "The Solution of the Palestine Problem," *Ahdath wa Watha'eq*, 15 May 1968, *IDP* 1968: 367–68.

29. Bourguiba, "News Conference Remarks," 26 April 1968, *IDP* 1968, 354.

30. "Speech by the Tunisian President Bourghiba at a Banquet in His Honor Given by the U.S. President Johnson," 15 May 1968, *IDP* 1968, 364.

31. Bergus to DOS, "Nasser and Palestinianism, or Carrying Water on Both Shoulders," Cairo 256, 3 February 1969, RG 59, Central Files 1967–69, POL 27 ARAB-ISR, Box 1818, NARA; Sayigh, *Armed Struggle*, 179–80; Cobban, *The Palestinian Liberation Organization*, 204–6; Hart, *Arafat*, 268.

32. Bergus to DOS, "Nasser and Palestinianism"; INR, Hughes, "UAR: Nasser's New Strategy Toward the Fedayeen," 14 February 1969, RG 59, Central Files 1967–69, POL 27 ARAB-ISR, Box 1818, NARA.

33. "Interview with Harrison M. Symmes," 25 February 1989, Foreign Affairs Oral History Collection of the Association for Diplomatic Studies and Training, Library of Congress, http://memory.loc.gov/ammem/collections/diplomacy (accessed July 2009).

34. Ibid.; "Prospects for King Hussein's Regime," 15 November 1968, RG 59, Records Relating to Iraq, Jordan, Lebanon, and Syria 1966–1972, Box 2, NARA; British Embassy to Seelye, "Fedayeen in Jordan," 7 October 1968, RG 59, Records Relating to Iraq, Jordan, Lebanon, and Syria 1966–1972, Box 3, NARA.

35. Hall to DOS, "West Bankers View King Hussein's Prospects for Survival," 12 September 1968, RG 59, Central Files 1967–69, POL 27 ARAB-ISR, Box 1813, NARA; Symmes to DOS, "Hikmat al-Masri's Views on Current West Bank Situation," Amman 7257, 30 October 1968, RG 59, Central Files 1967–69, POL 27 ARAB-ISR, Box 1814, NARA; Symmes to DOS, "Wasfi Tell's Prognostications," Amman 6114, 10 Augist 1968, RG 59, Central Files 1967–69, POL 27 ARAB-ISR, Box 1812, NARA.

36. INR, Thomas Hughes, "Jordan and the Fedayeen," 4 April 1969, RG 59, Central Files 1967–69, POL 13-10 ARAB, Box 1786, NARA; Duncan to DOS, "Some Jordanian Comments on Current Problems," 7 October 1968, RG 59, Central Files 1967–69, POL 27 ARAB-ISR, Box 1813, NARA.

37. State Department, "Memo on Shooting in Jordan Valley," 15 February 1968, RG 59, Records Relating to Iraq, Jordan, Lebanon, and Syria 1966–72, Box 1, NARA; Symmes, "GOJ Attitude Toward Guerrilla Warfare," Amman 3592, 27 February 1968, RG 59, POL 27 ARAB-ISR, Box 1807, NARA.

38. "Jordanian Political Assessment (for US Talks with UK)," RG 59, Records Relating to Iraq , Jordan, Lebanon, and Syria 1966–1972, Box 1, NARA.

39. Barbour Memcon with Eban, "Terrorism," Tel Aviv 2313, 15 March 1968, RG 59, POL 27 ARAB-ISR, Box 1806, NARA; Memcon with Rabin, Untitled, State 133284, 20 March 1968 RG 59, POL 27 ARAB-ISR, Box 1807, NARA.

40. Symmes to DOS, "Fedayeen Influence in Jordan," Amman 1211, 13 March 1969, RG 59, Central Files 1967–69, POL 13-10 ARAB, Box 1786, NARA; Duncan to DOS, "Developments in GOJ-Fedayeen Confrontation," Amman 7077, 16 October 1968, RG 59, Central Files 1967–69, POL 27 ARAB-ISR, Box 1814, NARA.

41. Battle to Under Secretary, Action Memorandum, "Jordan's Internal Defense," 29 August 1968, RG 59, Records Relating to Iraq, Jordan, Lebanon, and Syria 1966–1972, Box 2, NARA; Symmes to DOS, Amman 0716, 11 February 1969, RG 59, Central Files 1967–69, POL 27 ARAB-ISR, Box 1818, NARA.

42. Conversation Between Davies and Sharaf, "Arab-Israel Confrontation," 19 September 1968, RG 59, Records Relating to Iraq, Jordan, Lebanon, and Syria 1966–1972, Box 3,

NARA; Duncan to DOS, "Some Jordanian Comments on Current Problems," 7 October 1968, RG 59, Central Files 1967–69, POL 27 ARAB-ISR, Box 1813, NARA.

43. Porter to DOS, Beirut 14107, 6 November 1968, RG 59, Central Files 1967–69, POL 27 ARAB-ISR, Box 1813, NARA; Porter to DOS, "Fedayeen Activities in Lebanon," Beirut 14615, 29 November 1968, RG 59, Central Files 1967–69, POL 27 ARAB-ISR, Box 1815, NARA.

44. Cobban, *The Palestinian Liberation Organization*, 47; Smith, *Palestine and the Arab-Israeli Conflict*, 309.

45. Porter to DOS, "Repercussions in Lebanon of the HKJ-Fedayeen Confrontation," Beirut 14114, 7 November 1968, RG 59, Central Files 1967–69, POL 13-10 ARAB, Box 1786, NARA; Memcon Between Tucker and Majdalani, 27 August 1968, RG 59, Records Relating to Iraq, Jordan, Lebanon, and Syria 1966–1972, Box 3, NARA.

46. Porter to DOS, "Lebanese Disturbances over the Fedayeen Issue," Beirut 14240, RG 59, Central Files 1967–69, POL 13-10 ARAB, Box 1786, NARA; Porter to DOS, Beirut 14037, 4 November 1968, RG 59, Central Files 1967–69, POL 27 ARAB-ISR, Box 15, NARA.

47. Porter to DOS, Conversation with Chehab, "Fedayeen Activities in Lebanon," Beirut 14904, 10 December 1968, RG 59, Central Files 1967-69, POL 13-10 ARAB, Box 1786, NARA.

48. Porter to DOS, "Israeli Reprisal Actions on Lebanese Territory," Beirut 13923, 30 October 1968, RG 59, Central Files 1967–69, POL 27 ARAB-ISR, Box 1814, NARA; Porter to DOS, Beirut 14037, 4 November 1968, RG 59, Central Files 1967–69, POL 27 ARAB-ISR, Box 15, NARA.

49. Department of State Telegram to U.S. Embassy in Tel Aviv, 26 March 1968, RG 59, Central Files 1967–69, POL 27 ARAB-ISR, Box 1807, NARA; Symmes, State telegram, "Jordan Internal Situation and Future of Jarring Mission," Amman 4030, 26 March 1968, RG 59, Central Files 1967–69, POL 27 ARAB-ISR, Box 1807, NARA.

50. Barbour, "New Refugees and Jerusalem," Tel Aviv 2930, 18 March 1968, RG 59, Central Files 1967–69, POL 27 ARAB-ISR, Box 1807, NARA; INR, Hughes, "The Meaning and the Consequences of the Latest Violence in the Middle East," 26 March 1968, RG 59, Central Files 1967–69, POL 27 ARAB-ISR, Box 1807, NARA.

51. DOS Outgoing Telegram, "Middle East," 30 March 1968, RG 59, Central Files 1967–69, POL 27 ARAB-ISR, Box 1807, NARA; Porter to Rusk, "Deteriorating Prospects for Jarring Mission," Beirut 7935, 29 March 1968, RG 59, Central Files 1967–69, POL 27 ARAB-ISR, Box 1807, NARA; Symmes, "Assessment of *Fedayeen* Strength," Amman 4162, 7 April 1968, RG 59, Central Files 1967–69, POL 27 ARAB-ISR, Box 1809, NARA.

52. U.S. Defense Attache to DIA, 27 March 1968, RG 59 POL 27 ARAB-ISR, Box 1807, NARA.

53. See Yaari, *Strike Terror*; O'Neill, *Armed Struggle in Palestine*, 203.

54. The authority on Palestinian military—and many aspects of political and institutional—history is Sayigh, *Armed Struggle*; for more detailed lists of arms shipments and names of individual guerillas, see pp. 162, 182, and more generally 143–317. See also Cobban, *The Palestinian Liberation Organization*, 217.

55. O'Ballance, *Arab Guerilla Power*, 77.

56. "Persistence in Armed Struggle Means Victory," *Peking Review* 11, 21 (5 April 1968): 33; Abu Iyad, *My Home, My Land*, 66; "Fatah Men in China, Vietnam," *Fatah* 2, 6 (2 April 1970),

IPS; "Article on the Middle East in the Chinese Official Weekly *Peking Review*," 13 June 1969, *IDP* 1969, 104; "Article on the Palestinian Resistance Movement in the Chinese Official Weekly *Peking Review*," 23 May 1969, *IDP* 1969, 88, "Palestinian People Have Found the Way to Free Their Homeland," *Peking Review* 21 (24 May 1969): 34.

57. "Message of Greeting from the North Vietnamese President Ho Chi Minh to the International Conference for the Support of Arab Peoples," 24 January 1969, *IDP* 1969, 12. For Giap's meeting with Arafat, see David Meir-Levy, *History Upside Down*, 28–29.

58. "Joint Communique on the Visit of a Cuban Communist Party Delegation to Algeria," 10 July 1968, *IDP* 1968, 106; Abu Iyad, *My Home, My Land*, 70–71; "Joint Communiqué on the Algerian Foreign Minister Boutaflika's Visit to Cuba," December 1968, *IDP* 1968, 161; INR, Denney, "Algeria-Cuba: Running with the Hare and Hunting with the Hounds?" 7 March 1969, RG 59, Central Files 1967–69, POL 13-10 ARAB, Box 1786, NARA; "Appeal by the Executive Secretariat of the Afro-Asian-Latin American Peoples' Solidarity Organization to All Revolutionary Forces and Socialist Countries to Support the Arab and Palestinian Peoples' Struggle Against Israel's Aggression," 29 May 1969, *IDP* 1969, 92; Eagleton to DOS, "PFLOAG Activities," Aden 299, 24 April 1969, RG 59, Central Files 1967–69, POL 13-10 ARAB, Box 1786, NARA.

59. "Communiqué on the Consultative Meeting of Special Government Representatives of the Non-Aligned Countries," 11 July 1969, *IDP* 1969, 737.

60. "Joint Communique on the Yugoslav President Tito's Visit to Iran," 28 April 1968, *IDP* 1968, 59; "Speech by the Indian President Husain at a Dinner in Honour of the Ethiopian Emperor Haile Selassiee," 28 April 1968, *IDP* 1968, 59.

61. Wallner to SecState, "France in the Middle East—An Israeli View," 3 April 1969, RG 59, POL 27 ARAB-ISR, Box 1807, NARA.

62. Philippe Rondot, "France and Palestine: From Charles de Gaulle to Mitterand," *Journal of Palestine Studies* 16, 3 (Spring 1987): 87–100.

63. Dallek, *Nixon and Kissinger*, 113.

64. See Craig, "French Policy in the Middle East: Is There a Pay-Off?" 10 December 1974, FCO 93/532, UKNA.

65. Barbour, "Israel/Jordan," Tel Aviv 4773, 4 August 1968, RG 59, Central Files 1967–69, POL 27 ARAB-ISR, Box 1812, NARA; Symmes, "Jordanian Call for Urgent Security Council Meeting," Amman 6022, 4 August 1968, RG 59, Central Files 1967–69, POL 27 ARAB-ISR, Box 1811, NARA.

66. For the UNSC debate, see *Yearbook of the United Nations* 22 (31 December 1968), www.domino.un.org (accessed July 2008).

67. Ibid.

68. Ibid.

69. Untitled General Guidance Paper for Ambassador Ball Regarding UNSC Consideration of Salt Incident, n.d., RG 59, Records Relating to Iraq, Jordan, Lebanon, and Syria, 1966–72, Box 1, NARA.

70. Memcon Between Battle and Sharaf, "Israeli Air Attacks on Jordan and Subsequent Security Council Meeting," 6 August 1968, RG 59, Records Relating to Iraq, Jordan, Lebanon, and Syria, 1966–72, Box 2, NARA.

71. Symmes, "Aftermath of Israeli Air Strike on As-Salt," Amman 6059, 6 August 1968, RG 59, Central Files 1967–69, POL 27 ARAB-ISR, Box 1812, NARA.

72. Symmes, "U.S. Position on Salt Raid SC Resolution," Amman 6088, 8 August 1968, RG 59, Central Files 1967–69, POL 27 ARAB-ISR, Box 1812, NARA.

73. Porter, "U.S. Position on Current SC Debate," Beirut 11728, 9 August 1968, RG 59, Central Files 1967–69, POL 27 ARAB-ISR, Box 1812, NARA.

74. Telegram from the President's Special Assistant (Rostow) to President Johnson in Texas, 14 August 1968, *FRUS* 1964–68, 20:236; *Yearbook of the United Nations* 22 (31 December 1968). domino.un.org (accessed July 2008).

75. Barbour, "El Al Hijacking," Tel Aviv 4925, 15 August 1968, Digital National Security Archive; Memcon with Yosef Ben-Aharon, "Hussein and Jordan," 19 August 1968, RG 59, Central Files 1967–69, POL 27 ARAB-ISR, Box 1812, NARA.

76. Porter, "Arab-Israeli Deadlock," Beirut 11853, 14 August 1968, RG 59, Central Files 1967–69, POL 27 ARAB-ISR, Box 1812, NARA.

77. Cobban, *The Palestinian Liberation Organization*, 43, 143–44.

78. Up to this point, I have tried to distinguish the PLO from the fedayeen due to the fact that before late 1968, the organization was not controlled by the guerillas. By 1969, however, Palestinian fighters had gained de facto control of the PLO; my use of "PLO" to refer to the guerilla organizations reflects this change. Abu Iyad, *My Home, My Land*, 65; Morris, *Righteous Victims*, 367, Cobban, *The Palestinian Liberation Organization*, 218.

79. Gresh, *The PLO*, 28; "The Palestine National Charter Adopted by the Fourth Palestine National Assembly," 17 July 1968, *IDP* 1968, 393–95.

80. Sayigh, *Armed Struggle*, 195–96, 206–7.

81. "Memorandum by the PFLP to the Fourth Palestine National Assembly," 10 July 1968, *IDP* 1968, 389.

82. Cobban, *The Palestinian Liberation Organization*, 48.

83. Gresh, *The PLO*, 12.

84. Hart, *Arafat*, 334; Cobban, *The Palestinian Liberation Organization*, 165–67.

85. Sayigh, *Armed Struggle*, 208.

86. Morin, State Dept. Memo, "Israeli Plane," Algiers 1958, 23 July 1968, Digital National Security Archive; PFLP, "Statement by the PFLP on the Seizure of an El Al Aeroplane," 29 July 1968, *IDP* 1968, 409–10; Andrews, "Views of Shafiq al-Hut on Arab-Israel Problem, *Fedayeen* Activity, Etc.," 2 August 1968, RG 59, POL 27 ARAB-ISR, Box 1812, NARA.

87. Many guerilla groups tended to be more wary of hijacking and similar types of "external operations." Aside from the public relations problem of terrorist-style attacks, larger organizations including Fatah recognized that many of these operations were designed to increase the relative influence of extremist groups such as the PFLP at the expense of more moderate fedayeen. These tensions would become even more apparent during the 1970 crisis in Jordan. See Ali A. Mazrui, "The Third World and International Terrorism: Preliminary Reflections," *Third World Quarterly* 7, 2 (April 1985): 348–64.

88. Sayigh, *Armed Struggle*, 210–11, 214.

89. Porter to DOS, "Attack on El Al Plane," Beirut 15303, 27 December 1968, RG 59, Central Files 1967–69, POL 27 ARAB-ISR, Box 1816, NARA; Porter to DOS, "Fedayeen Attack Against El Al Plane," Beirut 15305, 28 December 1968, RG 59, Central Files 1967–69, POL 27 ARAB-ISR, Box 1816, NARA.

90. Barbour to DOS, "Israeli Reaction to Attack on El Al Plane," Tel Aviv 6618, 27 December 1968, RG 59, Central Files 1967–69, POL 27 ARAB-ISR, Box 1816, NARA.

91. Black and Morris, *Israel's Secret Wars*, 264.

92. Porter to DOS, "Israeli Attack on Beirut Airport," Beirut 15311, 29 December 1968, RG 59, Central Files 1967–69, POL 27 ARAB-ISR, Box 1816, NARA; Barbour to DOS,

"Statement of Prime Minister Eshkol Following Meeting of Cabinet," Tel Aviv 6626, 29 December 1968, RG 59, Central Files 1967–69, POL 27 ARAB-ISR, Box 1816, NARA.

93. Hoffacker to DOS, "Israeli Attack on Beirut Airport—Algerian Reaction," Algiers 2778, 30 December 1968, RG 59, Central Files 1967–69, POL 27 ARAB-ISR, Box 1816, NARA. Beirut told U.S. officials that it had been profoundly disturbed by the implications of the al-Khaldah raid and feared that the Israelis might be "determined to eliminate, as it has nearly succeeded in case of Jordan, a pro-Western Arab government which tended to divert some attention from Israel." Bruce to DOS, "British Press Reaction to Israeli Beirut Raid," London 15447, 30 December 1968, RG 59, Central Files 1967–69, POL 27 ARAB-ISR, Box 1816, NARA; Porter to DOS, "Lebanese Delegation to New York and Washington," Beirut 15341, 30 December 1968, RG 59, Central Files 1967–69, POL 27 ARAB-ISR, Box 1816, NARA.

94. Office of Public Information, United Nations, "Consideration by Security Council," 29–31 December 1968, *Yearbook of the United Nations* 22 (31 December 1968), domino.un. org (accessed October 2007).

95. Ibid.

Chapter 3 Nixon, Kissinger, and the Terror of a Postimperial World

1. Isaacson, *Kissinger*, 81–82.

2. Henry Kissinger, "Military Policy and Defense of the 'Grey Areas,'" *Foreign Affairs*, April 1955.

3. Nixon, *RN*, 343.

4. For more on this controversy, see Isaacson, *Kissinger*, 129–37, and Hersh, *The Price of Power*.

5. Nixon, *RN*, 340–41.

6. Ibid., 343, 346.

7. Kissinger, *Diplomacy*, 17, 104; see also Kissinger, *A World Restored*.

8. Kissinger, *A World Restored*, 84, 19. For more on Kissinger's suspicions of democracy, see Suri, *Henry Kissinger and the American Century*.

9. Kissinger, *Diplomacy*, 27, 706.

10. See Suri, *Power and Protest*; Kissinger, *Diplomacy*, 677, 704.

11. Nixon, "Address by Richard M. Nixon to the Bohemian Club," 29 July 1967, *FRUS* 1969–76, 1:2.

12. Kissinger, "Central Issues of American Foreign Policy," 1969, *FRUS* 1969–76, 1:4.

13. Ibid., 698, 763.

14. Kissinger, *Diplomacy*, 121, 704, 742–45.

15. Ibid., 745; Nixon, *RN*, 344. Nixon told Golda Meir, for instance, that the "Soviets are the main cause of Middle East tensions." Nixon, *RN*, 478, 483.

16. For a firsthand account of Kissinger's rivalries with Rogers and Secretary of Defense Melvin Laird, see Haldeman, *The Haldeman Diaries*.

17. For a broad look at the Nixon administration's policies toward the Arab-Israeli conflict and the impact of political dynamics inside the White House, see Quandt, *Peace Process*. On the development of a "special relationship" between Israel and the United States during the Nixon administration, see Douglas Little, *American Orientalism*. For grand strategy in the Middle East, see Salim Yaqub, "The Weight of Conquest: Henry Kissinger and the Arab Israeli Conflict," in Logevall and Preston, eds., *Nixon and the World*. For

earlier accounts of U.S.-Israeli relations, see Hahn, *Caught in the Middle East*, and Bass, *Support Any Friend*. For a broad overview of U.S. policy in the Middle East that charts the Nixon administration's lean toward Israel, see Stivers, *America's Confrontation*.

18. NSC Paper, "Basic Interests of the United States in the Middle East and a Proposed US Posture Toward the Area," Prepared for SRG Meeting 28 January 1969, NSC Meeting Files (1969–74), SRG Meetings, Box H-034, NPMP.

19. Ibid.

20. Ibid.

21. INR, George Denney, "Israel Looks at the US," 15 September 1969, NSC Files, Reel 12 (Israel Vol. 2, 1 June 1969–30 September 1969), Frames 325–33.

22. Laird to Kissinger, DOD Study, "American Interests in the Arab-Israeli Conflict," 22 August 1969, NSC Files, Reel 12 (Israel Vol. 2, 1 June 1969–30 September 1969), Frames 227–41.

23. Ibid.

24. Ibid.

25. This paper originated in the State Department's Near East desk. See Parker T. Hart to Kissinger, "Basic U.S. Interests in the Middle East," 28 January 1969, NSC Meeting Files (1969–74), SRG Meetings, Box H-034, NPMP.

26. Ibid.

27. Nixon, *RN*, 480–81.

28. Ibid., 283.

29. Kissinger, *Diplomacy*, 737–40.

30. Kissinger, *White House Years*, 341, 376. On the Rogers Plan, see Shlaim, *Iron Wall*, 307. This type of diplomatic subterfuge was consistent with another alleged move by Nixon and Kissinger in which they informed the South Vietnamese that they ought to hold out on peace negotiations in 1968 in hopes of achieving a better deal, which would be worked out by the incoming Nixon administration. For this controversial thesis, see Hersh, *The Price of Power*.

31. Kissinger, Memorandum for the President, 16 June 1970, NSC Country Files, Middle East, Box 645, NPMP.

32. Ibid.

33. Kissinger, "Military Policy and the Defense of the Grey Areas."

34. Quoted in Isaacson, *Kissinger*, 106, 115–16.

35. Ibid., 160.

36. Jochen Hippler, "Low-Intensity Warfare: Key Strategy for the Third World Theater," *Middle East Report*, January-February 1987, 33–38.

37. Fred Skolnik et al., eds., *Encyclopedia Judaica*, 2nd ed., vol. 13 (Detroit: Macmillan Reference, 2007).

38. "Suspected Guerrilla Bases in Jordan Raided by Israelis," *New York Times*, 18 March 1969; O'Neill, *Armed Struggle in Palestine*, 49; O'Neill, *Revolutionary Warfare*, 79.

39. Black and Morris, *Israel's Secret Wars*, 264–65.

40. Shlaim, *Iron Wall*, 310–13.

41. Ibid., 285, 287, 290.

42. Ibid., 286–89, 297, 310–11.

43. Maoz, *Defending the Holy Land*, 246; Van Creveld, *The Sword and the Olive*, 209–10.

44. Maoz, *Defending the Holy Land*, 235, 246–47. On the Samu raid, see Clea Lutz Bunch, "Strike at Samu: Jordan, Israel, the United States, and the Origins of the Six Day War," *Diplomatic History* 32, 1 (January 2008).

45. INR, Thomas Hughes, "Israel: The Concept of 'Active Defense,'" 28 March 1969, RG 59, Central Files 1967–69, POL 27 ARAB-ISR, Box 1819, NARA; see also Shlaim, *Iron Wall*, 309–10.

46. INR, Hughes, "Israel: The Concept of 'Active Defense.'"

47. Ibid.

48. DOS Outgoing Telegram, "Middle East Summary No. 1," 24 February 1969, POL 27 ARAB-ISR, Box 1818, NARA; Eilts to DOS, "Eritrean Casu[a]lties in Israeli Raid Against Fadayeen," 6 March 1969, POL 27 ARAB-ISR, Box 1819, NARA. See also reports of an elite force of Eritrean insurgents trained along the same lines as Fatah commandos that seem to support this information. Jackson to DOS, "Governor General Reviews Eritrean Security," 28 January 1969, POL 13-10 ARAB, Box 1786, NARA; on ELF fighters training with PLO instructors in Aden and Somalia, see Roy Pateman, *Eritrea: Even the Stones Are Burning*, 99–100.

49. NSSM 2, 24 January 1969, Digital National Security Archive.

50. Barbour to DOS, "Further Thoughts on Athens/Beirut," 2 January 1969, RG 59, Central Files 1967–69, POL 27 ARAB-ISR, Box 1816, NARA.

51. Clark to DOS, "Israeli Attack at Beirut," Bamako 001, 2 January 1969, RG 59, Central Files 1967–69, POL 27 ARAB-ISR, Box 1816, NARA; Oded, *Africa, the PLO, and Israel*, 6–8. For Nasser's policies, see Shlaim, *Iron Wall*, 194.

52. David Ben-Gurion quoted in Shlaim, *Iron Wall*, 194, 202.

53. AmEmbassy Fort Lamy to DOS, "Israeli Views on Chad and Its Arab Neighbors," 16 September 1970, RG 59, Subject Numeric Files 1970–73, POL 27 ARAB-ISR, Box 2056, NARA.

54. DOS Memcon, "Middle East Topics," 8 July 1969, RG 59, Central Files 1967–69, POL 27 ARAB-ISR, Box 1821, NARA.

55. *Al-Thawra al-Filastiniyya*, 15 August 1969.

56. "'Adwa'a 'ala 'Israel fi Afrika" [Spotlight on Israel in Africa], *Al-Thawra al-Filastiniyya* 17 (15 July 1969), IPS.

57. Skinner to DOS, "Arab Diplomacy Efforts in Upper Volta," 6 March 1969, RG 59, Central Files 1967–69, POL 27 ARAB-ISR, Box 1816, NARA.

58. Noel to DOS, Untitled, Khartoum 696, 20 June 1969, RG 59, Central Files 1967–69, POL 13-10 ARAB, Box 1767, NARA.

59. See, for instance, "Antaha Al-Sura al-'Askari bayna Biyafra wa Al-Athadeen Yiftah Al-Bab 'Amam Marhala Jadida Al- Jadida wa Musalaha Ankhat Al-'Amalaq Al-Afriki l-t'az Wajudha wa Sitratha," *Al-Hadaf* 1, 25 (17 January 1970).

60. McElhiney to DOS, "Ghana Repudiates Labor Ministers' Resolution on Israel," 5 April 1969, RG 59, Central Files 1967–69, POL 27 ARAB-ISR, Box 1819, NARA.

61. Yost to DOS, "Ethiopian Posture in Arab-Israeli Dispute," Addis Ababa 1669, 17 April 1969, RG 59, Central Files 1967–69, POL 27 ARAB-ISR, Box 1820, NARA.

62. Addis Ababa to DOS, Untitled Telegram, 15 April 1969, RG 59, Central Files 1967–69, POL 27 ARAB-ISR, Box 1820, NARA.

63. "Joint Communiqué on the Mauritanian President Ould-Dadah's Visit to Syria," 12 November 1968, *IDP* 1968, 151.

64. Jackson to DOS, "Governor General Reviews Eritrean Security," 28 January 1969, RG 59, Central Files 1967–69, POL 13-10 ARAB, Box 1786, NARA.

65. Eilts to DOS, "Eritrean Casualties in Israeli Raid Against Fadayeen," Jidda 762, 6 March 1969, RG 59, Central Files 1967–69, POL 27 ARAB-ISR, Box 1819, NARA.

66. "Resolutions of the First Meeting of the International Islamic Organisations," 6 October 1968, *IDP* 1968, 132.

67. DOS Outgoing Telegram, "Jerusalem Issue in Security Council," State 147753, 2 September 1969, RG 59, Central Files 1967–69, POL 27 ARAB-ISR, Box 1823, NARA.

68. Ramsey to DOS, "Al-Fatah in Karachi," 21 May 1969, RG 59, Central Files 1967–69, POL 13-10 ARAB, Box 1786, NARA.

69. Oehlert to DOS, "Al-Fatah Leader in Pakistan," Rawalpindi 5145, 23 May 1969, RG 59, Central Files 1967–69, POL 13-10 ARAB, Box 1786, NARA.

70. Winship to DOS, "Peshawar Support for Palestine Guerillas," 5 March 1969, RG 59, Central Files 1967–69, POL 13-10 ARAB, Box 1786, NARA.

71. Lydman to DOS, "Al Fath in Indonesia," Djakarta 464, 22 January 1969, RG 59, Central Files 1967–69, POL 13-10 ARAB, Box 1786, NARA.

72. Bell to DOS, "Al-Fatah Representative in Kuala Lumpur Makes Press Statement," 1 July 1969, RG 59, Central Files 1967–69, POL 13-10 ARAB, Box 1786, NARA.

73. The most comprehensive analysis of this debate appears in Gresh, *The PLO*, 17–18, 31; "News Conference Statement and Remarks by a Spokesman of the Palestine National Liberation Movement 'Fateh' on the Peceful Settlement of the Middle East Crisis," October 1968, *IDP* 1968, 453–54.

74. Gresh, *The PLO*, 33, 36.

75. Ibid., 40, 42.

76. Ibid., 42–44.

77. Ibid., 101–3.

78. Memcon between Sisco and Argov, "Attack on El Al Plane," 19 February 1969, RG 59, Central Files 1967–69, POL 27 ARAB-ISR, Box 1818, NARA.

79. Porter to DOS, "Fedayeen Attacks on El Al," Beirut 1634, 20 February 1969, RG 59, Central Files 1967–69, POL 27 ARAB-ISR, Box 1818, NARA.

80. Eleanor Glenn, "Memorandum for the Files," 8 September 1969, RG 59, Records Relating to Iraq, Jordan, Lebanon, and Syria, 1966–72, Box 6, NARA.

81. Khaled, *My People Shall Live*, 90–96, 146.

82. Memcon Davies and Williams, "TWA Hijacking," 31 August 1969, *FRUS* 1969–72, Vol. E-1, http://www.state.gov/r/pa/ho/frus/nixon/e1/45245.htm (accessed November 2007).

83. Rogers to Zurhellen, "TWA Hijacking," 31 August 1969, *FRUS* 1969–72, Vol. E-1, 11, http://www.state.gov/r/pa/ho/frus/nixon/e1/45252.htm (accessed November 2007).

84. Seelye to Sisco, "TWA Hijacking—Status Report," 8 September 1969, RG 59, Records Relating to Iraq, Jordan, Syria, and Lebanon 1966–1972, Box 6, NARA.

85. Seelye to Sisco, "TWA Hijacking," 10 September 1969, RG 59, Records Relating to Iraq, Jordan, Syria, and Lebanon 1966–1972, Box 6, NARA.

86. Richardson, "TWA Hijacking," State 159327, 20 September 1969, *FRUS* 1969–72, Vol. E-1, 24, http://www.state.gov/r/pa/ho/frus/nixon/e1/45265.htm (accessed November 2007).

87. Kissinger to Nixon, "TWA Hijacking," 21 September 1969, *FRUS* 1969–72, Vol. E-1, 25, http://www.state.gov/r/pa/ho/frus/nixon/e1/45266.htm (accessed November 2007).

88. See Gary Ostrower, "'I Hate It. I Hate It. I Hate It': The UN During the Nixon Years," *Diplomatic History* 31, 2 (April 2007): 353–56.

89. "Communications Concerning International Interference with Civil Aviation," 18–26 February 1969, UNISPAL, http://domino.un.org (accessed November 2007).

90. "Communications to and Consideration by the Security Council During Period 26 March–1 April 1969," UNISPAL, http://domino.un.org, (accessed November 2007).

91. Discussions on 14 August 1968, *Yearbook of the United Nations* 22 (31 December 1968), UNISPAL, domino.un.org (accessed November 2007).

92. Eilts to DOS, "Some Further Saudi Views on Current ME Situation," Jidda 953, 21 March 1969, RG 59, Central Files 1967–69, POL 27 ARAB-ISR, Box 1819, NARA.

93. Yost to Amman, Cairo, and Tel Aviv, "ME in SC—Israeli Raid on Jordan," State 047204, 27 March 1969, RG 59, Central Files 1967–69, POL 27 ARAB-ISR, Box 1819, NARA.

94. See Michael Hunt, *American Ascendancy* (Chapel Hill: University of North Carolina Press, 2007).

95. Yost to DOS, "Trip to Africa by Committee of 24," 13 March 1969, *FRUS* 1969–72, Vol. 5, http://www.state.gov/r/pa/ho/frus/nixon/v/42663.htm (accessed November 2007).

96. Editorial Note 50, *FRUS*, 1969–72, Vol. 5, http://www.state.gov/r/pa/ho/frus/nixon/v/42663.htm (accessed November 2007).

97. Editorial Note 81, *FRUS*, 1969–72, Vol. 5, http://www.state.gov/r/pa/ho/frus/nixon/v/42663.htm (accessed November 2007).

98. "Interview with Mr. Yasser Arafat, Chairman of the Executive Committee at the Palestine Liberation Organisation and Official Spokesman of the Palestine National Liberation Movement Fatah," August 1969, *IDP* 1968, 773.

99. "Speech by the Yugoslav President Tito During His Visit to Algeria," 5 November 1969, *IDP* 1969, 153.

100. "Speech by the Chinese Vice-Premier Hsieh Fu-Chih at a Reception Marking the 15th Anniversary of the Algerian Revolution," 1 November 1969, *IDP* 1969, 151.

Chapter 4: The Jordanian Civil War

1. Jordanian Prime Minister's Office, "Statement Concerning an Attempted Armed Attack on King Hussein of Jordan," 1 September 1970, *IDP* 1970, 900; Central Committee of the PLO, "Statement Concerning an Alleged Armed Attack on King Hussein of Jordan," 2 September 1970, *IDP* 1970, 900–901; King Hussein, "Speech on the 'Unusual Circumstances' in Jordan," 3 September 1970, *IDP* 1970, 901–2.

2. Most accounts of the September 1970 crisis have analyzed events from an American perspective. Some of the most valuable include Nixon, *RN*; Kissinger, *White House Years*; and Quandt, *Peace Process*. Recent works by Douglas Little and Salim Yaqub have contributed to the literature with the help of declassified U.S. documents. See Little, *American Orientalism* and Yaqub's essay in Logevall and Preston, eds., *Nixon in the World*. The recent *FRUS* vol. 24, *Middle East Region and Arabian Peninsula, 1969–1972: Jordan, September 1970*, is also of enormous value.

3. Quandt, *Peace Process*, 73–75.

4. PLO Central Committee, "No Letup in Liberation Struggle," *Fateh* 2, 12 (5 August 1970), IPS.

5. "Radio Interview Statements by Central Committee Chairman Arafat of the PLO on the Efforts Being Made to Reach a Peaceful Settlement," 25 July 1970, *IDP* 1970, 877.

6. "Press Conference Statements by Secretary-General Habash of the PFLP on the Front's Attitude Towards the Rogers Plan and Its Acceptance by Certain Arab Governments," 25 July 1970, *IDP* 1970, 878.

7. Fatah Information Office, "No to Submission, Yes to Revolution," *Fateh* 2, 12 (5 August 1970), IPS.

8. "Established Arab Policy Has Existed Within, Not Outside, a Peaceful Solution Sphere as Evidenced by the Policy and Make-up of Arab Regimes," *Fateh* 2, 13 (21 August 1970), IPS; Hart, *Arafat*, 304.

9. Central Committee of the PLO et al., "Statement of Palestinian Commando Organizations on Current Moves Aimed at Liquidating the Palestinian Cause," 9 August 1970, *IDP* 1970, 887.

10. "Commentary on Attitudes to the Middle East Cease-Fire and the Resumption of the Jarring Talks Published in the U.S.S.R. Weekly *New Times*," 7 August 1970, *IDP* 1970, 247.

11. "Commentary on the U.S. June 19 Proposals and the U.S.S.R. Attitude Towards Them Published in *China Weekly*," *IDP* 1970, 243.

12. Dannreuther, *The Soviet Union and the PLO*, 43–44. Christopher Andrew and Vasili Mitrokhin argue that the KGB established ties with the external operations wing of the PFLP under Wadi Haddad during 1970 in an attempt to exert a certain degree of influence over the organization. This channel would be severed when Habash renounced PFLP external operations in 1972, leading Haddad to split off from the PFLP. Andrew and Mitrokhin, *The World Was Going Our Way*, 246–52.

13. Primakov, *Russia and the Arabs*, 230.

14. Dannreuther, *The Soviet Union and the PLO*, 45–47.

15. "China Raps Faked Peace," *Fateh* 2, 12 (5 August 1970), IPS.

16. "World Liberation Movements to Attend National Congress Session at Wahdat," *Fateh* 2, 12 (5 August 1970), IPS.

17. "Declaration by the Democratic Republic of Vietnam on the Middle East Cease-Fire," 12 August 1970, *IDP* 1970, 250; "NLF Cables Support to Palestine Struggle," *Fateh* 2, 13 (21 August 1970), IPS.

18. "Palestine Emissaries Visit China, Vietnam, and Korea," *Fateh* 2, 12 (5 August 1970), IPS; "Fateh Delegates in Malaysia," *Fateh* 2, 12 (5 August 1970), IPS.

19. "World Conference in Japan Supports Liberation Movements, Raps Nuclear Armament and Presses for Okinawa," *Fateh* 2, 12 (5 August 1970), IPS.

20. "Students Meeting in Tunis Condemn Portugal," *Fateh* 2, 14 (5 August 1970), IPS.

21. "200 Delegates Pledge to Struggle for Aims of Palestinian Revolution," *Fateh* 2, 14 (17 September 1970), IPS.

22. Wheelock, "West Bank Reaction to Acceptance of American Initiative," 6 August 1970, RG 59, POL 27 ARAB-ISR, Box 2055, NARA.

23. Seelye Memcon with George Hishmeh, "United States Government Position on Palestinians," 4 August 1970, RG 59, POL 27 ARAB-ISR, Box 2055, NARA.

24. Fulbright, "Speech to the U.S. Senate by Chairman of the Foreign Relations Committee Fulbright Describing Middle East Settlement Terms the U.S. Should Support," 23 August 1970, *IDP* 1970, 269.

25. "Interview by Foreign Minister Eban of Israel on Arms Supply to the Middle East and on Israeli Policy Towards the Palestinians," 27 March 1970, *IDP* 1970, 76.

26. "Statement by Deputy Premier Allon of Israel Threatening Reprisals Against Lebanon for a Commando Attack Near the Lebanese Border," 22 May 1970, *IDP* 1970, 150.

27. "Radio Interview on Israel-U.S. Relations with Israeli Ambassador to the U.S. Rabin," 22 August 1970, *IDP* 1970, 254.

28. "U.S. Television Interview with Prime Minister Meir of Israel on Prospects for the Jarring Talks and Israeli Relations with the U.S.," 30 August 1970, *IDP* 1970, 277–78.

29. "U.S. Magazine Interview Statements by Secretary-General Eliav of the Israeli Lbor Party on Israeli Policy Towards the Palestinians," 26 January 1970, *IDP* 1970, 14.

30. INR, Teresita Currie, "Israel and the Palestinians," 31 August 1970, RG 59, POL 27 ARAB-ISR, Box 2055, NARA.

31. Houghton, "Radical Pressures in Lebanon," 10 April 1970, RG 59, POL 27 ARAB-ISR, Box 2055, NARA.

32. Phillips to FCO, Tunis 306, 10 October 1970, FCO 17/1055, UKNA.

33. INR, Teresita Currie, "Israel and the Palestinians," 31 August 1970, RG 59, POL 27 ARAB-ISR, Box 2055, NARA.

34. Sayigh, *Armed Struggle*, 260.

35. Donald Neff, *Warriors Against Israel*, 33–35; AmEmbassy Bonn to DOS, "Multiple Hijackings of Aircraft," 6 September 1970, *FRUS*, E-1, http://www.state.gov/r/pa/ho/frus/nixon/e1/45307.htm.

36. "Interview Statements by Two Officials of the P.F.L.P. on the Plane Hijackings Carried Out by Them," 9 September 1970, *IDP* 1970, 904–5.

37. Central Committee of the PLO, "Statements and Resolutions Suspending the PFLP from Membership in the Central Committee, "12 September 1970, *IDP* 1970, 909; Hart, *Arafat*, 315.

38. Cobban, *The Palestinian Liberation Organization*, 48, 150; Sayigh, *Armed Struggle*, 246–48, 256.

39. "Hadith Sahafi li-l Sayyid Yasir Arafat, Rayiss al-Lajanah al-Tanafithiyah al-Munathamah al-Tahrir al-Filastiniyah wa al-Munataq al-Rasmiy bi-Ism Harikat at-Tahrir al-Wataniy al- al-Filastiniyah 'Fatah,' Huwal Mu'atmar al-Muqamah al-'Arabiy Watatur ath-Thawarah Filastiniyah," 14 January 1970, WFA, 68; also *IDP* 1970, 749–50.

40. Sayigh, *Armed Struggle*, 238.

41. Haile Selassie, "Speech by Emperor of Ethiopia to Third Conference of Non-Aligned Countries," 8–10 September 1970, *IDP* 1970, 293; Kenneth Kaunda, "Speech by the President of Zambia Opening the Third Conference of Non-Aligned Nations," 8 September 1970, *IDP* 1970, 291; Josip Broz Tito, "Speech by the President of Yugoslavia to the Third Conference of Non-Aligned Countries," 8 September 1970, *IDP* 1970, 29.

42. Marien Ngoaubi, "Speech by the President of the Congo to the Third Conference of Non-Aligned Countries," 8–10 September 1970, *IDP* 1970, 292.

43. Léon Maka, "Speech by Parliamentary President Maka of Guinea to the Third Conference of Non-Aligned Countries," 8–10 September 1970, *IDP* 1970, 293.

44. Okoi Arikpo, "Speech by Foreign Minister of Nigeria to the Third Conference of Non-Aligned Countries," 8–10 September 1970, *IDP* 1970, 294.

45. Indira Gandhi, "Speech by Prime Minister of India to the Third Conference of Non-Aligned Countries," 8–10 September 1970, *IDP* 1970, 295.

46. Raul Roa Garcia, "Speech by Foreign Minister of Cuba to the Third Conference of Non-Aligned Countries," 8–10 September 1970, *IDP* 1970, 294.

47. In this regard, it could be said that the Third World was ahead of the First in discussions of human rights. Eduardo Mercado Jarrin, "Speech by Foreign Minister of Peru to the Third Conference of Non-Aligned Countries," 8–10 September 1970, *IDP* 1970, 295.

48. "Resolution on the Middle East Adopted by the Third Conference of Non-Aligned Countries," 10 September 1970, *IDP* 1970, 296.

49. Eagleton, Telegram to State, "Official Algerian Line on Hijackings," Algiers 1395, 10 September 1970, RG 59, POL 27 ARAB-ISR, Box 2043, NARA.

50. Cooley, *Green March, Black September*, 180; Vice Premier Li Hsein-Nien, "Speech at a Banquet in Honor of Special Envoy Yunis Representing the PLO Executive Committee Chairman Arafat," 5 September 1970, *IDP* 1970, 282–83.

51. Arnold Toynbee, "Samson Shakes the Pillar," *Fateh* 2, 13 (17 September 1970), IPS.

52. Kissinger, *White House Years*, 598–602.

53. Nixon, "Announcement of Plans to Combat Hijackings by U.S. President," 11 September 1970, *IDP* 1970, 297.

54. Central Committee of the PLO, "Statement on Security Measures in Amman," 5 September 1970, *IDP* 1970, 902; "It's the Showdown," *Fateh* 2, 14 (17 September 1970), IPS; King Hussein, "Letter from the King of Jordan to Brigadier Muhammad Daud Charging Him with the Formation of a Provisional Military Government," 15 September 1970, *IDP* 1970, 912–13; Sayigh, *Armed Struggle*, 262–63; Walker and Gowers, *Arafat*, 80; Dallek, *Nixon and Kissinger*, 225.

55. Alex Efty, "Devastation Seen All over Amman," *Fateh* 2, 15 (30 September 1970), IPS; Dallek, *Nixon and Kissinger*, 225;"It's the Showdown," *Fateh* 2, 14 (17 September 1970), IPS.

56. Black September appeared against the backdrop of Salvador Allende's victory in Chile and the discovery of a Soviet nuclear submarine base in Cuba. See Isaacson, *Kissinger*, 284–86.

57. Nixon, "Address in the Alfred M. Landon Lecture Series," Kansas State University, 16 September 1970, *Public Papers of the Presidents: 1970*, 295.

58. Ibid.

59. "Telegram from President Boumedienne of Algeria to Central Committee Chairman Arafat of the P.L.O. on Algeria's Support for the Palestinian Resistance," 17 September 1970, *IDP* 1970, 923.

60. "Cable from President Nasser of the U.A.R. to King Hussein of Jordan Calling for a Cease-Fire," 19 September 1970, *IDP* 1970, 923; "Cable from President Nasser of the U.A.R. to Palestinian Resistance Forces Commander-in-Chief Arafat Calling for a Cease-Fire in Jordan," 19 September 1970, *IDP* 1970, 924.

61. "Commentary on Hijackings Published in the U.S.S.R. Daily *Pravda*," 17 September 1970, *IDP* 1970, 305.

62. Davies, State Telegram, "Soviet Demarche Re: Jordan," 18 September 1970, Washington Special Action Group Meetings, Box H-76, NPMP.

63. WSAG, "Possible Outcome of Current Situation in Jordan and Implications," 18 September 1970, Washington Special Action Group Meetings, Box H-76, NPMP.

64. Ibid.

65. An excellent account of Israeli deliberations on the intervention can be found in Ashton, *King Hussein of Jordan*, 150–54; Memcon, Rabin, Argov, Kissinger, Haig, 22 September 1970, Mandatory Review Opening, 23 June 2009, Temporary Box 9, NPMP; Morris, *Righteous Victims*, 374–75, Quandt, *Peace Process*, 80–82.

66. Quandt, *Peace Process*, 80–81.

67. Haig Memorandum for the Record, "Kissinger's Briefing of White House Staff on Jordan," 25 September 1970 (recorded on 3 October 1970), Digital National Security Archive.

68. INR, Ray S. Cline to SecState, "Communist China/Middle East: Peking Hopes to Prolong Jordanian Crisis," 22 September 1970, RG 59, POL 13-10 ARAB, Box 2043, NARA.

69. Coon to DOS, "Soviet Line on Middle East," Kathmandu, 3179, 28 September 1970, RG 59, POL 27 ARAB-ISR, Box 2043, NARA.

70. Osborn to DOS, "Peking and Middle East," Hong Kong 3874, 25 September 1970, RG 59, POL 27 ARAB-ISR, Box 2056, NARA.

71. "Declaration on the Jordan Civil War Issued by the Government of China," 21 September 1970, *IDP* 1970, 308.

72. "Cable from Commander-in-Chief of the Palestinian Resistance Forces Arafat to the Conference of the Arab Kings and Presidents in Cairo on the Situation in Jordan." 22 September 1970, *IDP* 1970, 933; Hart, *Arafat*, 323.

73. U.S. Embassy in London to DOS, "British Press Favors Recognizing Status of Palestinian Movement," London 7862, 28 September 1970, RG 59, POL 13-10 ARAB, Box 2043, NARA.

74. Pompidou, Letter to Nixon, 21 September 1970, Washington Special Action Group Meetings, Box H-077, NPMP.

75. Paris to DOS, "France and the Palestinians," Paris 12888, 26 September 1970, RG 59, POL 27 ARAB-ISR, Box 2056, NARA.

76. "Statement by the Premier of Tunisia and Member of the Delegation of Arab Kings and Presidents, al-Adgham, Concerning an Operation to 'Annihilate the Palestinian People' in Jordan," 25 September 1970, *IDP* 1970, 939; *IDP* 1970, 947.

77. "Cable from President Nasser of the U.A.R. to King Hussein of Jordan on the Report Submitted by President Numairi to the Arab Kings and Presidents on the Situation in Jordan and the 'Plan to Liquidate the Palestinian Resistance,'" 27 September 1970, *IDP* 1970, 942–43.

78. Jordanian forces claimed to have lost 200 soldiers in the conflict, while the PLO reported 3,500 civilian and 900 guerilla casualties.

79. Morris, *Righteous Victims*, 375.

80. Quoted in Isaacson, *Kissinger*, 307.

81. Dallek, *Nixon and Kissinger*, 273.

82. Dayan, *Moshe Dayan*, 430–31.

83. "Message from Central Committee Chairman Arafat of the P.L.O. to the People and the Palestinian Revolutionaries on the Reasons for Accepting a Cease-Fire," 28 September 1970, *IDP* 1970, 957.

84. Houghton to DOS, Beirut 8325, 28 September 1970, RG 59, POL 27 ARAB-ISR, Box 2056, NARA.

85. Watson to DOS, "France, the US, and the Palestinians," Paris 14234, 19 October 1970, RG 59, POL 13-10 ARAB, Box 2044, NARA.

86. Eagleton to DOS, "USG Relations with Fedayeen," Algiers 1592, 20 October 1970, RG 59, POL 13-10 ARAB, Box 2044, NARA.

87. Buffum to DOS, "Radical Shift in the Fedayeen Movement," Beirut 9181, 21 October 1970, RG 59, POL 13-10 ARAB, Box 2044, NARA.

88. State Department Paper for the SRG, "U.S. Policy Toward the Palestinians," 22 October 1970, White House Senior Review Group Meetings, 26 October 1970, Box H-048, NPMP.

89. Ibid.

90. U.S. Embassy Moscow to DOS, "Are Soviets Warming to Fedayeen?" Moscow 6295, 22 October 1970, RG 59, POL 13-10 ARAB, Box 2044, NARA.

91. Klossen to DOS, "New Times Article on Fedayeen," Moscow 6518, 30 October 1970, RG 59, POL 13-10 ARAB, Box 2044, NARA.

92. "Speech on the Bases of a Middle East Settlement Delivered to a Conservative Party Meeting by U.K. Secretary of State for Foreign and Commonwealth Affairs Douglas-Home," 31 October 1970, *IDP* 1970, 359.

93. "Resolution on the Middle East Adopted by the Ninth Conference of the Afro-Asian Peoples Solidarity Organization," 12 November 1970, *IDP* 1970, 375–76.

94. "Final Statement Issued by the Third Annual Convention of the Association of Arab American University Students," 1 November 1970, *IDP* 1970, 363.

95. "An Appeal by a Group of Black Americans Against U.S. Support for Israel," 2 November 1970 (text from *Action*), *IDP* 1970, 364–69.

96. "Cable from the Central Committee of the P.L.O. to Chairman Mao Tse-Tung of the Council of State of the People's Republic of China, on the Twenty-first Anniversary of the Establishment of the Republic, Early October," *IDP* 1970, 963–64.

97. "Remarks on Yugoslav Policy in the Middle East Delivered by President Tito to the Federal Assembly of Yugoslavia," 18 November 1970, *IDP* 1970, 382.

98. "Foreign Policy Statement to the Knesset by Prime Minister Meir of Israel," 16 November 1970, *IDP* 1970, 377–81.

99. Saunders and Kennedy, Memo for Haig, "The Next WSAG/SRG Meeting," 2 October 1970, Washington Special Action Group Meetings, Box H-76, NPMP.

100. INR, Ray S. Cline, "Jordan: Uneasy Lies the Head," 2 October 1970, RG 59, POL 13-10 ARAB, Box 2044, NARA.

101. NSSM 103, Discussion Paper, "Middle East Policy Options," 13 October 1970, National Security Council Institutional Files, Meeting Files, Senior Review Group Meetings, Box H-048, NPMP.

102. "Speech Reviewing the History of the American June 19 Proposals by U.S. Assistant Secretary of State Sisco," 6 November 1970, *IDP* 1970, 370–73.

103. Yost to DOS, "US Policy RE Palestinians," State 169856, 15 November 1970, RG 59, POL 13-10 ARAB, Box 2044, NARA.

104. Ibid.

105. David Ignatius, "The Secret History of U.S.-PLO Terror Talks," *Washington Post*, 4 December 1988; see also Ignatius's fictionalized account, *Agents of Innocence*.

106. INR, "Jordan: The Fedayeen: Regrouping After the Jordanian Crisis," 17 November 1970, RG 59, POL 13-10 ARAB, Box 2044, NARA.

107. Brown to DOS, "GOT Views on Palestinian Question," Amman 5799, 10 October 1970, RG 59, POL 13-10 ARAB, Box 2044, NARA.

108. Brubeck to DOS, "Initiating Contacts with Fedayeen in Jordan," 12 October 1970, RG 59, POL 13-10 ARAB, Box 2044, NARA.

109. On the West Bank urban notables, see Chapter 1.

110. DOS to U.S. Embassies, 169856, 15 October 1970, RG, 59 POL 13-10 ARAB, Box 2044, NARA; Rockwell to DOS, Rabat 4582, 16 October 1970, RG 59, POL 13-10 ARAB, Box 2044, NARA.

111. Thacher to DOS, "USG Relations with Fedayeen," Jidda 03870, 19 October 1970, RG 59, POL 13-10 ARAB, Box 2044, NARA.

112. Ibid.

113. Kennedy and Saunders, Memorandum for Kissinger, "Senior Review Group Meeting on Jordan—December 17," 16 December 1970, Senior Review Group Meetings, Box H-050, NPMP.

114. Draft, "Background Paper: Additional Arms for Jordan," n.d., Senior Review Group Meetings, Box H-050, NPMP.

115. Kissinger to Nixon, "Mid-East Settlement—Palestinians and Hussein," 4 December 1970, Senior Review Group Meetings, Box H-050, NPMP.

116. Ibid.

117. See Saunders to Kissinger, "A Conversation on the Palestinians," 23 September 1970, NSC Files, Country Files, Middle East, Box 608, NPMP.

118. "Hadith as-Sayid Yasir Arafat, Rayiss al-Lajanah al-Tanafithiyah al-Munathamah al-Tahrir al-Filastiniyah wa al-Qaʾed al-ʿAm li-l-Tharah al-Filastiniyah, Huwal al-Taturat al-Rahanah al-Lamuqaf fi al-Urdun wa Mustaqbal al-ʿAmal al-Fidaʾi," *Al-Ahram*, 9 November 1970, *WFA*, 1970, 946; Gresh, *The PLO*, 105–6, 99.

119. Primakov, *Russia and the Arabs*, 231–32.

120. UNGA, "General Assembly Resolution 2649 (XXV) Condemning Denial of Self-Determination, Especially to the Peoples of Southern Africa and Palestine," 30 November 1970, *IDP* 1970, 721.

121. UNGA, "General Assembly Resolution 2672 (XXV) Recognizing That the People of Palestine Are Entitled to Self-Determination and Calling Once More on Israel to Take Immediate Steps for the Return of the Displaced Persons," 8 December 1970, *IDP* 1970, 722.

122. This latter figure would fall to $300 million in 1975, but the general increase would continue, averaging some $2.6 billion in U.S. assistance per year between 1971 and 2008. See Jeremy Sharp, "CRS Report for Congress: U.S. Foreign Aid to Israel," Congressional Research Service, Washington, DC, 25 April 2007, http://www.fas.org/sgp/crs/mideast/RL33222.pdf (accessed November 2007).

123. Saunders to Kissinger, "Where We Stand in the Mid-East," 22 October 1969, NSC Country Files, Middle East, Box 644, NPMP.

124. Laird to Nixon, "Middle East Arms Policy," 21 June 1971, NSC Country Files, Middle East, Box 647, NPMP.

125. Ibid.; NSC, Meeting on the Middle East and South Asia, 16 July 1971, Kissinger Transcripts, Digital National Security Archive; Rabin, Idan, Kissinger, and Haig, Memorandum of Conversation, 9 August 1971, Kissinger Transcripts, Digital National Security Archive.

126. "Radio Interview with Israeli Ambassador Rabin," 2 July 1971, *IDP* 1971, 201–2.

127. Cobban, *The Palestinian Liberation Organization*, 206; Sayigh, *Armed Struggle*, 216; Gresh, *The PLO*, 49.

128. The Philippeville massacre is often cited as the starting point of all-out war in the Algerian revolution. The incident itself was sparked by the killings of 123 *pieds-noirs* and suspected collaborators by the FLN; estimates of Algerians killed in the French retaliation run from 1,200 to 12,000. Philippeville is also cited as the moment in the war in which civilians were transformed into targets for both sides. *Fateh* 2, 16 (20 October 1970), IPS.

Chapter 5: A Worldwide Interlocking Terrorist Network

1. Black September Organization, "Statement Explaining the Munich Attack," 7 September 1972, *IDP* 1972, 224; "The Timetable of the Munich Disaster," 7 September 1972, *Times* (London).

2. Buffum to DOS, "The Fedayeen: Contradictions and Crisis," 5 September 1972, RG 59, Subject Numeric Files 1970–73, POL 13-10 ARAB, Box 2043, NARA.

3. Sayigh, *Armed Struggle*, 274–80; Walker and Gowers, *Arafat*, 84.

4. Buffum to DOS, "Reported Fedayeen Acquisition of Strategic Positions in Beirut," Beirut 9412, 28 November 1970, RG 59, Subject Numeric Files 1970–73, POL 23-8 LEB, Box 2447, NARA.

5. Buffum to DOS, "Likelihood of Israeli Attack in South Lebanon," Beirut 0315, 10 January 1972, RG 59, Subject Numeric Files 1970–73, POL 27 ARAB-ISR, Box 2059, NARA.

6. Buffum to DOS, "Israeli Attacks in South Lebanon," Beirut 0407, 12 January 1972, RG 59, Subject Numeric Files 1970–73, POL 27 ARAB-ISR, Box 2059, NARA.

7. Buffum to DOS, "Reassurances for Lebanon," Beirut 0773, 21 January 1972, RG 59, Subject Numeric Files 1970–73, POL 27 ARAB-ISR, Box 2059, NARA.

8. Buffum to DOS, "State Visit for Pres. Frangie," Beirut 845, 24 January 1972, RG 59, Subject Numeric Files 1970–73, POL 27 ARAB-ISR, Box 2059, NARA.

9. "Bayan al-Qayadah al-'Amah al-Thawrah al-Filastiniyah Huwal al-Mawaqaf al-Araby min a-'Atada'a Isra'yly 'ala Lubnan," 26 February 1972, *WFA* 69; Eliot to Kissinger, "Serious Trouble on Israel-Lebanon Border," 2 March 1972, RG 59, Subject Numeric Files 1970–73, POL 27 ARAB-ISR, Box 2059, NARA.

10. DOS to Beirut, State 32441, 25 February 1972, RG 59, Subject Numeric Files 1970–73, POL 13-10 ARAB, Box 2044, NARA.

11. Barbour to DOS, "Israel-Lebanon," Tel Aviv 1256, RG 59, Subject Numeric Files 1970–73, POL 27 ARAB-ISR, Box 2059, NARA.

12. DOS Telegram, "Lebanon-Israel," State 33207, 28 February 1972, RG 59, Subject Numeric Files 1970–73, POL 27 ARAB-ISR, Box 2059, NARA. See also DOS Telegram, "Call on Asst Secretaries Sisco and De Palma by Lebanese Ambassador, 6:30 PM Sunday, February 27," State 33211, 28 February 1972, RG 59, Subject Numeric Files 1970–73, POL 27 ARAB-ISR, Box 2059, NARA.

13. Brown to DOS, "Jordanian Comment on Events in Lebanon," 0904, 1 March 1972, RG 59, Subject Numeric Files 1970–73, POL 13-10 Arab, Box 2044, NARA.

14. Buffum to DOS, "Possible Lebanese-Fedayeen Confrontation," Beirut 3270, 24 March 1972, RG 59, Subject Numeric Files 1970–73, POL 27 ARAB-ISR, Box 2059, NARA.

15. "Radio Interview Statements by Chief of Staff Bar Lev of Israel, Assessing the Country's Military Preparedness and the Military Balance of Power in the Middle East," 11 September 1971, *IDP* 1971, 238.

16. "Article by Deputy Prime Minster Allon of Israel Outlining the Strength of Israel's Current Position," August 1972, *IDP* 1972, 211; "Statements on the Necessity for Israel to Retain Permanent Control of the Golan Heights, Sharm el-Sheikh, and the West Bank, Made by Defense Minister Dayan of Israel to the Tel Aviv Journalists' Association," 18 April 1971, *IDP* 1971, 118.

17. "Television Interview Statements by U.S. Secretary of State Rogers Commenting on the Role of the U.S. in Maintaining Political and Military Stability in the Middle East," 4 January 1972, *IDP* 1972, 102; "Report by U.S. President Nixon to Congress on U.S. Foreign Policy," 9 February 1972, *IDP* 1972, 140–44.

18. "Address by U.S. Assistant Secretary of State Sisco: The Step-by-Step Approach to Peace in the Middle East," 19 August 1972, *IDP* 1972, 217–20.

19. Cobban, *The Palestinian Liberation Organization*, 53.

20. For a general analysis of these factors, see INR, Curtis F. Jones, "Fedayeen: Frustration, Fractiousness, and Fragmentation," 20 October 1972, RG 59, Subject Numeric Files 1970–73, POL 13-10 ARAB, Box 2045, NARA.

21. Paul Martin, "Jordan Prime Minister Is Shot Dead in Cairo," 29 November 1971, *Times* (London).

22. "Bayan Munathamah 'Aylul al-Aswad Huwal Mus'uwalataha 'an Musar'a al-Sayid Wasfi al-Tal," 30 November 1971, *WFA* 777.

23. AmEmbassy Beirut to DOS, "Tal's Assassination," Beirut 10549, 1 December 1971, RG 59, Subject Numeric Files 1970–73, POL 15-1 LEB, Box 2447, NARA.

24. These reports contradict assertions, common in later years, that Arafat was implicated in Black September's actions and thus a terrorist. Rather, as this type of evidence suggests, the Black September faction was a challenger to the more moderate mainstream wing of Fatah led by Arafat. Buffum to DOS, "Tal Assassination," Beirut 10590, 2 December 1971, RG 59, Subject Numeric Files 1970–73, POL 15-1 LEB, Box 2447, NARA; see also Walker and Gowers, *Arafat*, 88.

25. On the controversy surrounding Hart's book, see Helena Cobban's review, "Biography or Hagiography?" *Journal of Palestine Studies* 14, 4 (Summer 1985); Cobban, *The Palestinian Liberation Organization*, 54; Hart, *Arafat*, 338, 347–49; Sayigh, *Armed Struggle*, 309.

26. "Hadith Sahafi Khas li-l Sayyid 'Abu Ayad,' Ahad Qadah Harikat at-Tahrir al-Wataniy al- al-Filastiniy 'Fatah,' Huwal Ba'd Shu'un ath-Thawarah Filastiniyah," 16 May 1972, *WFA*, 68; Sayigh, *Armed Struggle*, 307, 309.

27. "Magazine Interview with Palestine National Liberation Movement (Fateh) Leader Khalaf (Abu Ayyad) Commenting on the Effects on the Resistance of Opposition on the Part of Arab Governments and of Ideological Differences Within the Movement," *Jeune Afrique*, *IDP* 1971, 539–42.

28. "Five Killed in Gun Attack on Jordanians," 6 February 1972, *Times* (London); Buffum to DOS, "Fedayeen Activity in Europe," Beirut 1765, RG 59, Subject Numeric Files 1970–73, POL 13-10 ARAB, Box 2044, NARA.

29. Middendorf to DOS, "Sabotage of Natural Gas Pipeline," The Hague 488, 7 February 1972, RG 59, Subject Numeric Files 1970–73, POL 13-10 ARAB, Box 2044, NARA.

30. Buffum to DOS, "Reports of Fedayeen Sabotage in Europe," Beirut 1550, 11 February 1972, RG 59, Subject Numeric Files 1970–73, POL 13-10 ARAB, Box 2044, NARA.

31. Buffum to DOS, "Fedayeen Activity in Europe," Beirut 1765, RG 59, Subject Numeric Files 1970–73, POL 13-10 ARAB, Box 2044, NARA; Walker and Gowers, *Arafat*, 89.

32. Buffum to DOS, Untitled Telegram, Beirut 4778, 3 May 1972, RG 59, Subject Numeric Files 1970–73, POL 13-10 ARAB, Box 2044, NARA.

33. "Passengers of Hijacked Boeing Freed in Aden," 22 February 1972, *Times* (London); Dan van der Vat, "How Aden Hijackers Got 2 Million Pounds to Free Jet," 25 February 1972, *Times* (London).

34. Eric Marsden, "Palestine Guerillas Threaten to Blow Up Hijacked Belgian Jet," 9 May 1972, *Times* (London); Moshe Brilliant, "Israelis Kill Hijackers and Release Hostages," 10 May 1972, *Times* (London).

35. "Bayan Munathama 'Aylul al-Aswad Huwal 'Amaliyah Matar al-Lod" [Statement of the Black September Organization on the Status of the Lod Airport Operation], 9 May 1972, *WFA*, 222.

36. "Tasriyah li-Nataq bi-'Ism Munathama 'Aylul al-Aswad Huwal 'Amaliyah Matar al-Lod" [Statement of the Black September Organization on the Status of the Lod Airport Operation], 9 May 1972, *WFA*, 223.

37. "Bayan al-'Ahzab wa al-Qawah al-Wataniyah wa al-Taqadamiyah al-'Arabiyah Huwal 'Amaliyah Matar al-Lod" [Statement of the Arab National and Progressive Parties and Powers on the Lod Airport Operation], 11 May 1972, *WFA*, 224.

38. "Letter Dated 11 May 1972 from the Representative of Israel to the Secretary General," 11 May 1927, UNISPAL, www.unispal.un.org (accessed June 2009).

39. Paul Martin, "Arab Hijack Guerillas Think Again After Failure of Operation Against Airliner in Israel," 10 May 1972, *Times* (London).

40. "Japanese Gunmen Shoot 20 Dead in Suicide Raid at Tel Aviv Airport," 31 May 1972, *Times* (London).

41. "Amaliyah Matar al-Lod" [The Lod Airport Operation], *Al-Hadaf* 3, 154 (3 June 1972), IPS.

42. "Al-Jabhah Al-Sha'abiyah wa 'Amaliyah Matar al-Lod" [The People's Front and the Lod Airport Operation], *Al-Hadaf*, 3, 154 (3 June 1972), IPS.

43. George Habash, "Press Conference Statements by General Secretary Habash of the P.F.L.P. Outlining the Conclusions of the Front's Third National Conference and Discussing the Strategy of 'Revolutionary Violence,'" 14 March 1972, *IDP* 1972, 287.

44. "Risala al-Nidal al-'Amamy fi dur al-Feda'yeen al-Yabaniyeen" [Letter of National Struggle on the Role of the Japanese Fedayeen], *Al-Hadaf* 3, 154 (3 June 1972), IPS.

45. "Kozo Okamoto face à ses juges: La lutte se poursuivra" [Kozo Okamoto Faces His Judges: The Struggle Will Continue], *Fateh Informations* 13–14 (1 August 1972), IPS.

46. DOS Outgoing Telegram, "Attack at Lod Airport," State 96235, 31 May 1972, RG 59, Subject Numeric Files 1970–73, POL 13-10 ARAB, Box 2044, NARA.

47. DOS Outgoing Telegram for Buffum from Acting Secretary, "Attack at Lod Airport," State 95374, RG 59, Subject Numeric Files 1970–73, POL 13-10 ARAB, Box 2044, NARA.

48. Buffum to DOS, "Attack at Lydda Airport," Beirut 5943, 1 June 1972, RG 59, Subject Numeric Files 1970–73, POL 13-10 ARAB, Box 2044, NARA.

49. Buffum to DOS, "Lebanese Action Against Terrorists," Beirut 5873, RG 59, Subject Numeric Files 1970–73, POL 13-10 ARAB, Box 2044, NARA.

50. Irwin, Memorandum for the President, "Implications of Lod Airport Attack," 2 June 1972, RG 59, Subject Numeric Files 1970–73, POL 13-10 ARAB, Box 2044, NARA.

51. Buffum to DOS, "Israeli Attitude Toward Lebanon," Beirut 6045, 3 June 1972, RG 59, Subject Numeric Files 1970–73, POL 23-8 LEB, Box 1565, NARA.

52. Bush to DOS, "Proposal for Combatting International Terrorism," USUN 2090, 5 June 1972, RG 59, Subject Numeric Files 1970–73, POL 13-10 ARAB, Box 2044, NARA.

53. Buffum to DOS, "Reported Internal Strife in Fatah," Beirut 6370, 12 June 1972, RG 59, Subject Numeric Files 1970–73, POL 13-10 ARAB, Box 2044, NARA.

54. Buffum to DOS, "Internal Strife in Fatah," Beirut 6452, 13 June 1972, RG 59, Subject Numeric Files 1970–73, POL 13-10 ARAB, Box 2044, NARA.

55. Buffum to DOS, "GOL-Fedayeen Negotiations," Beirut 7144, 29 June 1972, RG 59, Subject Numeric Files 1970–73, POL 13-10 ARAB, Box 2044, NARA.

56. Shlaim, *Iron Wall*, 309–10. For more on Kissinger's standstill diplomacy, see Chapter 3.

57. Barbour to DOS, "Israeli Attitudes Toward Fedayeen Problem in Lebanon," Tel Aviv 4178, 27 June 1972, RG 59, Subject Numeric Files 1970–73, POL 13-10 ARAB, Box 2044, NARA.

58. Buffum to DOS, Beirut 6827, 22 June 1972, RG 59, Subject Numeric Files 1970–73, POL 27 ARAB-ISR, Box 2059, NARA.

59. Buffum to DOS, "Current Reaction," Beirut 6842, 22 June 1972, RG 59, Subject Numeric Files 1970–73, POL 27, ARAB-ISR, Box 2059, NARA.

60. Barbour to DOS, "Allon Demands Lebanese Action on Terrorists," Tel Aviv 4273, 30 June 1972, RG 59, Subject Numeric Files 1970–73, POL 13-10 ARAB, Box 2044, NARA.

61. Buffum to DOS, "Israeli Attacks on Lebanon," Beirut 6795, 21 June 1972, RG 59, Subject Numeric Files 1970–73, POL 27, ARAB-ISR, Box 2059, NARA.

62. DOS Outgoing Telegram, "Sisco/Kabbani Meeting RE Lebanese-Israeli Border Incidents," State 112742, 22 June 1970, RG 59, Subject Numeric Files 1970–73, POL 27 ARAB-ISR, Box 2059, NARA.

63. See Irwin and Bush, "Middle East in GA—African Group," 9 December 1972, State 221894, RG 59, Subject Numeric Files 1970–73, POL 27 ARAB-ISR, Box 2059, NARA.

64. Dar es Salaam to State, "President's Report on US Policies in Middle East and Africa Scored," Dar es Salaam 0370, 11 Feb 1972, RG 59, Subject Numeric Files 1970–73, POL 27 ARAB-ISR, Box 2059, NARA.

65. Klossen to DOS, "Proposal for Combatting International Terrorism," Moscow 5404, 7 June 1972, RG 59, Subject Numeric Files 1970–73, POL 23-8, LEB, Box 1565, NARA.

66. State Outgoing Telegram, "Foreign Involvement of Fedayeen," State 070888, 25 April 1972, RG 59, Subject Numeric Files 1970–73, POL 13-10 ARAB, Box 2044, NARA.

67. "Editorial Note," *FRUS* 1969–76, Vol. E-1, 91, http://www.state.gov/r/pa/ho/frus/nixon/e1/45434.htm (accessed December 2007).

68. "Conversation Between President Nixon and the President's Assistant for National Security Affairs," 6 September 1972, *FRUS* 1969–76, Vol. E-1, 93, http://www.state.gov/r/pa/ho/frus/nixon/e1/45513.htm (accessed December 2007).

69. "Conversation Among President Nixon, the President's Assistant for National Security Affairs, and White House Chief of Staff," 6 September 1972, *FRUS* 1969–76, Vol. E-1, 95, http://www.state.gov/r/pa/ho/frus/nixon/e1/45516.htm (accessed December 2007).

70. "Memorandum from Samuel M. Hoskinson and Fernando Rondon of the National Security Council Staff to the President's Assistant for National Security Affairs," 6 September 1972, *FRUS*, 1969–76, Vol. E-1, 96, http://www.state.gov/r/pa/ho/frus/nixon/e1/45517.htm (accessed December 2007).

71. Buffum to DOS, "Israeli Raids on Lebanon and Syria," Beirut 9587, 9 September 1972, RG 59, Subject Numeric Files 1970–73, POL 27 ARAB-ISR, Box 2058, NARA.

72. Buffum to DOS, "Israeli Raids on Lebanon and Syria," Beirut 9696, RG 59, Subject Numeric Files 1970–73, POL 27 ARAB-ISR, Box 2058, NARA.

73. INR, Curtis F. Jones, "Israeli Air Attacks on Fedayeen Bases in Syria and Lebanon," RG 59, Subject Numeric Files 1970–73, POL 27 ARAB-ISR, Box 2058, NARA; Saunders to Kissinger, "Israel's New Strategy of Pre-emptive War on the Fedayeen," 16 October 1972, NSC Country Files, Middle East, Box 610.

74. Paul Martin, "Lebanon Ultimatum to Guerillas as Israelis Withdraw," 18 September 1972, *Times* (London); Paul Martin, "Retreating Tanks Leave Trail of Misery," 19 September 1972, *Times* (London).

75. Horan to DOS, "Saudi Reactions to Munich Killings," Jidda 2902, 9 September 1972, RG 59, Subject Numeric Files 1970–73, POL 13-10 ARAB, Box 2043, NARA.

76. Horan to DOS, "Combatting of Terrorism," Jidda 2925, 10 September 1972, RG 59, Subject Numeric Files POL 23-8, Box 1565, NARA.

77. Buffum to DOS, "Current Reaction," Beirut 9643, 11 September 1972, RG 59, Subject Numeric Files 1970–73, POL 27 ARAB-ISR, Box 2058, NARA.

78. Buffum to DOS, "Current Reaction," Beirut 9576, 8 September 1972, RG 59, Subject Numeric Files 1970–73, POL 13-10, Box 2043, NARA.

79. INR-Merrick and Jones, "Syria: New Israeli Reprisal Policy Against Syria May Play into Soviet Hands," 20 September 1972, RG 59, Subject Numeric Files 1970–73, POL 13-10 ARAB, Box 2044, NARA.

80. DOS Outgoing Telegram for USUN, State 164995, 10 September 1972, RG 59, Subject Numeric Files 1970–73, POL 27 ARAB-ISR, Box 2058, NARA.

81. Office of Public Information, United Nations, "Consideration by the Security Council, September 1972," *Yearbook of the United Nations*, 1972, UNISPAL, www.domino.un.org (accessed July 2007).

82. Ibid.

83. Michael Leapman, "Americans Use UN Veto to Support the Israelis," 10 September 1972, *Times* (London).

84. AmEmbassy Tel Aviv to DOS, "Israeli Reaction to US Veto at UN," Tel Aviv 5972, RG 59, Subject Numeric Files 1970–73, POL 27 ARAB-ISR, Box 2058, NARA.

85. Verbatim Record of UN Security Council Debate, 1662th Meeting, 10 September 1972, UNISPAL, www.unispal.un.org (accessed June 2009).

86. Johnson to DOS, "Media Reaction—U.S. SC Veto," Belgrade 4378, RG 59, Subject Numeric Files 1970–73, POL 23-8, Box 1565, NARA.

87. Moore to DOS, "Combatting Terrorism," Khartoum 1220, 13 September 1972, RG 59, Subject Numeric Files 1970–73, POL 23-8, Box 1565, NARA.

88. AmEmbassy Tunis to DOS, "President Bourguiba Asks US Assistance in 'Grave' Middle East Situation," Tunis 4364, 17 September 1972, RG 59, Subject Numeric Files 1970–73, POL 27 ARAB-ISR, Box 2060, NARA.

89. Davis to DOS, "Secretary's Letter to Foreign Minister Regarding Measures Against Terrorism," Algiers 1599, RG 59, Subject Numeric Files 1970–73, POL 23-8, Box 1565, NARA.

90. DOS Outgoing Telegram, "Combating of Terrorism," State 164986, 9 September 1972, RG 59, Subject Numeric Files 1970–73, POL 23-8, Box 1565, NARA.

91. Annenberg to DOS, "Combating Terrorism," London 8504, 11 September 1972, RG 59, Subject Numeric Files 1970–73, POL 23-8, Box 1565, NARA.

92. Hanson to DOS, "Secretary's Letter to Foreign Minister on Consultation Regarding International Measures Against Terrorism," Accra 4754, 12 September 1972, RG 59, Subject Numeric Files 1970–73, POL 23-8, Box 1565, NARA.

93. AmEmbassy Pretoria to DOS, "Secretary's Letter to Foreign Minister on Consultation Regarding International Measures Against Terrorism," Pretoria 2939, 13 September 1972, RG 59, Subject Numeric Files 1970–73, POL 23-8, Box 1565, NARA.

94. Bush to DOS, "SYG's Initiative on Terrorism," USUN 3274, 15 September 1972, RG 59, Subject Numeric Files 1970–73, POL 23-8, Box 1565, NARA.

95. Bush to DOS, "SYG's Initiative on Terrorism," USUN 3340, 19 September 1972, RG 59, Subject Numeric Files 1970–73, POL 23-8, Box 1565, NARA.

96. Watson to DOS, "Israeli Reprisals and French Policy," Paris 17690, 20 September 1972, RG 59, Subject Numeric Files 1970–73, 1970–73, POL 27 ARAB-ISR, Box 2058, NARA.

97. DOS Outgoing Telegram, "French Briefed on Middle East," State 174648, 25 September 1972, RG 59, Subject Numeric Files 1970–73, POL 27 ARAB-ISR, Box 2058, NARA.

98. Bush to DOS, "Indications of Opposition to SYG's Initiative on Terrorism," USUN 3356, 20 September 1972, RG 59, Subject Numeric Files 1970–73, POL 23-8, Box 1565, NARA.

99. DOS Outgoing Telegram, "Terrorism Item in UN General Assembly," USUN 174105, 22 September 1972, RG 59, Subject Numeric Files 1970–73, POL 23-8, Box 1565, NARA.

100. Ibid.

101. DOS Outgoing Telegram, "Terrorism in UNGA," State 174387, 23 September 1972, RG 59, Subject Numeric Files 1970–73, POL 23-8, Box 1565, NARA.

102. DOS Outgoing Telegram, "UNGA—US Draft Convention on Terrorism," 25 September 1972, RG 59, Subject Numeric Files 1970–73, POL 23-8, Box 1565, NARA.

103. DOS Outgoing Telegram, "Partial Excerpt from Department Spokesman's Press Briefing," 22 September 1972, State 173851, RG 59, Subject Numeric Files 1970–73, POL 23-8, Box 1565, NARA.

104. Tasca to DOS, "GOG Meetings with Lebanese Ambassador and Israeli Diplomatic Representative," 27 September 1976, RG 59, Subject Numeric Files 1970–73, POL 23-8, Box 1565, NARA.

105. Ibid.

106. "Press Interview Statement by Foreign Minister Eban of Israel Outlining the Limitations to the Palestinians' Right to Self-Determination," 22 September 1972, *IDP* 1972, 234; "Statements by Foreign Minister Eban of Israel Surveying the Middle East Situation, Rejecting the Need for a New Palestinian State, and Describing the Conditions of the Palestinians Under Israeli Rule, Made in a Speech to the U.N. General Assembly," 28 September 1972, *IDP* 1972, 237–40.

107. Cobban, *The Palestinian Liberation Organization*, 55; Sayigh, *Armed Struggle*, 310; Hart, *Arafat*, 349.

108. "Bayan al-Duktur George Habash, al-Amin al-'Am al-Jabhah al-Sha'abiya l-Tahriah Filastin, Huwal al'M'uatamar al-Watan al-Thalath li-l Jabhah," 14 March 1972, *WFA*, 111–12; Cobban, *The Palestinian Liberation Organization*, 148; see also *IDP* 1972, 288.

109. Cobban, *The Palestinian Liberation Organization*, 148, 55.

Chapter 6: "The Torch Has Been Passed from Vietnam to Us"

1. "Hadith Sahafi khas Sayyid Yasir Arafat, Rayiss al-Lajanah al-Tanafithiyah al-Munathamah al-Tahrir al-Filastiniyah Huwal Qadaya al-Sa'ah," 28 November 1973, *WFA*, 473; Craig R. Whitney, "East Berlin Festival Week Ends," *New York Times*, 6 August 1973.

2. "Yasser Arafat in Berlin," *Journal of Palestine Studies* 3, 1 (Autumn 1973): 166–68.

3. Cobban, *The Palestinian Liberation Organization*, 223.

4. Dannreuther, *The Soviet Union and the PLO*, 51; "Tasriyah al-Sayid Kamal Nasir, al-Nataq al-Rasmiy bi-Ism Manathamah al-Tahrir al-Filastiniyah, Huwal Safir Wafd Yamithal al-Munathmah ila al-Itihad al-Sofiyatiy," 17 July 1972, *WFA*, 337.

5. Cobban, *The Palestinian Liberation Organization*, 224.

6. "Press Interview Statements by President Bourguiba of Tunisia Defending His Call for Israel to Withdraw to the Borders of the 1947 UN Partition Plan," 28 June 1973, *IDP* 1973, 450; Gresh, *The PLO*, 121.

7. Gresh, *The PLO*, 122–23.

8. "Hadith Sahafi Khas li-l Sayyid Yasir Arafat, Rayiss al-Lajanah al-Tanafithiyah al-Munathamah al-Tahrir al-Filastiniyah, Huwal 'al-Dawalah al-Filastiniyah,'" 29 June 1973, *WFA*, 203–4; Gresh, *The PLO*, 125–26.

9. Eban to Rogers, "Eban Letter to Secretary RE Terrorism Item in the UNGA," State 212279, 22 November 1972, RG 59, Subject Numeric Files 1970–73, POL 23-8, Box 1566, NARA.

10. DOS Outgoing Telegram, "Eban's Letter to Secretary RE Terrorism Item in UNGA," State 212685, 22 November 1972, RG 59, Subject Numeric Files 1970–73, POL 23-8, Box 1566, NARA.

11. DOS Outgoing Telegram, "UNGA Item of Terrorism," State 213790, 24 November 1972, RG 59, Subject Numeric Files 1970–73, POL 23-8, Box 1566, NARA.

12. Phillips to DOS, "Legal Comite [*sic*]: Terrorism General Debate Concludes: Reses Submitted," USUN 5028, 27 November 1972, RG 59, Subject Numeric Files 1970–73, POL 23-8, Box 1566, NARA.

13. Bush to DOS, "Legal Committee Terrorism," USUN 5086, 28 November 1972, RG 59, Subject Numeric Files 1970–73, POL 23-8, Box 1566, NARA.

14. Galbraith to DOS, "Terrorism in UNGA Legal Committee," Jakarta 12726, 11 December 1972, RG 59, Subject Numeric Files 1970–73, POL 23-8, Box 1987, NARA.

15. DOS Outgoing Telegram, "Terrorism Item in UNGA," State 227594, 16 December 1972, RG 59, Subject Numeric Files 1970–73, POL 23-8, Box 1987, NARA.

16. "Resolution 3034: Measures to Prevent International Terrorism," UN General Assembly, Resolution 3034, 18 December 1972, UNISPAL, www.unispal.org.

17. Bush to DOS, "Terrorism," USUN 5526, 13 December 1972, *FRUS* 1969–76, vol. E-1, 119, http://www.state.gov/r/pa/ho/frus/nixon/e1/45565.htm (accessed February 2007).

18. "Measures to Prevent International Terrorism," Official Records, 2114th Plenary Meeting, United Nations General Assembly, Twenty-Seventh Session, 18 December 1972, 20–32.

19. Ibid.

20. Ibid.

21. Bush to DOS, "Legal Committee—Terrorism Item," USUN 5582, 15 December 1972, *FRUS* 1969–76, vol. E-1, 120, www.state.gov/r/pa/ho/frus/nixon/e1/45566.htm (accessed February 2007).

22. INR, Perenyi, "External Research Study: State Department Conference on Terrorism," 29 December 1972, RG 59, Subject Numeric Files 1970–73, POL 23-8, Box 1987, NARA.

23. Barbour to DOS, "Israeli War on Terrorism," Tel Aviv 8366, 22 December 1972, RG 59, Subject Numeric Files 1970–73, POL 23-8, Box 1987, NARA.

24. Buffum to DOS, "Continuing Signs of Fedayeen Disarray," Beirut 13230, 7 December 1972, RG 59, Subject Numeric Files 1970–73, POL 13-10 ARAB, Box 2045, NARA.

25. DOS Memcon with Walid Khalidi, "Palestine and U.S. Policy Toward the Middle East," 20 November 1972, RG 59, Subject Numeric Files 1970–73, POL 27 ARAB-ISR, Box 2060, NARA.

26. Franklin to Rogers, "The Middle East Problem," 11 January 1973, RG 59, Subject Numeric Files 1970–73, POL 27 ARAB-ISR, Box 2060, NARA.

27. Ibid.

28. Buffum to DOS, "The Eleventh Palestine National Council—Elusive Unity," 24 January 1973, RG 59, Subject Numeric Files 1970–73, POL 13-10 ARAB, Box 2045, NARA.

29. "Muqararat al-Durah al-Hadyat 'Asharah lil-Majlas al-Watani al-Filastini," 2–16 January 1973, *WFA*, 13.

30. See, for instance, PFLP, *Military Strategy of the PFLP* (Beirut: Popular Front for the Liberation of Palestine, Information Department, 1970); INR, Jones, "Fedayeen: How Long Can a Symbolic Revolution Survive?" 26 January 1973, RG 59, Subject Numeric Files 1970–73, POL 13-10 ARAB, Box 2045, NARA.

31. Lowrie to DOS, "Visit of Yasser Arafat to Iraq," Baghdad 46, 5 February 1973, RG 59, Subject Numeric Files 1970–73, POL 13-10 ARAB, Box 2045, NARA.

32. "Bayan al-Lajanah al-Tanafithiyah al-Munathamah al-Tahrir al-Filastiniya bi-Munasibah Tawqiy'a 'Atafaq al-Salam fi Fiyatnam," 25 January 1973, *WFA*, 25; "Harb al-Sha'ab: Antasarat fi Fiyatnam…wa Satanasasar fi Filastine," *Filastine al-Thawra*, 31 January 1973, IPS.

33. Dayan, *Moshe Dayan*, 316.

34. "Hadith Sahafy Khas al-Sayid 'Abu Iyad' 'Ahad Qadah Harikah al-Tahrir al-Watany al-Filastiyny 'Fatah' wa al'Sayid 'Abu Yusuf' R'ayis Wafd Munathamah al-Tahrir al-Watany al-Filastiyny ila 'Ijtima'a Majslas Wazira'a al-Dafa'a al-'Arab," 1 February 1973, *WFA*, 32; Buffum to DOS, "Interview with Fatah's Abu Iyad," Beirut 1258, 11 February 1973, RG 59, Subject Numeric Files 1970–73, POL 13-10 ARAB, Box 2045, NARA.

35. "Backdown in Bangkok," *Time*, 8 January 1973, www.time.com (accessed February 2008).

36. DOS Outgoing Telegram, State 032680, 21 February 1973, RG 59, Subject Numeric Files 1970–73, POL 27 ARAB-ISR, Box 2061, NARA.

37. Scali to DOS, "Libyan Aircraft," USUN 571, 21 February 1973, RG 59, Subject Numeric Files 1970–73, POL 27 ARAB-ISR, Box 2061, NARA.

38. Kubisch to DOS, "Israeli Attacks on Libyan Airliner and Lebanese Bases," Paris 4339, 22 February 1973, RG 59, Subject Numeric Files 1970–73, POL 27 ARAB-ISR, Box 2061, NARA.

39. "Death in the Desert," *Time*, 5 March 1973, www.time.com (accessed August 2008).

40. Zurhellen to DOS, "Further Reaction to Downing of Libyan Plane," Tel Aviv 1469, 23 February 1973, RG 59, Subject Numeric Files 1970–73, POL 27 ARAB-ISR, Box 2061, NARA.

41. Zurhellen to DOS, "Libyan Plane: Israel's Public Defense and Private Doubts," Tel Aviv 1461, 23 February 1973, RG 59, Subject Numeric Files 1970–73, POL 27 ARAB-ISR, Box 2061, NARA.

42. AmEmbassy Tel Aviv to DOS, "Israeli Reaction to Libyan Plane Disaster Softens," Tel Aviv 1511, 26 February 1973, RG 59, Subject Numeric Files 1970–73, POL 27 ARAB-ISR, Box 2061, NARA.

43. "The Killers of Khartoum," *Time*, 12 March 1973, www.time.com (accessed 10/2011)

44. DOS Outgoing Telegram, " Terrorist Attack at Saudi Arabian Embassy Khartoum Involving U.S. Ambassador," State 03851, 2 March 1973, RG 59, Subject Numeric Files 1970–73, POL 13-10, Box 2045, NARA; Korn, *Assassination in Khartoum*, 202.

45. "The Killers of Khartoum," *Time*, 12 March 1973, www.time.com (accessed October 2011).

46. Buffum to DOS, "Current Reaction," Beirut 2492, 3 March 1973, RG 59, Subject Numeric Files 1970–73, POL 13-10, Box 2045, NARA.

47. Greene to DOS, "Terrorist Attack at Saudi Arabian Embassy Khartoum Involving US Ambassador," Cairo 0656, 3 March 1973, RG 59, Subject Numeric Files 1970–73, POL 13-10, Box 2045, NARA.

48. Greene to DOS, "March 4 Egyptian Press Reaction to Khartoum Killings," Cairo 0658, 4 March 1973, RG 59, Subject Numeric Files 1970–73, POL 13-10, Box 2045, NARA.

49. Eagleton to DOS, "Algerian Reaction to Khartoum Murders," Algiers 0520, 5 March 1973, RG 59, Subject Numeric Files 1970–73, POL 13-10, Box 2045, NARA.

50. Griffin to DOS, "Terrorist Attack at Saudi Arabian Embassy," Abu Dhabi 0317, 6 March 1973, RG 59, Subject Numeric Files 1970–73, POL 13-10, Box 2045, NARA.

51. Dubs to DOS, "Moscow Says BSO Terrorism Harms Palestinian Cause," Moscow 2395, 5 March 1973, RG 59, Subject Numeric Files 1970–73, POL 13-10, Box 2045, NARA.

52. Toon to DOS, "Media Reaction to Report: Khartoum Assassinations," Belgrade 0932, 6 March 1973, RG 59, Subject Numeric Files 1970–73, POL 13-10, Box 2045, NARA.

53. Buffum to DOS, "Arab Governments Support for Black September Organization," Beirut 2738, 9 March 1973, RG 59, Subject Numeric Files 1970–73, POL 13-10, Box 2045, NARA; Rogers to DOS, "Terrorist Leaders in Lebanon," State 041440, 7 March 1973, RG 59, Subject Numeric Files 1970–73, POL 13-10, Box 2045, NARA.

54. See DOS Memcon with Sisco and Naffa, "Khartoum Slayings of American Diplomats," 6 March 1973, RG 59, Subject Numeric Files 1970–73, POL 13-10, Box 2045, NARA.

55. See Walker and Gowers, *Arafat*, 96–97.

56. Ibid., 98–101; Cobban, *The Palestinian Liberation Organization*, 55.

57. DOS Memcon with Sisco and Naffa, "Khartoum Slayings of American Diplomats, 6 March 1973, RG 59, Subject Numeric Files 1970–73, POL 13-10, Box 2045, NARA.

58. DOS Outgoing Telegram, "Arab Governments Support for Black September Organization," 8 March 1973, RG 59, Subject Numeric Files 1970–73, POL 13-10, Box 2045, NARA.

59. Seelye to DOS, "Meeting with President Bourguiba: Black September Organization," Tunis 1276, 10 March 1973, RG 59, Subject Numeric Files 1970–73, POL 13-10, Box 2046, NARA.

60. Buffum to DOS, "Arab Government Support for Black September Organization," Beirut 2967, 14 March 1973, RG 59, Subject Numeric Files 1970–73, POL 13-10, Box 2046, NARA.

61. Seelye to DOS, "Meeting with President Bourguiba: Black September Organization," Tunis 1276, 10 March 1973, RG 59, Subject Numeric Files 1970–73, POL 13-10, Box 2046, NARA.

62. Seelye to DOS, "Khartoum Murders: Call on Chatti," Tunis 1372, 15 March 1973, RG 59, Subject Numeric Files 1970–73, POL 13-10, Box 2046, NARA.

63. Zurhellen to DOS, "Campaign Against Terrorism," Tel Aviv 2294, 23 March 1973, RG 59, Subject Numeric Files 1970–73, POL 23-8, Box 1987, NARA.

64. Ibid.

65. Ibid.

66. Fritts to DOS, "Soviet Ambassador's Views on BSO Terrorism," Khartoum 0647, 24 March 1973, RG 59, Subject Numeric Files 1970–73, POL 13-10 ARAB, Box 2046, NARA.

67. Klein to DOS, "GDR Reaction to Khartoum Murders," Berlin 0430, 9 March 1973, RG 59, Subject Numeric Files 1970–73, POL 13-10 ARAB, Box 2046, NARA.

68. Stoltzeus to DOS, "Arab Government Support for Black September Organization," Kuwait 0777, 12 March 1973, RG 59, Subject Numeric Files 1970–73, POL 13-10 ARAB, Box 2046, NARA.

69. Stoltzeus to DOS, "Arab Government Support for Black September Organization," Kuwait 0801, 14 March 1973, RG 59, Subject Numeric Files 1970–73, POL 13-10 ARAB, Box 2046, NARA.

70. Kubisch to DOS, "Terrorist Problem and Means to Combat It," Paris 6514, 15 March 1973, RG 59, Subject Numeric Files 1970–73, POL 13-10 ARAB, Box 2046, NARA.

71. Irwin to DOS, "Arab Government Support for BSO," Paris 7209, 22 March 1973, RG 59, Subject Numeric Files 1970–73, POL 13-10 ARAB, Box 2046, NARA.

72. He also argued that Yasir Arafat was involved not in planning but in the execution at Khartoum. Buffum to DOS, "PLO Role in Surrender of Khartoum Terrorists," State 045570, 13 March 1973, AAD.

73. Carter to DOS, "Reaction in Tanzania to Black September Slayings," 16 March 1973, RG 59, Subject Numeric Files 1970–73, POL 13-10 ARAB, Box 2046, NARA.

74. Cunningham to DOS, "Khartoum Events and Africa," Abidjan 1664, 12 March 1973, RG 59, Subject Numeric Files 1970–73, POL 13-10 ARAB, Box 2046, NARA.

75. Hillenbrand to DOS, "Arab Governments' Support for Black September and other Terrorist Organizations," Bonn 3922, 16 March 1973, RG 59, Subject Numeric Files 1970–73, POL 13-10 ARAB, Box 2046, NARA.

76. DOS Circular, "Arab Government Support for Black September Organization," State 051645, 20 March 1973, RG 59, Subject Numeric Files 1970–73, POL 13-10 ARAB, Box 2046, NARA.

77. Rogers quoting Crawford, "Campaign Against Terrorism," Sanaa 488, 28 March 1973, RG 59, Subject Numeric Files 1970–73, POL 23-8, Box 1987, NARA.

78. Ibid.

79. Parker to DOS, "Combatting Palestinian Terrorism," Rabat 01390, 29 March 1973, RG 59, Subject Numeric Files 1970–73, POL 13-10, Box 2046, NARA.

80. Buffum to DOS, "Closer Cooperation Between Fatah and PFLP," Beirut 3660, 30 March 1973, RG 59, Subject Numeric Files 1970–73, POL 13-10, Box 2046, NARA.

81. Zurhellen to DOS, "Campaign Against Terrorism," Tel Aviv 2294, 23 March 1973, RG 59, Subject Numeric Files 1970–73, POL 23-8, Box 1987, NARA.

82. Phillips to DOS, "Campaign Against Terrorism," USUN 1022, 23 March 1973, RG 59, Subject Numeric Files 1970–73, POL 23-8, Box 1987, NARA.

83. Buffum to DOS, "Arab Governments Support for Black September Organization," Beirut 2831, 12 March 1973, RG 59, Subject Numeric Files 1970–73, POL 13-10, Box 2046, NARA.

84. Volpe to DOS, "Arab Governments Support for Black September Organization: Possible EC Support for US Demarches: Suggested Direct Demarches to European Govts," Rome 1930, 12 March 1973, RG 59, Subject Numeric Files 1970–73, POL 13-10, Box 2046, NARA.

85. U.S. Embassy Amman to DOS, "How to Fight Fedayeen Terror," Amman 1339, 14 March 1973, RG 59, Subject Numeric Files 1970–73, POL 13-10, Box 2046, NARA.

86. Buffum to DOS, "How to Fight Fedayeen Terror," Beirut 2983, 15 March 1973, RG 59, Subject Numeric Files 1970–73, POL 13-10, Box 2046, NARA.

87. Ross, Sisco, and Meyer to Rogers, "Possible Actions Against Arab Governments for Continued Support of Black September Organization (BSO)," 16 March 1973, RG 59, Subject Numeric Files 1970–73, POL 13-10, Box 2046, NARA.

88. Ibid.

89. Stoltzeus to DOS, "How to Fight Fedayeen Terror," Kuwait 0810, 17 March 1973, RG 59, Subject Numeric Files 1970–73, POL 13-10, Box 2046, NARA.

90. Sisco, "Memorandum for the President," 11 April 1973, RG 59, Subject Numeric Files 1970–73, POL 13-10, Box 2047, NARA.

91. Buffum to DOS, "Analysis of Black September Operational Planning and Preparation," Beirut 3778, 3 April 1973, RG 59, Subject Numeric Files 1970–73, POL 13-10, Box 2046, NARA.

92. Ibid.

93. INR, Curtis F. Jones, "Middle East: The Evolution of Fedayeen Strategy," 5 April 1973, RG 59, Subject Numeric Files 1970–73, POL 13-10 ARAB, Box 2044, NARA.

94. Ibid.

95. Buffum to DOS, "Fedayeen Dilemma Continues," Beirut 4094, 9 April 1973, RG 59, Subject Numeric Files 1970–73, POL 13-10, Box 2046, NARA.

96. Hillenbrand to DOS, "Combating International Terrorism," Bonn 05283, 10 April 1973, RG 59, Subject Numeric Files 1970–73, POL 23-8, Box 1987, NARA.

97. "Terror to End Terror?" *Time*, 23 April 1973, www.time.com (accessed August 2008).

98. "Bayan al-Jabhah al-Tanfithyah al-Munthamah al-Tahrir al-Filastiniyyah Huwal 'Istashhad al-Munadaleen Yusuf al-Najar wa-Kamal Nasir wa-Kamal Adwan" [Statement of the PLO Executive Committee on the Assassination of Fighters Yusuf al-Najar, Kamal Nasir, and Kamal Adwan], 10 April 1973, *WFA*, 101; Ghorra to UN Security Council, Letter, 11 April 1973, UNISPAL, www.unispal.org; Buffum to DOS, "Fedayeen Reaction to Israeli Raid," Beirut 4172, 10 April 1973, AAD.

99. DOS Outgoing Telegram, "Israeli Raid on Beirut," State 06673, 10 April 1973, RG 59, Subject Numeric Files 1970–73, POL 27 ARAB-ISR, Box 2061, NARA.

100. Ibid.

101. Brown to DOS, "First Reactions to Israeli Beirut Raid," Amman 1922, 10 April 1973, RG 59, Subject Numeric Files 1970–73, POL 27 ARAB-ISR, Box 2061, NARA.

102. Rogers, "Memorandum for the President: Actions to Encourage Lebanon to Move Against Black September and Other Terrorist Groups," 11 April 1973, RG 59, Subject Numeric Files 1970–73, POL 13-10 ARAB, Box 2044, NARA.

103. Ibid.

104. "Bayan al-Qaydah al-'Amah li-Quwat al-Thawrah al-Filastiniyah Huwal Istashad Thalathah min Qadah Harikah al-Muqawamah al-Filastinyah fi Agarah Isra'ylyah ala Bayrut," 10 April 1973, *WFA*, 102; Day to DOS, "West Bank Reaction to Beirut Raid," Jerusalem 377, 11 April 1973, RG 59, Subject Numeric Files 1970–73, POL 27 ARAB-ISR, Box 2061, NARA.

105. Sayigh, *Armed Struggle*, 311.

106. Scali, "Department Press Briefing (Fedayeen Broadcast)," USUN 1366, 11 April 1973, AAD.

107. "War of Words," *Time*, 30 April 1973, www.time.com (August 2008).

108. Zurhellen to DOS, "Israeli Position on UNSC Debate," Tel Aviv 3026, 17 April 1973, AAD; Kissinger and Scali, Telecon, UN Proposal on Israel and Lebanon, 19 April 1973, Kissinger Telephone Conversations, Digital National Security Archive.

109. Zurhellen to DOS, "Eban on Occupied Territories and Jordan," Tel Aviv 3024, 16 April 1973, AAD.

110. Zurhellen to DOS, "Continued Israeli Ferment After Libyan Plane Tragedy," 31 March 1973, RG 59, Subject Numeric Files 1970–73, POL 27 ARAB-ISR, Box 2061, NARA.

111. George Jonas's *Vengeance*, which formed the basis for Stephen Spielberg's film *Munich* (2005), is based on a series of interviews conducted by the author with a man who claimed to be the leader of one of the Mossad's hit squads. The work is highly detailed, although politically charged, sensationalistic, and somewhat questionable due to the nature of unverifiable sources. Simon Reeve's *One Day in September* is a more sober journalistic account of the massacre and the Israel counterterrorist campaign in Europe.

112. Walker and Gowers, *Arafat*, 95, 129–30; "Deadly Battle of the Spooks," *Time*, 12 February 1973, www.time.com (accessed August 2008).

113. Black and Morris, *Israel's Secret Wars*, 263, 266–68, 273.

114. Ibid.

115. "Fatal Error," *Time*, 6 August 1973, www.time.com (accessed August 2008).

116. Buffum to DOS, "Alleged Israeli Terrorism," Beirut 9033, 1 August 1973, AAD.

117. Black and Morris, *Israel's Secret Wars*, 274, 276–77.

118. Statement by General Sharon of Israel expressing confidence in ISral's military strength," 25 July 1973, *IDP* 1973, 264.

119. "Press Conference Statement by US Secretary of State Kissinger Surveying Events Since the Outbreak of the War," 25 October 1973, *IDP* 1973, 333.

120. Buffum to DOS, "Lebanese Complaints to SC," Beirut 4373, 13 April 1973, AAD.

121. Walker and Gowers, *Arafat*, 95.

122. Porter, "Frangie on Fedayeen," State 75810, 21 April 1973, RG 59, Subject Numeric Files 1970–73, POL 13-10 ARAB, Box 2047, NARA.

123. Houghton to DOS, "Internal Security Developments in Lebanon," Beirut 4974, 30 April 1973, RG 59, Subject Numeric Files 1970–73, POL 13-10 ARAB, Box 2047, NARA.

124. "Bayan al-Lajanah al-Tanfithiyah li-l Munathamah al-Tahrir al-Filastiniyah Huwal al-Huwadath al-Jariyah fi Lubnan," 5 May 1973, *WFA*, 137.

125. Houghton to DOS, "Internal Security—Sitrep 3," Beirut 5047, 3 May 1973, RG 59, Subject Numeric Files 1970–73, POL 13-10 ARAB, Box 2047, NARA; Houghton to DOS, "Internal Security—Sitrep 2," Beirut 5021, 21 May 1973, RG 59, Subject Numeric Files 1970–73, POL 13-10 ARAB, Box 2047, NARA; Houghton to DOS, "Internal Security Developments in Lebanon," Beirut 4999, 20 May 1973, RG 59, Subject Numeric Files 1970–73, POL 13-10 ARAB, Box 2047, NARA.

126. Houghton to DOS, "GOL Attitude RE Lebanon," Beirut 5154, 7 May 1973, RG 59, Subject Numeric Files 1970–73, POL 13-10 ARAB, Box 2047, NARA.

127. Houghton to DOS, "Dayan Statement on Situation in Lebanon," Beirut 5379, 14 May 1973, AAD.

128. Brown, "Jordanian Views on Situation in Lebanon," Amman 2490, 8 May 1973, AAD.

129. Stoltzeus to DOS, "GOL Request for Assistance," Kuwait 1708, 21 May 1973, RG 59, Subject Numeric Files 1970–73, POL 23-8 LEB, Box 2447, NARA.

130. Maoz, *Defending the Holy Land*, 250.

131. Brown to DOS, "GOL Request for Assistance," Amman 2670, 18 May 1973, RG 59, Subject Numeric Files 1970–73, POL 23-8 LEB, Box 2447, NARA.

132. Ibid.

133. Houghton to DOS, "Situation in Lebanon," Beirut 7023, 14 June 1973, RG 59, Subject Numeric Files 1970–73, POL 13-10 ARAB, Box 2047, NARA.

134. Helms to DOS, "Former Lebanese President Doubts Lebanon Could Survive a Real Confrontation with Fedayeen," Tehran 3746, 30 May 1973, AAD.

135. "Ayar al-Aswad: Haqa'iq Hammah wa Durus Mafidah," *Al-Hadaf* 204 (2 June 1973); Houghton to DOS, "GOL-Fedayeen Relations," 20 June 1973, RG 59, Subject Numeric Files 1970–73, POL 13-10 ARAB, Box 2047, NARA.

Chapter 7: The Diplomatic Struggle

1. Arafat's Speech to the United Nations General Assembly, Agenda Item 108, "Question of Palestine," 13 November 1974, http://domino.un.org/unispal.nsf (accessed January 2007).

2. Lesch, *The Arab-Israeli Conflict*, 247–51.

3. "Statement by the PLO Executive Committee Stressing the Lack of Relevance of the UN Ceasefire Resolutions to the Palestine Revolution," 22 October 1973, *IDP* 1973, 305.

4. Buffum to DOS, "Further Leftist and Fedayeen Reaction to ME Cease-Fire," Beirut 12415, 24 October 1973, AAD.

5. Cobban, *The Palestinian Liberation Organization*, 56–58.

6. Dannreuther, *The Soviet Union and the PLO*, 50–52.

7. Ibid., 53.

8. Sayigh, *Armed Struggle*, 342.

9. Dannreuther, *The Soviet Union and the PLO*, 53–54.

10. Henceforth, this international movement for a comprehensive peace conference that would include the major belligerents in the Arab-Israeli conflict, the United States, Soviet Union, and the United Nations, will be referred to as the Geneva conference.

11. "Hatab al-'Arsh al-lathi 'Alaqaha al-Malik Husayn fi Afattaha al-Dura al-'Aadiya al-Saba'ah li-Majlas al-'Ama al-Urduni al-Tis'a," 2 December 1972, *WFA*, 489.

12. Day to DOS, "West Bank Attitudes on Palestinian Questions," Jerusalem 1516, 19 December 1973, AAD.

13. "Bayan al-Jabhah al-Wataniyah al-Filastiniyah fi al-'Ard al-Muhatalah huwal al-Tadamin fi Atar Munathamah al-Tahrir al-Filastiniyah wa al'Afadah min Nata'aj Harb Tishrin al-'Awal," 21 December 1973, *WFA*, 536; Houghton to DOS, " 'Notables' in Occupied Territories Again Urge PLO Attendance at Geneva Conference," Beirut 0739 18 January 1974, AAD. The Palestinian National Front was a popular organization created by the PNC which was intended to represent the population of the West Bank. For more on the National Front, see Tessler, *A History of the Israeli-Palestinian Confict*, 490, and Walker and Gowers, *Arafat*, 150.

14. "Barnamaj al-Jabhah al-Wataniyah al-Filastiniyah fi al-Watan al-Muhatalah," 15 August 1973, *WFA*, 252–53; Gresh, *The PLO*, 90, 133–35.

15. "Bayan al-Jabhah al-Wataniyah al-Filastiniyah fi al-Watan al-Muhatalah Huwal al-Tadamin fi al-Tar Munathamah al-Tahrir al-Filastiniyah wa al-Afadah min Nata'j Harb Tishrin al-Awal," 21 December 1973, *WFA*,539 ; "Letter to the Executive Committee of the Palestine Liberation Organization from the Palestinian National Front in the Occupied Territory," 1 December 1973, *Journal of Palestine Studies* 3, 3 (Spring 1974): 187–89; Gresh, *The PLO*, 134–36.

16. Cobban, *The Palestinian Liberation Organization*, 155; Gresh, *The PLO*, 138–39; Hadith al-Sayid Nayaf Hawatmeh, al-'Amin al-'Aam li-l Jabhah al-Shabiyah al-Dimaqratiyah al-Tahrir Filastin, Huwal Mus'alah 'al-Mahal al-Amriki-Isra'ili-al-Hashami,' " 6 December 1973, *WFA*, 507.

17. Buffum to DOS, "Fedayeen Political Activity in Wake of ME Cease-Fire," Beirut 12586, 31 October 1973, AAD.

18. "Muthakarah al-Jabhah al-Sha'abiyah li-Tahriry Filastin ila al-Lajanah al-Tanfithi-yah li-Munathmah al-Tahrir al-Filastiniyah huwal Muqafha min Mu'utmar al-Salam," 17 November 1973, *WFA*, 445.

19. Gresh, *The PLO*, 157; Press interview statement by PLO Executive Committee Chairman Arafat on USSR-Palestinian relations, the October War and its aftermath and negotiation possibilities," 28 November 1973, *IDP* 1973, 520–21; "Hadith Sahafi khas Sayyid Yasir Arafat, Rayiss al-Lajanah al-Tanafithiyah al-Munathamah al-Tahrir al-Filastiniyah Huwal Qadaya al-Sa'ah," 28 November 1973, *WFA*, 472; "Press interview statements by Fatah Central Committee member Khalaf (Abu Ayyad) commenting on the status of the Palestine revolution in Arab countries," Late August, 1974, *IDP* 1973, 484.

20. Cobban, *The Palestinian Liberation Organization*, 60–62.

21. Hart, *Arafat*, 383; Gresh, *The PLO*, 142–43; "Kalima al-Ikh 'Abu Salah' 'Adu al-Lajinah al-Mirkazia al-Harika al-Tahrir al-Watan al-Filastiniya 'Fatah' huwal Musa'la tumithiyl al-Sha'b al-Filastiniya, Waqama Sulta Wataniya Mistaqala," 7 January 1974, *WFA*, 5–6.

22. Said Hammami, "Article by the PLO's London Representative Hammami Suggesting Principles for Palestinian Participation in a Middle East Peace Conference," 16 November 1973, *IDP* 1973, 517–19; Hammami, "Making the First Move Towards Peace in Palestine," *Times* 17 Dec 1973; Gresh, *The PLO*, 144–46; Hart, *Arafat*, 392.

23. Ibid., 146–47.

24. Ibid., 147–48; "Mathakarah al-Jabhah al-Sha'abiyah al-Tahrir Filastin 'ila al-Lajanah al-Tanafithiyah al-Munathamah al-Tahrir al-Filastiniyah Huwal Muawafaha min M'uatamar al-Salam," 17 November 1973, *WFA*, 445–47.

25. Buffum to DOS, "Meeting Between Palestinian Leaders and Lebanese Foreign Ministry Secretary General Sadaqa," Beirut 13250, 16 November 1973, AAD.

26. "Hadith Sahafy Khas li-l Sayid Yasir Arafat, Ra'yes al-Lajanah al-Tanfithiyah al-Munathamah al-Tahrir al-Filastiniyah, huwal Qadaya al-Sa'ah," 28 November 1973, *WFA*, 383.

27. Quandt, "The Palestinian Issue in Arab-Israeli Negotiations," 23 November 1973, NSC Files, Saunders Files, Box 1178, NPMP.

28. Kissinger, *Years of Upheaval*, 627–29, Walker and Gowers, *Arafat*, 142.

29. Dinitz, Shalev, Scowcroft, and Rodman, Memorandum of Conversation, 26 November 1973, RG 59, Subject Numeric Files 1970–73, POL 13–10 ARAB, Box 2047, NARA.

30. Kissinger, *Years of Upheaval*, 352–53.

31. Ibid., 629.

32. Walker and Gowers, *Arafat*, 117; interview with Talcott Seelye, 15 September 1993, ADST.

33. Kissinger to Moscow, "INR Assessment of the Soviet Position on a Palestine Entity," State 229187, 20, November 1973, AAD.

34. "Message from President Podgorny and Prime Minister Kosygin of the USSR to the Arab Summit Conference in Algiers," 26 November 1973, *IDP* 1973, 203; Bassin to Secstate,

"Vinogradov on Need for Momentum at Geneva," 24 January 1974, NSC Files, Saunders Files, Box 1181, NPMP.

35. "The Algiers Summit Conference," *MERIP Reports* 23 (December 1973): 13–16.

36. "Hadith Sahafiy Khas li-Sayid Yasir 'Arafat, Ra'yees al-Lajnah al-Tanfiythyah al-Munathama al-Tahrir al-Filastiniyyah Huwal Qadiya Al-Sa'ah" [Press Statements by Mr. Yasir Arafat, President of the PLO Executive Committee, on the Current Affairs], 28 November 1973, *WFA*, 383.

37. "Khatab al-Sayid 'Abu Iyad,' Ahad Qadah Harikah al-Tahrir al-Watany al-Filastiny 'Fatah,' huwal Muwaquf al-Thawrah al-Filastiniyah min al-Qadaya al-Rahanah" [Speech by Fatah Central Committee Member Khalaf (Abu Iyad) Calling for Unity Among All Arab Quarters in Support of the Non-negotiable Rights of the Palestinians"], 27 November 1973, *IDP* 1973.

38. Buffum to DOS, "Increase in Public Caution Exercised by Fedayeen Leadership," Beirut 13717, 3 December 1973, AAD.

39. Buffum to DOS, "Fedayeen RE Palestinian State," Beirut 13930, 7 December 1973, AAD.

40. Keating to DOS, "Hussin [*sic*], Sadat, Faisal, and Palestinians: A GOI View," Tel Aviv 10050, 11 December 1973, AAD.

41. Keating to DOS, "Israel's Fears RE Palestinian Entity," Tel Aviv 10406, 12 December 1973, AAD.

42. Sayigh, *Armed Struggle*, 338.

43. Gresh, *The PLO*, 141.

44. Ibid., 157–59.

45. Sayigh, *Armed Struggle*, 343.

46. Hart, *Arafat*, 379.

47. PFLP, "Muthakarah al-Jabhah al-Sha'abiyah l-Tahrir Filastin 'ila al-Lajnah al-Tanfiythyah al-Munathama al-Tahrir al-Filastiniyyah Huwal Muqafha Mu'atmar al-Salam" [Memorandum of the People's Front for the Liberation of Palestine to the PLO Executive Committee on the Proceedings of the Peace Conference], 17 November 1973, *WFA*, 467.

48. Buffum to DOS, "Habash Rejects PLO Participation in Peace Talks, While West Bank Notables Urge PLO Attendance at Geneva Conf," Beirut 14362, 18 December 1973, AAD.

49. Buffum to DOS, "Reaction to Rome Airport Massacre," Beirut 14421, 19 December 1973, AAD.

50. "Bayan Munathamah Tala'a Harb al-Tahrir al-Sha'abiyah—Quwat al-Sa'iqah, huwal Wajub Rafad al-Musharakah al-Filastiniyah fi Mu'atamar Janif," 22 December 1973, *WFA*, 538.

51. Houghton to DOS, "Fedayeen Attitudes RE Terrorism and Peaceful ME Settlement," Beirut 1764, 13 February 1974, AAD.

52. Eilts to DOS, "Muhammad Al-Farra on Palestinian Role at Geneva," 20 March 1974, AAD.

53. Buffum to DOS, "Saeb Salam's Impressions of Arab Views on Peace Settlement," Beirut 13353, 20 November 1973, AAD.

54. Salim Yaqub, "The Weight of Conquest," in Logevall and Preston, eds., *Nixon and the World*, 236.

55. Quandt, *Peace Process*, 132–35.

56. Houghton to DOS, "Fedayeen 'Moderation,'" Beirut 2003, 19 February 1974, AAD.

57. Kissinger, Memorandum of Conversation, "Dinner Talks with Israeli Leaders," Kissinger Transcripts, 16 December 1973, 11–12, Digital National Security Archive.

58. Kissinger, "Secretary's Staff Meeting," 21 January 1974, Kissinger Transcripts, 4, Digital National Security Archive.

59. Ibid., 18, 21, 25–26.

60. Saunders to Kissinger, "Thoughts on Jordan-Israel Disengagement for Hussein's Visit," 13 February 1974, NSC Files, Saunders Files, Box 1184, NPMP.

61. Kissinger, Memorandum of Conversation, "The Palestinians; Syrian War Plans; Arms Aid to Jordan," 3 March 1974, Kissinger Transcripts, 5–6, Digital National Security Archive.

62. Ibid., 9, 14, 11, 13, 17, 20.

63. On Kissinger's strategic vision for the region, see Chapter 4; Yaqub, "The Weight of Conquest"; and Kissinger, *White House Years*, 352, 354.

64. "Memorandum from US President Nixon Cancelling $1000 Million Dollar Debt Owed by Israel for Military Equipment," 23 April 1974, *IDP* 1974, 283; "Statement to the Knesset by Israel Prime Minister Meir Presenting the Disengagement Agreement with Syria," 30 May 1974, *IDP* 1974, 290.

65. Houghton to DOS, "PLO Attitudes RE PFLP Terrorist Activity," Beirut 1636, 8 February 1974, AAD.

66. "Shock, Terror—and Slender Hopes," *Time*, 22 April 1974, www.time.com (retrieved August 2008).

67. Godley to DOS, "Psychological Impact of Kiryat Shemona Incident on Fedayeen Leadership," Beirut 4462, 16 April 1974, AAD; Godley to DOS, "Arafat Request for Encouragement from USG," 7 May 1974, NSC Files, Saunders Files, Box 1183, NPMP.

68. Godley to DOS, "Possibility of Additional Fedyaeen [*sic*] 'Spoiling' Operations," Beirut 4624, 19 April 1974, AAD.

69. "Bullets, Bombs and a Sign of Hope," *Time*, 27 May 1974, www.time.com (retrieved August 2008).

70. Godley to DOS, "Maalot Tragedy and Fedayeen Leadership," Beirut 5573, 16 May 1974, AAD.

71. Godley to DOS, "Trouble Ahead for Lebanon," Beirut 5740, 22 May 1974, AAD.

72. Godley to DOS, "Review of the Beirut Weekly Press," Beirut 7919, 10 July 1974, AAD.

73. "Arafat Talks with Egypt's *Rose Al-Yusuf*," 7 April 1974, and "Yasir Arafat Interviewed by Cairo's *Rose Al-Yusuf*," 8 April 1974, *Foreign Broadcast Information System*.

74. "Political Programme Adopted by the Twelfth Session of the Palestine National Council," 8 June 1974, *IDP* 1974, 449–50; Gresh, *The PLO*, 167.

75. Mishal quoted in Black and Morris, *Israel's Secret Wars*, 337.

76. "Recommendation by the Twelfth Session of the Palestine National Council to the PLO Executive Committee Concerning the Bases of Palestinian Action in the International Field," 8 June 1974, *IDP* 1974, 451.

77. Cobban, *The Palestinian Liberation Organization*, 148–49; "Bayan Siyasi Raqam Wahid li-Lajana al-Sha'biya l-Tahrir Filastin huwal al-Taturat al-Rahana fi majal 'al-Tasuyat al-Tasfuya' l-laqadiya al-Filastiniya," 20 July 1974, *WFA*, 248–50; "Al Bayan al-Sahafi al-Sadr 'an al-Jagha al-Sha'abiya l-Tahrir Filastin huwal Ansahabha min al-Lajina al-Tanfithia l-Munathama al-Tahrir al-Filastinia," 26 September 1974, *WFA*, 345.

78. Gresh, *The PLO*, 184–86.

79. "Al-Barnamaj al-Siyasi al-Marhali li-Munathama al-Tahrir al-Filastiniya al-lathi 'Aqra al-Majlas al-Watani al-Filastini fi Dura al-'Adiya al-Thaniya Ashara," 12 June 1974, *WFA*, 182.

80. Assad, Nixon, Kissinger, Memorandum of Conversation, 16 June 1974, Kissinger Transcripts, 18, Digital National Security Archive.

81. Ibid., 7, 5–6.

82. See Kissinger, *Years of Upheaval*, 629.

83. Quandt, "Middle East Trip Report," 2 August 1974, NSC Country Files, Middle East, Box 647, NPMP; Quandt and Oakley, "Approaches to Jordan-Israeli Disengagement," 19 June 1974, NSC Files, Saunders Files, Box 1184, NPMP; see also Eilts to DOS, "Palestine National Council," 11 June 1974, NSC Files, Saunders Files, Box 1184, NPMP, and Oakley, "Overall Strategy Paper for United States Action in Middle East Negotiations over Next Six Months," 5 July 1974, NSC Files, Saunders Files, Box 1185, NPMP.

84. Atherton to Kissinger through Sisco, "Next Steps in the Middle East: Strategy for the Next Six Months," 11 June 1974, NSC Files, Saunders Files, Box 1185, NPMP.

85. "High-Level U.S.-Palestinian Contacts May Develop," 12 July 1974; Golan, *Secret Conversations*, 219.

86. "Israel for the First Time Gives Basis of Talks with Palestinians," *New York Times*, 13 July 1974; Golan, *Secret Conversations*, 220–22; Quandt, *Peace Process*, 154.

87. Quandt, *Peace Process*, 154; Golan, *Secret Conversations*, 220–22.

88. Golan, *Secret Conversations*, 219.

89. Fred Skolnik et al., eds., *Encyclopedia Judaica*, 2nd ed., vol. 13 (Detroit: Macmillan Reference, 2007); David Shipler, "Israel Bars Rabin from Relating '48 Eviction of Arabs," *New York Times*, 23 October 1979.

90. Shlaim, *Iron Wall*, 328–29.

91. "Reported Press Interview with Prime Minister Rabin of Israel," late November 1974, *IDP 1974*, 364; "Statement Issued by Israel's Cabinet Insisting that Jordan Represent the Palestinians in Negotiations," 21 July 1974, *IDP 1974*, 314–15.

92. Shlaim, *Iron Wall*, 330.

93. Quandt, *Peace Process*, 155–57.

94. Kissinger, *Years of Upheaval*, 357–59.

95. "Bayan Sahafi huwal Zayara al-Sayid Yasir Arafat, Ra'yis al-Lajina al-Tanfithiya l-Munathima al-Tahrir al-Filastinia, l-l Itihad al-Sofiyati," 4 August 1974, *WFA*, 275; Cobban, *The Palestinian Liberation Organization*, 224; Gresh, *The PLO*, 154–56, 180–81.

96. Dannreuther, *The Soviet Union and the PLO*, 58–60, 62.

97. Statement by General Secretary Brezhnev of the CPSU Warning of the Dangers in the Current Middle East Situation and Calling for a Speedy Resumption of the Geneva Conference," 11 October 1974, *IDP 1974*, 335.

98. "Mashruw'a Qarar Muw'atmar al-Qamah al-Afriqiy bi-Sha'an al-Sharq al-Awsat" [Resolution of the OAU on Middle Eastern Affairs], 15 June 1974, *WFA*, 193.

99. "Bayan Filastini Masri Suri Mashtrik Bisha'an Husar Huq Tumithil al-Sha'ab al-Filastini fi Munathamah al-Tahrir al-Filastiniyah," 21 September 1974, *WFA*, 307; Pickering to DOS, "Jordan on the Eve of Kissinger Visit," Amman 5947, 6 October 1974, AAD.

100. "Hadith Sahafy Khasa Ra'ayees Huwary Bumidiyan, Ra'ayis Majlis al-Thawra wa-Ra'ayis Majlis al-Wajara al-Jaza'iriy" [Official Press Statements of President Houari

Boumedienne, President of the Revolutionary Assembly and Prime Minister of Algeria], 19 October 1974, *WFA*, 350.

101. "Khatib al-Sayid Faruq al-Qadumy 'Abu al-Lutif' Ra'ayees al-Wafd al-Filastiny, Amam Mu'atmar Wazira al-Kharjiyah al-Arab" [Speech by al-Sayid Faruq al-Qadumy "Abu al-Lutf," President of the Palestinian Delegation, in Front of the Conference of Arab Foreign Ministers], 22 October 1974, *WFA*, 352.

102. Pickering to DOS, "Jordan on the Eve of Kissinger Visit," Amman 5947, 6 October 1974, AAD.

103. Pickering to DOS, "Jordan and Rabat Summit," Amman 6294, 23 October 1974, AAD.

104. Cobban, *The Palestine Liberation Organization*, 60, 62.

105. Gresh, *The PLO*, 179; "Qarar Mu'atamar al-Qama al-'Arabi al-Sab'a bi-Sha'an 'Iqama al-Salta al-Wataniya al-Filastiniya wa Huq Tumithil al-Sha'ab al-Filastini," 29 October 1974, *WFA*, 420–21.

106. Godley to DOS, "The PLO After Rabat—What Next?" Beirut 13019, 30 October 1974, AAD.

107. Godley to DOS, "PLO Girds for UNGA Debate on Palestine," Beirut 13281, 6 November 1974, AAD.

108. Cobban, *The Palestine Liberation Organization*, 230.

109. "Wa Nawasul al-Kafa'a al-Musalla'a," *Filastine al-Thawrah*, Issue 114, 16 October 1974; Sayigh, *Armed Struggle*, 344.

110. Hart, *Arafat*, 408.

111. Gresh, *The PLO*, 180.

112. Sayigh, *Armed Struggle*, 344.

113. David Ignatius, "The Secret History of U.S.-PLO Terror Talks," *Washington Post*, 4 December 1988.

114. Gresh, *The PLO*, 181.

115. Kissinger, Memorandum of Conversation, "Off the Record Conversation with Media Executives," 14 November 1974, Kissinger Transcripts, 4, 12, Digital National Security Archive.

116. Kissinger, "The Secretary's 8:00 a.m. Regional Staff Meeting," 14 November 1974, Kissinger Transcripts, 13–14, Digital National Security Archive.

117. Houghton to DOS, "PLO Reacts Strongly to VC-10 Hijacking," Beirut 14095, 25 November 1974, AAD.

118. Gresh, *The PLO*, 190–91; "Public Meeting with Kissinger Possible," *Arab Report and Record*, 1974, 496.

119. My thinking on this topic owes much to Yezid Sayigh's discussion of the PLO's failure to take similar steps following the outbreak of the First Intifada. Sayigh, *Armed Struggle*, 616–17.

120. "Press Interview Statements by Executive Committee Chairman Arafat of the PLO Reviewing the Current Situation and Discussing the Policy Options of the Palestine Resistance," 7 January 1975, *IDP* 1975, 370–71; Gresh, *The PLO*, 181.

121. Ibid.; "Statement by General Secretary Brezhnev of the CPSU Asserting that Only a Full Settlement Will Bring About a Middle East Peace," 14 February 1975, *IDP* 1975, 168; "Bayan Sahafi huwal Zayara al-Sayid Faruq al-Qaddumi, Rayis al-Da'ira al-Siyasiya fi Munatham al-Tahrir al-Filastiniya, li-Bulgariya," 7 April 1975, *WFA*, 129–30.

122. "Television Interview Statements by US President Ford Discussing the Reassessment of US Middle East Policy and Attitude Towards the PLO," 25 April 1975, *IDP* 1975, 194–95.

123. Quandt, *Peace Process*, 165.

124. Ibid., 165; "Letter from 76 US Senators to President Ford Urging Renewed US Support for a Strong Israel," 21 May 1975, *IDP* 1975, 213.

125. "Press Interview Statements by US Secretary of Defense Schlesinger Discussing Actual and Potential US Military Involvement in the Middle East," 26 May 1975, *IDP* 1975, 209–10.

126. "Press Conference Statements by US Secretary of State Kissinger Discussing Current Developments of the Arab-Israeli Conflict in the UN and Warning of the Dangers of a Continued Stalemate," 15 July 1975, *IDP* 1975, 238.

127. Requests for the Pershing missiles would later be denied; Israel instead maintained its Jericho short-range ballistic missles—developed with French aid—into the 1990s. "Memorandum of Agreement Between the US and Israel Regarding the Reconvening of the Geneva Conference," 1 September 1975, *IDP* 1975, 267–68; "Statement of the US Government Assuring Israel of Continual Military and Economic Assistance," 1 September 1975, *IDP* 1975, 268.

128. "Radio Interview Statements by Defence Minister Peres," 5 September 1975, *IDP* 1975, 273; "Resolution of the Israel Knesset," 11 November 1975, *IDP* 1975, 312.

129. Resolution 3379 would later be repealed as a precondition for Israel's participation at the 1991 Madrid Peace Conference. "General Assembly Resolution 3379," 10 November 1975, *IDP* 1975, 129; UNGA Official Records, A/PV.2400, 10 November 1975, www.unispal. un.org (accessed November 2010).

130. "Television Interview Statements by Defence Minister Peres of Israel," 14 December 1975, *IDP* 1975, 352.

131. "Press Interview Statements by Prime Minister Rabin of Israel," 8 December 1975, *IDP* 1975, 346–48.

Conclusion

1. "Full Transcript of Abbas Speech," *Haaretz*, 23 September 2011; Neil MacFarquhar et al., "Palestinians Request U.N. Status," *New York Times*, 23 September 2011; Turki al-Faisal, "Veto a State, Lose an Ally," *New York Times*, 11 September 2011; Steve Coll, "Membership Dues," *New Yorker*, 26 September 2011.

2. Edward Said, "Reflections on Twenty Years of Palestinian History," *Journal of Palestine Studies* 20, 4 (Summer 1991): 6, 7.

3. For a contemporary example, see Jane Mayer, "The Predator War," *New Yorker*, 26 October 2009.

4. Gunning, *Hamas in Politics*, 33.

BIBLIOGRAPHY

Unpublished Primary Sources

1. UNITED STATES

National Archives and Records Administration, College Park, Maryland (NARA)
  General Records of the Department of State (RG 59)
  Central Foreign Policy Files, Subject Numeric Files, 1963–73
  Central Foreign Policy Files, 1973–75, Access to Archival Databases (AAD) (http://aad.
    archives.gov/aad)
  Office Files, Records Relating to Iraq, Jordan, Lebanon, and Syria 1966–1972
Nixon Presidential Materials Project (NPMP)
  National Security Files
  White House Central Files
Library of Congress, Washington, DC
Digital National Security Archive, Alexandria, VA, http://nsarchive.chadwyck.com.
  Kissinger Telephone Conversations: A Verbatim Record of U.S. Diplomacy, 1969–77
  Kissinger Transcripts: A Verbatim Record of U.S. Diplomacy, 1969–77
United Nations Information System on the Question of Palestine (New York: United Nations),
  http://domino.un.org

2. LEBANON

Maktabah al-Mu'assasat al-Dirasat al-Filastiniyyah [Library of the Institute of Palestine
  Studies (IPS)], Beirut

3. UNITED KINGDOM

National Archives of the United Kingdom, Kew (UKNA)
  Prime Minister's Files
  Records of the Foreign and Commonwealth Office: Near East and North Africa
    Department
  Records of the Foreign Office, Eastern Department (FCO 17)

Published Primary Sources

U.S. Department of State, *Foreign Relations of the United States* (*FRUS*) (Washington, DC:
  U.S. Government Printing Office, 1967–72)
International Documents on Palestine (*IDP*) (Beirut: Institute for Palestine Studies,
  1968–77)
Public Papers of the Presidents: Richard Nixon (Washington, DC: Federal Register Division,
  National Archives and Records Service, 1970–75)

Richard M. Nixon National Security Files, 1969–74. *Middle East* (Bethesda, MD: UPA Collection from LexisNexis, 2002)

Al-Watha'iq   al-Filastiniyyah   al-Arabiyah   (Palestinian-Arab   Documents)   (Beirut: al-Mu'assasat al-Dirasat al-Filastiniyyah, 1967–1975)

Newspapers, Journals, Magazines, and Series (Palestinian)

Dirasat wa-Tajarib Thawriyah (Fatah)
Fatah Informations (Fatah)
Fateh (Fatah)
Filastine al-Thawra (PLO)
Al-Hadaf (PFLP)
Hisad al-Asifa (Fatah)
Al-Thawra Filastiniyyah (PLO)

Newspapers, Journals, and Magazines (English and French)

Jeune Afrique
Le Monde
MERIP Reports
New York Times
Time
Times (London)

Secondary Works

Abdalla, Ahmed. *The Student Movement and National Politics in Egypt,* 1923–73. London: Zed Books, 1985.

Abu Iyad. *My Home, My Land.* New York: Times Books, 1981.

Aburish, Said. *Arafat.* New York: Bloomsbury, 1998.

Ajami, Fouad. *The Arab Predicament.* New York: Cambridge University Press, 1992.

Anderson, Benedict. *Imagined Communities.* New York: Verso, 1991.

Andrew, Christopher, and Vasili Mitrokhin. *The World Was Going Our Way.* New York: Basic Books, 2005.

Ashton, Nigel. *King Hussein of Jordan.* New Haven, CT: Yale University Press, 2008.

Baker, Raymond William. *Sadat and After: Struggles for Egypt's Political Soul.* Cambridge, MA: Harvard University Press, 1990.

Bass, Warren. *Support Any Friend.* New York: Oxford University Press, 2003.

Batatu, Hanna. *The Old Social Classes and the Revolutionary Movements of Iraq.* Princeton, NJ: Princeton University Press, 1978.

Batatu, Hanna. *Syria's Peasantry, the Descendents of Its Lesser Rural Notables, and Their Politics.* Princeton, NJ: Princeton University Press, 1999.

Beattie, Kirk. *Egypt During the Nasser Years.* Boulder, CO: Westview Press, 1994.

Beattie, Kirk. *Egypt Under Sadat.* New York: Palgrave, 2000.

Ben-Rafael, Eliezer. *Israel-Palestine: A Guerilla Conflict in International Politics.* New York: Greenwood Press, 1987.

Bhabha, Homi. *The Location of Culture*. New York: Routledge, 2004.

Black, Ian, and Benny Morris. *Israel's Secret Wars: A History of Israel's Intelligence Services*. New York: Grove Weidenfeld, 1992.

Brynen, Rex. *Sanctuary and Survival: The PLO in Lebanon*. Boulder, CO: Westview Press, 1990.

Chaliand, Gerard. *The Palestinian Resistance*. New York: Penguin, 1972.

Chomsky, Noam. *The Fateful Triangle: The United States, Israel and the Palestinians*. Boston: South End Press, 1983.

Citino, Nathan. *From Arab Nationalism to OPEC*. Bloomington: Indiana University Press, 2002.

Cobban, Helena. *The Palestinian Liberation Organization*. New York: Cambridge University Press, 1984.

Connelly, Matthew J. *A Diplomatic Revolution: Algeria's Fight for Independence and the Origins of the Post–Cold War Era*. New York: Oxford University Press, 2002.

Connelly, Matthew J. *Fatal Misconception: The Struggle to Control World Population*. Cambridge, MA: Belknap Press, 2007.

Cooley, John K. *Green March, Black September: The Story of the Palestinian Arabs*. London: Cass, 1973.

Curtis, Michael, et al. *The Palestinians*. New Brunswick, NJ: Transaction Books, 1975.

Dallek, Robert. *Nixon and Kissinger: Partners in Power*. New York: HarperCollins, 2007.

Dannreuther, Roland. *The Soviet Union and the PLO*. New York: St. Martin's Press, 1998.

Davis, Uri. *Israel, an Apartheid State*. London: Zed Books, 1987.

Dayan, Moshe. *Moshe Dayan: Story of My Life*. New York: Morrow, 1976.

Denning, Michael. *Culture in the Age of Three Worlds*. New York: Verso, 2004.

Dowty, Alan. *Israel/Palestine*. Cambridge: Polity Press, 2008.

Fink, Carole, Philipp Gassert, and Detlef Junker, eds. *1968: The World Transformed*. Cambridge: Cambridge University Press, 2003.

Fisk, Robert. *Pity the Nation: The Abduction of Lebanon*. New York: Atheneum, 1990.

Gaddis, John Lewis. *Strategies of Containment: A Critical Appraisal of American National Security Strategy During the Cold War*. New York: Oxford University Press, 2005.

Garthoff, Raymond. *Détente and Confrontation: American-Soviet Relations from Nixon to Reagan*. Washington, DC: Brookings Institution, 1985.

Gleijeses, Piero. *Conflicting Missions: Havana, Washington, and Africa, 1959–1976*. Chapel Hill: University of North Carolina Press, 2002.

Golan, Galia. *The Soviet Union and the PLO*. London: International Institute for Strategic Studies, 1976.

Golan, Galia. *The Soviet Union and the Palestine Liberation Organization*. New York: Praeger, 1980.

Golan, Matti. *The Secret Conversations of Henry Kissinger*. New York: Quadrangle, 1976.

Green, Stephen. *Living by the Sword: America and Israel in the Middle East*. Brattleboro, VT: Amana Books, 1988.

Gresh, Alain. *The PLO: The Struggle Within*. London: Zed Books, 1985.

Gunning, Jeroen. *Hamas in Politics: Democracy, Religion, Violence*. New York: Columbia University Press, 2008.

Habash, George. *Nous Vaincrons*. Beirut: Popular Front for the Liberation of Palestine, Information Department, 1973.

Hahn, Peter L. *Caught in the Middle East: U.S. Policy Toward the Arab-Israeli Conflict, 1945–61.* Chapel Hill: University of North Carolina Press, 2004.

Hahn, Peter L. *The United States, Great Britain, and Egypt, 1945–56.* Chapel Hill: University of North Carolina Press, 1991.

Haldeman, H. R. *The Haldeman Diaries: Inside the Nixon White House.* New York: G. P. Putnam's Sons, 1994.

Hämäläinen, Pekka. *The Comanche Empire.* New Haven, CT: Yale University Press, 2008.

Hanhimäki, Jussi. *The Flawed Architect: Henry Kissinger and American Foreign Policy.* New York: Oxford University Press, 2004.

Hart, Alan. *Arafat.* London: Sidgwick and Jackson, 1984.

Heikal, Mohammad. *Autumn of Fury: The Assassination of Sadat.* London: Andre Deutsch, 1983.

Hersh, Seymour. *The Price of Power.* New York: Summit Books, 1983.

Hirst, David. *The Gun and the Olive Branch: The Roots of Violence in the Middle East.* New York: Nation Books, 2003.

Hoffman, Bruce. *Inside Terrorism.* New York: Columbia University Press, 1998.

Ignatius, David. *Agents of Innocence.* New York: W. W. Norton, 1987.

Isaacson, Walter. *Kissinger.* New York: Simon & Schuster, 1992.

Jonas, George. *Vengeance.* New York: Simon & Schuster, 1984.

Kaplan, Robert D. *The Arabists: The Romance of an American Elite.* New York: Free Press, 1993.

Kennedy, Paul. *The Parliament of Man: The Past, Present, and Future of the United Nations.* New York: Random House, 2006.

Kepel, Gilles. *Jihad: The Trail of Political Islam.* Cambridge, MA: Belknap Press, 2002.

Kepel, Gilles. *The Prophet and Pharaoh: Muslim Extremism in Egypt.* London: Al Saqi Books, 1985.

Kerr, Malcolm. *The Arab Cold War: Gamal 'Abd al-Nasir and His Rivals, 1958–1970.* New York: Oxford University Press, 1971.

Khaled, Leila. *My People Shall Live.* Toronto: NC Press, 1975.

Khalidi, Rashid. *The Iron Cage: The Story of the Palestinian Struggle for Statehood.* Boston: Beacon Press, 2006.

Khalidi, Rashid. *Palestinian Identity: The Construction of Modern National Consciousness.* New York: Columbia University Press, 1997.

Kimmerling, Baruch, and Joel Migdal. *The Palestinian People: A History.* Cambridge, MA: Harvard University Press, 2003.

Kissinger, Henry. *Diplomacy.* New York: Simon & Schuster, 1994.

Kissinger, Henry. *Nuclear Weapons and Foreign Policy.* New York: W. W. Norton, 1969.

Kissinger, Henry. *White House Years.* Boston: Little, Brown, 1979.

Kissinger, Henry. *A World Restored.* New York: Grosset and Dunlap, 1964.

Kissinger, Henry. *Years of Renewal.* New York: Simon and Schuster, 1999.

Kissinger, Henry. *Years of Upheaval.* Boston: Little, Brown, 1982.

Kopilow, David. *Castro, Israel, and the PLO.* Washington, DC: Cuban-American National Foundation, 1984.

Korn, David. *Assassination in Khartoum.* Bloomington: Indiana University Press, 1993.

Kuniholm, Bruce. *The Origins of the Cold War in the Near East.* Princeton, NJ: Princeton University Press, 1980.

Lawrence, Mark Atwood. *Assuming the Burden: Europe and the American Commitment to War in Vietnam.* Berkeley: University of California Press, 2007.

Lesch, David. *The Arab-Israeli Conflict: A History.* New York: Oxford University Press, 2007.

Little, Douglas. *American Orientalism: The United States and the Middle East Since 1945.* Chapel Hill: University of North Carolina Press, 2002.

Logevall, Frederik, and Andrew Preston, eds. *Nixon in the World.* New York: Oxford University Press, 2008.

Louis, William Roger. *The British Empire in the Middle East, 1945–1951.* New York: Oxford University Press, 1984.

Malley, Robert. *The Call from Algeria: Third Worldism, Revolution, and the Turn to Islam.* Berkeley: University of California Press, 1996.

Manela, Erez. *The Wilsonian Moment: Self Determination and the International Origins of Anticolonial Nationalism, 1917–1920.* New York: Oxford University Press, 2007.

Maoz, Zeev. *Defending the Holy Land: A Critical Analysis of Israel's Security Policy.* Ann Arbor: University of Michigan Press, 2006.

Mattar, Philip, ed. *Encyclopedia of the Palestinians.* New York: Facts on File, 2000.

McAlister, Melani. *Epic Encounters.* Berkeley: University of California Press, 2001.

McMahon, Robert J. *The Cold War on the Periphery: The United States, India, and Pakistan, 1947–1965.* New York: Columbia University Press, 1994.

Meir-Levy, David. *History Upside Down.* New York: Encounter Books, 2007.

Merari, Ariel, and Shlomi Elad. *The International Dimension of Palestinian Terrorism.* Boulder, CO: Westview Press, 1986.

Mishal, Shaul. *The PLO Under Arafat: Between Gun and Olive Branch.* New Haven, CT: Yale University Press, 1986.

Morris, Benny. *Righteous Victims: A History of the Zionist-Arab Conflict, 1881–1999.* London: John Murray, 2000.

Neff, Donald. *Warriors Against Israel.* Brattleboro, VT: Amana Books, 1988.

Nguyen, Lien-Hang. *Hanoi's War: An International History of the War for Peace.* Chapel Hill: University of North Carolina Press, 2012.

Nixon, Richard. *RN: The Memoirs of Richard Nixon.* New York: Warner Books, 1978.

Norton, Augustus Richard, and Martin Greenberg, eds. *The International Relations of the Palestine Liberation Organization.* Carbondale: Southern Illinois University Press, 1989.

Nye, Joseph. *Soft Power.* New York: Public Affairs, 2004.

O'Ballance, Edgar. *Arab Guerilla Power, 1967–72.* Hamden, CT: Archon Books, 1973.

Oded, Arye. *Africa, the PLO and Israel.* Jerusalem: Leonard Davis Institute for International Relations, Hebrew University of Jerusalem, 1990.

O'Neill, Bard. *Armed Struggle in Palestine.* Boulder, CO: Westview Press, 1978.

O'Neill, Bard. *Revolutionary Warfare in the Middle East: An Analysis of the Palestine Guerilla Movement, 1967–72.* Boulder, CO: Paladin Press, 1974.

Oren, Michael. *Six Days of War.* New York: Oxford University Press, 2002.

Pateman, Roy. *Eritrea: Even the Stones Are Burning.* Lawrenceville, NJ: Red Sea Press, 1990.

Pedahzur, Ami. *Israeli Secret Services and the Struggle Against Terrorism.* New York: Columbia University Press, 2009.

Picaudou, Nadine. *Le Mouvement national palestinien: Gènese et structures*. Paris: Harmattan, 1989.

Posner, Steve. *Israel Undercover: Secret Warfare and Hidden Diplomacy in the Middle East*. Syracuse, NY: Syracuse University Press, 1987.

Prashad, Vijay. *Darker Nations: A People's History of the Third World*. New York: New Press, 2007.

Primakov, Yevgeny. *Russia and the Arabs*. New York: Basic Books, 2009.

Quandt, William. *Peace Process*. Washington, DC: Brookings Institution Press, 2005.

Quandt, William, Fuad Jabber, and Ann Mosely Lesch. *The Politics of Palestinian Nationalism*. Berkeley: University of California Press, 1973.

Rayyes, Riad El-, and Dunia Nahas. *Guerillas for Palestine*. London: Croom Helm, 1976.

Reeve, Simon. *One Day in September: The Story of the 1972 Munich Olympics Massacre, a Government Cover-up, and a Covert Revenge Mission*. London: Faber and Faber, 2000.

Rodinson, Maxime. *Israel: A Colonial Settler State?* New York: Monad Press, 1973.

Rubenberg, Cheryl. *The Palestine Liberation Organization: Its Institutional Infrastructure*. Belmont, MA: Institute of Arab Studies, 1983.

Rubin, Barry. *Revolution Until Victory? The Politics and History of the PLO*. Cambridge, MA: Harvard University Press, 1994.

Rubin, Barry, and Judith Colp Rubin. *Yasir Arafat: A Political Biography*. New York: Oxford University Press, 2005.

Said, Edward. *Orientalism*. New York: Vintage, 1979.

Saunders, Harold H. *The Other Walls: The Arab-Israeli Peace Process in a Global Perspective*. Princeton, NJ: Princeton University Press, 1991.

Sayigh, Yezid. *Armed Struggle and the Search for State*. New York: Oxford University Press, 1997.

Schiff, Zeev. *Fedayeen: Guerilla Against Israel*. New York: D. McKay, 1972.

Schoenberg, Harris. *A Mandate for Terror: The United Nations and the PLO*. New York: Shapolsky, 1989.

Seale, Patrick. *Asad of Syria: The Struggle for the Middle East*. Berkeley: University of California Press, 1990.

Sharabi, Hisham. *Palestine Guerillas: Their Credibility and Effectiveness*. Beirut: Institute for Palestine Studies, 1970.

Shlaim, Avi. *The Iron Wall*. New York: W. W. Norton, 2000.

Shulzinger, Robert. *Henry Kissinger: Doctor of Diplomacy*. New York: Columbia University Press, 1989.

Smith, Charles D. *Palestine and the Arab-Israeli Conflict*. Boston: Bedford St. Martin's, 2001.

Sobel, Lester, ed. *Palestinian Impasse: Arab Guerillas and International Terror*. New York: Facts on File, 1977.

Stein, Kenneth. *Heroic Diplomacy*. New York: Routledge, 1999.

Stephens, Robert. *Nasser: A Political Biography*. New York: Simon and Schuster, 1971.

Stivers, William. *America's Confrontation with Revolutionary Change in the Middle East*. New York: St. Martin's Press, 1986.

Suri, Jeremi. *Henry Kissinger and the American Century*. Cambridge, MA: Belknap Press, 2007.

Suri, Jeremi. *Power and Protest: Global Revolution and the Rise of Détente*. Cambridge, MA: Harvard University Press, 2003.

Tessler, Mark A. *A History of the Israeli-Palestinian Conflict.* Bloomington: Indiana University Press, 1994.

Tinnin, David. *The Hit Team.* Boston: Little, Brown, 1976.

Van Creveld, Martin. *The Sword and the Olive: A Critical History of the Israeli Defense Force.* New York: Public Affairs, 1998.

Walker, Tony, and Andrew Gowers. *Arafat: The Biography.* London: Virgin, 2003.

Westad, Odd Arne. *The Global Cold War: Third World Interventions and the Making of Our Times.* New York: Cambridge University Press, 2005.

Yaari, Ehud. *Strike Terror: The Story of Fatah.* New York: Sabra Books, 1970.

Yaqub, Salim. *Containing Arab Nationalism: The Eisenhower Doctrine and the Middle East.* Chapel Hill: University of North Carolina Press, 2004.

Yergin, Daniel. *The Prize.* New York: Touchstone, 1993.

{INDEX}

Abbas, Mahmoud, 263
Abu Daoud, 189, 204
Abu Iyad. *See* Khalaf, Salah
Abu Lutf, 245
Abu Nidal. *See* Banna, Hassan al-
Abu Nidal Organization, 173, 192
Abu Yusuf, 150, 206
Active Defense, 88, 91–92, 107, 138, 207, 217, 237, 255, 260
Adwan, Kamal, 150, 206
Afghanistan, 13, 80, 263
African Americans, 40–41, 130
African National Congress (ANC), 258–60
Al-Assad, Hafiz, 14, 219–20, 239
Al-Khaldah Raid, 73–74, 280n93
Al-Saiqa, 11, 223, 229–30
Algeria, 72, 258
    international influence of, 37–39, 93–94
    as model for PLO, 12, 19, 21–22, 26, 46, 48, 52, 53, 93, 101, 117–18, 152, 222, 260
    Revolution, 5, 19–20, 26, 39, 65, 290n128
    support for PLO, 48, 52–53, 61–63, 65–67, 69, 74, 105, 119–20, 122, 127, 149, 154, 158, 164, 167, 190–91, 209, 245
Algiers Summit, 228–29
Allon, Yigal, 36, 113, 147, 160, 241
Amman, 5, 16, 26, 44, 68, 108–10, 121, 125, 131, 141, 143
Angola, 13, 23, 25–26, 66, 80, 111, 130, 171
Arab League, 18, 149, 205, 219, 230, 246
Arab Liberation Front (ALF), 11
Arab Nationalist Movement (ANM), 11, 16, 19
Arafat, Yasir, 1, 3, 6, 11–12, 18–22, 26, 40, 43–44, 51–54, 62, 64, 70–71, 94, 98, 105, 109–10, 112, 117–18, 121–22, 125–26, 128, 133–37, 140, 142, 144, 148–50, 158–60, 173, 175–77, 185, 191–95, 200, 208–9, 213, 218, 220, 223–30, 232–53, 257, 259–60, 262–68
    background, 14–16
Arms shipments, 62, 86, 109, 139–40, 177, 184, 200, 220
Athens Airport attack, 73–74, 92
Atherton Jr., Alfred, 240

Baader-Meinhoff, 157
Ba'ath Party (Iraq), 11, 15

Ba'ath Party (Syria), 11, 15, 59
Baghdad, 173, 185, 204
Balfour Declaration, 53, 120
Ball, George, 67, 69
Bandung Conference, 19, 262
Banna, Hasan al-, 173
Bar Lev, Chaim, 45, 147, 219
Barbour, Walworth, 49, 57, 145
Battle, Lucius, 49–50
Beirut Raid, 206–10, 212, 216
Ben-Gurion, David, 94
Black Panther Party, 41
Black September crisis. *See* Jordan, Civil War
Black September Organization, 12, 142–43, 149–50, 152–54, 157–65, 172–73, 176, 185–93, 196–210, 213
Bouattoura, Tewfik, 48
Boumedienne, Houari, 53, 122, 245
Bourguiba, Habib, 53, 166, 177
Brezhnev, Leonid, 51, 244, 252
British Empire, 5, 10, 14, 21, 22, 32
Brown, L. Dean, 214–15
Buffum, William, 144–45
Burma, 25
Bush, George H. W., 158, 164, 168, 181–82

Cairo, 9, 14–16, 40, 44
Cairo Agreement (1969), 58
Carmichael, Stokely, 41
Castro, Fidel, 31
Central Intelligence Agency (CIA), 28–32, 39, 105, 102, 121, 133, 183, 192, 226, 250
Chamoun, Camille, 215
Che Guevara, 19, 25, 31, 40, 102
Chomsky, Noam, 40
Cohen, Baruch, 211
Colonialism, 14, 16, 22, 24–25, 39–40, 48–50, 53, 60, 62, 64, 93–95, 97, 105–6, 109, 111, 117–20, 122, 126, 130, 137, 156, 179–84, 218, 222, 255, 257, 259–60
Committee of, 24, 104–5
Congo, 39, 118
Congress of Berlin, 53
Counterterrorism, 7, 35, 92, 154, 173, 193, 201, 203, 207, 210, 212–16, 261
Cuba, 5, 12, 13, 19–22, 26–27, 64, 80, 85, 93, 105, 119, 124, 181, 219, 258, 260

Darwish, Mahmoud, 175–76
Davies, Rodger, 123
Davis, Angela, 175–76
Dayan, Moshe, 33–36, 73, 89, 126, 147, 185, 188, 233, 241
Decolonization, 6–7, 19, 22, 26, 104, 167, 259–60
Deir Yassin, 27, 46, 141, 160, 164
Democratic Front for the Liberation of Palestine (DFLP), 192, 221, 223–24, 228–30, 236–38
Détente, 31, 32, 79, 106–7
Dimona, 32

East Berlin, 3, 175, 177, 197
Eban, Abba, 33, 57, 89, 96, 112, 158, 159, 172, 178, 209–10
Egypt (Cairo)
    and Arab–Israeli conflict, 14–18, 33–37, 51, 90–93, 108–10, 140, 184, 187
    and Jordan Crisis, 122, 125, 127
    and Khartoum Murders, 190
    andx 1973 War, 219–20, 231
    and peace process, 231, 252, 254, 265
    and PLO, 11, 15, 19–20, 37, 52–54, 71, 143, 154, 223, 239, 251
    politics, 18, 262
    and Soviet Union, 50–52, 57, 132, 147, 177
Eid, Guy, 189
Eritrea, 25, 93, 95, 111, 204
Eshkol, Levi, 33, 35–36, 69, 73, 88, 90
Ethiopia, 64, 65, 80, 93–95

F-15 Phantom (fighter jet), 72, 86, 212
Fahmy, Ismail, 190
Fanon, Frantz, 19, 22, 26, 30, 52, 141, 258
Fatah, 11, 263
    and Black September, 142, 148–53, 158–59, 172–74, 191–93, 197–200
    formation, 15–19
    and guerilla war, 43–49, 51–65
    international influence of, 94–97
    and Israel, 34–35, 97–98
    and Jordanian war, 121–24
    and peace process, 178, 185, 200–229, 237–39, 251
    and PLO, 70–72, 117–18, 127–33, 136, 266–67
    and revolutionary models, 19–27, 40
Fedayeen, 5, 11, 12
    and consolidation of power over PLO, 70–75
    and Jordan, 34–36
    post-1967 rise of, 18, 20–29, 38–69
Ford, Gerald, 5, 242–43, 253

France, 10, 21, 25, 37, 39, 49, 53, 61, 64–65, 67, 74, 78, 94, 111, 120, 125, 127, 130, 131, 161, 162, 169, 181–82, 188, 197–99, 246
Franjieh, Suleiman, 157
Front de Libération Nationale (FLN), 26, 40, 46, 52–53, 128
Fulbright, William, 112

Gaza Strip, 10–11, 18, 33, 35
Geneva Conference, 5, 220–32, 237–45, 250–55, 267
Godley, McMurtrie, 235–37, 246
Goldberg, Arthur, 48
Great Britain, 10, 14, 32–33, 37, 57, 61, 74, 114, 129, 165
Greene, Joseph, 190, 195
Guerilla warfare, 3–7, 13, 15, 19–20, 24, 31, 38, 49, 72, 183, 258, 260–62
Guinea, 25, 118, 164–65
Gur, Mordechai, 89–90

Habash, George, 11, 16, 19, 52, 70, 101, 109, 117, 133, 156, 173, 225, 230, 232, 239, 260, 262, 285n12
Haddad, Sa'ad, 214
Haddad, Wadi, 173, 285n12
Haganah, 33, 241
Hamas, 11, 260, 262–63, 266
Hammami, Said, 224–25
Hasabaya, 160
Hassan, Khaled, 150, 224–25
Hawatmeh, Nayaf, 11, 178, 223, 228, 236
Hut, Shafiq al-, 153
Heikal, Muhammad, 54
Herzog, Chaim, 255
Hezbollah, 262
Hijacking (aircraft), 69–73, 100–103, 115, 117, 119–23, 153–54, 157, 166, 168, 173, 180, 195, 205, 251, 279n87
Houghton, Robert, 213–14, 232, 251
Human Rights, 24–25, 42, 64–65, 119, 171, 180
Hussein bin Talal, King, 34, 36, 44–45, 48, 54–61, 68–69, 81, 84, 81, 91, 148–49, 178, 211, 214, 221–23
    and 1970 War, 108–41
    and PLO's post-1973 status, 226–34, 237, 240–46, 250

Ignatius, David, 133, 289n105
Ikhwan Muslimun, 15–16, 262
India, 64–65, 67, 74, 119, 158, 165
Indonesia, 29, 96, 126, 130, 180
Intifada, 262–63, 266
Iran, 57, 64, 80–81, 94, 130, 158, 214, 258

Iraq, 11, 15, 18, 34, 56–57, 62, 110, 118, 123–24, 135, 158, 173, 181, 184, 204, 263
Irgun, 27, 54
Irish Republican Army (IRA), 171, 194–95
Israel, 10–11
  and Africa, 92–95
  and counter-guerilla operations, 43–50, 66–67, 153–54, 163–67, 183
  and Jordan, 55–58, 68–69, 126
  and Lebanon, 58–60, 144–48, 159–61, 207–12, 215–17
  and peace process, 17, 18, 187–89, 218–19, 221–29, 250–56, 267
  and PLO, 7, 15, 33–42, 112–14, 231–35, 239–46
  and the question of terrorism at sthe UN, 167–77
  and United States, 21, 22, 32–33. 60–61, 67–69, 81–92, 138–40, 261, 261–62
Israel Defense Forces (IDF), 14
  and counter-guerilla operations, 45, 88–92
  and al-Karama operation, 43–44, 45–46
  and Lebanon, 144–47, 160, 163
  occupation, 34–38
  and reprisals, 56, 58–59, 66–69, 73, 205

Japanese Red Army, 154–58, 236
Jaring Mission, 17–18, 85, 98, 109, 114, 123
Jarring, Gunnar, 17–18, 66, 82, 85–86
Jerusalem, 17, 35, 92, 95–96, 137, 243
Jeune Afrique, 40, 152
Johnson, Lyndon B., 5, 18, 32–33, 37–38, 41, 53, 77
Jordan, 12, 18
  and cross-border operations, 34–38
  and Israel, 89–91
  and Israeli reprisals, 43–52, 56–58, 66–69, 91
  and Lebanon, 146–48, 201–2, 213–15
  1970 war with PLO, 108–41, 143–44
  and Palestinian state, 221–29
  and United States, 54–58, 233–46
Jordan, Civil War 1970, 108–41
Jumblatt, Kamal, 213
June War. *See* 1967 war

Karama, Battle of, 12, 43–49, 61, 66–67, 69–71, 74–75, 141, 267
Kennedy, John F., 32–33
Kennedy, Richard, 131
Khalaf, Salah, 1, 97, 111–12
  and Black September Organization, 149–53, 172, 185, 187, 191–92, 209–11
  and emergence of guerilla movement, 26–27
  and al-Karama, 43–44
  and peace process, 220, 223, 226, 228, 230, 232

Khaldah Airport attack, 73–74, 280n93
Khaled, Leila, 101–2
Khalidi, Walid, 184
Khartoum Conference, 18
Khartoum murders, 189–205, 216–18
Kiryat Shmona, 235–36
Kissinger, Henry
  and Nixon Doctrine, 12, 76–78, 159, 261
  and peace process, 6, 102, 212, 218–19, 231–37
  and PLO, 134–40, 225–27, 239–44, 250–56, 264
  and views on diplomacy, 79–80
  and views on Middle East, 81–87, 106–07
  and war in Jordan, 108, 111, 121, 123, 131
Kenya, 53
Kuwait, 15–16, 44, 71, 102, 143, 159, 197, 199, 202–4

Laird, Melvin, 83, 139
Laos, 25, 130
Lebanese civil war, 11–13, 59, 145, 202–4, 208, 214, 262, 266
Lebanon
  and crackdown on PLO, 201–4
  and Israel, 58–60, 90–91, 100, 156–60, 163–65, 206–15
  and PLO, 68–69, 126–28, 141, 143–48
  U.S. Embassy, 28–29
Libya, 52, 153, 187–94, 202
Libyan airline disaster, 187–94
Lillehammeri, 211
Lod Airport Massacre, 154–61, 171, 173, 175, 195, 216, 218
Lydda, 16, 241

Ma'a lot, 236, 248
Mao Zedong, 19–20, 29, 31, 62, 258, 260
Maronite Christians, 262
Meir, Golda, 35, 88–90, 107, 109, 113, 131, 159, 210–11, 233, 235, 241–42
Moore, George Curtis, 189
Morocco, 52–53, 200
Mossad, 36, 201, 206–7, 210–12
Moynihan, Daniel Patrick, 255
Mozambique, 111, 130
Munich Olympics massacre, 12, 142–43, 161–76, 181, 187, 189–96, 204–5, 209–11, 216, 218
Muslim Brotherhood. *See* Ikhwan Muslimun
My Lai, 27

Nablus, 5, 18
Nasser, Gamal abdel, 14–18, 26, 29, 32, 41, 51, 53–54, 56, 61, 93–94, 109–10, 125–32
National Liberation Front of South Vietnam, 42, 61, 113, 117, 148, 168, 175, 194, 251, 259, 264

National Security Council, 81–84, 131, 134, 139,
        163, 226, 263, 239–40
Nehru, wJawaharlal, 29
1948 War, 11, 18, 23, 51, 203
        Arafat in, 15
        Dayan and, 33
        Habash and, 16
        Khalaf and, 44
        Khaled and, 101
        Rabin and, 241
        "Terrorism" and, 194
1967 war
        impact on the Arab states, 38, 54, 69
        impact on Palestinian guerillas, 14, 16, 18–20,
                39–40, 44, 54, 69, 82, 102, 136
        international diplomacy and, 17, 37, 50–51, 85,
                105, 263
        Israeli policy and, 33–36, 74, 89, 91
        United States and, 29, 33, 40–41, 54, 85,
                138, 211
1973 war, 219–45, 264–67
Nixon, Richard M., 1, 3, 5
        and Israel, 184, 225
        and Jordan crisis, 108–9, 111, 121
        and PLO, 138, 162, 189–90, 264–65
        resignation, 242
        views on diplomacy, 77–80, 183,
        views on the Middle East, 81–88, 102–7, 136,
                147, 204, 225
Nixon Doctrine, 6, 87, 91, 107, 138, 159, 196, 254,
        259, 261
Nkrumah, Kwame, 29
Noel, Cleo, 189
Non-Aligned Movement, 21, 64, 182, 216, 259
North Korea, 27, 93, 111

Oakley, Robert, 240
Occupied territories, 21, 33–34, 36, 44, 45, 51, 55,
        64, 67, 82, 90, 119, 126, 131, 136, 137, 147,
        158, 161, 187, 204, 221–24, 229–30, 237–38,
        261–63
October War. *See* 1973 war
Okamoto, Kozo, 156, 236
Organization of African Unity, 94, 118–19,
        245, 255
Ottoman Empire, 10, 15, 33

Pakistan, 48, 65, 67, 74, 96
Palestine Liberation Organization (PLO), 11
        and Africa, 92–94
        and Arab states, 15, 57–60, 69
        and China, 1, 30, 62, 111, 123, 130
        internal struggles, 44, 70–72, 96–100, 142,
                158–60, 184–85, 192–94, 205–6, 224–25,
                229–30, 235–39, 251–52, 266–67

international support, 64–65, 160–61, 175–76,
        244–46, 257–58, 262
and Israel, 33–35, 88–92, 112–13, 206–12, 229,
        241–42, 256, 260–61
in Lebanon, 143–48, 206–16
and peace process, 136, 220–68
and revolutionary warfare, 5–7, 13–14, 54,
        149–53, 257–58, 260, 267
and Soviet Union, 50–51, 177–78, 221, 223,
        228, 244
and United Nations, 165–66, 218–19, 246–50,
        255–57
and United States, 1, 7, 40–43, 81, 85, 105–7,
        112, 114, 132–36, 138–41, 147–48,
        171–74, 187, 195–205, 225–27,
        232–35, 239–44, 250, 253–55, 261,
        265–66
and war in Jordan, 108–41
Palestinian diaspora, 15, 18, 21, 23, 24, 38, 42, 70,
        71, 90, 93, 100, 132, 133, 184, 267
Palestinian National Council (PNC), 61, 70–71,
        98, 185, 238, 246
Palestinian National Front (PNF), 222, 224, 233
Palestinian refugees, 13, 16–18, 20, 23–25, 27, 34,
        40, 46, 49, 51, 64–65, 83, 90, 102, 112, 130,
        146, 175, 230, 247
Palestinian Student Union (PSU), 15–16, 44
People's Republic of China (PRC), 1–3, 29–30,
        50–51, 61–62, 106, 110–11, 114, 120, 124,
        130, 132, 145, 148, 161–62, 165, 178,
        175, 185
Peres, Shimon, 154, 241, 255–56
Popular Democratic Front for the Liberation
        of Palestine (PDFLP), 97–98, 117, 178,
        192, 213
Popular Front for the Liberation of Palestine
        (PFLP), 11, 26, 260, 267
        and Black September, 149
        and hijacking, 69, 72–73, 101–2, 173
        and Israel, 51, 58, 100, 206
        and Jordan, 115, 117–20, 125, 128
        and Lod Airport attack, 155–59
        and peace process, 177–78, 221, 223, 225, 230,
                235, 236–39, 260
        relations with Fatah, 44, 70–71, 97, 133, 201
        worldview, 19–20, 22, 26, 63, 94
Popular Front for the Liberation of Palestine–
        General Command (PFLP–GC), 192,
        235–36
Porter, Dwight, 28, 33, 56, 59–61, 68–69, 73,
        100, 145
Pravda, 50, 51, 122
Primakov, Yevgeny, 137
Provisional Revolutionary Government of the
        Republic of South Vietnam (PRG), 251

Quandt, William, 226, 239, 240, 243, 253

Rabat Summit, 219, 245–46
Rabin, Yitzhak, 35, 57, 85, 109, 113, 126, 140, 162,
    187, 225, 241–43, 256, 265
Reagan, Ronald, 13
Rejectionist Front, 230, 235–39, 246, 252
Revolutionary Studies and Experiences (Fatah
    Series), 20, 271n11
Rhodesia, 21, 26, 27, 48, 66, 67, 95, 105, 118, 130,
    165, 168, 171
Rogers Initiative, 108–11, 115, 118, 120, 133
Rogers Plan, 98, 112, 127, 130
Rogers, William, 81, 85–86, 147, 164, 178, 199, 202,
    204, 208
Rome Airport attack, 230
Rostow, Eugene, 37, 60
Rusk, Dean, 61, 68
Russell, Bertrand, 40

Sabena Operation, 153–54
Sadat, Anwar, 169, 177, 219–20, 231, 233, 239
Saiqa, 11, 223, 229, 230
Salameh, Ali Hassan, 133, 150
Salt, 66–69, 74
Samu Raid, 91
Saudi Arabia, 18, 52, 57, 71, 104, 136, 143, 159, 164,
    184, 189, 195, 204, 214, 231, 246, 257
Saunders, Harold, 38, 51, 131, 139, 233–34
Scali, John, 188
Schlesinger, Arthur, 76
Schlesinger, James, 253–54
Seelye, Talcott, 112, 227
Sharon, Ariel, 212
Shin Bet, 35–36, 90, 210–11
Shuqairy, Ahmed, 15, 97
Shuttle diplomacy, 231–32, 243, 252–54
Sinai II Agreement, 253–55, 262
Sino-Soviet Split, 29, 124
Sisco, Joseph, 132, 144–48, 160, 187, 193, 207, 231,
    240, 241
Six Day War. *See* 1967 war
South Africa, 5, 13, 23, 25, 27, 39, 41, 48, 67, 95,
    105, 111, 118, 130–31, 137–38, 161, 168, 170,
    199, 245, 250, 258
Soviet Union, 17, 25, 32, 62, 80–81, 84, 86, 110–11,
    165, 177, 199, 221, 230, 232, 243–44, 252,
    254, 264
Standstill Diplomacy, 86–87, 264
Student Non-Violent Coordinating Committee
    (SNCC), 41
Sudan, 94–95, 150, 162, 165–66, 177, 179, 189–90,
    199, 201, 209
Suez Canal, 41, 91, 108–9, 113, 219
Sukarno, 29

Symmes, Harrison, 54–57, 61, 68
Syria
    Fatah, 14–16, 18, 20, 95
    and Israel, 17, 34, 37, 91–92, 160, 163–65,
        174, 209
    and Jordan, 123–25
    and Lebanon, 58–59, 208, 214, 262
    and 1973 war, 219–20
    and peace process, 230–31, 235, 243,
        246, 254
    and PLO, 50, 52, 62, 90, 101–3, 143–44, 149,
        154, 177, 185, 190, 239

Tal, Wasfi al-, 143, 149, 152, 187
Ten-Point Program, 223, 238–39, 242, 246
Terrorism
    as concept, 7, 9–10, 51, 100
    controversy over, 12, 65, 153, 158–85, 258–59,
    efforts to control, 31, 35, 188–217, 260, 263,
        173, 193, 212
    Israel and, 89–90, 154, 210, 216, 261
    and peace process, 239–40, 256, 266
    as tactic, 100, 153, 158
    See also hijacking; *specific incidents*
Tito, Josip Broz, 64, 105, 118, 130
Toynbee, Arnold, 120, 181
Tripartite Declaration, 254
Tunisia, 52, 53, 125, 166, 177, 193–94, 266

UN General Assembly, 24, 105, 131–32, 137, 140,
    162, 167–70, 180–82, 198, 216–19, 224,
    246–50, 252, 255, 257, 259, 263
UN Resolution, 242, 17, 60, 67, 82, 85, 86, 89,
    106, 109, 112, 118, 123, 137, 158, 161,
    170, 171, 199, 220, 227, 238, 242, 247,
    250, 254
UN Resolution 3236, 247, 252
UN Resolution 3237, 247
UN Resolution 3379, 255, 309n.
UN Security Council, 17, 92, 183
    and efforts to curb "terrorism," 100–104
    and Khaldah raid, 74
    and al-Karama, 48
    and Lebanon, 145–46, 157, 207, 209
    and Salt attacks, 67–69
    and U.S. veto, 160–67, 174, 216, 263
United States, 2–3, 11
    and Arab-Israeli conflict, 17, 184, 199, 219–20,
        232–34, 264
    and Cold War, 32, 62, 64, 87, 93
    in eyes of PLO, 21–22, 105, 120, 152, 194–95,
        218, 225
    and Israel, 48, 52, 67, 92 94, 104, 123, 126–27,
        139–40, 180, 206–7, 212, 216, 253–57,
        265–66

United States (*continued*)
  and Jordan, 58, 68, 81, 114, 122, 134, 143
  and Lebanon, 58, 145, 160, 202, 208, 214
  and Middle East, 38–42, 66, 72, 83–84, 86,
    102, 147
  and PLO, 7, 106, 112–13, 127, 135, 143, 158, 178,
    200, 219, 226–30, 240–46, 250, 261,
    263–64
  and post-Vietnam containment, 3–5, 12,
    76–77
  students in, 30
  and "terrorism," 167–74, 181–82, 261
  and UN Security Council Veto, 160–67
  and Vietnam, 26–27
U.S. Congress, 102, 147, 192, 253, 255, 263
Urban notables, 15, 18, 55, 70, 134, 222

Vietnam, 258–60, 264
  as model for PLO, 12, 19–27, 40, 46, 48–49,
    53, 60, 95, 101, 106–7, 117, 124, 185–86, 215,
    220, 222, 236, 240
  and relations with PLO, 1–2, 5–6, 61–62,
    105, 175
  and United States, 29–30, 33, 37–39, 77–80,
    85, 87, 160, 168, 251, 254
Vo Nguyen Giap, 1, 3, 19, 64

Waldheim, Kurt, 167–69, 216
Walters, Vernon, 226–27
Washington Special Actions Group
    (WSAG), 123
Watergate, 242, 253
Wazir, Khalil al- (a.k.a. Abu Jihad), 62, 70
Weathermen, 157
West Bank. *See* Occupied territories
West Bank Insurgency (1967)
West Germany, 64, 144, 152–53, 157–58, 161, 189,
    198, 206
White House Senior Review Group (SRG),
    128, 135
Wilson, Woodrow, 53, 78
World Festival of Youth,
    175–76
Wrath of God, Operation, 210, 212

Yom Kippur War. *See* 1973 war
Yost, Charles, 132
Yugoslavia, 61, 65, 111, 162, 165

Zionism, 32, 35, 39, 41, 70, 88, 94, 98,
    112, 118, 130, 156, 185,
    245, 255
Zurhellen, Joseph, 194–96, 210

CPSIA information can be obtained
at www.ICGtesting.com
Printed in the USA
BVOW09s2227290717
490558BV00002B/40/P